Elizabeth Bishop and the Literary Archive

Edited by
Bethany Hicok

LEVER PRESS

Copyright © 2019 by Bethany Hicok

Lever Press (leverpress.org) is a publisher of pathbreaking scholarship. Supported by a consortium of liberal arts institutions focused on, and renowned for, excellence in both research and teaching, our press is grounded on three essential commitments: to be a digitally native press, to be a peer-reviewed, open access press that charges no fees to either authors or their institutions, and to be a press aligned with the ethos and mission of liberal arts colleges.

This work is licensed under the Creative Commons Attribution-NonCommercial 4.0 International License. To view a copy of this license, visit http://creativecommons.org/licenses/by-nc/4.0/ or send a letter to Creative Commons, PO Box 1866, Mountain View, CA 94042, USA.

The complete manuscript of this work was subjected to a partly closed ("single blind") review process. For more information, please see our Peer Review Commitments and Guidelines at https://www.leverpress.org/peerreview

DOI: https://doi.org/10.3998/mpub.11649332
Print ISBN: 978-1-64315-011-6
Open access ISBN: 978-1-64315-012-3

Library of Congress Control Number: 2019954592

Published in the United States of America by Lever Press, in partnership with Amherst College Press and Michigan Publishing

Contents

List of Abbreviations v
Member Institution Acknowledgments vii

Introduction 1
   Bethany Hicok

PART 1 THE QUEER ARCHIVE

Chapter One: "Too Shy to Stop": Elizabeth Bishop
and the Scene of Reading 17
   Heather Treseler

Chapter Two: Elizabeth Bishop's Sanity:
Childhood Trauma, Psychoanalysis, and Sentimentality 45
   Richard Flynn

Chapter Three: Elizabeth Bishop's Perspectives on Marriage 65
   Jeffrey Westover

Chapter Four: "Keeping Up a Silent Conversation":
Recovering a Queer Bishop through Her Intimate Correspondence
with Alice Methfessel 81
   Alyse Knorr

Chapter Five: Dear Elizabeth, Dear May: Reappraising the Bishop/Swenson
Correspondence 99
   David Hoak

Chapter Six: Odd Job: Elizabeth Bishop's
"The Fairy Toll-Taker" 115
   John Emil Vincent

PART II TRAVELS: SCALE, LOCATION, ARCHITECTURE, ARCHIVE

Chapter Seven: Elizabeth Bishop and Race in the Archive 131
   Marvin Campbell

Chapter Eight: "I miss all that bright, detailed flatness":
Elizabeth Bishop in Brevard 151
   Charla Allyn Hughes

Chapter Nine: "All the untidy activity": Travel & the
Picturesque in Elizabeth Bishop's Writings 173
   Yaël Schlick

Chapter Ten: The Burglar of the Tower of Babel:
Elizabeth Bishop, Architecture, Translation, Archive 193
   Douglas Basford

Chapter Eleven: Elizabeth Bishop's Geopoetics 227
   Sarah Giragosian

PART III THE WORK IN PROGRESS

Chapter Twelve: The Archival Aviary:
Elizabeth Bishop and Drama 249
   Andrew Walker

Chapter Thirteen: Archival Animals:
Polyphonic Movement in Elizabeth Bishop's Drafts 265
   Heather Bozant Witcher

Chapter Fourteen: "Huge Crowd Pleased by New Models":
Elizabeth Bishop's Cuttyhunk Notebook as Multimodal
and Multimedia Artifact 283
   Laura Sloan Patterson

Chapter Fifteen: The Matter of
Elizabeth Bishop's Professionalism 303
   Claire Seiler

Works Cited 319

List of Contributors 331

Acknowledgments 335

Index 337

Abbreviations

CP	The Complete Poems, 1927–1979
EAP	Edgar Allan Poe & the Juke-Box: Uncollected Poems, Drafts, and Fragments
EBNY	Elizabeth Bishop and The New Yorker
OA	One Art: Letters
P	Poems
PPL	Poems, Prose, and Letters
Pr	Prose
REB	Remembering Elizabeth Bishop
SCP	Swenson: Collected Poems
VC	Elizabeth Bishop Papers, Archives and Special Collections Library, Vassar College
WIA	Words in Air: The Complete Correspondence between Elizabeth Bishop and Robert Lowell
WUSC	Washington University Special Collections
USUSCA	Utah State University Special Collections and Archives

Member Institution Acknowledgments

Lever Press is a joint venture. This work was made possible by the generous support of Lever Press member libraries from the following institutions:

Adrian College
Agnes Scott College
Allegheny College
Amherst College
Bard College
Berea College
Bowdoin College
Carleton College
Claremont Graduate University
Claremont McKenna College
Clark Atlanta University
Coe College
College of Saint Benedict / Saint John's University
The College of Wooster
Denison University
DePauw University
Earlham College
Furman University
Grinnell College
Hamilton College
Harvey Mudd College
Haverford College
Hollins University
Keck Graduate Institute
Kenyon College
Knox College
Lafayette College Library
Lake Forest College
Macalester College
Middlebury College
Morehouse College
Oberlin College
Pitzer College
Pomona College
Rollins College
Santa Clara University
Scripps College
Sewanee: The University of the South
Skidmore College
Smith College
Spelman College
St. Lawrence University
St. Olaf College

Susquehanna University
Swarthmore College
Trinity University
Union College
University of Puget Sound
Ursinus College

Vassar College
Washington and Lee University
Whitman College
Willamette University
Williams College

INTRODUCTION

Bethany Hicok

In her 1971 poem "Crusoe in England," written at a time in her life when she contemplated where her own papers and effects would be placed, Elizabeth Bishop's avatar, Crusoe, safe in England after having been rescued from his island, notes that the local museum has asked him to "leave everything to them"—all the products of his island industry, for example, a flute, his knife, "shrivelled shoes," and "shedding goatskin trousers" (*PPL* 156). These objects, made by Crusoe on his island and used for his very survival, will now be placed in a museum as things torn from their original use and value. "How can anyone want such things?" Crusoe asks (156). Bishop herself was preoccupied with how objects separated from their original use might be interpreted. In a 1947 letter to her psychoanalyst Ruth Foster, Bishop wrote: "I am writing a poem about a litter of objects in a museum whose uses the spectator can't make out" (VC 118.33). In a life full of chaos and travel, Bishop managed to preserve and even partially catalog a large collection.

We find the largest share of that collection at Vassar College in more than 120 boxes filled with some 3,500 pages of drafts of poems, stories, and essays, notebooks, postcards, mementos, travelogues, photographs, artwork, and hundreds of letters, including those to major poets and writers of the twentieth century. And the archive continues to expand on a regular basis. Vassar recently catalogued more than 2,000 volumes from Bishop's library and made it available to scholars (the rest of her library is at Harvard). A number of these books contain Bishop's underlinings and annotations, so that scholars may trace her reading activity across her life. One can even peruse the card catalog Bishop prepared for these books (probably with the help of a graduate student at Harvard since the handwriting is not Bishop's).

Such "things" were important to Bishop; she was, in fact, a major curator of her own effects, which is why we have so many of them. The result is that Bishop's collection has become one of the great literary archives for the study of mid-century poetry and poetics, providing important documentary evidence of her creative process and the various social forces that help to shape a career. In addition, and perhaps most important for our collective project in this volume, Bishop's archival practice—her curatorial poetics—provides an excellent case study for understanding the value of archival research for teaching and scholarship in the humanities.

Bishop's archive at Vassar has been an important source for scholars and readers at least since Vassar made its initial acquisition in 1981. Work by Victoria Harrison, Barbara Page, Thomas Travisano, Lorrie Goldensohn, Eleanor Cook, Peggy Samuels, Camille Roman, Linda Anderson, myself, and others have provided a strong critical foundation for thinking about the relationship between the poet and her archive, as have Bishop's biographers Brett Millier, Megan Marshall, and, most recently, Travisano, whose biography was published by Penguin in November 2019.[1] With the contents of the archive being mined for new publications and editions, we might well ask the question: What actually constitutes Bishop's Archives? Bishop's papers can be found in other collections in the United States, Canada, and Brazil,[2] and some have not been "arrested" yet, to use Jacques Derrida's term.[3] When I was traveling in Brazil in 2011, I was pleasantly surprised to walk into the sitting room of Pousada do Chico Rei, the bed and breakfast where Bishop stayed in Ouro Prêto, only to find a letter signed by Bishop in a glass case. The letter is addressed to Lilli Correia de Araújo, who was the hotel's owner and with whom Bishop may have had an affair, as letters to Lilli in the Vassar archives suggest. But Bishop papers continue to find their way into institutional repositories throughout the United States. In 2004, a significant series of letters that Bishop wrote to Louise Bradley, a friend from summer camp and Bishop's first known correspondent and love interest, was acquired by Indiana University.[4] So the reassessment of Bishop continues.

Carolyn Steedman provides a definition of the concept of the archive that is useful when thinking about Bishop's case. "The Archive," Steedman writes,

> is made from selected and consciously chosen documentation from the past and also from the mad fragmentations that no one intended to preserve and that just ended up there.... [It is] a name for the many places in which the past (which does not now exist, but which once did actually happen; which cannot be retrieved, but which may be represented) has deposited some traces and fragments. (68–69)

More poetically, Steedman notes, it is "also a place of dreams"—a place "where the past lives, where ink on parchment can be made to speak" (70). Although Bishop's archive is certainly deposited in "many places," the major collection remains at Vassar, and so it makes sense to return to this particular space for a more theoretically informed approach to how the material archive as an institutional space has shaped our reading of this poet. No previous scholarly study takes Bishop's archive as both source and subject or considers how Bishop herself had a hand in curating her own reception. It is all the more important to undertake such work as recent developments in the digital humanities suggest a strong interest in blending literary and archival study.

In order to address this gap, I submitted a proposal, which was funded by the National Endowment for the Humanities (NEH), to lead a Summer Seminar for College and University Professors on Elizabeth Bishop and the Literary Archive in June 2017. Sixteen scholars, in various stages of their careers, joined me at Vassar College for three weeks of intensive study of Bishop, her material archive at Vassar, and the literary and cultural theory of archives. The seminar brought together literary scholars, archivists, translators, and poets who approached the archive both collaboratively and from multiple perspectives.[5] *Elizabeth Bishop and the Literary Archive* is the product of this memorable seminar. All but one of the fifteen chapters included in this volume were written by the NEH seminar participants, and they reflect the collaborative spirit of intellectual exchange that informed our seminar. Each chapter provides a case study of Bishop's multilayered creative process while exemplifying the varied forms of critical study that may be generated through archival interrogation, especially with the aid of new tools provided by advances in the digital humanities.

A SHORT HISTORY OF BISHOP'S ARCHIVES

Whether we are explicitly aware of it or not, the identities of literary figures, as many archivists agree, "are constructed and reconstructed through the experience of archival documents" (Craven 17). Archives themselves are shifting sites of knowledge that are incomplete, fragmentary, and subject to additions and deletions (Stead 2). The history of Bishop's archive at Vassar is a testament to these statements. Vassar purchased the bulk of Bishop's papers in 1981 from Bishop's final partner, Alice Methfessel, as part of the college's larger liberal arts mission to support the use of primary documents in undergraduate research.[6] Bishop graduated from Vassar, and the college was a significant influence on her poetic development.[7] Institutional context is important when we think about the archive, and Bishop's close connection to Vassar makes her archive there a particularly symbolic space for thinking about the literary archive's role in the liberal arts. Since Vassar's initial purchase, the college has made forty-eight additional acquisitions. We can map some significant shifts in our reading of Bishop across these acquisitions as they track with changes in literary scholarship.

Let us take as one example our comparatively recent reading of Bishop as a queer poet. We can mark the beginning of that reading with Adrienne Rich's reassessment of Bishop in 1983 when she began to reread Bishop's well-known poetry in terms of outsiderhood and lesbian identity. Rich's initial reading of Bishop found her sometimes "coy" and mannered, like the poet she was so often compared to, Marianne Moore.[8] Then, in 1988, Lorrie Goldensohn published a hitherto unknown poem by Bishop, the openly lesbian love poem "It is marvellous to wake up together," in *American Poetry Review*. At the time, the poem was in private hands—part of Bishop's "unarrested archive," to use Linda Morra's term.[9] Goldensohn was one of the first scholars to describe that moment in scholarship on Bishop when a major new discovery is made and the critical sands shift to accommodate a really new work of art, one that had a major impact on the criticism that followed. In *Elizabeth Bishop: The Biography of a Poetry*, in which the poem was reprinted in 1992, Goldensohn describes how during her time in Brazil, the then owner of Bishop's house in Ouro Prêto, Linda Nemer, handed over "a sheaf of papers . . . [and] a shoebox full of small notebooks" (27)—all in Bishop's hand. Goldensohn writes how she "unfolded a sheet of brittle onionskin and read through a typed, completed poem [she had] never seen before" (27). Vassar acquired the poem in 2002 along with other Bishop papers from the Portinari family of Brazil, and it has now been reprinted in several new editions of Bishop's previously unpublished work, including *Edgar Allan Poe & the Juke-Box* (2006), the Library of America edition of Bishop's *Poems, Prose, and Letters* (2008), and in *Poems* (2011), making it very much a part of the Bishop canon. By the early 1990s, following Goldensohn's discovery and under the influence of feminist, psychoanalytic, gender, and queer criticism, scholars began exploring in more depth the psychosexual tensions in Bishop's work and her lesbian identity, which culminated in a groundbreaking book of essays, *Elizabeth Bishop: The Geography of Gender* (1993).

Recently discovered materials acquired by Vassar, as well as the aforementioned letters to Louise Bradley at Indiana University, also deepen our understanding of Bishop as a queer poet. In *Elizabeth Bishop and the Literary Archive,* some of our scholars focus on Vassar's significant 2011 purchase, which includes Bishop's 1947 letters to her psychoanalyst, Ruth Foster, and 243 exuberant love letters exchanged between Bishop and her final partner and literary executor, Alice Methfessel, from November 1970 to June 1976. In the Foster letters, Bishop documents her alcoholism, the sexual abuse she suffered as a child, her candid exploration of her sexual identity as a lesbian, from her teens onward, at a time of extreme homophobia and persecution, and many facets of her traumatic childhood—each of which Bishop links explicitly to her own poetry. These pages constitute one of the most detailed psychosexual memoirs we have of any twentieth-century writer and provide insight into the relationship between trauma, sexual identity, and the creative process, a subject that Heather Treseler explores in our first chapter. Treseler reads the letters alongside Bishop's drafts of "In the Waiting Room" and a number of other archival documents that stage queer scenes of reading. The letters also make clear that Bishop understands her own sexual identity and, indeed, her poetic process through a psychoanalytic narrative, the master narrative for many mid-century writers, as Richard Flynn documents in his chapter.

The Bishop-Methfessel correspondence, according to Alyse Knorr in chapter 4, constitutes one of the most important series of queer love letters of the twentieth century, particularly as Vassar holds both sides of the conversation. They provide a rich material presence for this final love in Bishop's life and its influence on the final phase of her career. Knorr's work demonstrates just how important attention to the material archive can be in charting the dimensions of a new Bishop, one who is more open than the reticent figure that has been a stock trope of Bishop scholarship for so many years. But this new trove of material also adds another level of complex negotiation to Bishop scholarship in the archives. Knorr, for instance, was unable to represent Methfessel's voice as fully as she would have liked after Methfessel's heirs refused to grant permission to quote from her letters.

New editions of Bishop's previously unpublished work have also influenced how we read her. Those editions include *Edgar Allan Poe & the Juke-Box*, a collection of Bishop's "uncollected poems, drafts, and fragments" (edited and annotated by Alice Quinn in 2006); *Words in Air: The Complete Correspondence between Elizabeth Bishop and Robert Lowell* (edited by Thomas Travisano with Saskia Hamilton, 2008); and *Elizabeth Bishop and* The New Yorker (edited by Joelle Biele, 2011). These editions have added well over one thousand pages of previously unpublished or long out-of-print poetry, prose, drafts, and letters to Bishop's previously published work, a phenomenon that her readers began to address in the essay collection *Elizabeth Bishop in the 21st Century: Reading the New Editions* (2012). The Lowell-Bishop correspondence, as well as Quinn's edition, have sparked fresh readings of Bishop, but as we found when we worked with original documents in the archive, *Edgar Allan Poe & the Juke-Box* cannot be approached as a completely reliable edition of the work. John Emil Vincent's case study of Bishop's "The Fairy Toll-Taker," in chapter 6, demonstrates the problem of evaluating drafts that are missing information or transcribed incorrectly. Vincent reminds us that the roles of curator, editor, scholar, critic, and theorist all co-exist "in and around the archives"; any one role cannot exist without the others, and sometimes they converge in a single person.

Another issue associated with Bishop's material archive is reformatting.[10] Not long after the collection was acquired in the early 1980s, the Vassar Library created a duplicate set of preservation photocopies to ensure long-term access to this fragile, valuable, and soon-to-be heavily used collection (digital technologies had not yet been developed). A policy was established whereby researchers were first offered copies of the papers, although anyone could view originals upon request. While this approach has helped to preserve the collection, in recent years scholarly trends have emerged that highlight the material aspects of originals and the importance of examining them closely. As we worked in the archive, our seminar participants proved to be highly attuned to the physical nature of the collection. During the seminar, for instance, we examined the badly water-damaged and frayed original of Bishop's baby book, titled *A Biography of Our Baby*, which was acquired from Brazil by Vassar in 2002 with the Portinari family papers. For Thomas Travisano, Bishop's current biographer, who joined us during the seminar, the original of this document is important as the first account of Bishop's life, a book that despite its damage reveals much about a much-cherished and loved child (this was a deluxe version of a popular baby book) whose early days were documented with photographs and careful notations of weight and growth. Yet the pages also reveal the crisis that began to unfold with the death of Bishop's father and the mental deterioration of her mother. Although in this case some color photocopies are available, by their very nature these cannot convey all aspects of the original, nor can they replicate the overpowering experience of holding and examining the baby book directly.

    Photocopies of the Foster letters reveal very little beyond content, but the original documents tell a more complete story. Bishop's letters to Foster are originals, not carbons.[11] The letters have been folded in half, rather than tri-folded to fit in an envelope, so Bishop may not have sent them. In short, if we are going to use the archives, we must be attentive to the materiality of the archive and the stories these artifacts can tell. Photocopies distort our sense of the archive and Bishop's creative process. Her notebooks in their original form are a colorful collage of image and text, a layering of clippings, drawings, and ideas for poems and stories. Laura Sloan Patterson makes a case in chapter 14 for studying the originals of these notebooks as multimedia and multimodal artifacts that inform Bishop's method and art. In general, the essays and digital examples collected here provide insight into aspects of the collection that might be otherwise invisible to scholars working from photocopies. We would have liked to offer more digital reproductions of such vital material but were unable to because of the demands and restrictions placed on us by Farrar, Straus and Giroux (FSG).

    Here we come to one of the more pressing issues associated with using and reproducing Bishop's archive for scholarly purposes. FSG owns the copyright to

Bishop's unpublished and much of her published work and acts on behalf of the Elizabeth Bishop Estate regarding issues concerning permission to reuse material. Since the publisher stands to make further profit from a steady stream of publications coming out of the archives, as has happened in the last decade with more to come, its role in policing Bishop scholarship appears as a conflict of interest. The publisher is now also the copyright holder for May Swenson's papers. Claiming to represent the interests of the estate, FSG has placed an unfair financial burden on scholars seeking to publish selections from the archives, even though those selections are made for the purpose of advancing scholarship in the field and in no way compromise FSG's interests in continuing to produce new editions of Bishop's work. FSG's representatives were particularly concerned about the fact that Lever Press is an open access publication. This is a short-sighted approach to the question of copyright and scholarship, which results in exactly the opposite of the free exchange of ideas that exemplifies scholarship at its best. Moreover, many books and most scholarly journals, even those with conventional print runs, are now digitally available and downloadable through academic libraries. I chose to publish this edition with Lever Press because I believe strongly in making scholarly work available globally and to all, especially interested readers who do not have access to academic libraries.

Finally, good scholarship excites interest in a poet and her archives, encouraging more people to buy, teach, and read books by the author. As a scholarly treatment of Bishop's archives (not an edition of her work), fair use guidelines encourage us to support our arguments with representative work from the archives, since this is a book about the poet and her archives. That is what we have done here, choosing only those images and short sections of Bishop's notebooks that give the reader a sense of the extraordinary range of these materials. We would have liked to include more. But we feel that what we do offer provides an excellent beginning to opening up new archival readings of Bishop and, more broadly, mid-century poetry and its many archives. We have also sought on a number of occasions to correct the record in our readings. Our scholars have found transcription errors in an edition of Bishop's letters, *One Art,* and in *Edgar Allan Poe & the Juke-Box,* both published by FSG. We have corrected these errors wherever we have found them using original documents. Errors are inevitable but far less likely if editions are edited and checked by more than one scholar, rather than a single editor. It is FSG's responsibility, as the copyright holder that insists on restricting scholars' ability to present copies of Bishop's original work, to maintain the most exacting standards in the representation of those works, as the poet herself would have wished. FSG has an edition of Bishop's extraordinary notebooks planned for publication in the next few years. We hope that the publisher will take steps not only to present these notebooks as accurately as possible but to include facsimiles, as they sometimes did in *Edgar Allan Poe & the Juke-Box* and *Elizabeth Bishop and* The New Yorker. A digital component would also better represent Bishop's visual practice for teaching and scholarship.

Our contributors demonstrate that returning to the archive and describing original documents is crucial to understanding and accurately representing the powerful currents of this poet's career. From the poet's collage-like notebooks to her drawings and drafts that reveal a "polyphonic" process of composing, as Heather Bozant Witcher argues in chapter 13, these visual artifacts are essential to understanding the full range of Bishop's work. As a writer's reputation changes (as it has for Bishop), so does our reading of the archives and, indeed, of the poet's work, as we have seen so clearly in the shifts that our reading of Bishop has undergone over the last fifty years. We see here with Bishop what Anita Helle has called, in reference to Sylvia Plath's legacy, "an absorbing instance of archive formation as a cultural process, occurring through a variety of means (historical, popular, biographical, fictional) and engaging a range of public interests" (634). As with Bishop, new primary materials made available to Plath scholars at the beginning of this century led to a reassessment of the poet and the subsequent publication of an important and widely cited volume of essays in 2007, edited by Helle and titled *The Unraveling Archive: Essays on Sylvia Plath.* Since then, new archival research on Plath has presented readers with a poet "who is more historically located and multiple" (641). Working in the archive collaboratively for three weeks and now on this project has allowed us to study Bishop's material archive more thoroughly than would be possible under ordinary conditions in academic life.

ARCHIVAL STUDIES AND THE DIGITAL HUMANITIES

We have been inspired by a growing body of interdisciplinary work in literary studies and the digital humanities that brings together literary and archival study. The theme for the 2016 annual conference of the Pacific Ancient and Modern Language Association (PAMLA), for example, was Archives, Libraries, Properties, and at the Modernist Studies Association Annual Conference the same year, I co-directed (with Anita Helle) a seminar on Modern Poetry, Archives, and Estates. In May 2017, *American Literary History* published a special issue on archives. In the digital humanities, Marianne Moore scholars are working collaboratively to develop a digital and searchable version of Moore's notebooks that serve as an example of what could be done in Bishop studies if copyright restrictions can be renegotiated or lifted.

Also foundational to our work is interdisciplinary scholarship that takes the literary archive as its focus. For instance, *The Boundaries of the Literary Archive: Reclamation and Representation* (2013), an edited volume of interdisciplinary scholarship on the literary archive, brings together the expertise of both archivists and literary scholars. And Linda Morra provides a model for this kind of scholarship in her 2014 study of Canadian writers and their archives in *Unarrested Archives: Case Studies in Twentieth-Century Canadian Women's Authorship*. Our project is also informed by the theory and practice of archival research, including the work of historians and cultural critics (Carolyn Steedman's *Dust: The Archive and Cultural History*, 2001); genetic critics (Jed Deppman, Daniel Ferrer, and Michael Groden's edited volume *Genetic Criticism: Texts and Avant-textes*, 2004); and archivists (Randall Jimerson's edited volume *American Archival Studies: Readings in Theory and Practice*, 2000).

ELIZABETH BISHOP AND THE LITERARY ARCHIVE

The chapters in this collection are divided into three parts, reflecting the richness of the Bishop archive and the complexity of Bishop's creative process and professional self-fashioning. Part 1, The Queer Archive, brings together six chapters that read in and around the archives to make more visible and legible the traces, erasures, and reading and writing practices of the queer poet across her unpublished and published work. Part 1 begins with "'Too Shy to Stop': Elizabeth Bishop and the Scene of Reading," Heather Treseler's discussion of the queer scene of reading in the archival drafts of "In the Waiting Room," the Ruth Foster letters, and other documents. Richard Flynn's chapter, "Elizabeth Bishop's Sanity: Childhood Trauma, Psychoanalysis, and Sentimentality," follows with a return to the scene of childhood staged in the Foster letters and throughout the archive as it intertwines with Bishop's complex relationship to psychoanalysis. Treseler's and Flynn's exploration of archival documents not only reveal the importance of psychoanalytic discourse in shaping identity and influencing poetic craft during this period but also offer the most thorough investigation of this subject in Bishop scholarship to date.

Part of Bishop's efforts to craft a career for herself meant negotiating a society that considered homosexuality "as neurotic 'maladjustment.'" Jeffrey Westover's "Elizabeth Bishop's Perspectives on Marriage" investigates what the archive reveals about Bishop's relationship to the question of marriage as she negotiated her professional reputation. The chapter shows, too, how Bishop's archive pushes back against this medical discourse on homosexuality in two understudied stories that Bishop co-wrote with Pauline Hemingway in Key West. Treseler, Flynn, and Westover all see a "frankness" in Bishop's letters to Foster about her own sexuality that not only "resists the prevailing medical discourse" of the period, as Westover has argued, but also challenges the famous public reticence that continues to cling to scholarly discussions of Bishop's career. The archival record, however, reveals many Bishops, as the following three chapters demonstrate.

Alyse Knorr and David Hoak both focus on Bishop's unpublished correspondence. In "'Keeping Up a Silent Conversation': Recovering a Queer Bishop through Her Intimate Correspondence with Alice Methfessel," Knorr focuses for the first time on the love letters between Bishop and her final partner, Alice Methfessel, a relationship that also influenced this last phase of Bishop's career. Hoak's chapter, "Dear Elizabeth, Dear May: Reappraising the Bishop/Swenson Correspondence," reaches beyond the Vassar archives to explore the letters between May Swenson and Elizabeth Bishop housed in the Washington University Special Collections in St. Louis and the Utah State University Special Collections and Archives. Hoak's chapter does important work to highlight Bishop's extensive correspondence with other literary figures, besides Lowell, that can be found in the archives. The final chapter in part I, John Emil Vincent's "Odd Job: Elizabeth Bishop's 'The Fairy Toll-Taker,'" returns to this late prose poem as a case study in queer archival reading. The archive, these scholars argue, tells a more complex story of queer love than we have seen thus far.

With an attention to the material culture represented in the archives and beyond, this volume's second part, Travels: Scale, Location, Architecture, Archive, extends our understanding of Bishop as a traveler in the Americas at mid-century, placing her in a wider, more multidisciplinary framework and thereby expanding our sense of Bishop as a traveler as well as an archivist of those travels. We begin with the most thorough examination of race in the Bishop archives to date. Marvin Campbell's "Elizabeth Bishop and Race in the Archive" explores the material evidence of Bishop's exploration of race through a variety of documents—from clippings of advertisements to the interview that Bishop conducted in San Francisco in 1969 with Black Panther Party member Kathleen Cleaver. Campbell's study, which traces Bishop's exploration of race, class, and gender across the Americas from Key West to Brazil and back to San Francisco, places Bishop in an expanded Global South Atlantic context. Bishop's views on race are complex, Campbell argues. We should neither apologize for Bishop nor vilify these attitudes: "We need to be honest about them."

In "'I miss all that bright, detailed flatness': Elizabeth Bishop in Brevard," Charla Allyn Hughes studies Bishop's travel notebooks and uncovers a wealth of new information on Bishop's trips to Brevard, North Carolina, in the early 1940s and their important influence on her work. Located in the mountains of western North Carolina, about thirty miles southwest of Asheville, Brevard (and the region) has been "a popular vacation destination for the better part of the past two centuries,"

Hughes notes. Initially contrasting its mountains and abundant waterfalls to what she missed about Key West, Bishop warmed to Brevard and its collection of local characters during her time there. Whereas her trips to Brevard might be considered brief interludes in the extended stays that punctuated Bishop's travels, her time in Key West (where she lived part of the year for more than a decade in the 1930s and 1940s) has been the subject of a great deal of scholarly work. However, in "'All the untidy activity': Travel & the Picturesque in Elizabeth Bishop's Writings," Yaël Schlick offers a fresh look at Key West and its role in forming Bishop's creative imagination. Informed by theories of the picturesque, Schlick argues that Bishop's postcards from Key West (and other locales) offer an "intriguing space" where Bishop's travel experiences and touristic practices overlap. These archival materials, Schlick notes, are not a "means to search for origins" but rather offer "a pathway to plunge back into the temporal, palpable multiplicity of the travel experience." And Douglas Basford, in "The Burglar of the Tower of Babel: Elizabeth Bishop, Architecture, Translation, Archive," extends our understanding of Bishop's time in Brazil through the overlapping projects of translation and architecture. Basford makes a particularly important contribution to our understanding of Bishop's work in relationship to other Brazilian writers, such as João Cabral de Melo Neto.

Part II ends with a different conception of travel: the kind of time travel that working in the archives allows. "Every text," Claire Colebrook argues in "The Anthropocene and the Archive," "is a time capsule and a time machine, containing the present, but sending the present into a future that the present cannot control." Her statement could not be more applicable to Sarah Giragosian's examination of Bishop's geological imagination in "Elizabeth Bishop's Geopoetics," a term that positions Bishop's work at the intersection of science and poetry. In turning to a series of lesser-known poems, such as "The Museum," "Verdigris," and "The Mountain," Giragosian shows how engaged Bishop's poetry is with "anthropocentric understandings of memory, scale, and agency."

The chapters in parts I and II map Bishop's archival practice in the fragments and traces that we call the archive. Part III, The Work in Progress, becomes more intentional in its turn to how Bishop herself shapes her material and, indeed, her career. As Linda Anderson argues, Bishop's recursive writing process involved "returning to drafts, [and] using ideas and images from notebooks written years before" (7). This practice meant that Bishop actually gathered into her work "archival traces and memories which could also provide connections and echoes across time" (7). The chapters in part III provide detailed documentation of Bishop's archival practice. Andrew Walker turns to Bishop's early college translation of Aristophanes' *The Birds* in "The Archival Aviary: Elizabeth Bishop and Drama," illuminating the role that drama played in her evolving aesthetic process. Walker, like many of the scholars here, revises the idea of Bishop's self-presentation as "modest" and instead maps out Bishop's "extensive engagement with a modulating lyric practice" that involved experiments with "dramatic form, theatrical performances, and the intertwining of music and poetry."

Drawing on genetic criticism's attention to texts and *avant-textes*, Heather Bozant Witcher's "Archival Animals: Polyphonic Movement in Elizabeth Bishop's Drafts" attends to music and sound in Bishop's work as she explores Bishop's compositional process in her drafts for her Brazilian poem, "The Armadillo." In "'Huge Crowd Pleased by New Models': Elizabeth Bishop's Cuttyhunk Notebook as Multimodal and Multimedia Artifact," Laura Sloan Patterson explores the collaged notebook that Bishop kept in the 1930s as a "staging space" for her art, reading moments of visual overload in the notebooks as key points of production and productivity as Bishop developed her craft. Both chapters end with a discussion of how the archival materials can provide new ways of thinking about and teaching Bishop's art and craft.

Finally, Claire Seiler's "The Matter of Elizabeth Bishop's Professionalism" ends the collection with a full-scale rebuttal of another oft-repeated tenet of Bishop studies—Bishop's anti-professionalism, her retreat from self-promotion and refusal to participate in "Poetry as Big Business." As we have seen in the other chapters in this section, the evidence of Bishop's dramatic self-fashioning is extensive throughout her archive. Seiler turns to the "unremarkable" documents in the archives—a pair of Guggenheim applications—in order to explore Bishop's self-presentation at different points in her career within the context of the "increasingly institutional patronage and management of literature and the arts in the postwar United States" as well as in the context of the gendered politics of literary prizes. Seiler also warns her readers not to place too much interpretive weight on what might appear to be more remarkable documents, such as the Foster letters, for there are many stories to tell in the archives.

Our book begins with remarkable new literary finds and ends with the return to documents that might seem comparatively mundane in order to make the point that all archival materials tell important new stories about literary history. But, as Steedman reminds us, these stories are necessarily incomplete. Iain Bailey notes that we should consider the archive "as a place of work, rather than as a cache from which to draw certainties" (41). It could be argued that no poet knew this better than Bishop, for Bishop's poetic practice encourages a return to the archive. It is a practice that, like our work in the archives, requires her readers to understand "that sense of constant re-adjustment" that Bishop herself called our attention to very early in her career when she wrote "The Gentleman of Shalott" (*P* 12).

NOTES

1. Ron Patkus, Associate Director of Libraries for Special Collections at Vassar College, documented some of this scholarly activity in a special exhibition in 2011 commemorating the hundredth anniversary of Bishop's birth. See exhibition booklet, *From the Archive: Discovering Elizabeth Bishop*. I also want to thank Ron for his support of this seminar and the Lever Press publication as well as his detailed information on acquisition and preservation at Vassar.
2. For a thorough guide to Bishop-related materials held in institutions and private collections in Nova Scotia, see Barry, *Elizabeth Bishop: Archival Guide*.
3. In *Archive Fever*, Jacques Derrida notes that the word *archive* itself derives from the Greek *arkheion*—house of the archons—where the law is determined in Ancient Greece. Because of their recognized authority, official documents were kept in the house of the archons; hence, they are placed under house arrest (3).
4. William Logan writes on the correspondence between Bishop and Louise Bradley and the importance of Bishop's years at Camp Chequesset ("Elizabeth Bishop").
5. Two of the scholars, Marvin Campbell and Charla Allyn Hughes, graduated from Vassar and read Bishop for the first time while they were students, and Hughes had lived in Bishop's dorm, Cushing House.
6. The papers are held in Vassar's Archives and Special Collections Library, which holds the college's extensive rare book, manuscript, and archival collections. The Library has an active teaching and outreach program and each year responds to more than one thousand research requests. The Bishop collection is one among several heavily used collections.
7. See my discussion of Bishop at Vassar in Hicok, *Degrees*.
8. See Rich, "Eye" in *Blood* 125.
9. See Morra.
10. This has long been an accepted practice used by research libraries; see https://www.nedcc.org/preservation101/session-7/7paper-reproductions.
11. Lorrie Goldensohn misidentifies them as carbon copies in "Approaching."

PART I

THE QUEER ARCHIVE

CHAPTER ONE

"TOO SHY TO STOP"

Elizabeth Bishop and the Scene of Reading

Heather Treseler

In July of 1971, the poet Frank Bidart wrote a letter to Elizabeth Bishop, expressing his deep admiration for "In the Waiting Room." Addressing the older poet as "Miss Bishop," Bidart related the unlikely setting in which he first read her iconic poem:

> It's quite an experience to be sitting in the Hermit Hamburger, open the copy of The New Yorker you bought because-there's-a-poem-in-it-by-Elizabeth-Bishop, and find that it's not merely good, but about the kind of primal and radical experience it's usually quite impossible to talk about, or even face. What on earth does my I have to do with this body, these shoes, these people who insist we are connected, a "family"? Am I necessarily an I at all?—
> How "unlikely" to first read a great poem, one I'm sure I'll be living with for the rest of my life, in the Hermit Hamburger. (VC 1.14)

Cleverly, Bidart recreates the *mise-en-scène* of reading Bishop's poem at a restaurant in Berkeley, California, mirroring the child narrator of "In the Waiting Room," who undergoes epiphanies while reading *National Geographic Magazine* in a dentist's office. Indeed, Bishop's poem explores the "radical experience" of inhabiting an historical self, a biological body, and a network of social relation: her child narrator confronts what it means to be a person with a face and a pair of shoes, an aunt and a birthday, drawn into the nexus of identity marked by gender, race, class, and familial relation—and all that "family" was thought to include or shun in 1971.

Yet Bishop's "In the Waiting Room" is one of several poems that present a narrator's revelations while engaging with a para-literary text. She gives a topography

Frank Bidart describes his first encounter with "In the Waiting Room." Letter used by permission of Frank Bidart, © 2019. (VC 1.14; Courtesy of Vassar College)

of her sensibility in "The Map," an early *ars poetica*; meditates on the shocks and intrigues of travel vis-à-vis stock images in a family Bible in "Over 2,000 Illustrations and a Complete Concordance"; parodies martial display in the postcard-poem "View of The Capitol from The Library of Congress"; and employs the conventions of a personal letter to explore relational ambivalence in "Letter to N.Y." and "Invitation to Miss Marianne Moore." In these instances, para-literary media—the map, the family Bible, the postcard, and the letter—frame the narrator's engagement with the sub-genre at hand, each uniquely "widening the ego's field of perception," as the psychoanalytic critic Mary Jacobus posits (24). Thus, Bishop's reader enters the reading narrator's "inhabited solitude" (Jacobus 5), lending many of her poems their uncanny air of intimacy and "cognitive authority" (Ravinthiran xiv).

Bishop frames several poems, moreover, with sustained allusions that both tempt and temper the reader's initial expectations. She turns, for example, the popular nursery rhyme, "This Is the House that Jack Built" into a postwar dirge in "Visits to St. Elizabeths," drawing on her social calls to Ezra Pound's psychiatric ward. Similarly, she satirizes Cold War militarism within a Civil War travelogue in "From Trollope's Journal" and enlivens the domestic phantasmagoria of televised warfare in "12 O'Clock News." Borrowing from an array of texts and tableaux, references to elite and popular culture, private relation and public event, Bishop centers her poetics on the drama of perception: her narrators read—and are interpolated by—their environs and choice of textualities.

Staging interiority in connection with books, broadcasts, songs, letters, and other media, Bishop explores the dialectic of subjective thought and objective reality, imitating "the movement of the mind" that she admired in Gerard Manley Hopkins (*Pr* 468). In her collegiate essay on Hopkins, Bishop cites critic M. W. Croll's praise of Baroque writers: "Their purpose was to portray, not a thought, but a mind thinking.... They knew that an idea separated from the act of experiencing it is not the same idea that we experienced. The ardor of its conception in the mind is a necessary part of its truth" (*Pr* 473). To portray the development of thought as much as the thought itself, Bishop uses the metaphor of reading to frame, among other things, the unfolding nuance of cognitive process as well as what Jacobus identifies as a reader's "commitment to otherness" (13). And although the term *scene of reading* is often used in connection with Sigmund Freud's primal scene, or the child's traumatic discovery of parental intercourse as detailed in Freud's "From the History of an Infantile Neurosis" (1918), Bishop's poetry shows her knowledge of Freud's paradigm and, as in many of her generation, her conscious step beyond it in exploratory narratives about selfhood. The narrators in her poems do not always revisit anxieties spurred by induction into sexual or anatomical knowledge, although that is certainly one valence of "In the Waiting Room." They are, more often, subject to other climactic moments of discovery, which broaden the narrator's zone of cognizance: thus, Bishop's poem, with its child narrator studying a *National Geographic,* enlivened a "primal and radical experience" for Bidart in a Berkeley restaurant where, reading it, he was convinced he had encountered "a great poem, one I'm sure I'll be living with for the rest of my life" (VC 1.14).

For Jacobus, this transformative "scene of reading" is an instance of Winnicott's potential space, a zone in which the meaningful play of cultural experience transpires, and this definition generally characterizes Bishop's portrayal of reading, a motif in her writing about childhood and in many of her poems after 1947, following her analysis with Dr. Ruth Foster. As do Virginia Woolf's seminal essays "Reading" (1919) and "How Should One Read a Book?" (1926), Bishop's writing about reading suggests that it is not always a pleasurable activity but one that involves intimate, sometimes disconcerting encounters both with the self and with others. In "Time's Andromedas" (1933), another of Bishop's precocious collegiate essays, she describes an instance of being *unable* to read, unable to disengage her own "wordy racket" to contemplate the book before her:

> One afternoon last fall I was studying very hard, bending over my book with my back to the light of the high double windows. Concentration was so difficult that I had dug myself a sort of little black cave into the subject I was reading, and there I burrowed and scratched, like the Count of Monte Cristo, expecting Heaven knows what sudden revelation. My own thoughts, conflicting with those of the book, were making such a wordy racket that I heard and saw nothing—until the page before my eyes blushed pink. I was startled, then realized that there must be a sunset at my back, and waited a minute trying to guess the color of it from the color of the little reflection. (*Pr* 466)

There are several notable features in Bishop's account, including the "little black cave" she attempts to furrow "into the subject," where she hopes for "sudden revelation" as if she were a Biblical prophet, retreating to a rocky grotto. The narrative also suggests that epiphany—or climactic reading—is her tacit ideal and expectation, although she finds, in this instance, that her thoughts are so "conflicting with those of the book" that she cannot surrender to the book's import: she "heard and saw nothing," which implies that reading, for her, is an experience that summons both image and voice.

The failure to read, which Bishop describes, nonetheless underscores important elements—gathered attention, the possibility of "revelation," a conjuring of voice and image—that she associates with reading. As Jacobus observes, "reading the book, as opposed to seeing it, [ironically] depends on not-seeing the words" and allowing oneself to be swept up in the current of signification (7). Unable to absorb the book's content, Bishop discovers that the anthropomorphic page has "blushed pink" in a reflection of a sunset that might have otherwise gone unnoticed behind her (*Pr* 466). So although she is caught up in her own "wordy racket," the book's presence nonetheless intensifies and directs her focus. The "cave" of her intentional attention becomes suffused with light: the illuminated book induces the reader's heightened awareness of her physical environment. She cannot read the page or take in the words' semantic content, but she admires the sky's color caught there. The book, failing to serve as a window to another's subjectivity, becomes a mirror: Bishop's depictions of reading often engage this dualism.

An interest in the phenomenology of reading recurs throughout Bishop's oeuvre and with particular emphasis in "In the Waiting Room," nearly forty years after she wrote "Time's Andromedas." Scholars, commenting on this poem, have tended to focus on its autobiographical analogue, placing it among Bishop's late poems of "self-advice" (Schwartz 154); praising its "triumphs of tonality" (Howard 208); and noting its parallels with "Crusoe in England," the other lengthy first-person narrative poem in *Geography III* (1976) (Cook 217). Other critics have focused on

Bishop's truth-claims about the poem's veracity vis-à-vis its apparent source text, the February 1918 edition of *National Geographic* (Edelman, "Geography" 179-80), or legitimately examined the poem's complex engagement of gender and race, class and commodification. Keeping in mind Bishop's commitment to exploring "not a thought, but a mind thinking" and her worried reply to Bidart's letter—"The *Hermit Hamburger* sounds rather sad—everyone eating his hamburger in an individual booth?"—it seems appropriate to examine "In the Waiting Room" alongside its six manuscript drafts instead of by its New Critical lonesome (*PPL* 882). These drafts evince the poet's careful rendering of a "scene of reading" in a credulous narrator who bridges the perspectives of a "shy" inquisitive child and the reminiscing adult.

Other archival material relevant to a full understanding of this poem includes Bishop's recently unearthed letters to Dr. Ruth Foster, the psychiatrist and psychoanalyst with whom she worked in the late 1940s after a short, aborted attempt at analysis with Karen Horney in 1940 (Marshall, *Elizabeth Bishop* 78). These letters—twenty-two typed pages, including a timeline, with handwritten annotations—show Bishop meditating on the psychological experiences of reading and being read, extending and receiving recognition as she grappled with her troubling memories, creative process, and ambitions as a writer (VC 118.33). Discovered after Alice Methfessel's death in 2009 and acquired by the Vassar College Archives and Special Collections Library in 2011, Bishop's letters constitute both a revealing psychosexual memoir and a remarkable portrait of poetic sensibility during the interval in which her aesthetic was attaining its maturity. As Bethany Hicok has observed, the poet relates her personal history to her analyst in loose but decided connection with Freud's "sexual researches of childhood"—to include a focus on sexual initiation, maternal figures, and castration anxiety (Unpublished 4). But Bishop also investigates, more generally, the adventure of reading in connection with the language of dreams, analytic recognition, and the mortmain of memory, exploring ways in which these modes inform her poetics.

Several major poems—including "Insomnia," "View of The Capitol from The Library of Congress," "The Moose," and "In the Waiting Room"—derive imagery from the psychic loam of her richly descriptive letters to Foster, which grant readers not only a portal to Bishop's childhood travail, formative relationships, sexuality, and struggle with addiction but also an uncanny glimpse at her writing process as she came to newly understand it through psychoanalysis. Before the discovery of the Foster letters, I had hypothesized that Bishop's analysis, carried out over two years, helped to catalyze her mature aesthetic, evident in the intersubjective turn of *A Cold Spring* (1955). The Foster letters lend substance to that claim and show, moreover, that for poems such as "In the Waiting Room," Bishop drew upon specific tableaux articulated to her analyst decades earlier.

Remarkably, the letters contain the psychic grammar of Bishop's poem, to include the relationships between shyness and shame, trauma and compulsive reading; a vivid hallucination in a dentist's office; and the uncanny experience of melding voices with another older woman. Viewed alongside the Foster letters and archival substrate, "In the Waiting Room" appears to satirize the colonial gaze, to explore the interrelation of personal and public history, and to show Bishop's ingenious use of a para-literary conceit to engage her reader in the subtleties of "a mind thinking" (Pr 473). As does Bishop's narrator in "Time's Andromedas," we might find that the page "blushe[s] pink" as we confront what it might have meant to be "an *I* / . . . an *Elizabeth,* / . . . one of *them*" in the last year of World War I, as a white child and as a future queer woman with the privilege and punishment that might entail (P 180).

*

Combining insights from her analytic work with an ingenious imitation of *National Geographic*'s typography and idiomatic style, Bishop's "In the Waiting Room" melds lyric form and everyday media, fact and fiction, history and imagination. Her poem of internal geography aligns with her stated allegiance to the "more delicate" colors of mapmakers, rather than the limited palette of "historians," as she contests the disciplinary force of historicity, the burdens of being "an *I*" in human society with its acculturated violence and inequity (P 5). Drafts of the poem show the poet curating a scene of reading that implicates its narrator—as well as the readers of her poem—in the politics of spectacle and the epistemological hinge between self and other. "[P]unctuation?" is scrawled prominently in the top right-hand margin of the first extant draft of "In the Waiting Room," and it is one of the clear editorial tasks in this version, as Bishop orchestrates the poem's pacing by scoring end-stops, enjambments, and caesuras across fairly short lines.

What is also immediately intriguing is the draft's shape: Bishop writes in one continuous narrow column over two pages with two paragraph indentations in lieu of stanza breaks (marking the lines: "Suddenly, from inside," and "Then I was back in it"), which lend the poem the formatted look of a newspaper or magazine. These typographical choices are reinforced by the poem's first line, "In Worcester, Massachusetts," which imitates the place identifier in journalism, usually positioned below the article title and byline. Mimicking the look of a regional newspaper or *National Geographic*, the latter typically presenting stories in two or three narrow columns per page, Bishop's narrator relates her personal story as if it were the day's news—alongside the ramifying fact that "The War was on" (P 181).

Indeed, the first ten lines, written in declarative sentences and the

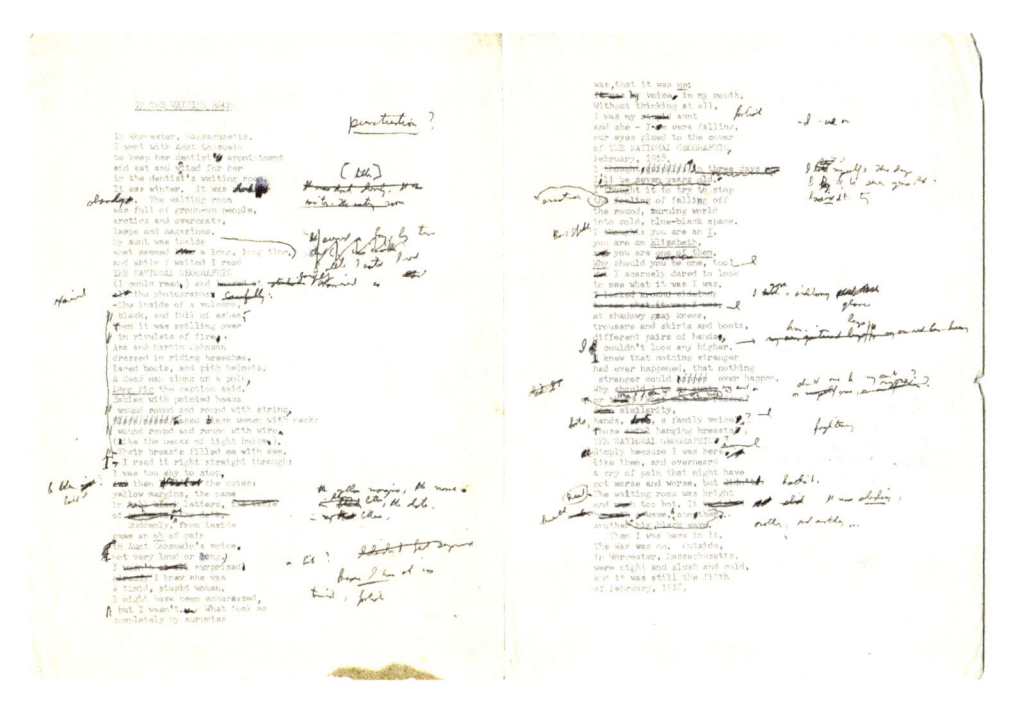

Bishop's annotated first draft of "In the Waiting Room."

"who-what-when-where" deictic mode of journalism, resemble the anecdotal style of *National Geographic* from the World War I era. Consider the opening lines of Bishop's published version of "In the Waiting Room" beside the folksy lead to "Helping to Solve Our Allies' Food Problem," an article from the February 1918 edition of *National Geographic* to which Bishop refers, specifically, in the poem's fourth draft:

In Worcester, Massachusetts,
I went with Aunt Consuelo
to keep her dentist's appointment
and sat and waited for her
in the dentist's waiting room.
It was winter. It got dark
early. The waiting room
was full of grown-up people,
arctics and overcoats,
lamps and magazines.
(P 179)

Mrs. Mulvany with her pet
pig is no longer an object of
ridicule and a topic for jest. She
is a patriot. The Solomons of conservation are sending Mr. Average Consumer
to her as a model of thrift, just as the
Wise Man of Biblical times sent the sluggard to the ant. By means of her pig
Mrs. Mulvany is helping to win the war,
for she is making from one to two pounds
of pork grow each day where none grew
yesterday.
(Graves 170)

Bishop's poem has less Calvinist flourish than the article about valorous Mrs. Mulvany, but both align individual experiences with the wartime context, anecdotal leads dilating to larger considerations. Tellingly, in the fourth draft of her poem, Bishop seems to have turned to a physical copy of the magazine to bolster her supply of narrative details. Thus she includes—and then removes in the fifth draft—lines that refer to the raising of swine, nationwide, in "pig clubs" of children who rear piglets for slaughter in support of the Allies (Graves 171).

Notably, however, Bishop's fourth draft begins with another porcine reference, one situated abroad. Indeed, the child narrator reports reading multiple "old NATIONAL GEOGRAPHICS," and the first image she highlights is that of "a dead man slung from a pole / -Long Pig (sic)it said." Tellingly, in the margin of the draft, directly across from these lines, she positions the American adventurers "Asa [sic] and Martin Johnson" as if they were offering a tour—to Western readers—of the magazine's voyeuristic images. As in the published draft of the poem, the narrator also encounters babies with bound "pointed" heads and naked women, and in this draft, she confesses of the latter that "their black breasts frightened me." Yet she also satirically stylizes herself as an intrepid reader, an adventurer like the Johnsons, and boasts that she reads all the *National Geographic*s available to her in that setting: "I studied all of them / up to the latest number." Thereafter, she details photographs from an active volcano crater in Alaska, Mount Katmai, and the "Valley of Ten Thousand Smokes" with its thousands of "fumeroles" or plumes of steam. The magazine editors, she indicates, have even included a line to show where the volcano had "blown its top off," lending a cartoonish note to the spectacle. In this fourth draft, the scene of reading is much more elaborate, detailed, and varied than in the published version, and it concludes with a reference to the national pig clubs in America, intended to supplement the Allies' food supply. The narrator's sympathies, however, appear to be with the "darling baby pigs" rather than with the military's "Food Problem," a phrase that links warfare's barbarity to the supply of and demand for bodies, human and animal.

Curiously, the narrator's proud parenthetical assertion, "(I could read)," is immediately—and perhaps ironically—followed by a detailed catalogue of photographs in this draft, which enlist the reader in the child narrator's interpretative gaze. As the phenomenologist George Poulet asserts, when reading, "I am on loan to another, and this other thinks, feels, suffers, and acts within me" (60). Bishop's draft, informed by featured stories in the actual magazine, heightens readers' experience of the narrator's perspective, *in propria persona*, as she confronts the spectacle of "Long Pig," learns the meaning of "fumeroles," and studies the line denoting the volcano's explosion.

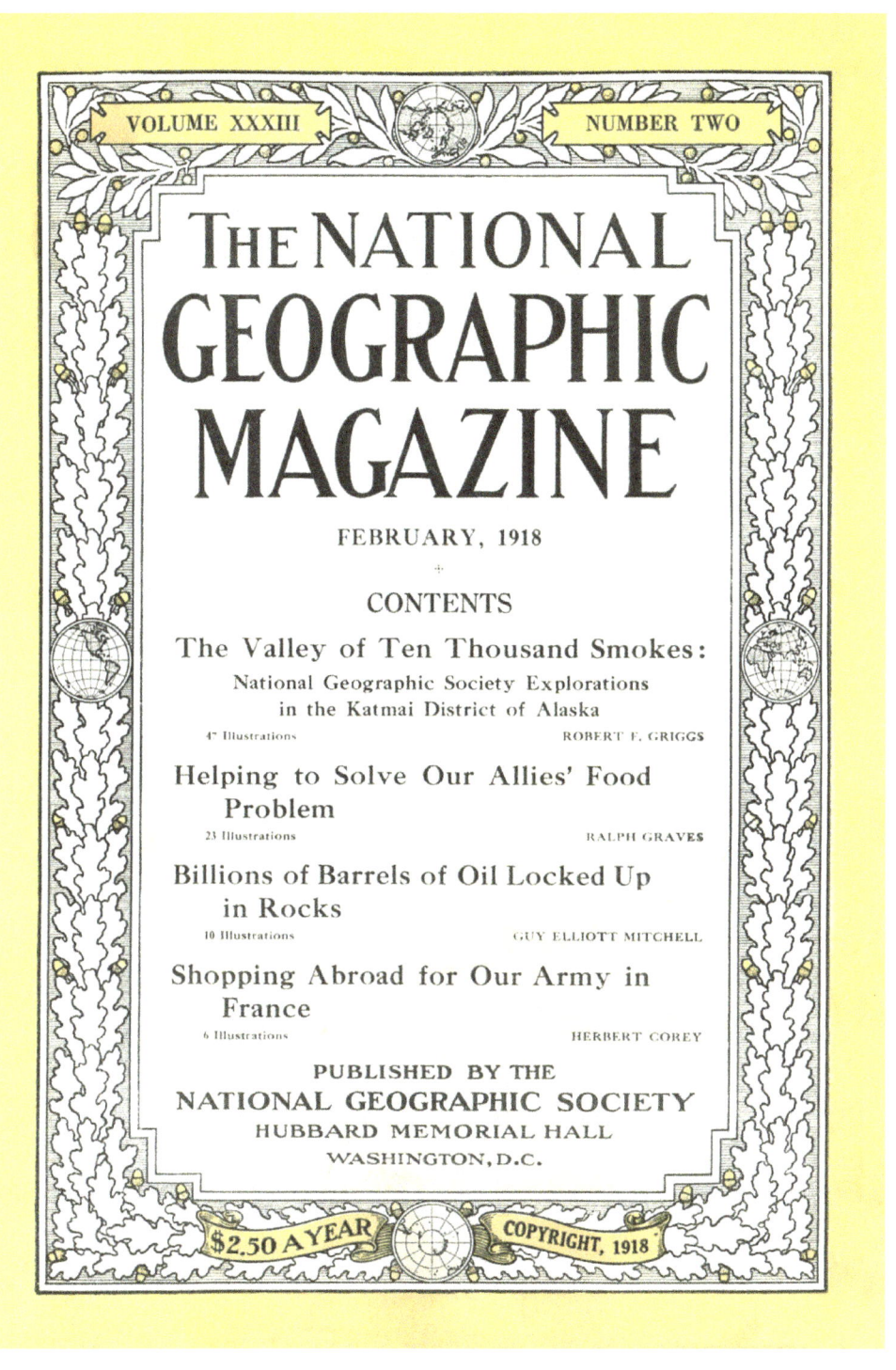

The cover of the *National Geographic Magazine* from February of 1918.

172   THE NATIONAL GEOGRAPHIC MAGAZINE

Photograph from Department of Agriculture

GROOMING A PIG FOR THE STATE FAIR

Eight years ago, before the inauguration of the pig-club movement in the South, most of the hogs in that section of the United States were of the razor-back variety—the kind which is so thin and scrawny that a wag has declared the farmer can prevent its going through a hole in his fence by tying a knot in its tail.

sive palmetto shrub tracts, was the only type of pig familiar to the farmer. To-day blooded swine are the rule rather than the exception, and it is a high tribute to the educational value of the boys' pig clubs that of the four States—Mississippi, Georgia, Virginia, and Delaware—reporting an increase in swine population on September 1, 1917, over the same date in 1916, Mississippi and Georgia stand second and third in pig-club enrollment. These two States reported an increase of 90,000 hogs, while the country at large showed a decrease of 5,000,000.

One of the strongly emphasized slogans of the pig-club organizers and supervisors is that it does not pay to raise a poor hog. On the other hand, the profits to be derived from pure-bred pigs are exceptionally large, considering the amount of capital invested. This preachment not only has had its immediate ef-fect in pig-club communities, where example has taken the place of precept, but it is causing the farmer to awaken to the fact that his son and his daughter are proving more efficient than he, simply because they are taking advantage of the information which has been gained by experts and specialists through years of experimentation and research.

THE "PRACTICAL" FARMER vs. THE PIG-CLUB MEMBER

The "theorists," as the college-trained agriculturists were once called, are no longer scorned by the "practical" farmer, whose "practicality" is seen in a very unenviable light when he is compelled to admit that it takes two years for his range-reared hog to acquire a weight of 150 pounds, while a pig-club member, like young Walter Whitman, of Indiana, presents as an exhibit his pet Duroc,

This article by Ralph Graves encourages American children to support the war effort by raising pigs.

Accompanying the narrator in her perusal, the reader of Bishop's draft has a redoubled experience of otherness as she allows for a "falling away of the barriers" between herself, the narrating subject, and the various secondary objects invoked and described (Poulet 57). Indeed, Bishop's curation of the magazine's content suggests that she was cognizant of the power of incorporating a para-literary text: using the child's apprehension of a magazine's images, she truncates readers' critical distance from the narrative she relates.

Tellingly, references to "Long Pig" and "pigs / with ~~darling~~ baby pigs" bookend Bishop's description of the magazine in this fourth draft, linking reports of cannibalism abroad to animal husbandry at home. Lee Edelman astutely notes that Bishop may have based the image of "a dead man slung on a pole" on Osa Johnson's best-selling memoir, *I Married Adventure* (1940), as no reference to cannibalism appears in the February 1918 edition of *National Geographic* ("Geography" 184, 190-91). Alternatively, Bishop may have remembered scenes from the Johnsons' popular film, *Among the Cannibals of the South Pacific*, which debuted in July of 1918 (Kansas Historical Society). And since Bishop misspells Osa Johnson's name as "Asa" in her poem drafts, it seems likely that she drew on her memory of the book or film instead of direct consultation with either.

In her memoir, Osa Johnson describes a trip with her husband Martin to the island of Malekula in Melanesia, the second largest island in the New Hebrides, where they meet some of the indigenous people residing there (116-22). In her narrative, Johnson notes that she and her husband are warned, as they approach, that residents of Malekula practice "cannibalism and head-hunting" (111), and a man on board their boat comments that the inhabitants of nearby Vao "still bury their old people alive and eat long pig" (112). The captain of their boat, Johnson reports, also disapproves of their plans: "If we were reckless enough to risk being served up as 'long pig,' that was our lookout, not his" (113). Notably, the *Oxford English Dictionary* (OED) associates the term *long pig* specifically with the South Pacific Islands, linking it to the Fijian phrase *vuaka balavu* and defining it, simply, as the consumption of human flesh as food.

Bishop retains the disturbing term *long pig* in her published version of the poem. Although many critics—and Bishop herself—have construed the poem's scene of reading as depicting tableaux from Africa, it seems that the poet blended continents, sources, and imaginings (*Conversations* 87). Indeed, she misattributed cultural practices and amalgamated geographic locales as if non-Western peoples were interchangeable, an elision that many contemporary readers find wholly unacceptable. Focusing on her narrator's reaction to the magazine, Bishop leaves the identities and nationalities of the photographed persons unspecified. In some readers, this might stir an awareness of how ways of looking and reading can

ing away continuously into the clouds far above. Down its sides tumble three magnificent glaciers broken to fragments by the steep descent. The tongues of all three come down to the level of the valley, where they stop abruptly without moraines, as though melted back by the heat.

Near the foot of these glaciers occurs the most conspicuous fissure to be found anywhere in the valley. It is 200 to 400 feet wide, with perpendicular walls, one of which stands about 35 feet higher than the other. The depth could not be ascertained because it is filled by a beautiful lake of clear, green water. Standing just at the foot of the glaciers, this fissure is one of the most picturesque spots in the whole valley (see page 146). Along the sides are numerous snow-drifts, from which miniature bergs break off and float away in the clear water.

WARM WATER FROM SNOW-DRIFTS

Fed by the glaciers and melting snows, Fissure Lake would be expected to be icy cold, but on the contrary it is decidedly tepid in spots, where heat evidently is received from below. One of the most amusing incidents of the whole trip occurred when our chemist, poking his thermometer into everything, discovered this fact.

I was coming along a little behind, and he, pretending to need my assistance, asked me to tell him the temperature of the water coming out from under the edge of a snow-field. Willing to answer even a foolish question, I had the words "ice cold" on the tip of my tongue when my fingers touched the water. The speaking expression froze on my face and I carefully dipped my hand in again. It was actually warm! How he did laugh at my discomfiture!

The snow-fields which surround the valley send trickling rills down the slopes, but these dry up and disappear long before the floor of the basin is reached. From the glaciers, however, comes a considerable stream, which runs, in spite of all obstacles, clear through the valley, dwindling to almost nothing before passing out of the hot area. These waters thus so nearly forget to run that we christened the stream the River Lethe.

The Valley of Ten Thousand Smokes in Alaska, which was explored by a *National Geographic* team in 1916.

coincide, concede to stereotype, and, in relation to the Johnsons, recycle myths of "the dark continent" (the pejorative phrase used in the Johnsons' films about Africa) as a colonial Eden ripe for commercial conquest and human exploitation. As Edelman asserts, most critics "have refrained from seriously reading Bishop's readings of reading" ("Geography" 180), and yet this poem "effectively positions itself to read its readers" (182). As in "Time's Andromedas," the reader of "In the Waiting Room" might catch a shadow on the page: the sanguinary "blush" of colonialism, its influence extending well into the twentieth century.

Curiously, in the fifth and final versions of the poem, Bishop abandons the passage about the domestic husbandry of pigs that, she states with a tinge of irony, was "supposed to solve" the Allies' wartime need for food. Had Bishop allowed both porcine references in the published poem, it would have drawn into connection the eating of human flesh, reportedly still practiced in Melanesia, and the raising of "baby pigs" for slaughter in the United States, insinuating parallels between cannibalism, wartime economy, and, by extension, total war's appetite for young bodies: as much an issue in February of 1918, during the United States' first year of involvement in World War I, as in 1971, when the United States was embroiled and incurring heavy casualties in the protracted, deeply unpopular war in Vietnam.

If wartime pig clubs—and "Long Pig"—had appeared in Bishop's published version of "In the Waiting Room," the poem would have acquired an additional layer of political provocation, one resembling the indictment of animals' suffering in "From Trollope's Journal," her "anti-Eisenhower" poem (*WIA* 594). There, she portrays cattle maintained in Washington, DC, during the Civil War, focusing on the animals' somatic distress—in lieu of the soldiers' bodies—as they too await programmatic slaughter:

> There all around me in the ugly mud
> —hoof-pocked, uncultivated—herds of cattle,
> numberless, wond'ring steers and oxen, stood:
> beef for the Army, after the next battle.
> Their legs were caked the color of dried blood;
> their horns were wreathed with fog. Poor, starving, dumb
> or lowing creatures, never to chew the cud
> or fill their maws again!
> (*P* 130)

In the persona of Trollope, the nineteenth-century British novelist, Bishop drew attention to the non-human bodies made to endure wartime barbarity, effectively writing an ecological indictment of war. But she chose not to take as direct an approach in "In the Waiting Room," removing the domesticated pigs and reversing the order of spectacles, such that in the fifth draft of the poem the narrator encounters—in a single edition of the magazine—a nameless volcano, the identically accessorized Johnsons (in a heteronormative romance of ethnographic adventure), a dead man ambiguously "slung" on a pole, babies "with pointed heads," and the metonymic parts of women with their "wound" necks and "terrifying" breasts.

Privy to the bare "necks," "heads," and "breasts" of indigenous women and children, the child-narrator reads their bodies figuratively and expressively. But she gives no elaborative commentary to the well-clothed Johnsons in their "riding breeches, / laced boots, and pith helmets" (*P* 179). Yet the Johnsons' gear, as Bishop describes it, is also telling: "riding breeches" conjure the Anglophone sports of horseback riding and hunting, and "pith helmets" or pith hats—constructed from the pith of tropical plants and covered in cloth—were the headgear worn by colonial armies in warm climates in the nineteenth and early twentieth centuries (OED). Pith helmets effectively became synecdoche for imperialism: George Bernard Shaw, in his 1934 play *Too Good to Be True*, describes a character as "wearing a pith helmet with a pagan" (OED), and Winston Churchill, in a famous photograph from 1898, poses in his martial uniform and pith helmet with the Egyptian pyramids in the background. So while Bishop's narrator subjects the bodies of indigenous men, women, and children to metaphoric interpretation, she focuses exclusively on the Johnsons' sartorial garb with its colonial and aristocratic connotations. Juxtaposing these descriptions, she aligns *National Geographic*'s entertainment of readers with the residue of colonial power: the pointing of guns replaced by the pointing of cameras.

Bishop's substantial revision of passages about the bodies of women and children in her drafts suggests the almost obsessive energy she lavished on this poem's scene of reading, encoding a queer subtext while constructing a racial imaginary that might provoke the poem's reader into recognition of his or her own hegemonic gaze. Indeed, the reader is conscripted into the narrator's voyeurism, epitomized by the magazine photographs as described in the published poem:

> Babies with pointed heads
> wound round and round with string;
> black, naked women with necks
> wound round and round with wire
> like the necks of light bulbs.
> Their breasts were horrifying.
> (*P* 179)

Winston Churchill poses in front of the Egyptian pyramids, 1898. Photo © Christie's / Bridgeman Images)

Seemingly staging the colonial gaze in order to satirize it, Bishop compares the women's necks, sonically "wound round and round with wire" to "the necks of lightbulbs," revealing her narrator's reflexive commercialism: she reads the photographed women as products of General Electric, related to her own place in time, surrounded as she is by "lamps" in the early dark. But the simile has a more sinister implication: compared to a light bulb, the female physique assumes disposable use value. When it ceases to produce (or reproduce), it can be replaced. Although Bishop's narrator describes another culture's technologies of beauty, she also implicates her own—through the two-way street that is metaphor—impugning constructed aesthetic value within a society's sexual economy.

As Kirstin Hotelling Zona observes in "Bishop: Race, Class, and Gender," the poet's descriptions of female anatomy, including the published clauses "Their breasts were horrifying" and "those awful hanging breasts," were the result of a long process of trial and revision, evident in the six drafts, in which the poet traffics between "allure and aversion" or, perhaps more accurately, between attraction and socialized fear in a conflation of sexual and racial difference (59). Within the persona of a prepubescent girl, Bishop tries on a range of responses to the naked female body. Notably, in the first draft, she writes "Their breasts filled me with awe" and refers, in the second mammary passage, to "those ~~awful~~ hanging breasts" with "frightening" as a margin annotation. Thus, the speaker begins in a state of Wordsworthian "awe" and admiration for the "awful," in the Romantic sense, but almost immediately qualifies this reaction with fear. Given that in other drafts Bishop addresses herself in the margins rather magisterially with instructions (e.g., in the third draft, alongside the volcano passage, she writes, "but I'll find something—maybe better—in the actual one [*National Geographic*]"), one cannot help but wonder if "frightening" could be, in part, her commentary on the speaker's unmitigated admiration of the female form, a "frightening" admission for a poet who, professionally, tried to keep her personal life tidily in the closet. Venturing boldly, if awkwardly, to depict relationships across class and racial lines in such poems as "Faustina, or Rock Roses" and "Manuelzinho," Bishop, for the most part, kept queer perspectives discreetly sub-textual, although her drafts of "In the Waiting Room" tell a different story.

In the second draft, for example, "filled me with awe" is crossed-out and replaced with "terrified me." (The word "dread" also appears crossed out in the margin along with a separate, virtually indecipherable phrase, which could be "transfixed me" or "horrified me.") What begins in wonder and fascination is transposed into varieties of fear, Bishop modulating queer attraction into something, for her era, more generic: a frightened response to the unclothed black body that might catch her readers in the crosshairs of their own prejudice and apprehension.

The third draft shows yet another permutation: Bishop writes, in her trademark parentheses, which often contain her poem's crux or *cri de coeur*, "(their black breasts ~~terrified~~ me)" and, in a margin annotation, posits "frightened" as a substitute for "terrified." Playing adjectival scales, Bishop composes an anxious fixated melody. She also wavers between "dreadful" and "awful" as the qualifier for "hanging breasts" in the third draft, converting a potentially erotic image of untrammeled flesh into a source of horror, a word she aligns with the "darker darkness" of sexual desire in the unfinished poem "Edgar Allan Poe & the Juke-Box" (*EAP* 49-50). Having once expressed her preference for "closets, closets, and more closets" to Bidart (*REB* 327), Bishop hides queer attraction in colonial subjugation—and sexualization—of the black body, composing a text with intertwined valences of meaning. As Zona astutely notes, "These drafts also underline the link that exists for Bishop between race and gender and, given the focus on 'I' in this poem, the central role this link occupies in the articulation of identity for the poet" ("Bishop" 59). Reader and writer, child of 1918 and poet of 1971, Bishop presents an array of textual encounters and masks in the published poem, while the "understory" of her drafts evinces a fascinating dialectic of concealment and mimicry.

By the fourth draft, Bishop posits that reading itself is an exhilarating, endangering adventure, one that can obliterate a reader's sense of self in radical identification with other bodies as sources of pain or pleasure. What similar feature, the narrator wonders, links this cohort of human beings, sitting in a Worcester waiting room? She wonders if witnessing "dreadful breasts" in the magazine has established their shared vulnerability or their collective hearing of a cry of pain, one that could worsen and fill the waiting room with "bruising / senseless waves of sound." The narrator also asks if she herself has been misled by a "family voice" into a volcanic "crater of ashes," and *family* in this context might invoke the word's etymological sense of "household members" to include slaves, women, and children: all those governed by the "paterfamilias" or adult male head of the household (OED). Whatever historical, etymological, or biographical analogs the poet might have had in mind, there is certainly more connection in this early version of the poem between what the child reads and interrogates as the possible source of her realizations: How has she arrived at an understanding of human suffering and peril? Has reading the *National Geographic* and confronting "those dreadful breasts" conscripted her into cognizance of human violence and her future liabilities as a woman? Bishop's narrator suggests that reading itself might be to blame for the "big black wave" of her epiphanies (*P* 181).

Notably, the "dreadful breasts" in the fourth draft are rendered as "those awful hanging breasts" in the published poem, which subtly echoes the "filled me with awe" phrasing of the first draft. Indeed, these "hanging breasts" are akin in their symbolism to the "rocky breasts" in Bishop's "At the Fishhouses," which offer something "dark, salt, clear, moving, utterly free" connected to "knowledge . . . historical, flowing, and flown" (*P* 64). Critics have instinctively paired these poems in their assessments, though they were published many years apart. Schwartz, for example, writes of "In the Waiting Room": "Perhaps not since her uncanny 'At the Fishhouses' (P 62), with its final acknowledgement of the tragic double bind—the desire for knowledge and the pain of its necessity—had Bishop written a poem so thoroughly immersed in the complexity of human suffering" (144).

In both poems, the female breast is a site of metaphysical meditation whether as an icon of desire or suffering, individuation or collectivity. In "In the Waiting Room," for instance, Bishop's narrator asks if the "awful hanging breasts" have "held us all together / or made us all just one," a question that puns on the paradoxical definitions of cleavage as a bringing together or a pulling apart (*P* 181). Confronted with our origin in the maternal body and universal need for sustenance and nurture, we are both individuated in hunger and united in that vulnerability. And here Bishop's narrator, positioned in Worcester, plays with scales of proximity and distance, connection ("What similarities") and objectification as she gazes at the women in the magazine. Scripted onto the "awful hanging breasts" is the colonizer's dependence upon the bodies of the colonized for material gain; for objectification of abject fear; and, in the case of Bishop's narrator, for disguised enactment of poetic epistemology and queer desire (*P* 181).

Tellingly, in Bishop's letters to Foster, she links the mammary image in "At the Fishhouses" explicitly to her experience of psychoanalysis. She reports, in one letter, having taken a bus ride in Keene, New Hampshire, while drunk. Falling asleep, she dreamt that "everything was very wild & dark & stormy and you [Dr. Foster] were in it feeding me from your breast" (VC 118.33; qtd. in Goldensohn, "Approaching" 10). As if to leaven the significance of this dream, Bishop adds, parenthetically, "I should think this would be a common dream about a woman analyst." Yet the image, for Bishop, remained freighted with meaning, and she states in her letter to Foster that she intends to dedicate the poem, "this particular number," to her if it proves to be "any good" (VC 118.33).

Revealingly, when Robert Lowell protested in his letter to Bishop about "At the Fishhouses" that the poem's mammary imagery was "a little too much in its context" (*WIA* 7), she did not alter her poem, and she offered no defense of that decision in her subsequent letters to Lowell. Similarly, in speaking about "In the Waiting Room" with George Starbuck in 1977, Bishop insisted that what she termed "the African things" were strictly based on content from the *National Geographic*, obfuscating the constitutive role of her imagination:

My memory had confused two 1918 issues of the *Geographic*. Not having seen them since then, I checked it out in the New York Public Library. In the February issue there was an article, "The Valley of 10,000 Smokes," about Alaska that I'd remembered, too. But the African things, it turned out, were in the *next* issue, in March. . . . I should have had a footnote. (*Conversations* 87)

In addition to Bishop's frank racial objectification in her phrase "African things," the poet was also inaccurate in her account. Edelman, in analyzing the *National Geographic* issue from March of that year, notes that it does not contain images of "Babies with pointed heads," or "black, naked women with necks / wound round and round with wire" (184). Moreover, neither the February nor March issue of the magazine has any "essay about Africa at all" (Edelman, "Geography" 184). Bishop's strenuous assertions about the literality of these images suggest her anxiety to appear as the reporter, rather than the conjurer, of scenes with blatant ethnic caricature and sexual undertones. As in Bishop's drafts of "View of The Capitol from The Library of Congress," in which she initially characterizes the Congressional Dome as an "elaborate sugar-tit for a / nation / that likes sugar" (VC 77.4) before changing the image to a "big white old wall-eyed horse" (*P* 67), the poet obscures the political and erotic connotations evident in her drafts of "In the Waiting Room," although queer desire is not entirely absent from the child narrator's dramatized fixation.

Reversing the antagonism in "Time's Andromedas" between an internal "wordy racket" and the book in hand, Bishop's narrator in "In the Waiting Room" becomes thoroughly engrossed in the magazine's content and cover. In the fourth draft of the poem, she lavishes attention on the latter, noting "the yellow margins, the oak leaves / the name in black, the table / of contents that I knew" (VC 53.19). As if to reassure herself, she meditates on the serial's familiar typography including its bright margins, which cordon the list of contents like a gilt frame; its decorative oak leaves, which may allude to the oak as the official tree of the British Empire; and its annunciatory title, which invokes both the powers of state ("national") and worldly knowledge ("geographic"). The magazine cover, in this draft, reifies cultural imperialism in resembling a framed portrait or museum case: it offers a curated, labeled, highly mediated tour of artifacts and natural resources.

Bishop shortens her lengthy description, however, to a terse couplet in the published poem: "And then I looked at the cover: / the yellow margins, the date" (*P* 179). The effect of this editorial excision is that it lessens the emphasis on the disciplinary conventions of the magazine as an institution of colonial connoisseurship and, instead, draws closer together female bodies from two different continents.

To wit, there is less auxiliary narration between "Their breasts were horrifying" and the "*oh!* of pain / —Aunt Consuelo's voice—" (*P* 179-80). Thus, Bishop maintains in her final draft a focus on the female body, albeit one parceled into parts: necks, breasts, a pained voice, and the narrator's seated self in the anteroom to these presumed future developments.

The aunt's exclamation draws the narrator from her textual absorption—and the shyness that forbids her to stop reading—back to her surroundings in the dentist's office, where patients' teeth are doctored against decay and loss and where her aunt's cry recalls the narrator to her own body with renewed intensity. "Without thinking at all / I was my foolish aunt, / I—we—were falling, falling" (*P* 180). Radical identification induces a swoon in Bishop's narrator who feels herself tethered to her aunt in somatic sympathy, spinning out of time and space, held only by the date on the magazine, a mark of historical time and historicized consciousness. Confronting the existential contingencies of personhood, the so-called accidents of birth, the narrator returns with resigned relief to chronological time and an individuated self at the end of the poem: she is only one historical person on "the fifth / of February, 1918," a day on which her aunt's "cry of pain . . . could have / got loud and worse but hadn't" (*P* 181).

The latter detail ominously intimates more sustained, anguished cries in situations threatening the integrity of women's bodies inside and outside of clinical settings. Biographically, a "scream, the echo of a scream, [that] hangs over that Nova Scotian village" had preceded Bishop's mother's permanent psychiatric hospitalization in 1916 (*Pr* 62) and catalyzed the familial rearrangements that led to Bishop's unhappy stay in Worcester and, thereafter, an uncle's perpetration of her sexual abuse as Bishop documents in the Foster letters. In 1971, when the poem first appeared in *The New Yorker*, the Supreme Court's decision in *Roe v. Wade* was still two years in the offing. In a variety of settings, women's cries of pain often became worse, sometimes catastrophically so.

Readers of these archival drafts can see the poet shuttling from her imagination (or reminiscence) to a reconnaissance of concrete details from the physical magazine and back again. Carefully, Bishop construes a scene of reading that undercuts *National Geographic*'s imperial hauteur and depicts a child's horror as she enters a world in which black bodies, female bodies, bodies of babies, and those of dead men are subject to cameras and commodification, distortion and dehumanization. Indeed, founded in 1888 by Alexander Graham Bell and Gardiner Hubbard, the National Geographic Society did not include African Americans in its membership until the 1940s and, as chief editor Susan Goldberg recently acknowledged, "Until the 1970s *National Geographic* all but ignored people of color who lived in the United States. . . . Meanwhile it pictured 'natives' elsewhere as exotics, famously and frequently unclothed, happy hunters, noble savages—every type of cliché." Bishop's poem undeniably animates *National Geographic*'s imperialist framework and culture of ethnic caricature even if her intention was to ironize these postures.

And despite her insistence on the poem's literality, Bishop took great liberty with strict fact. As a poet-cartographer, not a "historian," she conflates, anachronistically, the Johnsons' explorations in Africa, which began in 1921, with their expeditions to the South Seas in 1917 and 1919, remixing tableaux from Africa, America, and the South Pacific in her poem's imagery.[1] Thus Bishop's interest in the para-literary extends to the archive but does not neatly conclude there: her motivations in replicating stock *National Geographic* narratives about non-Western cultures are not entirely clear.[2] Was the poet complicit with the magazine's racist codes or did she construct a scene of reading meant, in part, to provoke her readers' recognition of hegemonic stances in the popular magazine and culture at large? Perhaps Bishop's narrator falls into a *symptomatic* vertiginous swoon: cultural imperialism was, in 1918 and 1971, a practice and point of view that could not hold without pulling its beneficiaries into the vortex of its contradictions. Bishop, in the ten poems of *Geography III*, proves herself to be a citizen of such paradoxes and discomforting ironies. Despite its errors in fact, "In the Waiting Room" is a profoundly civic poem, one that enlivens in miniature the legacy of Western colonialism, American commercialism, and the moral devastation of war through the terror of a precocious child, coming into consciousness of her position—and implication—in historical narrative.

※

In *Psychoanalysis and the Scene of Reading*, Jacobus observes that "The world of the poem (a world in which privacy and privation are inseparable from reading) can be calm: it has become available to be thought" (51). And in many ways, Bishop's "In the Waiting Room" is a thoughtful—if not "calm"—revisiting of the headlong, anguished, affectionate letters she wrote to Foster in 1947. Both the letters and the poem meditate on selfhood and desire, the mechanics of empathy and shame, trauma and compulsive reading, initiation into carnal and worldly knowledge, reverie and the creative process. Although the poem's "Elizabeth" does not venture backward in time to the colonization of Africa and the Atlantic slave trade, that genocide—causally linked to the fact that "The War was on"—is a subscript in the poem's imagery of commercial imperialism (*P* 181). Read in connection with the Foster letters and archival drafts, "In the Waiting Room" is clearly both an elegy to childhood innocence and to any notion of human history, unscored by violence.

Dated "February 1947," the Foster letters include several scenes of reading that closely parallel "In the Waiting Room." Biographer Brett Millier states that Bishop and Foster "spent a good part of . . . two years . . . [exploring] the origins of [Bishop's] depression and alcoholism" (*Elizabeth Bishop* 194), and Foster assured her that she was "lucky to have survived" her childhood (180). Megan Marshall adds that Foster was one of the first American women to train as a psychoanalyst, and treating "creative people" was a mainstay of her practice (*Elizabeth Bishop* 78).

Born to a "proper Bostonian family" and educated at Goucher College and the elite Winsor School, Foster rebelled against familial expectations in attending medical school and interning at clinics with Freudian inflections in Baltimore, London, and New York (Marshall, *Elizabeth Bishop* 78). By 1937, Foster had established a private practice in New York City while also treating patients at the Northside Center for Child Development in Harlem (Marshall, *Elizabeth Bishop* 78-79). Bishop, who began working with Foster in the spring of 1946, testifies to Foster's loyal following among her patients, professing to her analyst that "laying all transferences [sic] aside . . . I really do love you very much in which sentiment I am doubless [sic] joined by countless others" (VC 118.33; qtd. in Goldensohn, "Approaching" 7). En route to the Yaddo Writers' Colony in 1950 when she heard that Foster had died of pancreatic cancer at the age of fifty-six, Bishop wrote revealingly to Marianne Moore that Foster was "so good and kind" and had "certainly helped [her] more than anyone in the world" (*OA* 206).

Fortuitously discovered by Angela Leap, Methfessel's heir, and purchased by Vassar College in 2011, Bishop's letters to Foster show the poet "dar[ing] to look / to see what it was I was" around the time of her thirty-sixth birthday and about a half a year after the publication of *North & South* (*P* 180). In them, Bishop describes living in the home of her paternal grandparents in Worcester for several difficult months in 1917-18, where her uncle Jack cruelly teased the newly parentless child about "why didn't I laugh and play" and threatened her with "a spanking or a whipping" (VC 118.33). Meanwhile, her well-intentioned grandmother outfitted her in uncomfortable neo-Edwardian dresses and insisted that she play with dolls (*Pr* 88, 96-97).

Failing to thrive in Worcester, where she developed debilitating asthma and eczema sores, Bishop was sent to live with her maternal aunt Maud Shepherdson, whose husband George, a "real sadist," abused Bishop sexually, a trauma that she repressed, she writes to Foster, until after her aunt's death (VC 118.33; qtd. in Marshall, *Elizabeth Bishop* 18). Bishop details in the "long sad tale of Uncle George" that the abuse began when she was eight years old and continued into her mid-adolescence (VC 118.33). An accountant for the General Electric Company and a former school principal, Shepherdson fondled Bishop in a bathtub, dangled her by her hair "over the second story verandah railing," broke his wife's ribs, and threatened to beat his niece (VC 118.33). He also, Bishop reports, "gloats over violence, despises any other race but his own, hates colored people, etc., believed in the Ku Klux Klan and the protocols of Zion" (VC 118.33). Shepherdson's racism, anti-Semitism, pleasure in violence, and domestic abuse are—in Bishop's account—all part of his pathology. She offers, in effect, an amateur psychological profile of her abuser, one that reads his harmful injury of her and her aunt as connatural with his racial prejudices and white supremacism: women, Jews, and African Americans were all subject to his vitriol and loathing.

Describing to Foster a particularly intense period of Shepherdson's abuse, Bishop notes that she "would read harder & harder & try not to hear him" (VC 118.33; Marshall, *Elizabeth Bishop* 19). This detail serves as an analogue to the child in "In the Waiting Room" who appears to displace her anxiety onto studying a magazine, which she "reads" with absorption until her aunt's cry recalls her to her surroundings. Moreover, Bishop's insight about her uncle, that "the streak of cruelty ... [and] dreadful sentimentality ... often go together," provides a purview into poems such as "View of The Capitol from The Library of Congress" and "From Trollope's Journal," in which Bishop parodies military machismo and jingoist feeling (VC 118.33; qtd. in Marshall, *Elizabeth Bishop* 19).

Tellingly, as she works up to writing to Foster about her uncle, Bishop comments on her shyness, linking—through narrative adjacency—a personal source of shame, the reticence she shared with Foster, and a deepening trust in her analyst:

> Ruth you once said that I wouldn't think you had once been shy would I and I said yes. I should have been more emphatic I think – I felt right away that you had once and probably for a very long time been frightfully shy and that was an other [sic] reason why I took to you. (VC 118.33; qtd. in Goldensohn, "Approaching" 16)

Addressing Foster as "Ruth," as one formerly "frightfully shy" person to another, Bishop concludes that section of her letter with a vaunt about her growing confidence: "I feel that in some ways I could bet you are shyer than I am right now" (VC 118.33; qtd. in Goldensohn, "Approaching" 16). Therapeutic playfulness aside, Bishop establishes a circuitry in this letter between the survival of trauma; the affective states of shyness, estrangement, and shame; and, on the other end of the relational spectrum, the liberating bonds of empathic understanding.

A similar circuitry of affects recurs in "In the Waiting Room" as the narrator, like the traumatized boy in "Visits to St. Elizabeths," rhetorically "pats the floor / to see if the world is there, is flat" (*P* 132). Reading the *National Geographic* "straight through / ... too shy to stop," the speaker practices habits of deflection and avoidance that Bishop employed in managing her Uncle George's chronic abuse. Indeed, the Foster letters show the poet looking "to see what it was I was" as a writer and reader, as a de facto orphan and a profoundly visual dreamer, as a lover of women and as an American distrustful of the lauded institutions of state and family.

Less traumatic but significant scenes of reading with ties to "In the Waiting Room" also appear in the Foster letters. In passing, Bishop details how she acquired a portion of her sex education from the nursing textbooks her Aunt Grace and mother had used; the textbooks had "awful photographs" that haunted her for a long while (VC 118.33). Like the child narrator in "In the Waiting Room," Bishop grappled with anatomical knowledge without an adult intermediary to offer explanations or reassurances.

But the epistolary passage in the Foster letters that aligns more closely with "In the Waiting Room" is a lengthy detailed account of a dream Bishop reports having had after reading a book titled *The History of Impressionism*. In her reverie, she found herself in "a large almost chateau building in a small French village" (VC 118.33). Exploring the house, she gravitates toward the bookshelves, where she studies a book about "sexual Rites -or marrige [sic] rites" of tribes, full of illustrations. As she studies the book, she becomes aware of an attractive girl reading over her shoulder. Initially, she feels embarrassed but convinces herself that feeling ashamed is "silly." Soon the attractive girl, whom Bishop describes as resembling a younger "idealized" version of Foster, makes a comment about the book, and both women turn the page and encounter an anecdote about the classical conductor Leopold Stokowski, who boasts about the longevity of his orgasm. Bishop and the Foster-esque figure laugh at Stokowski's bravado, and then, at the end of the recounted dream, they venture from the library to the "village" outdoors (VC 118.33).

This epistolary passage shares many parallels with "In the Waiting Room," including the narrator's study of photographs of "Savege [sic] tribes" wearing "sexual decorations" in an "Oceanic" style (VC 118.33). Indeed, this last detail connects Bishop's dream to the South Pacific where the Johnsons, in their travels, photographed and filmed indigenous peoples for commercial gain. It also suggests that Bishop's reverie, as she related it to Foster, may have been as much a source text for "In the Waiting Room" as the *National Geographic*; in her vivid dream, she may have conflated images from the Johnsons' books or films, her study of art history, her childhood fright at graphic photographs in medical textbooks, and her deeply intimate trust of her analyst, with whom she reads and laughs.

Bishop also confesses, in her letter, to being self-conscious about "the book I was reading" and yet continuing to read, having rationalized that her sense of shame is "silly" in contradistinction to the narrator of "In the Waiting Room," who appears to feel both shameful and compelled (VC 118.33). Another ramifying difference between Bishop's epistolary account and "In the Waiting Room" is the figure of the "nic[e]-looking girl," a younger "rather idealized" version of her analyst, who helps diffuse Bishop's embarrassment at being caught reading (and viewing) "sexual decorations" (VC 118.33). Indeed, the Foster figure joins Bishop in perusing the book, turning the pages, and sharing a laugh about the supposed erotic stamina of Stokowski.

Notably, in the poem, it is an anguished cry of pain instead of mutual laughter that is shared between the narrator and an older woman. Laughter about performative masculinity (and heterosexuality) in the epistolary dream is transmogrified into a shared scream, the child's voice melding with her aunt's in the neighboring room. But in the letter to Foster, sexuality and anatomical knowledge do not remain "flightening [sic]" or hinge into vocalized pain emanating from the "inside." Instead, the laugh opens outward, into "the village," which subtly recalls the archetypal Great Village of Bishop's childhood story in which, against the backdrop of reassuringly agrarian life, Bishop perceived her mother's scream as hanging "forever, a slight stain in those pure blue skies" in an eerie naturalization of her mother's psychosis (*Pr* 62).

Finally, the Foster letters and "In the Waiting Room" share a dentist's office: Bishop recounts a hallucination in the former, which she experienced when given gas for a tooth extraction. She relates to Foster that John Dewey had assured her that a daydream, while under anesthetic, was not unusual: "I was whirling away in space in the dark but I could see all the planets – they were beautiful, a sort of fiery white – and I was telling myself that I had 'solved the problem of the universe'" (VC 118.33; qtd. in Goldensohn, "Approaching" 6). In addition, Bishop states that her hallucination was connected to Margaret Miller, her unreciprocated love from Vassar College. Just as she was about to "place" Miller among the planets, she suddenly regained consciousness and discovered that she was kicking her dentist in the chest while the nurse tried to restrain her. To Foster, Bishop recalls her dental procedure with a touch of comedy and eros. Yet the sensation she describes in "In the Waiting Room" of "falling off / the round, turning world / into cold, blue-black space" (*P* 180) conjures the interstellar travel of her hallucination but with the beauty of the planets and her desire for Miller removed. As in the early drafts of "In the Waiting Room," the queer text all but disappears in the published analogue to the biographical event.

Although Bishop's work with Foster did not relieve her alcoholism or asthma, as she had hoped (*OA* 163-64), analysis seems to have inaugurated for her a new sense of ease in reading and being read, writing and repeating. In one letter to Foster, she cites Edgar Degas's observation that "'Art doesn't grow wider, it recapitulates,'" and she credits analysis with freeing her from viewing each poem as a necessarily singular "isolated event" (VC 118.33; qtd. in Goldensohn, "Approaching" 11). She now considers her writing a continuum: her poems "go on into each other or over lap [sic]" and are "one long poem anyway" (VC 118.33; qtd. in Goldensohn, "Approaching" 11). Later in her letters to Foster, Bishop reports that upon receiving a proof for a poem in *The Nation*, she felt "pleased"—for the first time—by seeing her work in print, a poignant remark, given that Bishop's first book had appeared six months earlier (VC 118.33). Perhaps Bishop's analysis had already moved her toward a new approach and appraisal of her poetry, one that did not avoid "repetition" as it drew from dreams and memories in an increasingly intersubjective, biographical aesthetic.

The Foster letters position their contemporary readers in the waiting room: reading these intimate documents, we are privy to "a cry of pain that could have / got loud and worse" (P 181). We witness some of the travail Bishop survived as a functional orphan, shuttled among relatives' homes; as the victim of verbal, physical, and sexual abuse; as an alcoholic, increasingly cognizant of her loss of control; and as a "shy" woman, struggling to make sense of the relationships she experienced and desired. In the Foster letters and in the drafts of "In the Waiting Room," which draw substantially from them, Bishop explores what Bidart termed the "primal and radical experience" of selfhood that, by his measure, are moments "usually quite impossible to talk about, or even face" (VC 1.14). Incorporating a para-literary text into the traditional lyric poem, Bishop created a mode that enabled psychological intimacy with her reader as well as a pointed satire of the colonial postures of the *National Geographic Magazine* and American culture at large. Indeed, the dialogic architecture of Bishop's poem allows its speaker to "face" her selves—and those of her readers—with an uncanny sense of honesty.

As Jacobus writes of eighteenth-century novels, "Too easily, perhaps, we tend to claim that such epistolary novels or memoirs are 'psychologically' realistic, when what we really mean is that they create in us the very forms of subjectivity which we think of ourselves as sharing" (203). Writing to Foster, Bishop gathered insights and images that inform the world of "In the Waiting Room," in which colonial violence and war delimit the privacy of subjectivity: that which calls from "inside" to challenge the "big black wave" of historical narrative. Taking the metaphoric place of Foster in reading over "Elizabeth's" shoulder, we may find ourselves newly conscious of our reading practices, peering into an archive that testifies to the poet's deliberative process and wary status as a citizen. Bishop's twenty-first-century readers may find themselves "too shy to stop," held by whatever the page—serving as both portal and mirror—might divulge or deliver.

NOTES

1. According to the Kansas Historical Society, the Johnsons took their first trip together to the South Seas in 1917 and a second in 1919. Their first trip to Africa took place in 1921.
2. In the April 2018 edition of *National Geographic*, "The Race Issue," Susan Goldberg's "From the Editor" column cites the observations of John Edwin Mason, professor of history at the University of Virginia, who notes that "*National Geographic* comes into existence at the height of colonialism, and the world was divided into the colonizers and the colonized. That was a color line, and *National Geographic* was reflecting that view of the world." Bishop's poem engages with the magazine's racist legacy, mimicking and ironizing its reinforcement of the hegemonic colonial gaze.

CHAPTER TWO

ELIZABETH BISHOP'S SANITY

Childhood Trauma, Psychoanalysis, and Sentimentality

Richard Flynn

Reviewing *Questions of Travel* (1965) in the *Kenyon Review*, Howard Moss wrote,

> The credibility of these poems derives from a shocking fact: Miss Bishop is completely sane. . . . A clearly lighted equanimity allows for every note of the scale, including that intensity from which every blur and distraction has been erased. Disinterestedness has become passionate. She has made sanity interesting without lecturing us about it. (256)

For many years this was the standard view of "Miss Bishop." When I was a senior in college, I bought the newly published *Geography III* (1976) and, having been familiar with the Noonday paperback of the 1969 *Complete Poems*, I was blown away as soon as I read the first poem in the book, "In the Waiting Room." This was a different Bishop—her voice was more personal, the poem more accessible. There was no "Elizabeth Bishop Phenomenon" then: no biography, no letters, no "uncollected poems, drafts, and fragments." There was one Twayne book by Anne Stevenson.

I had been working on a senior capstone paper about Bishop's onetime Vassar classmate Muriel Rukeyser (there was not even a Twayne book about her work). I had fallen in love with Rukeyser as a freshman in high school; our assignment was to pick any poem in the second edition of John Malcolm Brinnin and Bill Read's then brand-new anthology *The Modern Poets* (1970—the one with Rollie McKenna's photographs) and to reflect on it in a personal essay. I chose Rukeyser's "Effort at Speech Between Two People," a poem with great appeal to the troubled adolescent I was. Though I would defend it even now, it is certainly a poem open to charges of sentimentality. Rukeyser was barely past adolescence when she wrote it. Bishop undoubtedly would have found it both sentimental and self-pitying. No fan of Rukeyser, she wrote in her notebook: "M. Rukeyser - like having a Wurlitzer automatic pipe organ in the home" (VC 75.3, p. 30; qtd. in Goldensohn, "In the Footsteps" 25).

Bishop is represented by four poems in the Brinnin and Read anthology: "Letter to N.Y.," "A Cold Spring," "Florida," and "The Prodigal"—all of which had been either published or accepted for publication before Bishop left for Brazil in November of 1951. From the biographical note we see that the anthology was published during what we now know was one of the most troubled times for Bishop: "Elizabeth Bishop, born February 8, 1911, in Worcester, Massachusetts, makes her home part of the time in San Francisco and part of the time in Ouro Preto, Minas Gerais, Brazil" (47). In some sense, one could say that the fifteen years she spent living with Lota de Macedo Soares, the productive period that produced the poems in *Questions of Travel* and the story that lies at its center, "In the Village" (1953), had been erased by the anthology, and, of course, the poems for *Geography III* were yet to come. There was certainly no indication that the elegant woman depicted in the photograph (in a tweed suit smoking a cigarette at her desk) was the type to have taken up with a young woman in her twenties with a very young son and to have become fond of the same Beatles and Janis Joplin records I loved. Likewise, except for the inclusion of the double-sonnet "The Prodigal," there was no hint of the poet's intense struggle with alcoholism that, in the 1940s, led her to seek treatment with the psychoanalyst Dr. Ruth Foster. Nor is there a hint of the haunted childhood that Bishop began to explore with Foster. As Bishop confided to Jane Shore years later, Foster had told her that "given my childhood, I shouldn't have survived, but I did" (*REB* 314; Millier, *Elizabeth Bishop* 180).

Once Bishop's Vassar archive became available to scholars in 1982, the "sane" "Miss Bishop" Moss described in his review began to give way to the complex, troubled, and prolific Bishop we know now. New additions to the archive (there have been forty-eight), along with the explosion of scholarship and biographical studies based on extensive use of the archive, have both deepened and darkened the picture, with an increasing emphasis on childhood trauma. The recent acquisition of Bishop's 1947 letters to Foster (VC 118.33) intensifies this emphasis by revealing childhood trauma beyond the circumstances surrounding Bishop's well-known virtual orphanhood,[1] including the details of her abuse by her Uncle George Shepherdson.

This chapter will focus on two moments when Bishop was at her most troubled: February 1947, when struggling intensely with her alcoholism and the end of her relationship with Marjorie Carr Stevens, she wrote the extraordinarily revealing set of letters to Foster, and the spring of 1970, when her relationship with Roxanne Cumming finally blew up in Ouro Prêto, reflected in letters "telling all" to her Seattle friend Dorothee Bowie. Although it might seem counterintuitive, I will enlist these intimate letters written in extreme circumstances to complicate our sense of a "sane" Bishop, by reexamining and revising some of the qualities Moss discusses in his review. As her friend James Merrill knew, Bishop's public persona, her "instinctive, modest, lifelong impersonations of an ordinary woman" (259) masked a much more extraordinary and idiosyncratic poet. Yet Bishop insisted on her sanity, even in her most unguarded moments, and, as Moss notes, her "equanimity" includes "intensity," her "disinterestedness" is "passionate," and her "sanity" is "interesting, without lecturing" in part because it is so hard won and so precarious. These revelatory letters are written as Bishop breaks out of extended periods of writer's block to create important work that signals new directions in her writing, specifically work that revisits scenes of childhood trauma. In the poems and stories about childhood published during her lifetime, including "In the Village," the Nova Scotia childhood poems in the "Elsewhere" section of *Questions of Travel*, and poems such as "In the Waiting Room," Bishop deftly avoided "playing up [her] sad romantic plight." In her letters to Anne Stevenson, she makes a point of downplaying self-pity and emphasizing the "cheerful" rather than the "awful," expressing her admiration for stoicism and courage: "Although I think I have a prize 'unhappy childhood', almost good enough for the textbooks—please don't think I dote on it" (*Pr* 431).

Bishop's famous distrust of sentimentality—and the fine line between genuine feeling and the "false position" of sentimentality—is, I believe, a key to understanding her artistic preoccupation with childhood, a preoccupation informed by her vexed relationship with psychoanalytic treatment and texts. Bishop had a lifelong intellectual interest in psychoanalysis, and her reading ranged far beyond Freud and orthodox Freudian theory. Her experience with psychiatric and psychoanalytic treatment was largely confined to the 1940s, and her most significant stretch was her analysis with Foster from the spring of 1946 through sometime in 1948.[2] Shortly after Foster's death from pancreatic cancer in 1950, Bishop wrote Marianne Moore, "Dr. Foster was so good and kind, and certainly helped me more than anyone in the world" (*OA* 206). In her last interview with Elizabeth Spires in 1978, Bishop tied her 1940s analysis with Foster to her uncanny ability to remember her childhood:

> My memories of some of those days are so much clearer than things that happened in 1950, say. I don't think one should make a cult of writing about childhood, however. . . . I went to an analyst for a couple of years off and on in the forties, a very

nice woman who was especially interested in writers, writers and blacks.[3] She said that it was amazing that I would remember things that happened to me when I was two. (*Conversations* 125-26)

Bishop believed that her "total recall" (*OA* 249; *EAP* 306) enabled her to treat potentially sentimental subjects without sentimentality.

Bishop also associated sentimentality with cruelty. Near the end of her "long sad tale" about her abusive Uncle George, she remarks, "What I dislike even more than the streak of cruelty almost is his dreadful sentimentality - I guess they often go together. His eyes were always filling up with tears, etc." (VC 118.33; qtd. in Goldensohn "Approaching" 19). She writes, "I can never forgive myself as long as I live," referring to her adolescent embarrassment and shame about "living . . . in that apartment in Revere and later for a while in that dreadful little house in a place called Cliftondale" (VC 118.33). She even confesses that "for years I was intensely ashamed of Aunt Maud, all that part of my life." When her adolescent love interest, Judy Flynn, drops by unexpectedly, Bishop becomes "suddenly so painfully aware of the poverty of the place that I lost my head completely and burst into tears" (VC 118.33). Ordinarily, however, she seems to have "concealed [her shame] pretty much from everyone," preferring to appear "brave." Flattered when a camp counselor compares her with the hero of Hugh Walpole's *Fortitude* (1913), Bishop remarks that although Walpole wasn't "highbrow" enough for her, "being brave" was her "major theme" for "years and years" (VC 118.33).

In "The Country Mouse," Bishop's autobiographical narrator recalls becoming aware of "falsity and the great power of sentimentality" when she lies to her friend Emma that her mother is dead: "I didn't know then, and still don't, whether it was from shame I lied, or from a hideous craving for sympathy, playing up my sad romantic plight. But the feeling of self-distaste, whatever it came from, was only too real. I jumped up to get away from my monstrous self that I could not keep from lying" (*Pr* 98). This feeling of self-distaste is the first of three great truths—reflected in this story—that came home to Bishop during the short "stretch of [her] life" when she lived with her paternal grandparents in Worcester. The second, somewhat ironically, was her social consciousness, as she became aware of her class privilege and its precariousness ("I had never felt secure about my status," 99). The third is the famous prose genesis of what would become "In the Waiting Room" approximately ten years later: "I was one of them, too, inside my scabby body and wheezing lungs. 'You're in for it now,' something said. How had I got tricked into such a false position?" (99).

SUMMER 1946–FEBRUARY 1947, NOVA SCOTIA AND NEW YORK CITY

Brett Millier characterizes January and February 1947 as "miserable" for Bishop, but they were also momentous. In addition to her first meeting in January with Robert Lowell at Randall Jarrell's apartment, she was quite productive, finishing "Faustina, or Rock Roses," "Varick Street," and "At the Fishhouses." In the letter to Foster marked "Sunday morning" [February 9],[4] Bishop writes that she feels pleased for "the first time" at seeing her work in print; she also notes that she has been more productive than she has been in "two or three years," even "while in my cups - kegs, I should say," but then she worries: "If only I didn't feel I were that dreadful thing an 'alcoholic'" (VC 118.33; qtd. in Goldensohn, "Approaching" 5).

Appended to the Foster letters, a chronology she apparently prepared for the doctor is telling; the years 1943 through 1946 are virtually lost, with only the notation "K.W & NY - worked in the Navy Yard. Marjorie, K.W. acquaintances NY people." Beginning in August of 1944, when she moved to the apartment at 46 King Street that Loren MacIver found for her, Bishop struggled with living alone, her asthma, and her drinking. Her relationship with Marjorie Stevens was in a protracted decline, and she was in such distress after an October visit from Marjorie that she moved in with her friend Anna B. Lindsey and underwent a brief and unsuccessful psychiatric treatment with a Dr. Jameson (see Millier, *Elizabeth Bishop* 172-74). Sometime during the spring of 1946, Bishop began seeing Foster, and, in early March, Marjorie wrote Bishop to say that she shouldn't return to Key West.

In the summer of 1946, Bishop interrupted her sessions with Foster and, nervous about the appearance that year of her first book of poems, *North & South*, made what was perhaps her most significant trip in adulthood to Nova Scotia. Her first visit to the province of her childhood in sixteen years, the trip provided her with the seeds for several important poems, including "At the Fishhouses," which she completed quickly, submitting it to *The New Yorker* on February 13, 1947, and "The Moose," which would not be finished for twenty-six years. On the same trip, she sought and may or may not have obtained the records of her mother's treatment at Nova Scotia Hospital in Dartmouth.[5] The February 1947 Foster letters are written a few months after this pivotal trip, just as the publication of her first book gave her greater visibility. Given Bishop's previous unsatisfactory experience with psychiatry and psychoanalytic treatment, it is important that we understand what made her intimate and frank letters to Ruth Foster different.

Although very little is known about Ruth Foster, the Foster letters lead to other traces in the archive. For years, I had been interested in an offhand reference in a 1957 letter Bishop wrote to Robert Lowell, in which she mentions Harry Stack Sullivan (*OA* 351; *WIA* 247). Sullivan's theories, as Philip Cushman writes in his lively cultural history of psychotherapy, *Constructing the Self, Constructing America*, represent a "road not taken" (159), an alternative to "American psychoanalysis under the influence of ego psychology" (187) emphasizing that interpersonal relations are influenced by the social and the political as opposed to the "ego psychologist's . . . idea that the ego is structured in an ahistorical, universal, acultural, and apolitical manner" (191). As the Foster letters reveal, Bishop spent a considerable amount of time with Lloyd Frankenberg and his wife, the artist Loren MacIver, when she lived in her King Street apartment, and it appears that she discussed not only poetry with him but also psychoanalysis.[6] Frankenberg was a devotee of Sullivan for whom he had worked during his alternative service as a conscientious objector[7] and had published a long, didactic poem, "Lifecycle of an Interperson," in the July 1946 issue of the British journal *Horizon*. As Sullivan's personal assistant during a period in which Sullivan was seriously ill, Frankenberg was also aware that Sullivan was gay, as he had to intervene in the increasingly strained relationship between Sullivan and his "adopted son," James Inscoe. In August of 1947, Frankenberg's *New York Times* review of the privately printed edition of Sullivan's *Conceptions of Modern Psychiatry* (1947) resulted in it becoming an unexpected bestseller. When I noticed that the book was in the portion of Bishop's newly catalogued library in the Vassar archive, I requested her edition of Sullivan's book and discovered that Bishop had inserted a copy of Frankenberg's review. Soon after I discovered that there was an important connection between Sullivan and Foster.

Foster was not, as Lorrie Goldensohn has written, a "Kleinian analyst" ("Approaching" 2). Although there is scant information about Foster, it seems likely that she was, at least by the mid-1940s, allied with the unorthodox culturalist-interpersonal school of neo-Freudians. We know from her obituary that she had practiced psychiatry in New York City beginning in the mid-1930s. A draft history[8] of the William Alanson White Institute written by Ralph Crowley and Maurice Green reveals that she graduated from the institute in 1947 and that she had, as a student, supported Clara Thompson, Erich Fromm, and others when they split from Karen Horney's Association for the Advancement of Psychoanalysis in 1943 and joined with Harry Stack Sullivan to found the White Institute.[9] We also know that Foster was one of three founding staff psychiatrists for Kenneth and Mamie Clark's Northside Center for Child Development in Harlem (Markowitz and Rosner 264). In "Efforts of Affection: A Memoir of Marianne Moore," Bishop described her as "a doctor of almost saintly character":

> One of the very few occasions on which we [Moore and Bishop] came close to having a falling out was when, in the forties, I told her I had been seeing a psychoanalyst. She disapproved quite violently and said that psychoanalysts taught that "Evil is not

evil. But we know it is." I hadn't noticed that my analyst, a doctor of almost saintly character, did this, but I didn't attempt to refute it, and we didn't speak of it again. (*Pr* 139)

Bishop had been familiar with the work of the cultural school at least since the fall of 1940 when, at the behest of Louise Crane, she had several sessions with a founder of that school, Karen Horney. Moore expressed her disapproval in a letter to her brother: "Elizabeth is very heavy in soul, so weary & discouraged now & again that Louise [Crane] took her to a psychiatrist" and notes that she had counseled Bishop to rely instead on the "quiet heroisms of faith" (*Selected Letters* 405).[10] Although that treatment was short-lived, Bishop thought highly enough of Horney to recommend (in a 1942 letter to Moore from Mexico City) Horney's controversial first book *The Neurotic Personality of Our Time* (1937). In that book, Horney writes "that neuroses are generated not only by incidental individual experiences but also by the specific cultural conditions under which we live. . . . When we recognize the great import of cultural conditions on neuroses the biological and physical conditions, which are considered by Freud to be at their root, recede into the background" (viii). Bishop's remark about Freud's limitations as "the perfect interpreter of *touch* only" illustrates why a form of psychoanalysis less focused on Freud's drive theory might appeal to her (qtd. in Ellis, *Art* 58).

One major difference between orthodox Freudian analysis and the culturalist/interpersonal psychoanalysis of the White Institute involved the relationship between the analyst and her patient. Clara Thompson writes in her 1950 treatise *Psychoanalysis: Its Evolution and Development* that "the analytic situation is essentially a human relationship in which, while one person is more immediately detached than the other and has less at stake, he is nevertheless an active participant" (108). Culturalist and interpersonal analysts, then, departed from strict Freudian notions of transference and resistance. In particular, as Stephen Mitchell and Margaret Black write, they "tilted the balance between past and present more toward the present," emphasizing how "the patient's early formative relationships . . . shaped an approach to living in the present," and they regarded countertransference as "a crucial feature of the psychoanalytic project" (79). As Donnel Stern notes in his article on the history of interpersonal psychoanalysis, a major point of its departure from Freudian orthodoxy rested on the rejection of "concepts of transference neurosis and standard psychoanalytic technique, including rigid definitions of analytic neutrality and anonymity" (77). The work of the culturalist/interpersonalist analysts at the White Institute where Foster was trained prefigures the "relational model" of psychoanalytic technique as it is distinguished from the "drive/structure" model (Greenberg and Mitchell 388-89). The analyst, then, is encouraged to see herself not as an aloof authority but rather as a "participant-observer."

As the first letter to Foster (labeled "Saturday") demonstrates, Bishop's emotional investment in her analyst was intense: "laying all transfernces [sic] aside which is not impossible no matter what you think, I really do love you very much in which sentiment I am doubless[sic] joined by countless others . . ." (VC 118.33; misquoted in Marshall, *Elizabeth Bishop* 78). And Bishop's breach of the boundaries between analyst and analysand, in the form of her late-night drunken phone call to Foster (VC 118.33), illustrates the potential pitfalls of seeing the analytic situation as a human relationship. Foster appears to have been quite ethical in pointing out to Bishop that Bishop's love was transference-love. In this letter Bishop apologizes for being "[i]nconsiderate yes and unreliable," and she relates a "confused nightmare" about the aftermath of the 1937 accident in France in which Margaret Miller's arm was severed. In the nightmare, Foster replaces Louise Crane who, unlike Crane, is not "responsible for the accident in any way." Betraying the depth of her erotic attachment to Foster, instead of reading "some Shakespeare to Margaret Miller, as she had in 1937," Bishop imagines that she has written a poem for Foster "about the shape and size of a sonnet although the meter is wrong" (VC 118.33). Awake, Bishop remembers only a few words and the first line: "Alive alive and with blue eyes," a line that anticipates the blue eyes featured in love poems written years later, such as "Dear, my compass . . ." and "Breakfast Song."

Heather Treseler brilliantly and presciently analyzed the letter-poems addressed to Foster in her essay "Dreaming in Color: Bishop's Notebook Letter-Poems," written before the Foster letters became available. She notes that the poems in the notebook in which Bishop records her 1946 Nova Scotia observations (VC 75.3) "figuratively extend[]" the "analytic conversation" (98). That conversation and the color blue appear in the same notebook in a poem titled "Blue Postman."

Jonathan Ellis provides a nuanced reading of the second of these drafts in *Art and Memory in the Work of Elizabeth Bishop*, comparing it to the nonsense verse of Lewis Carroll and Edward Lear (167-69). "Despair," writes Ellis, "punctuates the poem's whimsical form and sound as in Lear, though what matters to both poets is the 'transference' of pain into language" (169). However, Ellis's transcription of "Blue Postman" is inaccurate. Examining the two drafts, it appears that the poem in the draft he transcribes ends after the couplet "—But on & on in despair / he vanishes in blue blue air" (VC 75.3, p. 99). Ellis omits this couplet, which nearly repeats the couplet that ends stanza 3, in which he also mistranscribes "blue blue air" as "thin blue air" (167). After the couplet, Bishop has drawn a solid line before

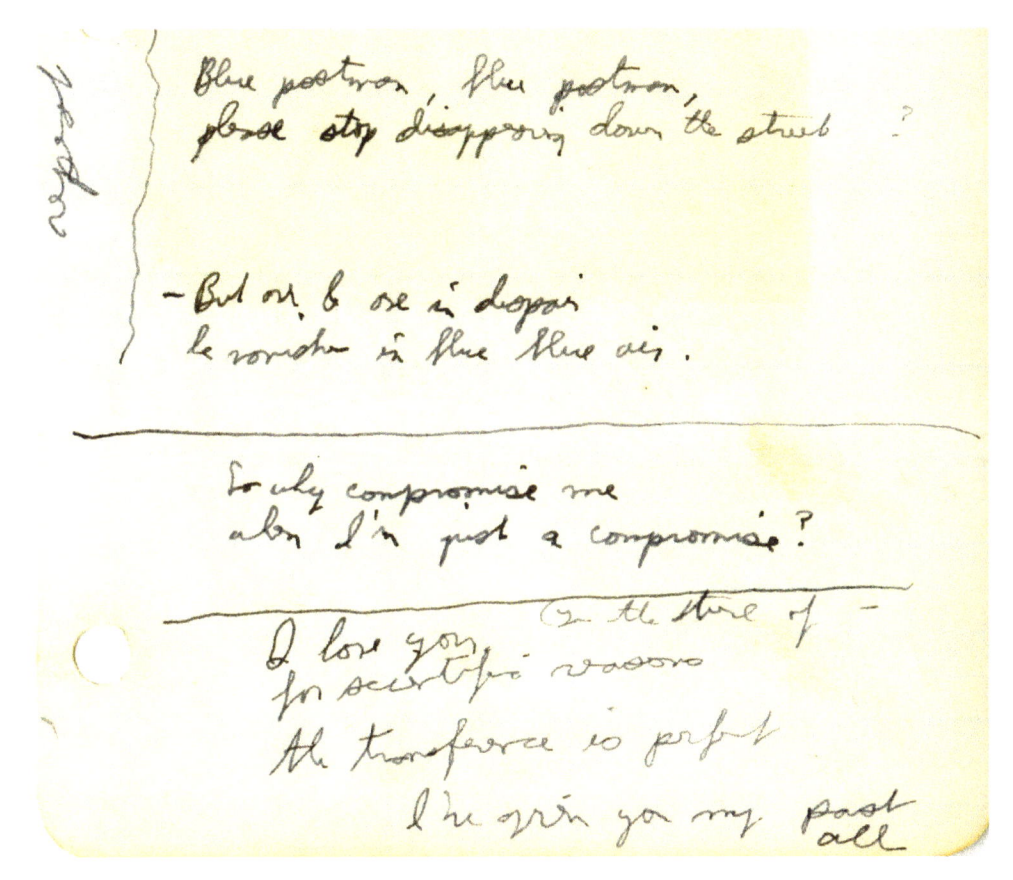

An excerpt from a page of Bishop's notebook with a draft of "Blue Postman." (VC 75.3; Courtesy of Vassar College)

the lines "So why compromise me / when I'm just a compromise?" and another solid line before the lines about transference that Ellis also mistranscribes:

> I love you
> for scientific reasons
> the transference is perfect (168)

As the manuscript shows, the last lines on the page actually read:

> (To the tune of –
> I love you
> for scientific reasons
> the transference is perfect
>   I've given you my past
>   all (VC 75.3, p. 99)

ELIZABETH BISHOP'S SANITY

The additional line "I've given you my past / all" coupled with the use of the psychoanalytic term *transference*—the process by which the patient transfers unconscious feelings from childhood to the analyst in order to recognize and work through them—suggests that Bishop might have been thinking about Foster. In the 1947 Foster letters, it is clear that Bishop became conscious of her transference as she recounted the dreams during her trip to Nova Scotia, in which her analyst played key roles. Ellis dates "Blue Postman" to the 1946 Nova Scotia trip and ties it to the now-destroyed letters Bishop wrote to Marjorie Stevens, and it is on this trip that Bishop makes the notes on which she bases several major poems and writes the "Dear Dr. Foster" drafts as well.

I suspect that these final lines are not part of "Blue Postman" at all but a later commentary on the poem or a commentary on the letters to Foster.[11] The lines are tonally quite different from the rest of the poem and appear to be written in pencil rather than pen.[12] Although dating the entries in the two Key West notebooks is difficult,[13] one may speculate that the lines about "transference" were penciled in later in 1946 or even in 1947 after Bishop had resumed her sessions with Foster. Perhaps the note "(To the tune of –" is a wry allusion to the popular song then dominating the jukeboxes: "(I Love You) For Sentimental Reasons."[14]

Whether "perfect" or not, Bishop's transference provided the inspiration for the dreams that inspired her poems. "At the Fishhouses" was already finished when she commented on it to Foster in the February 1947 letters. Noting that the poem grew out of a "dream or a drunken doze" on a bus ride during her "awful week" at Keene, New Hampshire, in June of 1946, she wrote,

> I had a dream in which everything was very wild & dark & stormy and you were in it feeding me from your breast. (I should think this would be a common dream about a woman analyst) anyway you were much bigger than life size, or maybe I was just reduced to baby size, and it seemed to be very calm inside the raging storm. It was not milk, it was some rather bitter dark gray liquid. (VC 118.33; qtd. in Goldensohn, "Approaching" 10-11)

This dream certainly illuminates the image of the rocky breasts at the end of the poem, but Bishop goes on to say that she "saw this poem when I was in Lockeport," connecting "the appearance of the water with my dream on the bus" and connecting the seal with Foster:

> I told you how I connected the seal with you once but I didn't like to say the rest. I think there may be something in the double meaning of the word seal, too also

there is at the end a sort of interchange between kissing & feeding (or is this all too obvious to you and I don't need to pt. it out at all?) and I suppose a kiss is always considered a sort of seal. "knowledge is historical" besides being a random thought I wrote down yrs ago also refers obviously to the process of psychoanalysis I know. Well I could go on analyzing my own poem indefinitely, I'm afraid. (VC 118.33; qtd. in Goldensohn, "Approaching" 11-12)

In Bishop's desire to get to the source of that bitter, imagined knowledge "derived from the rocky breasts / forever" (*P* 64) and to give her analyst her "past" or her "all," the transference provides a much-needed comic relief in the form of the analyst/seal that serves to lighten the somber "gray and blue-gray" atmosphere and tone of the rest of the poem. The notes from the Nova Scotia trip are marked GM for "Geographical Mirror," which Millier suggests "were part of an attempt to find herself reflected in the land and the sea" (*Elizabeth Bishop* 182). Or perhaps it is an attempt to find some form of imagined knowledge that could somehow transform the "historical" knowledge she was confiding to her analyst into something "utterly free" or at least "flowing and flown" (*P* 64). If Bishop imagined "Geographical Mirror" to be a series of poems, the 1946 Nova Scotia trip portions of the notebook contain not only the genesis of "At the Fishhouses" but also images that find their way into "A Summer's Dream" ("dwarfs are 'cheerful' & giants seemed morose," VC 75.3, p. 114) and "Cape Breton" ("The little calf that bawls," VC 75.3, p. 115), poems generally attributed to her Nova Scotia trip of 1947. Although the mid- to late 1940s seem very painful for Bishop, they are also very productive: "At the Fishhouses," "A Summer Dream," "Cape Breton," "The Bight," and "Over 2000 Illustrations"—all completed between 1947 and 1948—show her geographical reflections, with the help of Foster, turned into art. While her treatment with Ruth Foster did not help to cure her asthma or her alcoholism, Bishop was able to work through a debilitating writer's block and overcome her "fear of repetition" (VC 118.33).

Bishop's analysis with Foster seems to have been terminated sometime before her year as Consultant in Poetry to the Library of Congress. Foster's subsequent death from pancreatic cancer on September 29, 1950, contributed to Bishop's sense that the year 1950 was "Just about my worst, so far" (VC 77.4). Despite her positive feelings for Foster, Bishop never underwent analysis again, although she did continue to read psychoanalytic texts, including Ernest Jones's biography of Freud and Melanie Klein's *Envy and Gratitude* (1957), which she described to Robert Lowell as "a grim little book . . . superb in its horrid way" (*WIA* 294).

Page from Bishop's notebook featuring images that would later be used in "Cape Breton," "A Summer's Dream" and "At the Fishhouses" (VC 75.3, p. 115; Courtesy of Vassar College)

JUNE 1970, OURO PRÊTO

The period immediately following the apparent suicide of Bishop's longtime partner Lota de Macedo Soares was even more challenging for her than the period during the 1940s when she was treated by Foster. By the spring of 1970, in addition to her continuing unresolved grief for Macedo Soares, her relationship with her young lover Roxanne Cumming was falling apart. Quoting a letter Bishop wrote to Lowell on "December 15 or 16," 1969, Millier characterizes the years between 1968 to 1970 as "a totally wasted stretch" (*Elizabeth Bishop* 399; *WIA* 661). By the spring of 1970, however, Bishop completed two of her best poems, "Crusoe in England" and "In the Waiting Room." At the same time, Bishop pours out her distress in a series of long letters to Dorothee Bowie, the assistant to the English department chair when Bishop taught at the University of Washington in 1966 and Bishop's "chief troubleshooter, devoted helper, and willing excuse-maker when drinking interfered with her duties" (Millier, *Elizabeth Bishop* 377). Bowie was one of her few friends who knew the history of Bishop's relationship with Cumming. Bishop's letters to Bowie from Ouro Prêto are frank and at times frantic, revealing the details of what she believed to be Cumming's nervous breakdown, her hospitalization in Belo Horizonte, and her eventual return to the United States in late April. In her June 14, 1970, letter to Bowie, Bishop expresses concern that Cumming may not be receiving the treatment she needs in Seattle, as well as her concern for Cumming's three-year-old son, Boogie. Connecting Boogie's predicament to her own early life with her mother before Gertrude's permanent hospitalization, Bishop also conflates Cumming's illness not only with her mother's illness but also with Macedo Soares's illness, lamenting her own "guilt feelings" while at the same time depicting herself as "feeling pretty tough and like myself for the first time in five years" (VC 27.5, June 14, 1970, p. 3).

While she recognizes that Boogie's experience is "harrowing," she portrays herself as having survived her own childhood trauma but without Boogie's "resiliency": "I was alone with my mother until I was 4 ½ or so ... and no father, as well. But some loving aunts and grandparents saved my life, and saved me - a damaged personality I know, but I did survive" (VC 27.5, June 14, 1970, p. 2; qtd. in Lombardi, *Body* 222).

Although the Bowie letters are not new to the Vassar archive, they reveal the same commitment to writing poetry as a "sane" response to emotional turmoil as the Foster letters. In the intimate space of letters "telling all" to Bowie, Bishop notes her creative breakthrough in the midst of personal chaos, writing her "first poetry in over three years" (VC 27.5, p. 1). She completed "Crusoe in England" the day after Cumming entered the hospital in Belo Horizonte,[15] and the night before

> I am feeling pretty tough and like myslf again for the first time in five years. The very fact that I have stopped drinking with the wrst provocations of my life going on at the same time, is a good sign, I know. My own life has been darkened always by guiltfeelings, I think, about my mother—somehow children get the idea it's *their* fault - or I did. And I could do nothing about that, and she lived on for twenty years more and it has been a nightmare to me always. I feel I should have been wiser about Lota, too, somehow, and maybe, maybe, I could have saved her,— But she is lost to me forever, and by God, I am going to save someone, if I can. Schizophrenia CAN be cured - my mother was too early a case. Look at Robert Lowell (all my friends are mad) - with a new drug, he hasn't had a breakdown for over three years, I think- no psychiatry or anything, just PILLS.
>
> I am typing electrically full tilt- many mistakes no doubt - and telling you all, Dorothee. The only prose book I ever thought I wanted to write is a book about the life of Dorothea Dix - her real name - a wonderful young woman who devoted herself to the insane, and the awful asylums in the US, in the 19th century - she died quite young,- shipwrecked, I think. She has never been properly known about and I have had this in mind for years to do. I probably never will do it - but I think I'd like to try to save Roxanne's life and sanity if there is the slightest possibility of it. I'm going to ask her to go back to Dr Victor again- if she will, perhaps you could, as I said, talk to him- he is probably too busy to write letters - and see what he thinks. You neednt spare my unstable personality - 'queer, drunk, and all the rest, I am sane.& I've never felt saner.
>
> Dr Ralph Vinta -

A passage from Bishop's June 14, 1970 letter to Dorothee Bowie. (VC 27.5; Courtesy of Vassar College)

this June 14 letter, she completed "In the Waiting Room," a poem she had been working on since before Macedo Soares's death in 1967.

Bishop had moderated her drinking during the first few months of 1970, although it appears that she was using an unhealthy combination of prescribed medicines including tranquilizers, antidepressants, and amphetamines. Feeling that her "life has always been darkened by guilt feelings," she writes of her mother's illness that

> somehow children get the idea that it's their fault - or I did. And I could do nothing about that, and she lived on for twenty years more and it has been a nightmare to me always. I feel I should have been wiser about Lota, too, somehow, and maybe, maybe, I could have saved her. But she is lost to me forever, and by God, I am going to save <u>someone</u> if I can. (VC 27.5, June 14, 1970, p. 3; qtd. in Lombardi, *Body* 222)

Having completed both "In the Waiting Room" and "Crusoe" in the "last, or / next-to-last, of three loved houses" may have helped her work through childhood trauma and a sense that Brazil, once a home, had become a place of exile, or shipwreck.

Marilyn May Lombardi is one of the few Bishop critics to pay attention to this letter to Bowie, and she reads it in terms of "Shipwreck and Salvage," as she titles the concluding chapter of her book *The Body and the Song*. Bishop expresses her need to "save <u>someone</u> if I can" by referring to her wish to write a book about Dorothea Dix. In this dense, single-spaced letter filled with handwritten marginalia and corrections (see letter above), resembling the Foster letters in that regard, she writes, "I am typing electrically full tilt- many mistakes no doubt - and telling you all, Dorothee," as she describes "[t]he only prose book I ever thought I wanted to write . . . a book about the life of Dorothea Dix" (VC 27.5, June 14, 1970, p. 3; qtd. in Lombardi, *Body* 224-25). Dix, Bishop writes, "devoted herself to the insane, and the awful asylums in the US, in the 19th century." Recognizing that it is a book she "probably will never write," Bishop expresses a wish "to save Roxanne's life and sanity" (VC 27.5, June 14, 1970, p. 3). It becomes clear, however, that she is more concerned with saving (or asserting) her own precarious sanity: "You needn't spare my unstable personality - queer, drunk, and all the rest, I am sane,& I've never felt saner" (VC 27.5, June 14, 1970, p. 3; qtd. in Lombardi, *Body* 222).

As Lombardi notes, Bishop refers to Dix in the drafts of her unfinished Sable Island piece (VC 53.18), which she abandoned sometime in the mid-1950s, and she notes Bishop's reading of *The Life of Dorothea Lynde Dix*, by Francis Tiffany. Although Lombardi goes a bit too far when she says that Bishop "had come to think of herself as a Dorothea Dix for the literary world, an architect of asylum and a rescuer of shipwrecked souls" (219), no doubt the notion of shipwreck was heightened for Bishop at this time, having recently completed "Crusoe" as she contemplated returning in the fall to the Boston area of her youth to take Robert Lowell's place at Harvard. As Bishop knew from the Tiffany book, Dix's two great contributions to Nova Scotia were helping to found the asylum where Gertrude Bulmer was later to be hospitalized and raising money to modernize the lifesaving station on Sable Island.[16] Family legend had it that Bishop's great grandfather Robert Hutchinson had died at sea in a wreck off Sable Island (Barry, *Elizabeth Bishop: Archival Guide* 30-31). She would also have known that Dix was instrumental in establishing St. Elizabeths, the hospital where she had paid her visits to Ezra Pound during her unhappy stint as Consultant in Poetry to the Library of Congress, during that worst year, so far.

Bishop ends her letter to Bowie empathizing with Boogie's predicament, lamenting that his mother couldn't satisfy his craving for affection and tying that craving to that of "all these particualr [sic] three of my loony friends"—Cumming, Macedo Soares, and Robert Lowell—who, she remarks, "crave affection" and are far less "*demonstrative*" than she. Accusing Cumming of not being affectionate enough with her son, she writes, "Well, thank God for my little Aunt Maud, and I hope she went straight to Heaven - she deserved to, the way she devoted herself to me" (VC 27.5, June 14, 1970, p. 4). Bishop comes close to succumbing to nostalgia and sentimentality as she invokes her Aunt Maud, who had nursed her back to health with both devotion and Romantic and Victorian poetry, without mentioning the intense shame about Maud she had confessed to in the Foster letters or the cruelty of her Uncle George. Nevertheless, Bishop's wish to save the sanity of others belies her more pressing need to save herself.

MARCH 1971, OURO PRÊTO

When Bishop began teaching at Harvard in September 1970, she met her last love, Alice Methfessel, who became the closest thing to a savior Bishop was to find. Having returned to Ouro Prêto in the spring of 1971 to organize her papers and other personal belongings in order to ship them back to the United States, Bishop writes a letter to Methfessel dated "March Night of 23 or 24 - Tuesday -," in which she encloses a typed extract from Melanie Klein's essay "Love, Guilt and Reparation." In this letter she writes that she loves Methfessel because she is "probably less neurotic than anyone else I know" (VC 116.5, March 23 or 24, 1971, p. 2). Bishop developed her interest in Klein in the 1950s in Brazil.[17] Klein's brand of object-relations psychoanalysis had not yet made a great impact in the United States, but its influence was already widespread in England and South America. Macedo Soares had a great interest in psychology and psychoanalysis and had a fairly extensive library. Macedo Soares's analyst near the end of her life was Dr. Decio Souza, who had been trained by Klein. Although Bishop writes Methfessel that she now prefers Klein to "Freud and Freudians," she nevertheless confesses that she is "not sure" how much of Klein she still believes (VC 116.15, March 23 or 24, p. 1). Bishop excerpts a lengthy passage about female friendship, assiduously avoiding Klein's discussion distinguishing female friendship "from a homosexual love relation"[18]:

> Let us take as an instance a friendship between two women who are not too dependent upon each other. Protectiveness and helpfulness may still be needed, at times by the one, at other times by the other, as situations arise. This capacity to give and take emotionally is one essential for true friendship. Here, elements of early situations are expressed in adult ways. Protection, help and advice were first afforded to us by our mothers. If we grow up emotionally and become self-sufficient, we shall not be too dependent upon maternal support and comfort, but the wish to receive them when painful and difficult situations arise will remain until we die. (Klein and Riviere 100; qtd. in VC 116.15, March 23 or 24, p. 3)

Bishop reassures Methfessel that this description of friendship "doesn't all apply exactly": if she had had a more ordinary upbringing, Bishop writes that she might be "happier and easier to love." But she vows to "do my best. As I said I am *aware* of all this- & really trying, baby -" (VC 116.15, March 23 or 24, p. 3). Bishop deflects the portion of the typed excerpt in which Klein cautions that "an unresolved conflict from infancy plays an important part in the breakup of the friendship," noting that a friendship is "unlikely to succeed" if "we expect the friend to make up for our early deprivations." Bishop was able to achieve with Methfessel a kind of stable instability in which her "early sorrow" seemed to recede somewhat.[19]

In 1972, given the deadline of delivering the Phi Beta Kappa poem at Harvard, Bishop, while she remained "queer, drunk, and all the rest," was able to summon the stoic sanity she had long craved in order to finish "The Moose" after twenty-six years: the poem that had its genesis in the 1946 bus trip home from Nova Scotia, which Bishop had written about in her 1947 letter to Foster. In that letter Bishop recalls that her Aunt Grace had given her some rum and a sleeping pill, and she was half asleep listening to "two women seated far back behind me and they kept talking all night" (VC 118.33). The louder voice that spoke in "a *comiserating* [sic] tone" was the Nova Scotian voice of Aunt Grace. "The other voice I couldn't hear so well," she wrote Foster, "was you." In the poem, those voices, now transformed to "Grandparents' voices" (*P* 191) utter that "peculiar / affirmative" (*P* 192) that lulls the speaker to sleep. Just before this in the same letter, right after her analysis of "At the Fishhouses," Bishop writes, "The sentence I woke up saying to myself . . . was 'The image falls gratefully from the light, turning a little, back to the levels we are told no sunbeam ever reaches.' and I had a clear picture of something like a piece of jewelry say - I think it was gold- falling down through the water only the feeling about it was the reverse of its being lost - it was very happy" (VC 118.33; qtd. in Goldensohn, "Approaching" 13-14). Like the seal, the "grand, otherworldly" moose arrives to bring Bishop and all of us, after so many years, a hard-won, fleeting, and "sweet / sensation of joy" (*P* 193).

NOTES

1. The biographical facts about Bishop's virtual orphanhood are well known. Bishop's father William Thomas Bishop died of Bright's disease when she was eight months old, and her mother, Gertrude Bulmer Bishop, was committed to Nova Scotia Hospital in Dartmouth in June of 1916 when her daughter was five. Bishop never saw her mother again, and Gertrude Bishop remained in the hospital until her death on May 29, 1934, shortly before Bishop graduated from Vassar College in June. After her mother was hospitalized, Bishop remained with her maternal grandparents until October 1917 when she was "brought back unconsulted and against my wishes" (*Pr* 89) to live with her paternal grandparents in Worcester, Massachusetts. Her brief time in Worcester is detailed in "The Country Mouse," first published in 1984. In May of 1918, her grandfather John W. Bishop arranged for her to live with her mother's oldest sister Maud and her husband George Shepherdson in the working-class Boston suburb of Revere.
2. By most accounts, Bishop began seeing Foster in the spring of 1946. A reference in an August 5, 1948, letter to Anny Baumann seems to indicate that she was still in treatment with her: "I had

hoped that going to Dr. Foster might help [cure asthma], but it didn't seem to—at least not yet, at any rate—I suppose it might eventually" (*OA* 163-64).

3. Foster was generally interested in treating creative clients, and she treated several of Bishop's friends, including Louise Crane and Tommy Wanning (*OA* 206). Bishop's reference to "blacks," undoubtedly refers to Foster's work at the Northside Child Development Center in Harlem.

4. Frankenberg and MacIver had taken Bishop to see Shaw's one act *Androcles and the Lion* the night before—her thirty-sixth birthday. Bishop makes no mention of Sean O'Casey's *A Pound on Demand*, the other one-act on the program, which is a slapstick farce about a drunk and his sober sidekick trying to withdraw money from the post office so he can keep on drinking.

5. A digitized photocopy of these records are available as pdfs as part of the Bulmer-Bowers-Hutchinson-Sutherland family fonds (Accession No. 1997.002) in the Acadia University Digital Collections: http://openarchive.acadiau.ca/cdm/landingpage/collection/BBHS. They are not labeled but begin at the bottom of page 19: http://openarchive.acadiau.ca/cdm/search/collection/BBHS/page/19.

6. Bishop's interest in the cultural-interpersonal school is reflected in the parenthetical remark she makes in her retelling of her dream in the "Sunday Morning" Foster letter: "Lloyd and I talked some about psychoanalysis last night. I showed him Dorothy Parker's review of the Farnham book & at one point he remarked 'good old penis envy'" (VC 118.33). There is no evidence Parker ever wrote a review of Farnham's anti-feminist, pop-Freudian tome *Modern Woman: The Lost Sex* (though she is quoted in a June 16, 1947, *Life* magazine article). In any event, Frankenberg's remark about penis envy is humorously disdainful. Bishop seems to have maintained her interest. In an April 1949 letter to Frankenberg and MacIver, it appears that Bishop was acquainted with Patrick Mullahy, who edited and explained the Sullivan lectures and also wrote *Oedipus—Myth and Complex: A Review of Psychoanalytic Theory,* which Frankenberg reviewed in the March 19, 1949, issue of *The New York Times*: "Tell Lloyd ... that I saw his review of Patrick's book and liked it. I've had the book ordered for some time but it hasn't come yet" (Bishop, *One Art* 185). Through serendipity (and a used book dealer), I recently bought the copy of *Oedipus—Myth and Complex* that Mullahy inscribed to "Loren and Lloyd."

7. For an account of Frankenberg's work for Sullivan during the war, see Wake, particularly chap. 6. Frankenberg's association with Sullivan began in the 1930s when he attended meetings of what F. Barton Evans calls "the famous Zodiac Group, a regular meeting on Monday evenings in a local bar of friends sharing social and professional interests" that included Karen Horney, Clara Thompson, and Erich Fromm (42).

8. A PDF of an unpublished draft history of the White Institute is available to download from the "Erich Fromm Document Server": https://opus4.kobv.de/opus4-Fromm/frontdoor/index/index/start/0/rows/10/sortfield/score/sortorder/desc/searchtype/simple/query/revolution+white+institute/docId/24509.

9. For a brief summary of the origins of the White Institute, see Kwawer.

10. Moore's letter to her brother was written shortly after the "Roosters" debacle. Another reason for Bishop's being "heavy in soul" was the unexpected death of her Aunt Maud the previous August.

11. The draft of "Blue Postman" on page 98 of the notebook shows that Bishop worked on different projects sometimes on the same page. The canceled line running down the left side of the page—"It is raining women's voices as if they were dead even in the memory"—is Bishop's translation of a line from "Il Pleut," the most famous of Guillaume Apollinaire's *Calligrammes*. On folio 97 of the notebook, she is working on translations of Apollinaire's "La Blanche Neige" ("The White Snow") and "Automne" ("Autumn").

12. Alice Quinn reproduces "Blue Postman" in her notes on another version, "Dream-" (*EAP* 36), and omits the final lines altogether (*EAP* 261-62).
13. Quinn notes that the sequence of the pages of each of the notebooks "can't be relied upon to date the drafts accurately. All that can safely be said is that all the drafts [in the two notebooks] date from 1936 or 1937 to the late 1940s" (*EAP* 258). Nevertheless, internal evidence suggests that much of this notebook dates from the mid-1940s, roughly from 1944 to 1948.
14. Nat King Cole's version entered the Billboard charts in November of 1946. In the February 8 issue—the date of Bishop's thirty-sixth birthday—around the time she was having trouble "laying all transfernces aside," there were four recordings of the song on Billboard's "Most Played Jukebox Records" chart: Nat King Cole's version and versions by Eddy Majestic, Ella Fitzgerald, and Charlie Spivack. Bishop's lines seem to parody the popular song's lyrics: "I love you for sentimental reasons / I hope you do believe me / I've given you my heart."
15. Although Millier states that Bishop sent "Crusoe in England" to Howard Moss in the spring of 1971, she actually sent it on May 18, 1970, and Moss wrote her to accept it on June 2 (*EBNY* 317-19). The copy that is marked up for the typesetter bears the date June 2, 1970 (VC 58.17).
16. See Goldman.
17. Although it is uncertain when Bishop first read Klein, her interest in Klein's writing intensified in Brazil. Millier notes that her recent reading of Klein influenced "Sestina" (*Elizabeth Bishop* 267), and Victoria Harrison mentions a March 1956 letter to Kit and Ilse Barker in which she mentions rereading Klein's *Psychology of Children* and Ernest Jones's three-volume biography of Freud (227-28). In a March 1959 letter to Robert Lowell, she recommends *Gratitude and Envy* (*WIA* 294).
18. Bishop's copy of Klein and Joan Riviere's *Love, Hate and Reparation* is dog-eared on page 99, where Klein offers the following explanation in a footnote: "The subject of homosexual love relations is a wide and very complicated one. To deal with it adequately would necessitate more space than I have at my disposal, and I restrict myself, therefore, to mentioning that much love can be put into these relationships."
19. Alyse Knorr takes up this correspondence in detail in chapter 4.

CHAPTER THREE

ELIZABETH BISHOP'S PERSPECTIVES ON MARRIAGE

Jeffrey Westover

> *Marriage can never be renewed except by that which is always the source of true marriage: that two human beings reveal the You to one another.*
> —Martin Buber

In a number of texts, both published and unpublished, Elizabeth Bishop addresses the themes of marriage, love, and courtship. Such issues were vexed ones for her. As a young woman, she rejected Robert Seaver's marriage proposal (Millier, *Elizabeth Bishop* 112). Later, her friend Pauline Hemingway wondered in a letter whether she and Tom Wanning were engaged (Millier, *Elizabeth Bishop* 201), and Robert Lowell famously confessed to her that she was the one who got away (*WIA* 225-26).[1] Given that Bishop's most important romantic relationships were lesbian at a time when same-sex relationships (much less marriages) were not socially sanctioned, Bishop had to confront the issue of marriage and adopt a quasi-public stance toward it to pursue a career as a professional writer.[2] In Frank Bidart's words,

> One must remember that for the vast majority of her life, in both social and literary terms, *not* to be in the closet was to be ghettoized; people might know or suspect that one was gay, but to talk about it openly in straight society was generally considered out-of-control or stupid.... Out of her distrust of the straight world she didn't want people to know she was gay. (*REB* 327)

Stephen Vider provides a general context for thinking about Bidart's comments. In the America of the 1950s and 1960s, Vider writes, "[a]dapting to marriage became not only socially desirable—it was widely understood as developmentally normal. As heterosexual marriage was made a mark of maturity, homosexuality was increasingly understood as a neurosis: a symptom of maladjustment" (703). Three unpublished archival documents (two stories and a letter Bishop wrote to her psychoanalyst Ruth Foster) provide important insights into Bishop's attitudes toward marriage and her resistance to the medical designation of homosexuality as neurotic.

Bishop's letters demonstrate that she felt the social pressure of other people's expectations that she should marry. On March 11, 1941, for instance, Bishop wryly pointed out to Frani Blough that her housekeeper, Mrs. Almyda, wants her to have a baby (*OA* 99), and in 1948, she joked with Lowell about finding her a husband, writing that "I'd settle for some form of dignified concubinage as long as it was guaranteed" (*WIA* 49). In what follows, I address Bishop's treatment of this topic primarily in the context of letters and unpublished work, including two virtually undiscussed stories from the Vassar archives, "Eula Wiggle" (VC 53.19) and "The River-Rat" (VC 53.4), to account for a pattern of indirection she displays regarding the institution, or enterprise, to borrow terms used by Bishop's mentor, Marianne Moore, in her own important long poem about marriage (Moore, *New Collected Poems* 63). In particular, these two stories reveal that marriage was on Bishop's mind not only as material for fiction and poetry but also as a matter to reckon with in personal terms. The unpublished stories can enrich and deepen our sense of Bishop's attitude toward marriage and same-sex desire in relation to her own long-term "marriages" with women, her ambitions as a professional writer, and her fraught relationship to home and travel.

In several texts, courting characters or married spouses are observed and commented on by a narrator so that Bishop can treat the topic through a distanced perspective, such as in the poem "House Guest" as well as in the two unpublished stories.[3] In the first two "Songs for a Colored Singer," moreover, Bishop invents a persona who expresses her dissatisfaction with marriage, which has gotten so bad that she is "going to go and take the bus / and find someone monogamous" (*PPL* 37). In "Roosters," Bishop tartly comments on the subordination and even disposability of wives. The title character of "Penelope Gwin" blithely informs her listeners that "This family life is not for me" (*EAP* 3). In addition, a youthful Bishop published "The Thumb," the story of a courtship that goes singularly awry. The character-narrator of this story is a suitor who is both attracted to and repelled by the woman he pursues. In the posthumously published story "Was It in His Hand?" two female friends (the narrator being one of them) consult a psychic who assumes they want to know what their future husbands will be like (*PPL* 558). As she indicates in an unpublished letter to her psychoanalyst Ruth

Foster, Bishop watched at least one woman whom she cared for, Judy Flynn, lose her intellectual liveliness after many years of marriage (VC 188.33). Finally, in "Mr. and Mrs. Carlyle," dated 1978, she wittily figures marriage as "One flesh and two heads" (*PPL* 264).

Bishop humorously expresses dismay regarding marriage in work she composed even before she attended college. The protagonist of "Penelope Gwin" eschews marriage in favor of travel and cosmopolitan culture:

> I introduce Penelope Gwin,
> A friend of mine through thick and thin,
> Who's travelled much in foreign parts
> Pursuing culture and the arts.
> "And also," says Penelope
> "This family life is not for me.
> I find it leads to deep depression.
> And *I* was born for self expression." (*EAP* 3)

As Alice Quinn points out, the name of Bishop's heroine plays on the word *penguin* (Pen Gwin), an association reinforced by the picture of a penguin on the manuscript copy of the poem reproduced in *Edgar Allan Poe & the Juke-Box* (*EAP* 3). Bishop inserts the underlined words "Our Heroine" as a caption beneath the picture. As Quinn explains, moreover, Penelope's surname plays on *gouinne*, a French slang word for lesbian (*EAP* 244). Near the end of the poem, Penelope humorously confirms her commitment to remaining unmarried:

> Of course, while in Romantic France
> I met with Cupid and Romance.
> One glimpse at my rejected suitor—
> He was a handsome German tutor.
> But no! I would be no man's wife,
> The stark reality of life
> For me, and he was past his prime.
> His mouth hung open half the time.
> It gave my senses quite a jolt
> To find he had begun to molt. . . . (*EAP* 4; ellipses in original)

In these amusing lines, Bishop treats the topics of marriage and female independence comically, but her heroine also takes a definite stand against heterosexual marriage to defend Gwin's preference for travel and cosmopolitan culture. The

Adrienne Rich of "Compulsory Heterosexuality and Lesbian Existence" would have recognized Penelope Gwin as a marriage resister (*Blood* 56).

One may compare the breezy humor of "Gwin" with the darker tone of "The Thumb," a short story that echoes Hawthorne's "The Birthmark" and Poe's "Imp of the Perverse." In both the light verse and the unsettling and accomplished short story, Bishop repudiates the institution of marriage as unsuitable or unavailing to certain persons. In the poem, Bishop portrays Gwin as a free-spirited alter ego who finds her bourgeois aunts to be irrelevant and oppressive. Although the narrator of "The Thumb" is presumably male, he is unnerved by the hypermasculine right thumb that mars the beauty of Sabrina, a woman who otherwise strikes him as an epitome of femininity. By combining the physical qualities of both sexes, Sabrina simultaneously arouses and disgusts the narrator. She becomes the object of his obsessive fascination, a woman who keenly appeals to him but whose thumb ultimately discomfits him when he abruptly halts his courtship. As Lorrie Goldensohn points out, the narrator's "choking rage and madness" are "directed at the courtship pattern toward which Sabrina invites him" ("Body's Roses" 75). This situation sums up Bishop's sense of her predicament as a lesbian woman in a heteronormative environment.

Sabrina's thumb is that of a "brute" (*PPL* 514). Bishop calls attention to its ungainliness. The thumb is covered by several "coarse, black hairs," which intensify its repulsiveness by making its manliness contrast the more starkly with the feminine perfection of Sabrina's physical charms and engaging demeanor (*PPL* 515). Those hairs, like the shape and quality of the eponymous appendage, make the thumb a symbolic phallus. They provoke the kind of sexual anxiety that J. Alfred Prufrock feels when he considers the fine hairs on the arms of "the women who come and go / Talking of Michelangelo" (132). At the same time, the "obscene" starkness of the thumb might figure the clitoris (*PPL* 514). By noticing and not noticing Sabrina's flawed right thumb, the narrator shows that he is obsessed with it, both seeking to avoid it and finding himself staring at it—and even dreaming of touching it (*PPL* 516). In this respect, Bishop offers a symbol of the homosexual who is unable to accept the truth of his or her same-sex desire. In Thomas Travisano's view, "The question of gender reversal is unavoidable: one has to wonder if Bishop is not using an implicitly male narrator (neither his sex nor his name are ever actually specified) to explore her attraction to forbidden beauty" ("Emerging Genius" 46).

The ambivalence of "The Thumb" is not evident in "Penelope Gwin." However, in "The River-Rat" and "Eula Wiggle," two unpublished stories Bishop composed as an adult, a dim or outright negative view of marriage prevails. This view is anchored in the character-narrators of both stories, which are set in Arkansas (Pauline Hemingway, with whom Bishop collaborated on the stories, was from Piggott, Arkansas, the setting of "Eula Wiggle"). Bishop's archive at Vassar does not indicate a date for "Eula Wiggle," but it does identify "The River-Rat" as having been written circa 1948. There is no evidence of who assigned this date or how, and Brett Millier does not discuss either story in her biography nor does Megan Marshall in *Elizabeth Bishop: A Miracle for Breakfast*. Nonetheless, these stories are worth considering in light of Bishop's stated intention that she would never marry and in light of constraints on women's freedom and independence in the middle of the twentieth century. "The River-Rat" portrays marriage as a physically damaging, sickly state, whereas "Eula Wiggle" addresses the institution in comic terms, spoofing courtship as a form of calculated self-fashioning and marriage as primarily a means of achieving upward mobility.

Both items are in Box 53 of the archive, and in a letter to an editor at *The New Yorker*, Bishop mentions stories set in Arkansas composed by herself and Pauline Hemingway (*EBNY* 36), suggesting that both texts were collaborations. In addition, both stories are in typescript and feature numerous emendations in ink and in pencil, indicating that Bishop-Hemingway revised the story in several stages. Since insertions in ink are crossed out and replaced with emendations in pencil, the pencil markings seem to represent a later stage of revision.[4] There are also two drafts of each story. An archivist has placed the drafts inside folded sheets to label each one as the first or second. Although Bishop (and Hemingway) may well have preferred to revise further (especially as there are unfilled textual gaps in some cases), both stories have some form of conclusion and a comparatively clear logic to their plots. Unlike the drafts of some poems in the archive, which often feature alternate options for specific words without indicating a definitive preference for either, the revisions of these prose documents arguably provide more clues to readers about overall structure and particular choices regarding diction. For example, the first draft of "The River-Rat" is titled "The Water- (River) Rat," with "River" inserted in parentheses as a potential substitute for "Water." The second draft is simply titled "The River-Rat," with "Water" crossed out in pencil. Seeing these material features of the archival documents gives one a sense of the process of composition and raises questions about the nature of Bishop's collaboration with Hemingway.

Both typescripts are on onionskin paper and feature rust marks from paper clips at the upper left-hand corner. Both are paginated. Some of the typeface is relatively faded, but all of the text is comparatively legible, even when typed alterations have been made. Some of the sheets are folded in the corners and marked by minor stains. Revisions, as I have mentioned, are indicated in both ink and pencil. In every case except one, the emendations are legible or discernible because of the textual context. There are some blanks in the typescript of "Eula Wiggle" without any handwritten insertions. In at least one other blank appearing in "The River-Rat," an indecipherable word has been inserted by hand.

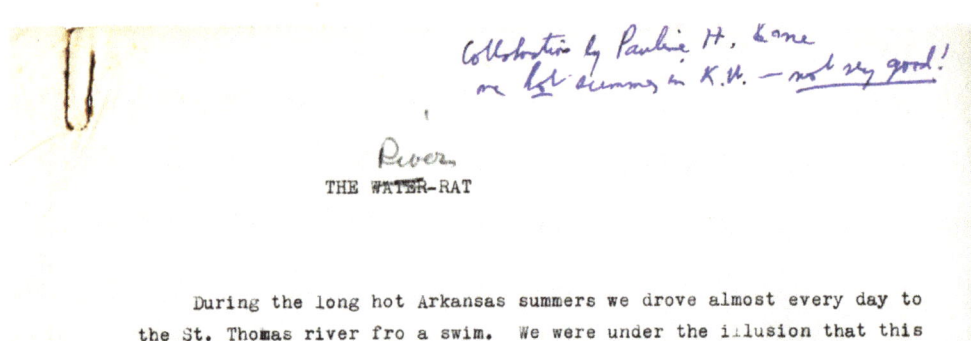

> *River*
> THE ~~WATER~~-RAT
>
> *Collaboration by Pauline H. & me one hot summer in K.W. — not very good!*
>
> During the long hot Arkansas summers we drove almost every day to the St. Thomas river fro a swim. We were under the illusion that this would 'cool us off', although it really did nothing of the sort. The St. Thomas river, or that section of it near *Kerbil* where we went

Part of the first page of the second draft of Bishop's unpublished short story "The River-Rat"

At the top of "The River-Rat," there is an inscription in purple ink that reads, "Collaboration by Pauline H. and me one <u>hot</u> summer in K.W.—<u>not very good</u>!" Nevertheless, the handwriting for the revisions appears to be by the same person and looks similar to the handwriting of Bishop's notebooks, letters, and draft poems. Such manuscript annotations and emendations indicate that although the collaboration was playful and Bishop felt some doubts as to the quality of at least one of them, she also decided they were worth pursuing to the extent of typing and revising them. Another piece of evidence supports the idea that Bishop considered the stories worth her time and energy. She tested the waters regarding the publication of "The River-Rat." On April 26, 1948, she wrote William Maxwell the following letter:

> My friend, Mrs. Pauline Hemingway, and I have been amusing ourselves in our spare time here by collaborating on some little stories. They mostly grew out of anecdotes she has told me about her life in Arkansas twenty or thirty years ago. We have been doing it more or less for fun but I have decided to send one ["The River-Rat"] on to you to see if you think there is any possibility of making New Yorker material out of it. We have a couple more and ideas for several more—one trouble is that some of the tales just don't seem credible, although they are perfectly true.
>
> I should be grateful if you could give me an opinion. (*EBNY* 35-36)

No reply from Maxwell seems to have survived, but perhaps he discouraged Bishop from pursuing the material any further, given that she never published either story. Joelle Biele does not state whether a typescript of "The River-Rat" appears in *The New Yorker* files along with a copy of the letter she reproduces in her edition of Bishop's *New Yorker* correspondence, but she points out in a footnote that "Bishop submitted the story under the name 'Katherine Burns'" (36). The content of Bishop's letter to Maxwell accords with the handwritten note at the top of a typescript copy of the story in the Vassar archives identifying Pauline Hemingway as the coauthor. In the other story, the name of the family for whom the eponymous Eula Wiggle works is "Bishway." The character-narrator of the story is a member of this family, and the moniker seems to be a comical portmanteau of Bishop and Hemingway's surnames. The name may also play on *bushwa* ("bunkum, hooey").

Let me provide a brief summary of the story lines for each piece, beginning with "The River-Rat." The protagonist is Linnie May Blackshire, a fourteen-year-old female Huckleberry Finn (she lives in a shack with her father and belongs to a clan of "river people"). The story is told by a character-narrator whose younger eleven- or twelve-year-old sister, Winnie Burns, befriends and admires Linnie. (Given her doubts about fictional credibility in the letter to Maxwell, Bishop may have wanted to intensify the story's verisimilitude by giving the narrator the same surname as Bishop's *nom de plume*, implying that it was a personal memoir.) The story begins when the unnamed narrator joins other prepubescent and adolescent boys and girls for a picnic lunch and swimming. The narrator carefully explains that the boys are able to cross the river easily, but many of the girls ask a male to spot them. The narrator refers to these boys as "boosters." When the narrator encounters some trouble, she shouts to her booster, Robert, "'You go and get help. You can make it by yourself'" (VC 53.4, p. 2). After Robert balks, she repeats the command and he finally complies (VC 53.4, p. 2).[5] Then she remarks, "It was a relief to be going to death alone anyway. The water was a very pleasant temperature, very soft and soothing" (VC 53.4, p. 2). At this point in the story the narrator seems to have become "a believer in total immersion" like the speaker of "At the Fishhouses" (*PPL* 51). As she struggles to stay above water, she decides that life isn't worth the effort and succumbs to the current, sinking and rising several times. On one of her descents, she is suddenly yanked to the surface and saved. The narrator identifies her savior as "the already slightly legendary Linnie May Blackshire," informing the reader that this is her first close encounter with the legend and that she admires her (VC 53.4, p. 2). Linnie May speaks in a matter-of-fact dialect and tells the narrator, "You hadn't orter try that with the river rising" (VC 53.4, p. 2).

Winnie and the narrator decide to thank Linnie May for her valor by inviting her on an outing with them in "Uncle Philp's [sic]" attractive green canoe, which, like Linnie May, is characterized as "legendary" (VC 53.4, p. 4). The canoe has a cosmopolitan provenance, coming from Germany and having been used on trips in Mexico. The narrator emphasizes the enviable beauty and glamor of the canoe, portraying it as a kind of *object d'art* and sign of her family's social status. She reports that the girls embark on several outings. Incidentally, the boat is called

Merde Alors, a name which Linnie May finds "poetic" and repeats aloud for the pleasure of it, as charmed by the sound of the phrase as though it were "Juanita" or "Ramona" (VC 53.4, p. 4; underlining in original). In the course of one canoe trip, Linnie May displays her keen visual acuity (just as she had done in saving the narrator). She shushes the sisters on the canoe when she notices movement on the shore. She quickly picks up her rifle and shoots into the bush on the bank, deftly bagging a squirrel. Her good marksmanship is the result of an almost preternatural eyesight, which Winnie admires and obviously wants to emulate. After killing the squirrel, Linnie May informs the sisters that she will retrieve it on the return journey and serve it up for supper to her father (VC 53.4, p. 4).

Linnie May's powers of perception and communion with her landscape are similarly on display in another important scene. She notices a snake swimming across the river and concludes that it must be getting late. When the sisters ask her how she knows this, she explains that the snake swims across the river every day at 5 o'clock, which means she must return home because it is "Time to fix supper" for her father and herself. The narrator takes pains to underscore Linnie May's independence and vigor. It is clear that she is a paragon of American self-reliance and that both sisters admire her because of this. "Although her father was a religious man and inclined to be strict about such things as dancing," we are told, "Linnie May managed their house to suit herself, shot squirrels, fished and swam whenever she felt like it. It was her belle epoque" (VC 53.4, p. 5; underlining in original). Both sisters regard Linnie May's freedom as "ideal" (VC 53.4, p. 3), and on their outings they form a positive female community together.

The pastoral summer comes to an end when Winnie goes off to boarding school and Linnie May and one of her friends hire themselves "out as maids-of-all-work" (VC 53.4, p. 6). The turning point in the story happens when Linnie May comes back home and announces her plans to marry. Her groom is a kind of twin; he is a "long, thin, sharp-eyed river-type, and . . . a good squirrel shot" (VC 53.4, p. 6). In the first days of their marriage, they prove to be a handsome and distinctive couple instead of "humdrum like the people in town" (VC 53.4, p. 6). They even seem a bit like E. E. Cummings's heroic outsiders in "anyone lived in a pretty how town" (1940). But two summers later when Winnie is hailed by an unrecognizable figure in the post office, the person turns out to be Linnie May with a squalid child by her side and another one on the way. The narrator explains that "both the child and the woman looked pale and unhealthy; the woman's hair was stringy, and when she smiled, she revealed several missing teeth" (VC 53.4, p. 6). In the final paragraph, "Katherine Burns" foreshortens the picture of Linnie May's current state and ends her tale abruptly, noting the change in her demeanor from "cheerful" to "whining" and her nostalgia for the "good times" they shared. She talks about those times as if they happened in the distant past instead of within recent memory (VC 53.4, p. 6).

To a degree, Linnie May's fate parallels that of Bishop's childhood friend Judy Flynn, whom she describes in an unpublished letter of February 1947 to her therapist, Dr. Ruth Foster. The date of the letter and the "circa 1948" on the typescript of "The River-Rat" suggest that Bishop may have written both within a comparatively short span of time. If so, Bishop's attitudes toward Flynn may be reflected in her story. In any case, Bishop's remarks in the archival letter reveal a frankness about lesbian experience and an attitude toward it that resists the prevailing medical discourse characterizing homosexuality as neurotic "maladjustment" (Vider 703). The conflict between Bishop's expressed view of same-sex love and the prevailing one exemplifies the idea that the archive can sometimes give voice to the experience of oppressed people and provide a fuller, more complex understanding of the past.[6] As Kenneth E. Foote points out, "Any view of the past conserved by the archival record can be placed, profitably, in the context of the representations maintained by other institutions" (380). In this case, the professional psychiatric community is a relevant institution to consider, since it codified homosexuality as a "sociopathic personality disturbance" in the first *Diagnostic and Statistical Manual of Mental Disorders* in 1952 (Marshall, *Elizabeth Bishop* 107).

Comparing Bishop's letter to Foster with the heteronormative view of sexuality promulgated by such medical discourse produces a dissonant record of the meaning of same-sex relations, revealing the moral bankruptcy of medical taxonomies that seek to master and control instead of heal. As Adrienne Rich observes, "Heterosexuality has been both forcibly and subliminally imposed on women. Yet everywhere women have resisted it" (*Blood* 57). In her letter, Bishop remembers her love for Judy Flynn, "one of the most beautiful adolescent girls" she had known. A fragment of an erotic lyric about Judy in the archive shows just how struck Bishop was with Judy's beauty. At the top of the notebook page, underneath the title "Judy," Bishop writes the line "-At school we sat in rows," which is followed by blanks left for more lines. Bishop then tries out some possible lines that might be placed somewhere in the poem and carries on with lines set in a stanza that seem to complete the poem:

> I still am proud
> that then I stared so hard
> upon the back of Beauty's neck.
> I'd know it in a crowd. (VC 73.2)

From this brief lyric, written in a notebook dated 1934-37, one can see that Bishop tries to capture the experience of sitting in a row in Walnut Hill behind her beautiful friend Judy, staring at her beautiful neck.[7] Judy returned her feelings and the two girls were talked about, but the principal, Miss Farwell, dismissed the rumors as empty gossip and even treated the girls to drives and picnics. Bishop explains to Foster that "Miss Farwell was wrong in a way but I think her attitude was quite right" (VC 118.33). Bishop cherished one particular visit from Judy while at camp: "I remember sleeping with her during a wild summer storm at some little inn on the Cape & being very happy" (VC 118.33). She also remembered Judy's mother commenting that Judy seemed to love Bishop more than her fiancé. Finally, Bishop recalls seeing Judy years later in New York after she had married and had children. Bishop found that "she had become such a bore poor dear - very overtalkative and not nearly as beautiful though still quite handsome" (VC 118.33).

Despite the pleasure Bishop reveals when remembering her adolescent friend, she is somewhat condescending when she describes her as a married woman. Although the adult woman is still handsome, Bishop finds her less enchanting than she was when young. In "The River-Rat," Linnie May's transformation happens faster and is more shocking than Judy Flynn's decline, but the changes in both women are negative. Although Bishop mentions in letters that she enjoyed being around young babies, in both the story and the letter to Foster, she is quite frank about her distaste for the physical tolls that motherhood (and not just marriage) can take on women. On this score, Bishop might have savored Charlotte Perkins Gilman's epigram in "The Commonplace": "It's very queer / The dreadful trials women have to carry; / But you can't always help it when you marry" (5).

Bishop's commentary on Miss Farwell's behavior and attitude regarding the crush between the young Bishop and Flynn also reflects the poet's clear resistance to the idea that love between two people of the same sex is pathological. Her confident assertion of the legitimacy and value of her youthful romance exemplifies the idea that "the archive is a space where queer subjects put themselves together as historical subjects" (Marshall et al. 2). Bishop's epistolary remark should be considered as an important private counterpoint to her famous public reticence about such matters.

In "Eula Wiggle," Bishop tells a more rollicking but also more sardonic story about courtship and marriage. The tale shares something of the comedy of Flannery O'Connor. Like "The River-Rat," Bishop tells this story via a character-narrator. She also triangulates the story's action and characterization around the narrator, the narrator's younger sister, and the title character in a way reminiscent of "The River-Rat," so that even though the narrator is a witness to the action, she is also at a significant remove from the protagonist and the events she describes. Eula and Linnie

May both speak in an obviously marked dialect that differentiates them from the narrator in each story. The assumed name Bishop used when she showed "The River-Rat" to Maxwell compounds this pattern of social differentiation, because the character-narrator's surname is the same as that of the pseudonymous author.

The problem of "Eula Wiggle" is that the main character wants to get married but believes she must obtain a divorce first. This situation is the basis for comedy, but it is also a means for Bishop to express her scorn for marriage and the rituals of courtship that can repress and infantilize women. Eula works as a cook in the Bishway household. When her employer Mr. Bishway learns that Eula's marriage to an out-of-town engineer is bogus, Eula is slow to comprehend. She seems impervious to enlightenment on this score. Indeed, her unflappable optimism suggests that she remains constitutionally gullible in the wake of her sham wedding. Her behavior throughout the story frequently derives from an excessive readiness to conform to social mores concerning sex and marriage because she thinks they benefit her, but the ironic perspective of Bishop's character-narrator links Eula's foolishness with her eagerness to marry.

Bishop offers Eula Wiggle as a comic caricature to satirize marriage as a social institution and question the social expectations associated with it. Once Eula finally accepts the fact that she was never legitimately married to the engineer, for example, she is quick to resume her quest for a husband, and soon she is conspiring with Ginnie, the narrator's eleven-year-old younger sister,[8] to compose letters responding to one Mr. Filbert, an Oklahoma farmer who has posted a want ad for a wife in the newspaper. In the process, she never gives a thought to her previous romantic debacle. In fact, Eula proves herself quite capable of manufacturing half-truths about herself to entice Mr. Filbert, and she succeeds in tying the knot with him.

Although Eula is the butt of the narrator's comic irony throughout the story, she nevertheless gets her man in the end, and her sunny disposition as a married woman remains as hardy and unexamined as ever. Eula and Linnie May are alike in terms of their complacency as married women, but marriage doesn't seem to exact the kind of physical toll on Eula that it does on Linnie May. In Eula's case, Bishop seems to be suggesting that marriage is only viable for the comparatively witless, something she suggests in a remark she once recorded in a notebook: "Sometimes it seems—this is probably profoundly untrue but anyway—sometimes it seems—as though only intelligent people are stupid enough to fall in love, & only stupid people are intelligent enough to let themselves be loved" (qtd. in Millier, *Elizabeth Bishop* 246). With apologies to Wallace Stevens, if we doctor the following lines from "The Sense of the Sleight-of-Hand-Man," it is possible to read them as an apt description of Bishop's portrait of marriage in "Eula Wiggle": "It may be the ignorant [wo]man, alone, / Has any chance to mate h[er] life with life / That is the sensual, pearly spouse . . ." (205). In Bishop's storytelling, marriage is suitable to a rube like Eula Wiggle but not to a sophisticate like Penelope Gwin.

Like Gwin, however, the narrators of "Eula Wiggle" and "The River-Rat" do not portray marriage in a favorable light. While Bishop cherished her long partnership with Lota de Macedo Soares, she adopts a more distant and jaundiced view of heterosexual marriage in these prose stories, all of which appear to precede that relationship. Although Eula is the object of the narrator's comic scorn, she succeeds in achieving fulfillment. If she is a naive or unintelligent hayseed whose emotional life is on the same plane as the narrator's younger sister, Ginnie, Eula is also happily married and rises in class by the end of the story. This achievement is rendered with so much irony as to be a parody of the comic plot paradigm that culminates in marriage, as in many of Shakespeare's comedies. By suggesting that a foolish woman is an ideal candidate for marriage, the narrator signals her disillusionment with matrimony as a bourgeois and patriarchal institution. By pairing Eula with Ginnie in Eula's scheme to land a husband, the story reflects on the way romantic ideology outfits girls for marriage, potentially warping them in the process. As their collaboration on the composition of the personal ad suggests, Ginnie presumably wants to grow up to share Eula's fate as a happy bride whose marriage raises her station in life. For Ginnie as much as for Eula, romance is "the great female adventure, duty, and fulfillment" (Rich, *Blood* 59). The narrator, by contrast, renders Eula's fatuousness for comic effects. Through the insider/outsider stance of a character-narrator, Bishop casts a cold eye on marriage. As the plot of "The River-Rat" shows, moreover, marriage can turn out to be a destructive enterprise for an intelligent and independent woman.

If the attitudes toward marriage range from desire and disgust to ironic amusement and tragic bafflement in "The Thumb" (1930), "Eula Wiggle," and "The River-Rat" (both ca. 1948), Bishop seems to offer a gentler form of comic satire in her late poem, "Mr. and Mrs. Carlyle" (ca. 1978). Given that the poem seems to have reached its final configuration much later than the stories did,[9] Bishop's view of matrimony may have been tempered by her years with Macedo Soares, who provided Bishop with "the affectionate protection of a home" (Bell 34). In a 1961 letter to the recently remarried Pearl Kazin Bell, Bishop even revels in marriage and domestic life[10]:

> [I] have had "conjunctivitis" for the first time in my life. My eyes felt so horrible and I couldn't read or type for a few days and I kept feeling if only I could cry I'd be all right. So finally I sat down and read *Little Women* for about two hours and wept a great deal, as I always do at sentimentality, and my eyes felt much better. This is just to say that since then, yesterday, I have been in a golden haze of matrimony,

"womanhood," death by—what on earth is it Beth dies of? *Little Women*, plus having a baby in the house, convinces me that probably matrimony, womanhood, babyhood, and all of it are Best. The baby particularly . . . (*OA* 393; ellipses in original)

By portraying the sentimentality of a well-known nineteenth-century female author as a guilty but dependable pleasure, Bishop can share her indulgence in a funny but sympathetic way with her fellow professional woman friend. Famously unsentimental in her poems, Bishop nonetheless savors the "golden haze of matrimony" in her weakened state, lapping up the convivial comforts of domesticity as the cure for her illness. With this dose of acceptable emotion, Bishop presumably recovered enough to see straight and polish off her letter. Bishop's little lampoon depicts marriage and family life with an off-kilter, comically rosy glow, but it also expresses a measure of real tenderness. Similarly, but more significant, Bishop mentions the anniversary of her relationship with Macedo Soares in a letter she wrote to the musicians Arthur Gold and Robert Fizdale. She closes her letter to the gay couple with the following postscript: "That gold ring I usually wear says inside (or did I show you?) 'Lota—20-12-51.' Twenty years ago was the day I told Lota I'd stay in Brazil & she had [the ring] made for my birthday the next February. —I think I miss her more in New York than any place. She liked it so much & had such good times here—and with you" (*OA* 551).

"Mr. and Mrs. Carlyle" shares the air of amusement of the letter to Pearl Bell, without its reference to sentimentality. Bishop's portrait of the couple calls attention to the miscommunication that often characterizes if not defines the marital state, but (like the epistolary picture of domestic bliss) it nonetheless allows for a certain wistfulness in its outlook. The poem recounts a story of missed connections: the husband plans to meet his wife at an inn called the Swan with Two Necks, but the rendezvous goes awry. Mr. Carlyle is working on a book, so his wife is trying to protect his peace and quiet, but the contretemps at the inn annoys her. Bishop's freakish figure of the double-headed swan deftly expresses the conundrum that love and companionship inevitably entail situations of conflict. Bishop's image ("One flesh and two heads") comically depicts marital unity as an unnatural monstrosity (*EAP* 180).

Siobhan Phillips offers a sophisticated reading of this poem by putting it in the context of Bishop's epistolary practice. Bishop's "swan with two necks," she writes,

> uses its source to suggest a literary-humanistic possibility, recognizing the white of the page as an almost erotic field of affection and resistance, in which the exchange of words can turn into a dialogue of kisses and pecks and in which those kisses and pecks can turn into each other. The "Swan" of "Mr. and Mrs. Carlyle" honors the

genre in which this poem began, evincing Bishop's appreciation for writing as an ethical relationship rather than subjective expression or objective account. ("Elizabeth Bishop" 346)

Phillips's approach is complex and rich. At the same time, it seems important that the letter on which Bishop bases this poem was addressed not to Thomas Carlyle but to Jane Carlyle's aunt (Carlyle 163-65). While the poem focuses on the doings of both Mr. and Mrs. Carlyle, it portrays marriage as a kind of comedy of errors. There is a double edge to the poem, for it depicts marriage as both a form of union and of "seething" conflict (which, after all, was a factor in Bishop's "marriage" to Macedo Soares). Swans may be an ideal metaphor for the faithful love that unites a couple over the course of a lifetime, but Bishop certainly portrays marriage as a form of the grotesque in the paradoxical image of "One flesh and two heads." Phillips emphasizes the way "pecks" can become kinds of kisses, which is surely apt, but Bishop's syntax ("or") also calls attention to the more aggressive meaning of *pecks*, and this more negative sense aligns well with other diction in the poem such as "fuss" and "vex." Mrs. Carlyle's part in her marriage is not without its costs, for she must "save" herself fuss through ingenuity and circumscribe her activity to avoid bothering her husband.[11]

Bishop expresses her amusement with Mrs. Carlyle's complaints in a letter she wrote to Howard Moss in 1970, admitting in the course of her account of "woeful trials" that "I do sound just like Mrs. Carlyle" (*EBNY* 311).[12] She rounds out the letter to Moss by explaining that she "re-read" Mrs. Carlyle's letters "to let her do my complaining for me" (*EBNY* 313). One detects in Bishop's amusement a kind of affection for Mrs. Carlyle's crankiness as well as a recognition that marriage sometimes drives a wife to "fight to be affectionate" (Moore, *New Collected Poems* 66). Bishop confesses in a letter to Frani Blough Muser that she "loathe[d]" Mr. Carlyle but "like[d] his letters" (*OA* 514). Like the poem, this remark bespeaks a realistic or pragmatic attitude toward marriage. By the time Bishop reached the later stages of the poem's revision, she had become well acquainted with both the charms and challenges of marriage, or at least of the long-term same-sex relationships that in our own time might have become legal marriages.

NOTES

1. Hugh McIntosh reads the epistolary exchanges between Lowell and Bishop as a figurative or queered form of marriage (231). According to him the poets shared "a fantasy of heterodomesticity that is typical of realist fiction" (238). By imitating and echoing each other in letters and poems, they expressed their mutual attraction. Moreover, their relationship "brought together

a conventional logic of marriage, seeing oneself with the other, and a more subversive cross-gendering, identifying oneself as the other" (238).
2. For a nuanced treatment of Bishop's negotiation of this situation, see Pollak 238-40.
3. By contrast, when she wrote love poems, they were about lesbian desire and same-sex love, not heterosexual marriage. The love poetry she published during her lifetime was subtle and coded, but she did choose to publish it. In much of her posthumously published work, however, she was more forthright about her love of other women.
4. Regarding the genesis of a text, Wim Van Mierlo observes that "[p]en and paper are not neutral in the writing; they can stimulate or inhibit, and thus determine both the rhythm of composition and the shape of what is being written" (33).
5. Perhaps the booster's name echoes that of Robert Seaver, the man who proposed to Bishop and committed suicide after she rejected his proposal. The following passage may hint at a memory of Seaver's death: "'Maybe I'd better take your hand' gasped my booster, seizing it and trying to steer us both upstream. But giving up one hand destroyed my coordination completely and we both slid faster down the river. I was dragging my helper with me and he, - 'the only son of his mother and she a widow', raced through my head" (VC 53.4, p. 2). In any case, it is significant that a female, not a male, saves the narrator and bonds with her emotionally afterward.
6. At the same time, it is worth bearing in mind that the scholarly review of private documents not intended for publication is a delicate matter, particularly in the case of so famously private a poet as Bishop. In historian Carolyn Steedman's words, the scholar "who goes to the Archive must always be an unintended reader, will always read that which was never intended for his or her eyes" (73). In effect, the scholar in the archive "always reads . . . [a] purloined letter" (73).
7. Megan Marshall mangles her transcription of the last line of the poem as "upon this best of Beauty," rendering it unintelligible (*Elizabeth Bishop* 121). This misquotation (and many others throughout critical work on Bishop) exemplifies the continuing problem of relying on secondary sources rather than primary ones when discussing Bishop's archive.
8. Pauline Hemingway's sister, with whom Bishop was also acquainted, was named Virginia ("Jinny") Pfeiffer.
9. Bishop's 1948 letter to William Maxwell, together with the inscription "ca. 1948" at the top of the "The River-Rat" typescript, provides an approximate date of composition for that story and perhaps also "Eula Wiggle." In a letter of July 9, 1978, to Frank Bidart, Bishop refers to the poem as "a very slight affair" that she "started long ago" but is now "almost done" (*OA* 625).
10. In an earlier, unpublished letter, Bishop congratulates her friend on her marriage to Daniel Bell, pointing out in a marginal comment that "Sino" is Portuguese for bell (VC 24.11, p. 1). Bishop closes with a playful postscript playing on her friend's new surname, quoting from Edgar Allan Poe's "The Bells" ("Hear the mellow wedding bells - / Golden bells!") (VC 24.11, p. 3).
11. Mrs. Carlyle's pragmatism may be the antithesis of Eula Wiggle's sentimentality. Bishop might have agreed with Oscar Wilde that "A sentimentalist is simply one who wants to have the luxury of an emotion without paying for it. . . . As soon as you have to pay for an emotion you will know its quality, and be the better for such knowledge" (639). In Bishop's poem, Mrs. Carlyle may not be altogether better for her emotional knowledge, but she surely seems to pay for it.
12. In a less comical remark two years later, Bishop wrote to Bidart that she had recently attended "the first wedding of my life" and "found it pretty depressing" (*OA* 557).

CHAPTER FOUR

"KEEPING UP A SILENT CONVERSATION"

Recovering a Queer Bishop through Her Intimate Correspondence with Alice Methfessel

Alyse Knorr

In his review of *Words in Air: The Complete Correspondence between Elizabeth Bishop and Robert Lowell* (2008), William Logan calls Bishop and Lowell "two poets in love" and "star-crossed lovers," comparing them to several famous long-distance literary couples before noting, with disappointment, that "this love was impossible, as [Lowell] must have known. Bishop was an alcoholic and a lesbian, as well as half a dozen years older" (par. 8). Logan's reading of the Lowell-Bishop relationship, further romanticized in *Dear Elizabeth*, Sarah Ruhl's theatrical adaptation of *Words in Air,* has the odd effect of re-closeting Bishop. So much so that readers may be surprised to learn of the existence, in the Bishop archives at Vassar, of 243 actual love letters, postcards, and greeting cards between Bishop and her partner Alice Methfessel, totaling more than 500 pages of correspondence.

    These letters provide new information about Bishop's life in Brazil, her writing process, and her late poems. Moreover, Bishop's letters to Methfessel are more intimate than any of the nearly 2,000 pages of correspondence published across *Words in Air, One Art: Letters* (1994), and *Elizabeth Bishop and* The New Yorker (2011). In the four decades since Vassar purchased Bishop's papers in 1981, a number of critics have discussed her epistolary writing,[1] including but not limited to that with Lowell. However, Vassar did not acquire the Methfessel letters or Bishop's letters to her psychoanalyst Ruth Foster until after Methfessel's death in 2011. Since this acquisition, more attention has been placed on the Foster letters.[2] In her Bishop memoir/biography *Elizabeth Bishop: A Miracle for Breakfast* (2017), Megan Marshall dedicates a chapter to the Bishop-Methfessel relationship, using the letters as her primary source of information about the couple. She also published a *New Yorker* profile about the two women featuring excerpts from the letters that foreground the importance of this relationship. A more detailed analysis of the content and physical characteristics of the Bishop-Methfessel letters reveals a remarkable correspondence: at once an entertaining read, ranging in tone from lighthearted to tragic; a treasure trove of information about one of the twentieth century's most important poets; and a love story about two women from different generations. In short, the Bishop-Methfessel correspondence can serve for Bishop studies as the same kind of major scholarly intervention and queer recovery initiative as the publication of Vita Sackville-West's letters to Virginia Woolf or of Emily Dickinson's love letters to Susan Huntington Gilbert Dickinson. As physical artifacts, the letters function as a technology of intimacy for the correspondents by allowing them to conjure one another in tactile form. Ultimately, the "untranscribable" material elements of the letters carry significant implications for future archival research and publication of letter volumes.

REVELATIONS FROM THE CORRESPONDENCE

Bishop's late work, including many of the poems from *Geography III* (1976), can be better understood by comparing it to her letters to Methfessel. During the summers of 1971 and 1972, the women wrote letters almost daily and often even multiple times per day, as indicated by their frequent time marking. These time stamps range from the very precise, as in "Friday; 8:45 a.m. June 30," to the more general, as in "Later" or "Morning." Although Bishop wrote many letters daily during her summers in Brazil, her letters to Methfessel tend to be much longer than those to any other correspondent. Given these factors, the peak of Bishop's correspondence with Methfessel between 1970 and 1973 may have been one of Bishop's most prolific writing periods. Because of this dailiness, Bishop's letters read like a diary of her life in Brazil, and she even worries sometimes that she writes to Methfessel too much, that her letters are too dull, and that she should "try to curb [her] impulse to sit down and tell [Methfessel] every little boring and unpleasant thing that happens" (VC 114.31, February 13, 1971).

On the contrary, Bishop's verbal snapshots of life in Brazil are far from tedious. She describes life in Ouro Prêto in vivid, colorful detail, narrating the antics of her cat Suzuki and her maid Vitoria—quite often the only two friends she has around. She describes the way Carnival sweeps the town (referenced in "Pink Dog") and pokes fun at the "smelly drunk hippies" who visit as part of the Living Theatre. She recounts reading detective novels, making jelly and fudge, and, on one occasion, carrying six pounds of meat home on her back from the butcher's office, staining a new white shirt along the way. The self-portrait Bishop paints in these letters is

Bishop and Methfessel met in 1970 at Harvard, where Methfessel worked as a secretary. The women were partners until Bishop's death in 1979. (snapshot 1972; photographer unknown; VC 100.16; Courtesy of Vassar College)

of a complicated, highly intelligent artist: someone as quick to humor as she is to sorrow, constantly observing her environment for all its small idiosyncrasies and rich details, as she does in her Brazil period poems.

Methfessel, in turn, catches Bishop up on the news from America, covering Vietnam, Muhammad Ali, the Pentagon Papers, and Russian cosmonauts. The pop culture and fads of the 1970s appear everywhere in her letters, from Carol Burnett to waterbeds. Through the exchange of these everyday accounts of their lives, the women develop a deep intimacy. They flirt, fight, plan vacations together, share inside jokes and memories, and commit to each other, with Methfessel reminding Bishop that she still wears her ring.

The Bishop-Methfessel correspondence contains significant information about Bishop's writing life and literary opinions. She shares thoughts on William Shakespeare, Norman Mailer, Octavio Paz, Sylvia Plath, W. H. Auden, Oscar Wilde, and Adrienne Rich. She disparages Allen Ginsberg's wordiness and imprecise descriptions and laments that her Seattle poetry students have never been taught form and have "tin ears" (VC 118.37, April 24, 1973). She takes delight in being the first (she assumes) to use the word "piss" in *The New Yorker* and discusses her struggle to find motivation to write: "But oh dear 'motivation' was on my list of forbidden words," she laments. "How to replace it? Being extremely interested in any one thing is just a matter of luck, don't you think? (One of my really lucky breaks in this world.)" (VC 115.2, May 6, 1971). In another letter, she writes about her distaste over having to give a talk at a Vassar alumni event because, she says, "my modest contribution to social criticism shd. be in the poems, I shd think, if anywhere . . . Don't you think that is right?" (VC 115.4, July 3, 1971). This reference is a rare one for Bishop, who did not often make such remarks about her poetry serving as social commentary. In other letters, Bishop describes to Methfessel her revision process of "The Moose" and references ideas and images from several of her other published or proposed works, including "Grandmother's Glass Eye," "Primer Class," "Visits to St. Elizabeths," and the Life World Library's *Brazil*.

Perhaps most significant, this correspondence contains early evidence of the language Bishop would eventually use in her famous villanelle "One Art." Brett Millier writes in her essay "Elusive Mastery" that "One Art" was produced in a two-week period at the end of October 1975. In a letter dated October 8, 1975, Bishop writes to Methfessel of their recent breakup, saying that "*I think I've managed to cope with disasters, etc. fairly well*—Please don't think I am self-pitying here; it's true—even Dr. Baumann says so! So I think I'm still tough enough to weather whatever other blows life brings along" (VC 118.39, October 8, 1975; emphasis mine). The word *disasters* is an obvious precursor to the villanelle's refrain and final line, "the art of losing's not too hard to master / though it may look like (*Write it!*) like disaster," and the rest of the letter shares the villanelle's tone of stalwart, insistently forced optimism and stubborn pride at surviving personal tragedy after personal tragedy.

One of the reasons the Methfessel letters reveal so much new information about Bishop's life and work is that Bishop is more open in these letters than she is with any other correspondent. Her candor when discussing her emotions, her writing challenges, and even her daily life in letters to Methfessel, as compared to her letters to Lowell or even her doctor and close friend Anny Baumann, is striking. Bishop herself corroborates this openness in a 1971 letter to Methfessel in which she worries about writing too many "indiscreet" letters and asks Methfessel if she will eventually destroy them (VC 114.32, February 14, 1971). Methfessel in turn writes the following year asking Bishop to take her letters with her when she returns from Ouro Prêto so that no one can read them in Bishop's absence (VC 116.28, July 17, 1972).

The noteworthy candor of these letters is paralleled by an equally unique level of spontaneity that clearly shows Bishop's mind in an unedited process of thinking, moving in frequent stuttering parentheticals, asides, abbreviations, typos, self-contradictions, and self-censorship. She sometimes bleeps out words like "pot" or "sex" as "p—" or "s—" and on one occasion writes a sweet little lyric for Methfessel and then vigorously scratches it out. "All for now, Alice darling," she begins. "I think about you most of the time I'm afraid and am trying hard to write some of it but not much luck so far" (VC 115.5, July 14, 1971). The next two lines of type are blacked out with a marker, followed by more typing: "(More to follow), all popular, and tending toward indecency)." Handwritten next to these sentences is "Very bad—I'll try again." However, the blacked-out lyric is still legible enough to decipher beneath the marker, and it reads: "My love is young / She cannot sing on key / Who cares? Whatever song she's ever sung / Was quite all right with me" (VC 115.5, July 14, 1971).

Bishop's late poems, in turn, have an epistolary quality to them: as a whole, they are chattier, prosier, more autobiographical, and more narrative than her earlier work. In short, they have the quality of a speaker telling a story to an imagined audience, or a letter writer sharing anecdotes with a correspondent. Likewise, Bishop's frequent conversational asides, parentheticals, and interjections (including "Heavens,"[3] a favorite epistolary exclamation) appear more often in late poems like "In the Waiting Room," "The Moose," and "Crusoe in England." These three poems—as well as "Sonnet," with its portrayal of a "creature divided"—are also noteworthy for their themes of outsiderhood, a subject Bishop often touched on in her letters to Methfessel from Brazil and that Methfessel apparently helped to alleviate in Bishop. In one 1971 letter from Brazil, for example, Bishop tells Methfessel that she feels homesick for the first time ever and that her relationship with Methfessel has developed in her a greater attachment to her home country (VC 114.36, March 23, 1971).

This theme of outsiderhood surfaces again in "Pink Dog," whose main character may have been partly inspired by "Drop of Fire," a traveling beggar who frequently visited Bishop with her dog "Little Cake." Bishop writes to Methfessel in 1971 describing Drop of Fire as a former or possibly current prostitute. She writes that "She is quite idiotic and obviously diseased—still rouges her cheeks in the 19th century manner" (VC 114.29, February 11, 1971). Bishop remarks that although Methfessel would love the dog, Drop of Fire "would make [her] cry" (VC 114.29, February 11, 1971). A month later, Bishop writes to Methfessel that Little Cake has had four puppies and confesses a far greater amount of sympathy for Little Cake than for Drop of Fire. "She is so clever," Bishop writes of the dog, "and when she comes with her poor drunken whore she looks into my face and really seems to be trying to explain the situation, and how she is doing her best, and how hard it all is" (VC 114.39, March 28, 1971).

The beggar in "Pink Dog" seems a kind of amalgamation of Drop of Fire and Little Cake. Like Little Cake, she is a "poor bitch" and "nursing mother" to be pitied. Like Drop of Fire, she is diseased with "a case of scabies" yet is still encouraged to

"Dress up! Dress up and dance at Carnival," perhaps with her nineteenth-century rouged cheeks. The pink dog, like Drop of Fire, is one of the city's many "idiots" and "parasites," at risk of being drowned in the river along with the city's other "drugged, drunk, or sober" beggars.

This new information from the Methfessel correspondence adds to existing scholarship on the origins of "Pink Dog" by Bethany Hicok, Regina Przybycien, and Elizabeth Neely. In *Elizabeth Bishop's Brazil* (2016), Hicok connects the poem to allegations in 1962 that one of Brazilian governor Carlos Lacerda's police agencies was dumping homeless beggars into a river; Hicok notes that Brazilian readers tend to cite this scandal as the inspiration for Bishop's poem and that she likely began drafting it after the scandal in 1962. However, since the poem's final version was not published until 1979, there is room to believe that Drop of Fire and Little Cake—as Bishop described them in 1971 to Methfessel—could have also influenced the pink dog character.

THE BISHOP-METHFESSEL CORRESPONDENCE AS QUEER ARCHIVAL RECOVERY

In addition to providing a wealth of new information about Bishop's late life and work, Methfessel letters also serve as a way of further recovering Bishop's queerness. Jack Halberstam (writing as Judith) points out that "lesbianism has conventionally come to be associated with the asexual, the hidden, the 'apparitional' and the invisible" (56). Without visiting the archives, there is no way for a Bishop scholar or reader to gain a sense of the relationship that was integral to Bishop's late life and writing. And yet it is only by reading these letters that one can complicate long-standing myths about Bishop's poetic "reticence." What does it mean, for instance, to call a poet "reticent" and then glimpse a greeting card from her lover with text reading, "My love for you is pure . . . LUST" (VC 117.4)? In effect, the absence of Bishop's erotic epistolary writing in the vast canon of her other published letters serves to re-closet her.

However, archival queer recovery projects can correct this phenomenon, as they have in the cases of Emily Dickinson and Virginia Woolf. *Open Me Carefully* (1998), a collection of Emily Dickinson's love letters to her sister-in-law Sue Dickinson, served as a major intervention in scholarly interpretations of Dickinson's poems, further opening her work up to feminist and queer theoretical criticism. Likewise, *The Letters of Vita Sackville-West to Virginia Woolf* (2001) has offered transformative insights into Woolf's life and work.

What is unique and fortunate about the Bishop-Methfessel correspondence is that, unlike the Dickinson or Sackville-West letters, *both* sides of it survive and in a highly condensed time frame, creating, in effect, a complete, intimate conversation. When read together in order, the letters follow a classic narrative arc. The correspondence begins with several letters from the fall and winter of 1970, when the two women first met and fell in love after Bishop joined the faculty at Harvard, where Methfessel worked as a secretary. From this point, the letters fall into five major time periods. The period of longest and most regular correspondence is the spring and summer of 1971, during which Bishop lived in Ouro Prêto, Brazil, with no phone. The second period of most frequent correspondence takes place in the summer of 1972, when Bishop was again in Ouro Prêto. The third major period takes place during March of 1973, when Bishop traveled by train to her new teaching job in Seattle and wrote to Methfessel recounting the journey along the way. A two-year gap in the letters follows, with the next major period of correspondence occurring in the fall and winter of 1975. During these months, the couple had separated, and Bishop wrote desperately to Methfessel with apologies and revisions to her will. Finally, in the summer of 1976, Methfessel wrote several letters to Bishop during a family vacation, the content of which indicates that the couple was happily reunited again by this time. Although the letters do not extend past 1976, the couple remained together until Bishop's death in 1979.

Reading both sides of the correspondence reveals a more complete picture of the women's relationship, as well as significant new contextual grounding for queer readings of Bishop's late poems. A queer reading of "The Moose," for instance, might foreground the otherworldly strangeness of the female moose figure but ignore as merely heteronormative the married "grandparents" (98) in the back of the bus "talking, in Eternity" (100), "the way they talked / in the old featherbed, / peacefully, on and on" (124-26). However, in a 1947 letter to her psychoanalyst Ruth Foster, Bishop remembers a night bus ride from her aunt Grace Bulmer Bowers's home back to New York in which she overheard "two women seated far back behind me ... talking all night or so it seemed to me" (VC 118.33, n.d.). She describes one voice of the voices in this "endless conversation" sounding like her Aunt Grace, and the other like Foster herself.

Combining this archival information with content from the Methfessel letters lends a queerer interpretation of those grandparents in "The Moose" (which Bishop dedicated to Grace Bulmer Bowers). Mornings spent in bed together with croissants and the newspaper is a common theme to which both Methfessel and Bishop return in their letters; in one letter, Bishop reminisces about how comfortable Methfessel's bed was and how much she enjoyed starting the day with her (VC 114.32, February 14, 1971). Just as the two women from the night bus trip blur into Aunt Grace and Ruth Foster in Bishop's imagination, Bishop's and Methfessel's domestic happiness in bed together is represented by the long-married grandparents on the bus. And, in turn, Aunt Grace and Ruth Foster share a featherbed together in the evasive, imaginary space of the poetic genesis moment, as interpreted through the archive.

The Methfessel letters also contain useful clues to Bishop's feelings about gender and homosexuality. In her germinal article "Survival of the Queerly Fit: Darwin, Marianne Moore, and Elizabeth Bishop," Susan McCabe argues that Bishop and Moore "shroud aberrant desire" (565) and that the "horrifying" breasts in "In the Waiting Room" and the "hanging teats" in "Pink Dog" (both written after 1970) are expressions of Bishop's "ambivalence about femaleness" (564). However, Bishop's letters to Methfessel (written around the time of the poems' generation) add another perspective to the discussion, seeming—much like the dog in "Five Flights Up" (which Bishop wrote in Methfessel's Chauncy Street apartment)—to have "no sense of shame" about her gender or sexuality. Although the women occasionally write about "indiscreet" lust and encourage each other to burn their letters, they very rarely mention homosexuality and never refer to themselves or their relationship as lesbian. Their anxiety over "indiscretion" seems to stem not from the relationship being a same-sex romance but from the vast age difference between them.

This age difference is the most recurring source of tension in the letters. Bishop, born in 1911, lived through two world wars and McCarthyism. Methfessel, however, came of age during the civil rights era. Throughout the course of their exchange, both women adopt each other's generational slang, with Bishop picking up Methfessel's "Gee, I miss you," and Methfessel trying out Bishop's "Horrors," "ye Gods," and even the Portuguese term of pitying endearment, *coitada*. Their age difference even comes up in how they negotiate their terms of endearment, with Methfessel eventually insisting that, while Bishop may call her "baby" or "Mouseketeer," "infant" is taking it too far (VC 116.21, July 13, 1971). And although this age difference is sometimes a source of humor (for instance, when Bishop describes her false teeth falling out at a lunch[4]), Bishop also worries that Methfessel only loves her for her "grandmotherly" qualities (VC 115.5, July 7, 1971), and she often writes with the melancholy assumption that, due to Methfessel's young age, she will eventually marry and separate from Bishop. At one point, Bishop even suggests (perhaps humorously) that Methfessel marry a "nice, rich" Brazilian so that the two women can be in the same country during Bishop's "declining years." Early on in the correspondence, Bishop establishes the expectation that Methfessel will continue dating men but asserts that she does not want to know the details or have to think about it, as "[t]here's no point in encouraging a tendency to masochism" (VC 118.34, December 29, 1970). However, Bishop frequently puts herself down, calling herself an "OLD WOMAN" (VC 114.40, March 31, 1971) and chastising herself to "act [her] age" (VC 118.34, December 30, 1970).

Bishop also worried about how she was reaching the end of her life while Methfessel's was just beginning. Early in the relationship, for instance, she describes a dream in which she and Methfessel had three hours to share in an airport before they had to separate on different flights. "The problem," Bishop writes, "was what to do in the three hours. I woke up panicky, before we had decided" (VC 114.33, February 22, 1971). The dream's central metaphor of the two women "going to different places" on separate planes hints at Bishop's anxiety over their lives diverging due to their different ages. The most apparent example of Bishop's awareness of her own mortality lies in her October 1975 letter to Methfessel about her will, during which time the couple was separated. In this letter, she asks Methfessel to "help [her] die" if she ends up in a vegetative state. She asks Methfessel to watch for a wink from her left eye or a left finger twitch (correcting herself and suggesting the right side, should a stroke incapacitate her left side) and to give her 20 Nembutal upon seeing the signal.

Methfessel responded to letters like this one by cheerfully chastising Bishop—admonishing her to stay healthy, buffeting back her self-criticisms, and denying Bishop any room for self-pity. However, one telling excerpt may hint at Methfessel's deeper feelings about the age difference. In 1971, Methfessel wrote to Bishop about Gabrielle Russier, a thirty-two-year-old French teacher who committed suicide after being arrested for conducting an affair with a sixteen-year-old male student. In a striking parallel to Methfessel and Bishop's own age difference and anxiety over "indiscretions," Methfessel expressed sympathy about Russier's case, which deeply affected her emotionally (VC 116.20, July 10, 1971).

Thus, only Bishop perceives an impossibility or impropriety to their relationship—never Methfessel. And that impropriety is rooted, again, not in sexuality but in age. Bishop is aware that Methfessel's youth and dating life might make her sexually active—an anxiety she expresses with one mention of her birth control pills and frequent mentions of wondering what Methfessel is doing at night. On one occasion, after re-reading several of Methfessel's letters and looking at her photos, Bishop writes to her anxiously, in a letter that begins with her characteristic exclamation "Heavens!" She confides that she has been obsessing over what Methfessel might have been doing that evening, assuming the worst: "Damn it all," Bishop writes, "You are much too young for me . . . [a]nd . . . really much more sensible than I am, I know—so that I know you'll probably do what's right for you, and I'll *know* it's right for you—but I dread it terribly at the same time" (VC 114.32, February 19, 1971). Despite Bishop's fears that Methfessel loved her for her "motherly" or "grandmotherly" qualities, if there was a maternal role to their relationship, Methfessel was the one filling it. In dozens of letters, Methfessel excoriates Bishop for drinking and urges her to take her Antabuse pills. She encourages her to get writing, reminds her of deadlines, and validates her idea for a letter-writing course at Harvard.

Bishop's concerns over their age difference, as well as her complicated feelings of loss after her Brazilian lover Lota de Macedo Soares's death, are all apparent in her poem "Crusoe in England," which provides a particularly rich case study for a queer reading guided by the Methfessel letters. In the poem, Crusoe, the narrator, is clearly much older than his lover Friday, whom he calls a "boy," and, like Bishop, clearly conflicted about his declining age:

> Now I live here, another island,
> that doesn't seem like one, but who decides?
> My blood was full of them; my brain
> bred islands. But that archipelago
> has petered out. I'm old.
> I'm bored, too, drinking my real tea,
> surrounded by uninteresting lumber. (*P* 186)

McCabe calls the poem "both frank and masked, its irony infusing [Bishop's] male persona's intimation of the love that dare not speak its name" ("Survival" 566). She argues that the island Crusoe is trapped on is a symbol of queer isolation "alternatively wrought with depression and self-pity" (567) until the "crisis of desire" marked by the arrival of Friday (567). McCabe interprets the loss of Friday as inspired by Bishop's loss of Macedo Soares, with Crusoe's island representing a kind of "microcosm of impossible love" (566). Some evidence from the Methfessel-Bishop letters supports these interpretations. For instance, Bishop writes often to Methfessel about her loneliness and isolation in the solitude of Brazil, where she continues to grieve Macedo Soares. Indeed, after Macedo Soares's death, Brazil was never the same for Bishop. She frequently opines to Methfessel about her ambivalence about the country, which she blamed for Macedo Soares's death; these mixed emotions over Brazil surface in her late poems "Santarém" and "Pink Dog."

The Bishop-Methfessel letters, however, also add to and complicate McCabe's analysis, revealing a poem just as influenced by Methfessel as it is by Macedo Soares. The tropical landscape of "Crusoe in England" could have been as easily inspired by the islands that Bishop and Methfessel saw during a joyful 1971 trip to the Galapagos as it might have been by Brazil. And when Crusoe states, "Just when I thought I couldn't stand it / another minute longer, Friday came," we could just as well read this as a description of Methfessel's invigorating arrival late in Bishop's life. Like Friday for Crusoe, Methfessel's youth liberated Bishop and inspired in her a new energy for life. In her letters, Methfessel frequently calls Bishop out on the "self-pity" that Crusoe describes feeling, and her "loud, cheerful voice" (VC 118.34, December 29, 1970), possibly rendered as a "joking voice" in "One Art" and as a bubbly nature in "Sonnet," gave Bishop hope and kept her lighthearted.[5]

Indeed, in many of her letters to Methfessel, Bishop seems to shift moods suddenly, contradicting herself and forcefully or wistfully amending previous statements. "I'm not really blue, Alice," she writes in one example, "Sad, I must confess—but it makes me happy to think of you" (VC 115.4, July 5, 1971). Statements like these, in which Bishop is trying desperately not to be sad and seems genuinely cheered by Methfessel, are quite common. Methfessel, however, is a much more effusive, cheerful, and practical letter writer. In one letter, she observes that she tends to fret less than Bishop and keep a generally more positive, optimistic outlook about their relationship, which she sees as a wonderful gift that fills her with joy (VC 115.1, April 16, 1971).

Methfessel's youthful energy, captured succinctly in the above passage yet apparent throughout all the correspondence, meant a great deal to Bishop during her declining years. Again and again, Methfessel's ebullient energy lifted Bishop out of her gloom. Bishop puts it best herself in a letter referring to a recent flight: "Yesterday as we whooshed up above the rain and gloom of Boston into the bright blue sunlight above it, I thought it was exactly what your coming into my life has done for me, Alice—not that fast, maybe, but pretty fast—and the wonderful difference is just the same" (VC 118.36, March 23, 1973). Conversely, as noted above in the "One Art" letter excerpt, when Bishop felt she had lost Methfessel, her thoughts turned toward her own aging and death—much like Crusoe after losing Friday in "Crusoe in England."

Finally, the museum artifacts Crusoe mentions at the end of the poem mirror the thoughtful self-archiving process Bishop often described to Methfessel that same year. Much of Bishop's work during her two long summers in Brazil in 1971 and 1972 involved archiving, sorting, reading, and burning her papers, including letters to Robert Lowell and Flannery O'Connor. Bishop reports to Methfessel—her secretary as well as her lover—about what to hold on to and what to file away, and in this sense, we can consider Methfessel to be Bishop's first archivist. Indeed, after Bishop died, Methfessel preserved their love letters for the rest of her life, locking them in a safe discovered by her partner only after her death in 2011. Clearly, Methfessel knew the value of these letters and safeguarded them accordingly.

THE LOVE LETTER AS ARTIFACT

I wish now to address the physical properties of the Bishop-Methfessel letters, arguing that they functioned for their correspondents as a technology of intimacy—as physical artifacts that convey much more than the words alone. To begin with, Bishop and Methfessel treasured each other's letters and often used them to conjure each other in a tactile way. Bishop carried Methfessel's letters in her shirt, re-read them until she had almost memorized them, "pat[ted] them lovingly" (VC 115.1, April 1, 1971), and even slept with them. Methfessel, in turn, cried on at least one of the letters (and indicates with an arrow the smudged word on which the tear fell) (VC 116.9, February 7, 1971) and later propped one of Bishop's postcards up in front of her typewriter so that she could imagine herself looking out at the same view as her partner.

The women both express often that they miss holding, hugging, touching, and sleeping with each other. Writing multiple letters per day was a way for the correspondents to demonstrate their faithfulness and to make themselves physically immediate to each other. As Bishop writes, "I feel cheerful as long as I keep typing to you" (VC 115.2, May 7, 1971), and "I hate to leave my desk and typewriter—it's the only place I feel a bit closer to you" (VC 115.1, April 1, 1971). For her part, Methfessel stated that she loved creating a written record of her deep affection for Bishop (VC 116.9, February 1, 1971).

Bishop usually begins and ends her day by writing to Methfessel, and frequently writes her throughout the day as well, "just so [Methfessel] wouldn't seem quite so far away" (VC 114.34, February 25, 1971). Bishop's loneliness and depression often felt worse in the evening, and writing to Methfessel at night was one remedy, as was receiving her letters: "I don't know what I'd do without your letters, really," she writes to Methfessel. "I'd be so much blue-er" (VC 115.1, April 27, 1971). At times, this relief spirals into dependency, with both women expressing anxiety over how often they receive letters or even keeping "score" of how many letters they'd received. At other times this sentiment gets expressed in a more lighthearted manner, as in a *Peanuts* cartoon enclosed in one letter that shows Snoopy rifling through the day's mail and thinking, "Rats! I hate it when I don't get any love letters!"

Bishop makes clear in a July 1971 letter that written correspondence cannot adequately replace physical proximity or oral conversations, lamenting that "I miss talking to you—the way I do—all the time . . . Writing is just no substitute—and I do hope when I talk I'm a bit more entertaining than when I type" (VC 115.4, July 2, 1971). However, letters undoubtedly provided more than just a feeling of comfort and connection across the miles; they also provided a physical embodiment of love, with both women noting often that, despite the distance, writing made them feel nearer to each other. For both women, the letters were a way to "kee[p] up a silent conversation," in Bishop's words (VC 118.36, March 23, 1973).

One note in particular captures the significance of letters in this relationship. On August 7, 1971, during a vacation together, Bishop writes a handwritten note to

Methfessel on "Galapagos Cruises" letterhead while sitting on her bunk with Methfessel in the room, as sunburned and sandy as Bishop herself. Bishop says she's writing simply to remind Methfessel that "whenever & wherever you get this—I'll undoubtedly still be loving you as much as I do this very minute" (VC 115.7, August 7, 1971). Given that Methfessel was apparently in the room with Bishop at the time she wrote the letter, the document seems to represent less a form of practical communication across distance and more a ritualistic declaration of love—the creation of an artifact that would persist beyond the boundaries of space and time and return Methfessel to this moment "whenever & wherever" she chose to re-read the letter.

Historical material culture theory provides a useful lens through which to consider the letters as physical artifacts in this way. Jacques Maquet, for instance, argues in his essay "Objects as Instruments, Objects as Signs" that it is the recipient or user of an object who confers upon it its symbolic meaning, not the object itself or the object's maker. Although Maquet's examples focus on large-scale, nationally symbolic objects, his theory can be applied to this correspondence in the sense that each recipient in the exchange shaped the meaning of the letters in symbolically meaningful ways that transcended their instrumental or practical uses. Along these same lines, in his essay "Why We Need Things," Mihaly Csikszentmihalyi points out the ways that objects are often used in "commemorating" friendships and "giv[ing] permanence" to relationships (27), as evidenced in the Galapagos Cruises letter, which serves to commemorate the women's first vacation taken together. Csikszentmihalyi continues, "Our addiction to materialism is in large part due to a paradoxical need to transform the precariousness of consciousness into the solidity of things" (28). In the case of Bishop and Methfessel, their letters became solid, tangible manifestations of each other's consciousness.

Thus, the key to understanding how the love letters offered a physical embodiment of Bishop and Methfessel's relationship is the materiality of the letters themselves. In his essay "Some Matters of Substance," Robert Friedel argues that the material from which historical artifacts are made must be the starting place of any analysis of their content: "[t]he material itself conveys messages, metaphorical and otherwise" (42). What, then, can be gleaned from a close study of the materiality of the Bishop-Methfessel letters? To begin with, the letters' visual appearance reinforces a sense of the women's personalities and a sense of their roles in relation to each other. This fact becomes abundantly clear when comparing the original color images of this correspondence with black-and-white photocopies. Color is critical for understanding these letters. Methfessel's bouncy cheerfulness saved Bishop at the end of her life; the vibrant colors of Methfessel's cartoonish greeting cards teach us something about the nature of their relationship and in turn about the joyful tone of late Bishop poems and drafts like "Sonnet" or "Breakfast Song." In addition, Methfessel's letters are literally colorful (she uses pink, purple, red, green, and blue ink, but rarely black). Color can also provide important information on amendments and additions; in one letter, for instance, Methfessel uses green ink but adds a note at the top in red (VC 116.19, May 15, 1971).

Handwriting is another untranscribable element of these letters. Methfessel's handwriting, like her personality, is large, bright, and effusive; Bishop notes to Methfessel that her handwriting is "nice and loud and cheerful like your voice on the telephone" and that just seeing this handwriting at the post office gives her a feeling of "relief" (VC 115.5, July 14, 1971). Bishop's microscopic scrawl, in contrast, seems to hide any sentiments as soon as it utters them. Bishop ends one letter to Methfessel with a tiny handwritten "xxxxx," beneath which is written "(you can select the spots)" (VC 115.11, June 26, 1972), whereas Methfessel scrawls bold declarations of love in ALL CAPITALS twice at the top and bottom of a typewritten letter, in enormous pink and purple ink respectively (VC 116.11, February 19, 1971). She could be just as effusive when angry as when joyful, writing a profanity in large letters in the middle of a letter in which she is angry at Bishop for not writing for many days (VC 116.14, March 14, 1971). Although her large handwriting is lost in her typed letters, Methfessel's effusiveness still comes across in moments when she seems to practically bang on her keyboard with joy to enumerate all her kisses and hugs to Bishop (VC 116.26, June 29, 1972).

As Bishop scholars who have worked in the archive know all too well, Bishop's handwriting is almost illegible, and her typing skills aren't much better. However, Bishop's letters to Methfessel are even messier than those she writes to her other close correspondents, with sloppy typing, last-minute corrections, additions, and postscripts running up and down all margins. The messy quality of Bishop's letters signifies both the amount she was usually writing to Methfessel on any given day as well as her level of spontaneity and openness; perhaps she was comfortable enough with Methfessel that she wasn't especially worried about how her letters to her looked.

Transcriptions that correct Bishop's typos and spelling errors may make her letters more readable, but they also leave no sense of when Bishop may have been typing while intoxicated, while freewriting (as in the Ruth Foster letters), or even while she's writing with her typewriter balanced on a train toilet seat, bumping along painfully and making many typos (VC 118.36, March 23, 1973).

Methfessel, however, being a secretary, has much more legible handwriting and excellent typing skills. She constantly corrects Bishop's terrible spelling and, in one letter, turns a rare typo into a flirtatious joke (VC 116.20, July 8, 1971). Our awareness of her as Bishop's secretary is reinforced when we see her writing on Harvard

> (Pill- Day)   2.
>
> Next morning -
>
> (& I really will change this ribbon) - The plum jam is a great success - pale green - & just for fun I showed Vitoria how to make foamy coffee with powdered milk this A M - so I probably had the best breakfast for hundreds of miles around, with toasted cornbread, plum jam, and capuccino - but it's no fun at all, alone. The sun comes in my window very early - the cocks crow - the bells at Santa Ephigenia strike the hours - it is lovely, really, and I like waking up early here, but damn it, it is lonely. I woke up about 4 and tried your little radio- they seem to go right on with the loud advertising even at that hour... I think I'll have to indulge myself and buy a radio, however - a slightly stronger one - once in a while there are good things - and the Ministry of Education has some good music - but I can only make my present radio (yours) work at night -

Bishop's typed letters to Methfessel are full of corrections, additions, and postscripts; the "messier" quality of these letters reveals a level of openness and spontaneity that Bishop had with few, if any, of her other correspondents. (Bishop to Methfessel, February 16, 1971, VC 114.32; Courtesy of Vassar College)

letterhead, which is also an interesting access point for considering the tangled roles these women played to each other as mother and daughter figures, friends, lovers, and employer/employee. In one letter on Harvard letterhead, for instance, Methfessel begins by formally addressing Bishop the way one would an employer, then immediately reassures Bishop that she has nothing to fear about their relationship; it is just that the students have a habit of looking over her shoulder and making snarky comments when they think she's writing a personal note (VC 116.12, February 26, 1971).

Another untranscribable element of the Bishop-Methfessel correspondence is the frequent ephemera and clippings included within letters. These little mementos and offerings are often included without comment, referencing private memories and inside jokes between the two that we may never fully understand. Some of the clippings are filed separately from their original letters in the Vassar archive, making them difficult to date. News articles, Snoopy cartoons, brochures, a stamp, and even a hotel "do not disturb" sign all fill the folders of the archive. One cartoon, telling in its playful response to heteronormativity, features a man and a woman with the caption "Love is . . . not correcting her all the time," beneath which Methfessel makes a flirtatious joke about how she'll avoid doing this to Bishop since she loves her so much (VC 116.23, September 25, 1971). And in a manner typical of her letter writing, Bishop applies a child's sticker of a cat to the top of one letter but then self-consciously comments on its sentimentality: "Yucky, isn't it . . ." ("yucky" seems to be a common feature of their pet language for each other) (VC 114.29, February 11, 1971).

In the case of a February 11, 1971, letter from Bishop, the page actually contained a gift for Methfessel—the top left corner of the page is missing, with an arrow pointing to it and a note from Bishop explaining that the small poem printed there was to be cut out and put into the mouth of a decorative fish Bishop had given Methfessel.

The frequently tiny size of the clippings and ephemera Bishop and Methfessel sent back and forth are in line both with Susan Rosenbaum's notion of Bishop the archivist's "miniature museum" as well as Bishop's frequent use of the word *little* throughout her poems.

For instance, the painting "the size of an old-style dollar bill" in "Poem" may have resembled a tattered 1000 cruzeiros note Bishop sent Methfessel in a letter dated July 4, 1972. Unfortunately, the size of the clippings is impossible to understand by looking at Vassar's photocopies. In order to appreciate their smallness, the original objects must be handled and photographed alongside items for scale.

In addition to ephemera, the women sometimes exchanged photos; however, they each seem ambivalent about any sense of intimacy that photos could provide. At one point, Methfessel reports that she felt odd about displaying images of Bishop on the wall of her room (VC 116.12, February 28, 1971) and tells Bishop that she would prefer for Bishop to remember her appearance rather than hang up her photo (VC 116.16, April 1, 1971). For her own part, Bishop often warmly describes visual memories of Methfessel in the past, but when she imagines herself sharing physical space with Methfessel in the future, she grows anxious about her age and "physical decay" (VC 114.32, February 21, 1971). While planning a trip to the Galapagos Islands, Bishop puts down her own aging body, worrying that she will have to stay sitting on the beach holding Methfessel's robe and watching her youthful athletics in the water. Thus, exchanging letters *without* photographs allowed the women to feel intimate physical proximity without the baggage of age anxiety.

Finally, letterhead and envelopes can also convey a great deal and are often overlooked when letters are transcribed. Methfessel uses strikingly vaginal flower letterhead to write to Bishop at one point (VC 116.16, April 18, 1971), while in another letter, written during a visit to her parents' house on borrowed paper (VC 116.9, February 7, 1971), she playfully corrects her party affiliation at the top of the "Women's National Republican Club Inc." letterhead. Envelopes from different greeting cards show all the different names Methfessel may have called Bishop, which together reflect the many different roles the women played for each other at different times, ranging from highly formal, professional terms of address to more intimate nicknames.

The insights gleaned from this material study imply that, because these letters as artifacts meant such a great deal to their recipients as physical objects, scholars should treat them as such in archival research as well. While it is obvious that working from an original document is superior to working from a photocopy, both

Stickers like the one at the top of this letter are an untranscribable element of the love letters that convey an understanding of the correspondents' playfulness and tenderness. In a typical move, Bishop self-consciously comments on the sentimentality of the sticker with "yucky, isn't it?" (Bishop to Methfessel, 11 Feb 1971, VC 114.29; Courtesy of Vassar College)

Bishop and Methfessel frequently exchanged ephemera and clippings in their letters. Many of these tokens—such as this hotel stamp—were very small, which exemplifies Susan Rosenbaum's notion of Bishop as an archivist constructing a "miniature museum." (Hotel Stamp, VC 116.32; Courtesy of Vassar College)

are preferable to working from a typed transcription alone, which renders invisible any material, untranscribable elements of the letters. And yet, as Catharine Labio points out, "We refer, almost invariably, to the contents of . . . letters, not to their physical properties" (7). In the case of the Bishop-Methfessel correspondence, to neglect the letters' physical properties would mean missing their symbolic resonance and metaphorical function as a technology of intimacy. As such, standard practice for future transcriptions of archival documents should ideally include photos or detailed references to the material's physical qualities in addition to its content. Likewise, digitization of archival materials will both democratize access privileges and enhance the quality of analysis by providing visuals instead of secondary copies or tertiary transcriptions.

CONCLUSION

The Bishop-Methfessel correspondence is key to understanding Bishop as a passionate, erotic writer, inspired and paralyzed, at various times, by love. As Daniel Marshall, Kevin Murphy, and Zeb Tortorici put it, "the drama of existence is a central, compelling narrative or mystery inhering in queer archives, a drama borne out by countless scholars' efforts to find lost queer things" (1). On the one hand, Bishop's love letters are not lost—they have been preserved and are open to readers in the Vassar archive. On the other hand, because none of them have been published, and they are only available to those who can travel to Vassar, they are, unlike letters with Bishop's other frequent correspondents, very much absent from the conversation about Bishop's life and work. Therefore, I argue for the publication of a new edition of Bishop's letters that includes selections from the Methfessel correspondence and/or a scholarly edition of these letters, chronologically ordered, with letters from both writers. To continue to ignore these letters in discussions of Bishop's life and epistolary writing is to re-closet this writer; to incorporate these letters into future dialogue is to recover the queerness so integral to the poems themselves.

NOTES

1. Most notably, see Ellis, *Art*; Hammer.
2. See Goldensohn, "Approaching"; Treseler, "One Long Poem"; McClay, "'This Suffering Business.'"
3. In "Poem" from *Geography III*.
4. Bishop writes, "We went to the local restaurant for dinner and my tooth, or teeth, fell out again" on February 10, 1971 (VC.114.29).
5. Of course, the "joking voice" could also have been Macedo Soares's, as early drafts of an elegy for her seem to indicate (*EAP* 219-21).

CHAPTER FIVE

DEAR ELIZABETH, DEAR MAY

Reappraising the Bishop/Swenson Correspondence

David Hoak

In her book on the poetics of Marianne Moore, Elizabeth Bishop, and May Swenson, Kirstin Hotelling Zona devotes a chapter to the nearly three-decade exchange of letters between Elizabeth Bishop and May Swenson. She finds the correspondence, numbering more than 275 items, a trove of insight into the two women's poetics but opines that perhaps little has been made of it, in part, because the letters seem free of clues to Bishop's intimate life details. She further adds that in the letters, "Bishop appears most often . . . as the Bishop of self-restraint, an advocate of personal distance, a remarkably Moore-like mentor in diction and self-expression" who is "at times condescending, competitive, elitist, and, as Bishop herself put it, 'nasty'" (Zona, *Marianne Moore* 97).

The twin Bishops of self-restraint and interpersonal distance do emerge in the letters, even punctuated by the occasional flare of condescension or sarcasm, but more often I find in them the Bishop of wit and warmth, even of vulnerability and domesticity. While there are echoes of Moore and her discomforts, I cannot embrace Zona's description of Bishop as a "Moore-like mentor." For one thing, if we've learned anything about Bishop in the last fifteen years it is that she was categorically not a prude. Bishop's great obsession was accuracy. A word that served that purpose was always a candidate for the right word. Her genius, which obsessed Swenson, was to marry mystery to accuracy, the personal in the shadow of the impersonal. What needs to be treasured in the Bishop/Swenson letters is how much humor, warmth, and support spring from exchanges that find each woman frankly, and often bluntly, standing her poetic ground and, especially in the case of Swenson, insisting on the validity of her poetic instincts. If little has been made of the letters, perhaps we can begin to give them their due now that we have learned to embrace Bishop fully, in her myriad strengths and weaknesses, triumphs and faults. Still unpublished in full,[1] the letters reveal two women with so much in common that their differences slide out of focus, leaving me inclined to view them as opposite sides of one coin.

Apart from their well-rounded portrait of Bishop, it is Swenson's remarkable analyses of Bishop's poems that are perhaps the greatest prize in the letters. Early and late, her comments and observations, especially her intimations of erotic feelings, command Bishop's attention and startle her with their emotional depth and sharp detail. Swenson's astute readings mark her as one of Bishop's most probing early readers, and her criticism of Bishop's poems and stories holds up well even after decades of Bishop scholarship and critical writing.

The two poets met at Yaddo, an artists' community in Upstate New York, in the fall of 1950. It was Bishop's second visit and Swenson's first: "There was a little poet, May Swenson, not bad, & a nice girl" (*WIA* 110), Bishop wrote Robert Lowell from Yaddo that November, sounding a curiously offhand note in describing the thirty-seven-year-old Swenson. There was no great difference in physical stature between the two; perhaps Bishop was struck by the youthful impression Swenson made. We may wonder if she was surprised to learn that she was only two years older than Swenson or that both had graduated college in 1934. Although close in age, Swenson would have conceded she was much the younger poet in measure of accomplishment. Bishop had already published a prizewinning first book and was a past Guggenheim Fellow with a first-read contract with *The New Yorker*. And while not by any means wealthy, a significant inheritance had allowed her to travel extensively after college and left her free of the need to find regular employment to support herself. Swenson, by contrast, was the classic nearly starving artist, who by 1950 had been living her bohemian dream in New York City's Greenwich Village for almost fifteen years, sharing rent and expenses with friends and doing what writing she could while taking a series of office and editing jobs. She had seen her first poem printed in a major publication only the year before.

Whatever her first impressions, let's ponder what Bishop might have made of the following, from a letter written by Swenson, during her stay at Yaddo, to Pearl Schwartz, the bright young graduate student ten years her junior whom she had met the year before and with whom she would live until 1966:

> My Dearest One: Well at last I am getting to know Elizabeth Bishop. She wears skirts with back pockets, has very tiny feet . . . wears knee-length woolen ribbed sox, spent her childhood in Nova Scotia, wears no rings on her fingers, is fond of Tennyson's "In

Memoriam," is two years older than I am . . . likes to drink beer, and can't hold her water. . . . She's about my height, kind of square shaped, rather chunky in chest and shoulders compared to her hips—the buttocks look square, the effect heightened by narrow pelvic bones and a wide waist—nice adolescent legs. Her eyes are round and brown, half scared, half bold, and her tone of voice no matter what she's talking about is spoofing.[2]

The "little poet" could not only write, but she rivaled Bishop as an observer. Reading our way into their long correspondence, her words to her lover remind us that, behind her natural modesty, steady generosity, and loving appreciation, the piercing eye of Anna Thilda May Swenson never ceased to keep a sharp lookout.

Zona and others have framed Swenson as frustrated by Bishop's sexual reserve or "masking." No doubt she was, but her frustrations were perhaps more artistic than personal. I believe Swenson often knew "who was addressed, or ever undressed" as she put it in her brilliant late poem "Her Early Work," in which she invokes the revelatory power of Bishop's "wraparounds, overlaps and gauzes" (*SCP* 471). The letters are full of passages that make it clear the two poets took each other's sexuality for granted. Many of these are charming and funny.

In a 1955 letter, Bishop relates the substance of a Guggenheim recommendation she has sent off for Swenson. She felt certain Swenson would finally be selected because she had known her for five years and was, as she put it, "familiar with your way of life (!) . . ." (WUSC 103/3999, January 9, 1955, p. 1). A year later, early in 1956, during perhaps her happiest summer with Lota de Macedo Soares, Bishop writes: "Lota and I both wish you were here this morning to go for a swim right now and slide in the waterfall with us and have ripe figs and prosciutto for lunch. . . . I'd love to see you there! [in the pool]. (Come to think of it, I haven't seen a real blond in an awfully long time.)" (WUSC 103/4000, February 5, 1956).

In November, Bishop writes to say a male friend is coming to New York and would be the ideal person to bring back the blue jeans Bishop has requested. In fact, Bishop suggests, "Why don't you captivate this friend, marry him and return to Brazil with him. He's partial to American girls" (WUSC 103/4001, November 10, 1956, p. 1). Bishop's use of "captivate" rather than, say, "capture" seems calculated to pique Swenson, who impatiently parries her sly provocation. To her next letter she adds an addendum containing no reference whatsoever to Bishop's suggestion until it suddenly ends with an abrupt paragraph of a single line: "Do I have to marry him to go to Brazil? Come to New York. Love, May" (WUSC 103/4001, November 15, 1956, p. 4).

For a glimpse of truth in Zona's assessment of Bishop as critic, let's consider a letter from April 1962 that finds Bishop wearing her poet-mentor hat and, in a moment of runaway critical candor, getting carried away. Swenson had asked her to look at the manuscript of her third book, *To Mix with Time* (1963), and to help her identify the "no-good" poems. Bishop had admired many of the book's poems she'd seen earlier but now reading them in typeset manuscript, with their clever index and experimental typography, sent her to the woodshed. She objects to Swenson's obsession with imposing an extra system, or order, on her poems. "Style alone," Bishop tells her, should give unity and shape to a book of poems. She closes: "I really think that the best poems are quite complete enough in themselves and that you don't have to start in outer space, descend, take a thorough view of everything, and finish off our own planet" (WUSC 103/4006, April 3, 1962, p. 1). Then, a parenthesis: "(I hope you hear my joking tone of voice—heavens, letters are dangerous—I'm not being sarcastic—just affectionate!)." Having exchanged 140 letters over twelve years, Bishop may have felt entitled to claim affection. But if "nasty" doesn't describe this reproach, "sarcastic" isn't a big stretch. Bishop can't help herself when her "fiend" persona emerges in discussions of poetics and style. It is a word she returns to again and again to apologize for or excuse a particular critical tone.

Bishop's letter stands out for its rare examples of criticism that caused Swenson to make changes in her work. *To Mix with Time* contained poems Swenson had written during her 1960 trip to Europe. Her poem "The Pantheon, Rome" was based on a rainy day visit to the ancient site. Bishop had seen the building, too, and for both it was an indelible memory of their time in Italy. The poem included a line with the phrase "the rain ruining the floor." Bishop, unable to abide the inaccuracy of asserting that rain could have any effect on a centuries-old stone floor, objected: "Why not just contradict yourself? 'The rain ruining the floor. No, it isn't ruining the floor'" (WUSC 103/4006, April 3, 1962, p. 3). There is no small irony in this advice, which finds Bishop recommending to Swenson an alternative we might label one of her few mannerisms. Indeed, as quickly as we smile, Bishop, only a sentence later, is hedging: "But that probably sounds too much like me." Swenson's published version of the poem includes the line, "The rain that cannot ruin the floor" (*SCP* 174), changing her point of view while managing not to sound "too much like me."

Bishop's painstaking rumination on *To Mix with Time* is her longest letter to Swenson and actually included a separate page ranking and grading Swenson's poems. It meant a lot to the younger poet, whose reply took her several weeks to organize. She described Bishop's letter as "careful and extremely helpful" and signed her long reply, "Love to you, and so many thanks." Swenson's letter, unique in its density of detail among the missives she sent Bishop, rises to this distillation of where she hoped to take her art:

What I have resolved—and wonder if I can stick to it—in my future work, is to *stop* comparing things and depend on *precision*, on emphasizing the uniqueness of things, their *un*likeness to other things—can it be done? Not entirely, maybe, but it's healthy to try. (*You* solve this problem by absolutely unused comparisons...) (WUSC 103/4006, May 21, 1962, p. 2; qtd. in Swenson, *Made with Words* 235)

Swenson's reply also suggests that by this time she had learned to read Bishop's criticism without much injury to her feelings.

However, Bishop may have bruised Swenson's feelings a few years earlier, nearing the publication of her second book, *A Cage of Spines* (1958). Having already admired many of its poems, and even written a moving tribute for its cover, Bishop volunteered in a 1958 letter to look at the whole book. In mid-May, the manuscript arrived in Bishop's mail and, awakened by a raging storm the next morning, she read it all the way through. She sent Swenson a short letter generally praising the book, listing about eight poems she liked best and then six or so that she liked but a little less. She caviled with a few of Swenson's choices then added, "BUT—I am not going to write criticism. In my excitement I did write you a long letter full of all kinds of it—but on thinking it over I don't believe it's a good idea." For good measure, she added, "You are old enough to know your own mind!" (WUSC 103/4002, May 14, 1958, p. 1). It was, in fact, two weeks before Swenson's forty-fifth birthday.

Swenson shot back a letter begging, with no doubt unintended humor, "I hope you didn't destroy the 'criticism letter' you wrote—please let me have it" (WUSC 103/4002, May 22, 1958, p. 1; qtd. in Swenson, *Made with Words* 224). Bishop replies about ten days later, beginning her letter, "Since you bravely invite me to 'criticize'" (WUSC 103/4002, June 4, 1958, p. 1). She spends nearly the whole first page of her four-page letter apologizing in one way or another for her remarks to come. The "criticism letter" is one of the better-known examples from their correspondence, a catalog of Bishop proscriptions, cited by Zona and others, that has invited comparison with Moore. Bishop uses Swenson's growing interest in "shape" poems to make a point about what she considers "eccentricities of form." She continues: "I think if there is a novelty in a poem the reader likes to discover it for himself.... He isn't going to ... like the poem because the eccentricities have been pointed out to him" (WUSC 103/4002, June 4, 1958, p. 2). She adds rather harshly, "of course one should experiment—but not all one's life—."

Bishop goes on to cite the long list of words she thinks mar some of Swenson's poems, warning that this "will make you think I am a hopeless reactionary and a prude as well": "I don't like ... 'loins,' 'groins,' 'crotch,' 'flanks,' 'thighs,' ... 'torso,' 'armpit,' 'pelvis,' ... 'buttock,' 'udder' ... those words stick out too much and distort the poem. They ... startle the reader in a directly physical way, perhaps more than you realize" (WUSC 103/4002, June 4, 1958, p. 2). Bishop closes her long apologia with a final summing up: "I don't want to sound like a fiend—I give this just as an example of all the things you must think of if you want to keep the reader with you without a hitch" (WUSC 103/4002, June 4, 1958, p. 4).

When her "fiend" really starts fuming, Bishop can make us laugh, and we have to wonder if Swenson smiled too when confronted with the following: "In 'News From the Cabin' the first creature is a woodpecker, isn't it? If so, birds don't have scrotums.... 'Loins' is archaic sounding to me, too (except loin of pork).... Actually, I like the word 'armpit'—but it would have to be very carefully placed" (WUSC 103/4002, June 4, 1958, pp. 2-3). Bishop then allows what to Swenson must have seemed a mysterious exception but which we understand today having access to Bishop's unpublished poems: "(Where you've used 'crotch' for the doll, in the Chirico poem—that's all right . . .³)" (WUSC 103/4002, June 4, 1958, p. 3). Bishop has worked herself into such a critical lather that she ends in a burst of uncharacteristic didacticism, loosely quoting Igor Stravinsky's *Poetics of Music*, "The more art is controlled, limited, worked over, the more it is free . . . My freedom thus consists in my moving about within the narrow frame of what I have assigned myself for each of my undertakings . . . it will be so much the greater and more meaningful the more I surround myself with obstacles" (WUSC 103/4002, June 4, 1958, p. 4).

After eight years of exchanging letters, Swenson must have grasped the irony of these words in relation to Bishop's life and work. Having glimpsed some of the obstacles that had and still surrounded her fellow poet's life, perhaps now she could see as well that Bishop needed to create her poems in an atmosphere Swenson would scarcely have been able to breathe. Perhaps she recalled the bay in the "The Bight," with its litter of correspondences and the little ocher dredge clicking away at its endless untidy activity? One thing she couldn't have known is that only a few years before they met, Bishop had written to her therapist Ruth Foster:

> I think I like old fashioned things and also slightly uncomfortable things.... I liked privies up until a few years ago, and I liked reading by oil lamps and I always prefer straight chairs and people are always saying to me how can you read or write or whatever in that uncomfortable position . . . (VC 118.33, February 1947)

Whatever insight she gained reading Bishop's "criticism letter," it caused Swenson heartache. Bishop didn't have a comfortable next three weeks either, apparently. It took that long for Swenson to reply, and when she did, Bishop shot back a letter almost immediately beginning, "I was so relieved to receive your letter night before last—I had worried about mine and thought I'd been awfully mean.... It was a mess of a letter" (WUSC 103/4002, 7/3/1958, p. 1; qtd. in *OA* 360). Swenson's reply begins quietly: "I do, very much, appreciate—and might even benefit from—your long letter about my poems. I've taken so long before answering . . . mainly because I thought I'd better let it soak in, and then re-read, trying to be objective. Which I think I can be, pretty well, now" (WUSC 103/4003, June 24, 1958, p. 1; qtd. in Swenson, *Made with Words* 224-25). Swenson wanted to address each of Bishop's points and manages to do this without becoming defensive. Her reply is both a frank self-appraisal and an inspiring and moving declaration of independence. Typing her way into a deep reverie, she admits that many of Bishop's comments add weight to suspicions she has about her work.

> From the very beginning I came at poetry backwards. . . . I never studied prosody . . . never acquired a background in what had . . . been done by others. . . . Following a strict form, that doesn't work for me—I don't *enjoy* that. . . . The physical is the beautiful to me—it's awfully strong in me. . . . I don't see, logically, why buttock is an uglier word than, say, thumb. . . . I write as I eat and drink: for the taste. There's a self-centeredness, too, in my work that keeps it limited. . . . I don't know if it's in me to write important poetry. I don't know if my life will turn out to be important, except to myself. (Significant poetry comes out of a significant life.) (WUSC 103/4002, June 24, 1958, pp. 1-3; qtd. in Swenson, *Made with Words* 226-28)

A few years later Swenson would send Bishop as fervid a summary of her poetics as she would ever write. A poem, she said,

> should isolate the present moment, vivify it—it's alright to use the future, too, because that belongs to the imagination, and to intuition—the present belongs to the color of one's feelings, and to one's point of view (a particular way of squinting at things). The past is all so settled, and trampled over. It's no fun unless you stand on the end of the diving board, alone, naked, not thinking of "how" or "why" or the best technique, but just the sensation—let impulse do it, instead of heavy knowledge. And not to care whether anyone's watching or not, is very important. (WUSC 103/4007, June 19, 1962, p. 1; qtd. in Swenson, *Made with Words* 238)

It would be hard to imagine a manifesto less likely to have been written by Elizabeth Bishop. Her past might be trampled over, but it would resist being settled. Her poems would portray a mind thinking, and that mind would often be sifting the past. There would be no diving board but repeated slow descents into reverie and memory. Swenson, by contrast, was a busy camera clicking away at the present. For her, a poem was a thing taking place. She even called her 1978 book *New and Selected Things Taking Place*. Swenson's Mormon Utah childhood brimmed with love and security. She was always the adored, "famous daughter" of her mother and father. She was the revered eldest sibling of her eight brothers and sisters. She seems to write out of, up and away from her beginnings, looking always forward. Her poems can explicitly contemplate her death, but they rarely meditate on loss. Bishop, at work on the other side of the coin, is the great alchemist of loss, and when death occurs in her published poems, it is often submerged.

Almost thirty years after her death, Swenson, while hardly neglected, has not attained the level of academic and public popularity that her life and art clearly merit. In 1998, Gardner McFall edited a volume of her prose and letters, *Made with Words*, in the Poets on Poetry series. Zona's book, *The Feminist Poetics of Self-Restraint*, appeared in 2002. In 2006, *Body My House* appeared, the first collection of critical essays on Swenson. In 2013, the Library of America's publication of her *Collected Poems* would seem to have heralded her arrival as an important voice in American poetry. Still, she remains one of the few major twentieth-century poets not to have a comprehensive critical biography. Swenson should be a hero to environmentalists and ecologists and people who dream of space travel. She should be a touchstone for people who study evolution and species conservation. Yet much of the poetry-loving public knows only the other May. The "other May" is, of course, May Sarton, who bedeviled Swenson for decades. Even the other May has a biography. Swenson was regarded by everyone who knew her as perhaps the kindest, steadiest, most loving person they had ever known. However, she could fall off this pedestal when it came to Sarton. Near the end of their correspondence, in late 1978, after she had discovered her books misshelved with Sarton's one more time in one more bookstore, she complains to Bishop: "It bugs me to be confused with her. One May S. is a weak poet with a big rep; the other is the opposite" (WUSC 104/4015, December 2, 1978, p. 2; qtd. in Swenson, *Made with Words* 254).

This statement is striking for a person whom friends treasured for her steady sweetness of character and down-to-earth modesty. A clue to this outburst may lie in a comment of Jane Mayhall's from an interview she gave to Gardner McFall in 1995 about her longtime friend.[4] Among descriptions of her sterling character, she makes the startling assertion that Swenson was "drenched in the desire to be important" (USUSCA MSS 485, Series 1, Box 1, Folder 7, p. 5). This observation adds to the received image of Swenson a component of drive and ambition.[5] These may be related as much to aspirations for her work as they are to the stark fact of having to earn a living in the competitive world of mid-century New York publishing. Swenson allowed very little to impede her daily production of writing, and we might well wonder: If Elizabeth Bishop had decided she needed to publish five hundred poems, and set about doing so, would she be the Bishop we recognize today?

If a healthy ambition fueled Swenson's effort to get her correspondence with Bishop underway, we must also credit her patience in managing such a long writing relationship with a poet we know was a master of arm's-length emotional reserve. She did this not only by being as good a letter writer as Bishop but also by being able to elicit playful teasing and even flirting from the older poet. Bishop, a public agnostic and almost certainly a private atheist, loved hearing about Swenson's Mormon upbringing and prodded her to write stories based on her religious memories. She teases Swenson in a 1953 letter after Swenson wrote describing ancestor baptism: "Mormonism must be very strange," she writes, "I had known about saving dead souls, but I didn't realize you actually were baptized over and over again for them—poor little May—no wonder you still look so clean" (WUSC 103/3997, December 26, 1953, p. 2). Bishop's poking fun here may betray a wistful envy of Swenson's childhood, which she no doubt imagined as blissful.

McFall also drew from Mayhall a reflection on whether she thought Swenson was infatuated with Bishop physically. Mayhall said she couldn't be certain but tended to doubt it. She added, however, that Swenson "knew Bishop was a power and so she hung onto power" (USUSCA MSS 485, Series 1, Box 1, Folder 7, p. 5). There are reasons to be skeptical that Swenson's focus on Bishop was based on a physical infatuation. No doubt Swenson was dazzled by Bishop at their first Yaddo meeting. She had loved the mysterious poems of *North & South* (1946) and there, in the flesh, was their mysterious author with her "half scared, half bold" eyes. When the two met, however, Swenson was in the early years of her relationship with Pearl Schwartz, and her letters to Schwartz at this time are full of passionate ardor and longing. To join Mayhall in harboring a skepticism about a major physical attraction to Bishop, we must somehow reckon with Swenson's dazzling, unfinished poem about her, "Somebody Who's Somebody." This poem from the early 1960s harks back to their stay at Yaddo and rises to an astounding close, with Swenson casting herself as an "unhobbled hound wild for love," suggesting a considerably more than room temperature affection for Bishop.

Rozanne Knudson, Swenson's last partner and first literary executor, in a letter to the poet Edward Field, wrote that "Somebody Who's Somebody" is "the only spoof poem that touches E.B.'s sacred (to her fans) life."[6] In what sense might "Somebody Who's Somebody," begun ten years after Swenson's first stay at Yaddo, be a spoof? Could the "unhobbled hound wild for love" be an ironic or cartoon mask overlaying more complex but platonic feelings for Bishop? In any case, I trust Swenson's sincerity in the poem's beautiful final lines: "I have never *known* you years / and years—and love / the unknown you" (*SCP* 596). In Swenson's feelings for Bishop, both private and shared, there is something complicated and conflicted that we have yet fully to account for.

Perhaps her infatuation was an intense longing to possess the attention of the writer of Bishop's austere and hermetic early poems? Some chords in this key are struck in the early letters. When Bishop resumes writing, in early 1953, after the hiatus of settling in Brazil, Swenson is thrilled:

> I loved getting your letter and so much news about you on one soft, thin page. The blue of the paper, I decided, must be the color of your toucan bird's eyes. . . . Let me know if I can be of any use to you, sending books or something—I will be your representative in "The States." (WUSC 103/3996, March 10, 1953, p. 1; qtd. in Swenson, *Made with Words* 198-99)

Swenson might not have realized how eagerly Bishop would take this as an audition to become her personal shopper. Like many before and after her, Swenson won the part. Far from just books, the Bishop wish list would come to include records, household items, games and puzzles, binoculars, and clothes. Bishop also hired her at fifty cents a page to type her stories for publication. At the end of this long project, Swenson wrote to Bishop, getting her girlhood church wrong, but with the piercing eye wide open, "I have tentatively concluded that you are a blend of Lewis Carroll, Kafka and Jean Genet, laced with some home-distilled Presbyterian bitters" (WUSC 103/3997, December 11, 1953, p. 1; qtd. in Swenson, *Made with Words* 202).

Early and late, the letters abound with such quips, observations and asides, often rendered, particularly by Bishop, in punch lines worthy of a practiced comic. Both women loved cats and birds, and Bishop, who was often away from New York, was always hungry for gossip from the world of poets and poetry. In addition, neither drove and each shared a deep insecurity about being photographed. "Will you send me a better picture of yourself than the one from the [Village] Voice?" Bishop writes in 1956. "I rather like the Voice one, though. . . . You look like a nice young Russian Nihilist of 1890" (WUSC 103/3997, February 5, 1956, p. 1; qtd. in OA 315). When Swenson wrote admiring Bishop's well-known 1954 profile photograph in front of the rock wall behind Samambaia, the poet replied, "I loved appearing against my rocks . . . in an old shirt by way of contrast with Amy Lowell in her comfortable armchair and velvets and laces. . . . I'm forty-five Wednesday and never felt foolisher" (WUSC 103/4000, February 5, 1956, p. 1). In 1956, Swenson received word that an elderly mutual acquaintance from Bishop's New York City days, a Mrs. Gates, had died at a movie theater in Florida. May reported to Bishop that her companions had assumed she'd fallen asleep and were shocked when they couldn't rouse her after the picture ended. Bishop replied, "I was sorry to hear about Mrs. Gates's death—did they tell you what the movie was?" (WUSC 103/4000, June 1, 1956, p. 2).

Swenson's long 1960 camping adventure in Europe inspired both humor and introspection from Bishop. In a lengthy letter, handwritten while she and Pearl Schwartz were in France, Swenson described a dental emergency and how she had found a dentist in Chartres who was able to treat the problem. In a postcard she sent after reading Swenson's long travelogue, Bishop writes, "Oh dear, a toothache in Chartres is worse than Death in Venice" (WUSC 103/4004, 1960, p. 1). Swenson's densely detailed letter is also remarkable for a small, carefully articulated drawing she interpolates in her discussion of driving in Spain and France.

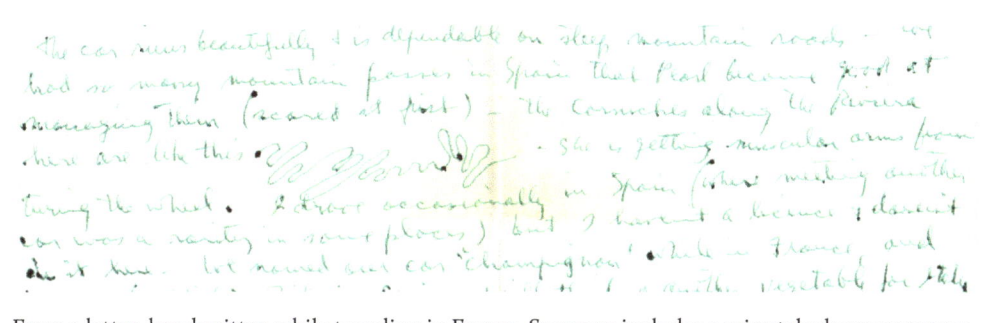

From a letter, handwritten while traveling in France. Swenson includes a minutely drawn representation of the switchbacks on the Riviera corniches.

Her rendering of the vertiginous corniches along the Riviera manages, like many of her poems, to convey both playfulness and a startling impression of accuracy. Swenson, like Bishop, was a lifelong non-driver but apparently took the wheel at times for deserted stretches in Spain. By contrast, Bishop's own "driving" almost certainly consisted of little more than short bursts in driveways and other off-road locations. Swenson's subsequent descriptions of the many adventures and economies that might be had by staying out of hotels and sleeping in cars and tents were, according to Bishop, so persuasive that the aristocratic, never-roughed-it-one-day-in-her-whole-life Macedo Soares actually "considered camping for one minute and a half." She added alliteratively that if Macedo Soares changed her mind "we may end up by pitching a pup-tent in the Peloponnesus" (WUSC 103/4004, December 26, 1960, p. 1).

Bishop's huge, handsome cat, Tobias, with his black-and-white tuxedo coat is one of the cameo stars of the correspondence. He appears in at least three well-known photographs of Bishop. Almost every potential subject, human or feline, in Bishop's Brazil, scorned the camera, but not Tobias. He "likes photographers," Bishop told Swenson, "and hams terribly" (WUSC 103/4000, May 10, 1956, p. 3).

Although he was an "unreconstructed" cat, who climbed "all over the most unfavorable guests," he could be a courtly presence with the household's other pets. Bishop's devoted little Siamese, Suzuki, would try to groom the immense cat but always gave up. It was, she told Swenson, "like washing a Cadillac" (WUSC 103/4004, 1960, p. 2). Bishop had heard that cats were sometimes eaten in Brazil and kept an eye on one older worker who seemed to pay a little too much attention to Tobias. She told Swenson that whenever she saw the two together, she'd make sure to point out that Tobias hadn't reached such a venerable old age without getting "pretty tough" (WUSC 104/4009, December 30, 1963, p. 1).

When Zephyrino, Bishop's favorite canary, died, she was told it was from complications of being overweight. She lamented to Swenson, "But how do you reduce a canary?" (WUSC 103/4008, May 22, 1963, p. 2). In the late 60s, when she still had her San Francisco property, Bishop wanted Swenson to know that during a West Coast trip, she and Rozanne Knudson were welcome to use the apartment and visit Jacob, her talented mynah bird. "I'd love to have you call on him. He tells you his name and that he loves you, and was working on 'Awful but Cheerful' when last seen" (WUSC 104/4014, July 21, 1969, p. 2).

No consideration of the Bishop/Swenson correspondence would be complete without devoting time to its emotional high-water mark, the pair of letters the poets exchanged over two weeks starting at the end of August 1955. The first of these, from Swenson, was written after she had made her way through Bishop's second book, *A Cold Spring* (1955). We might call it the "Rapture Letter." Although she had seen eight of the eighteen new poems in it elsewhere, she writes, even "they seemed new in their new setting." She finds "At the Fishhouses" the most "moving" but quickly adds the provocative remark that "most of your poems are not—they engage something else than the emotions." "What is it?" she writes. "Something else, and something more important. They are hard, feelable, as objects—or they give us that sensation—and they are separate from the self that made them" (WUSC 103/3999, August, 24, 1955, p. 1; qtd. in Swenson, *Made with Words* 208). These words anticipate later appreciations of Bishop: that she writes with a painter's eye; that she resists the intellectual; that she allows description, painstaking and accurate, to accrete in such a way that the thing described rises spontaneously before the reader, a vision all but literally, in Swenson's words, "hard, feelable." Swenson seems even to foreshadow the moving elegy, "In the Bodies of Words," that she would write for Bishop more than twenty years hence, which closes:

> But vision lives, Elizabeth. Your vision multiplies,
> is magnified in the bodies of words.
> Not vanished, your vision lives from eye to eye,
> your words from lip to lip perpetuated. (*SCP* 470)

After reading Bishop's "Four Poems," Swenson writes that she has had "to furnish them with 'meanings' from my own experiences because you've left yours out . . .—you had to, I suppose, to get them said at all. This makes them nonobjective, which I sense is necessary for you are trying to say—not say but record—what can't [be] or isn't ordinarily recorded. And an originality occurs that way" (WUSC 103/3999, August 24, 1955, p. 1; qtd. in Swenson, *Made with Words* 208). This observation seems to prefigure what Bishop would write to Anne Stevenson, ten years later, one of her most quoted comments about art: "glimpses of the always-more-successful surrealism of everyday life, unexpected moments of empathy . . . catch a peripheral vision of whatever it is one can never really see full-face but that seems enormously important" (*Pr* 414).

In "Invitation to Miss Marianne Moore," Swenson hears all the "ings" popping out like "triangles being struck at the back of the orchestra" (WUSC 103/3999, August 24, 1955, p. 2; qtd. in Swenson, *Made with Words* 209). She finds "an enfolded, unexpected prize" in many of the *Cold Spring* poems: the "slack strings plucked by heavy thumbs" from the title poem; a "nobody-ever-used-it-before" rhyme like "extraordinary geraniums" and "assorted linoleums" or a "person improbably in the setting"; the preacher carrying his frock coat on a hanger; or Miss Breen in "Arrival at Santos" (WUSC 103/3999, August 24, 1955, pp. 2-3; qtd. in Swenson, *Made with Words* 209-10). She credits Richard Eberhart with finding the prize in "The Bight": the water that "doesn't wet anything" (WUSC 103/3999, August 24, 1955, p. 3; qtd. in Swenson, *Made with Words* 210). Swenson ends her letter with one of her most beautiful encomiums to Bishop: "Not to need illusion—to dare to see and say how things really are, is the emancipation I would like to attain, as you have—but I guess you don't need to try, you just do see that way, being you" (WUSC 103/3999, August 24, 1955, p. 3; qtd. in Swenson, *Made with Words* 210).

Bishop's reply, of September 6, 1955, is one of the most profoundly personal letters she ever wrote to anyone. It must have nourished Swenson for years and, in turn, suggests how much their writing meant to Bishop. Its magnificent opening paragraph deserves to be quoted in full:

> Dear May: I am a rosy glow because of your letter for eighteen hours or so and I must answer you right away. I am still in a glow—I imagine my temperature is about 100 Fahrenheit right now. . . . If I had 1,000 readers like you I'd feel life had been worthwhile—no, that's asking too much—500 would do nicely. No more of that nobody-appreciates-me feeling . . . but I shall try to make one reader like you do me, and be properly grateful for that. . . . (WUSC 103/3999, September 6, 1955, p. 1)

Bishop announces she will clear up Swenson's "dubious points." "The Four Poems are pretty mysterious, I'm afraid." She goes on, cagily as Swenson would have it,

"I'd hoped they'd have enough emotional value in themselves so that I wouldn't have to be more specific." She adds, getting even cagier, "Any meanings you want to attach are all right, I'm sure—the wilder the better. It should be a sketch for an acute, neurotic, 'modern' drama—or 'affair,' that's all" (WUSC 103/3999, September 6, 1955, p. 1).

Bishop unties the ending of "Rain Towards Morning," perhaps her trickiest syntactical knot, which had puzzled Swenson. Bishop quietly confirms that the face belongs to the hands, that we are to imagine "a confused image of a person in the half-light of dawn" taking her slowly awakening partner's face in her hands and alighting on it a kiss (WUSC 103/3999, September 6, 1955, p. 1). A moment later she discloses an intimacy: "I am touched," she writes, "to think of your reading these poems aloud. . . . I mumble to myself sometimes but mostly it embarrasses me too much even to do that" (WUSC 103/3999, September 6, 1955, p. 2). We are struck wondering if Bishop really did "hang her words in air," as Robert Lowell asked, only to see them and never to say them?

Bishop waits until near the end of her long letter finally to address Swenson's statement that her poems engage something other than the emotions. Bishop liked to say that poetry was a way of thinking with one's feelings. She seems genuinely puzzled by Swenson's assertion: "Maybe that's not what you mean by 'emotion,'" she offers, adding that her most successful poems seem somehow distant and objective. She closes with a reflection that brings to mind what others have called Bishop's personal within the impersonal: "I don't think I'm very successful when I get personal,—rather, sound personal—one always is personal, of course, one way or another" (WUSC 103/3999, September 6, 1955, p. 4).

Bishop, having reached the bottom of a well of soul searching, must resurface to close her letter. In an abrupt change of scene, she brings Swenson into the kitchen for a glimpse of ruffled domesticity. She's lost a whole batch of Josephine Baker Pudding, full of rare and costly ingredients, blaming Alice B. Toklas's cursory cookbook advice: "I might have known I couldn't trust that woman to get a recipe straight . . . and now the damned thing . . . is curdled." Finally, she adds, in a touching nod to their shared predicament as poets, "I'm getting expert at bread, too—it rises like a dream—rolls, brioche, anything you want. When the muse gives up the ghost I can set myself up with a little shop in Rio, an impoverished gentlewoman, selling doughnuts and brownies" (WUSC 103/3999, September 6, 1955, p. 4).

Two of Swenson's most insightful tributes, both from 1960 letters, followed her seeing poems that would appear in Bishop's third book, *Questions of Travel* (1965). On reading "Brazil, January 1, 1502," she wrote,

Deceptively plain and conversational at first—so relaxed in its form—and then in other readings, and read aloud, becoming brilliantly colored and symbolized like the birds and the lizards behind the screening leaves and against the rocks... everything is placed and described accurately, rather than flamboyantly (which would have been easier)—and there is much to see and to find, having to do with time, season, place, history but all sewed with a very personal yet modest stitch. (WUSC 103/4004, January 10, 1960, p. 1; qtd. in Swenson, *Dear Elizabeth* 20-21)

Swenson had happened to see Bishop's "The Riverman" in a copy of *The New Yorker* while in Rome. At first, she had had to read it in a hurry but on later reflection fell under its spell. Calling it "a magic poem about magic," Swenson says that it absorbed her first as a story. Only later did she become attuned to what she calls its "sensations," finding it a "lulling, drugged, intense rhythmic thing—." Hailing the riverman as "real" and "contemporary," she sums up, "I experience his feelings, his belief in his power" (WUSC 103/4004, December 5, 1960, p. 4).

Beginning in the mid-1960s, Bishop's and Swenson's lives underwent wrenching change. Each lost her partner of over fifteen years and began anew. It would be years before Bishop regained solid footing, both in her relationships and in her surroundings. Swenson was more fortunate. She met a new partner, the accomplished teacher and writer Rozanne Knudson in 1966 during a teaching residence at Purdue and spent the rest of her life in domestic contentment, moving between homes in Sea Cliff, New York, on Long Island, and Bethany Beach, Delaware. Starting in 1970, Bishop took up the teaching career, in and around Boston, that she would pursue until her death in 1979. Their letters to each other begin to thin out. During the last decade of Bishop's life, they exchanged fewer than thirty cards and letters, but many of these, especially Swenson's, are among their most emotionally charged. Swenson seemed to grasp that the dynamic had changed between them, that Bishop was now the party that needed support and a kind word; her last letters are full of affection and gratitude for Bishop's years of encouragement, and she lavishes extra praise on Bishop's late poems.

Writing in 1969, her first letter in over six months, Swenson is contrite, uncertain whether Bishop is still in Ouro Prêto or has returned to San Francisco. She closes her short letter, "I hope you are happy and working, and well. I love you a lot, you know" (WUSC 104/4014, October 27, 1969, p. 1; qtd. in Swenson, *Made with Words* 252). Of "Crusoe in England," she writes Bishop in 1971,

Wonderful, and sad, and absurd, and true. The one of a kind, the explorer, marooned, mateless—who showed uniqueness, invented his survival equipment and lived on his own world—only to find in the end that he's no exception to the common fate of all those others who never ventured.... A great and remarkable poem, on all its levels—there are at least three levels that I see.... (WUSC 103/4014, December 2, 1971, p. 1; qtd. in Swenson, *Made with Words* 253)

Bishop answers with her trademark self-deprecation, "You so beautifully got the point . . . of the Crusoe poem that I want to write you a note to thank you. (I'm afraid it *isn't* very good...)" (WUSC 103/4014, December 5, 1971, p. 1; qtd. in *OA* 550).

Swenson's last two letters, in 1979, are especially tender. Writing from Los Angeles in 1979, after being made a Fellow of the American Academy of Poets, she tells Bishop, "I know that *you* had much to do with it. If only I could make you feel my joy and thanks! . . . your influence is most immense, and without your nod I'm sure this could not have happened. Please know that I love you—always will" (VC 21.6, 2/12/1979, WUSC 103/4016, February 12, 1979, p. 1; qtd. in Swenson, *Made with Words* 255).[7] Six weeks later, after reading Bishop's "Pink Dog" in *The New Yorker*, she writes in what would be her final letter to Bishop, "Some people have told me they hate it. I think it's one of the most powerful poems you've ever published. I love it." Swenson's last words to Bishop on "Pink Dog" make a fitting coda to the life and art of both women: "So vulnerable; so tough" (VC 21.6, March 28, 1979, p. 1).

NOTES

1. Seventeen of Bishop's letters to Swenson (with edits and portions omitted) are included in Bishop, *One Art*; forty-one are published (with some editing and omissions) in Swenson, *Made with Words;* and three appear in Swenson, *Dear Elizabeth*.
2. Swenson to Schwartz, October 19, 1950, Utah State University Special Collections and Archives. COLL MSS 485, Series I, Box 1, Folder 17, p. 1. Reprinted by permission of The Literary Estate of May Swenson, copyright © 2019.
3. Bishop must have had in mind her unpublished, and perhaps unfinished, poem beginning, "Where are the dolls who loved me so . . . ," which includes the word "crotch" and is collected in *Edgar Allan Poe & the Juke-Box* (2006).
4. Jane Mayhall to Gardner McFall, from an interview, November 27, 1995.
5. Also corroborated by conversations and interviews with Edward Field (b. 1924) and Ann Grifalconi (b. 1929), close friends of Swenson's for many years. Field still resides in the same Greenwich Village neighborhood where Swenson lived until 1966.
6. Letter given to the author by Edward Field.
7. Few of Swenson's original letters to Bishop have survived. We have both sides of the correspondence because Swenson, whenever possible, kept carbon copies of her letters and donated these, along with Bishop's originals, to Washington University in St. Louis. In perhaps fifteen cases, the Vassar archive contains a letter (presumably received by Bishop) that corresponds to one of Swenson's copies. These can differ in minor ways. The text cited here is the Vassar version, which differs very slightly from Swenson's copy.

CHAPTER SIX

ODD JOB

Elizabeth Bishop's "The Fairy Toll-Taker"

John Emil Vincent

The Bishop archives pose unique challenges for archivist, curator, editor, scholar, publisher, critic, and theorist, and sometimes these figures are consolidated to the same person. For example, when Alice Quinn assembled *Edgar Allan Poe & the Juke-Box* (2006), she made choices that touch on each one of these activities, identities, and more to the point, fields of expertise. However, her apparatus abjures her status as scholar or critic for the role of curator, as her stated goal is to get things out of the archives and before the eyes of eager readers. But this chapter hopes to show with a small case study that in and around the archives there is no curator without scholar and no scholar without critic and no critic without theorist, and the more explicit we can be about the activity and the purview of our projects, the greater felicity for each, however synchronous, role we play.

 The manuscript discussed here—"The Fairy Toll-Taker"—was posthumously published in a cleaned-up version in *Edgar Allan Poe & the Juke-Box* (215-16). It appears in the appendix with other, in the words of Helen Vendler, "maimed and stunted siblings," which are there as adjuncts to material appearing in the more respectable neighborhoods of the volume (37). "The Fairy Toll-Taker," interestingly, is not only relegated to the outskirts, but it is primarily meant, according to Quinn's explicit commentary, to fill out and support a footnote Quinn made for another poem, "Far far away there, where I met . . . ," that Bishop wrote when she was in San Francisco from the beginning of 1968 into 1969. And both poems, Quinn implies by putting them together, comment on how ugly the dirty hippie sexual revolution was and how little Bishop liked the milieu. The footnote for which Quinn presents

"The Fairy Toll-Taker" as support, however, actually says more about the music of the moment, about the music's sexuality and organization of sexuality, than about sex per se. Quinn quotes from an unpublished account Bishop wrote "of attending a rock-and-roll practice session":

> All the sexuality is in the bumping and grinding bodies and of course in the music driving to a climax—the sexuality of the instrument, guitars, violins etc (think of the cubists, etc), the serenade, flamenco—all gone—the sexual quality of the human voice and all its infinite variety of appeals, caresses, even gratitudes, and so on—none of that—nothing of it left in the instruments and only the mechanical physical working part of it in the performers—all has been transferred to a machine. (*EAP* 341)

Bishop laments the consolidation of the sex in music to machinic bumping and grinding. She misses the play of sexiness, the play of signs. She really doesn't like this music. She wants more sexiness, more concealment and display, more play. And she thinks the involvement with the music makes even the very forthcoming dancers unsexy. She continues:

> when they stop they probably say nothing to each other—each one ... exhausted before they start. It is hard to imagine any delicate sex-play—flirtation—a kiss that is led up to by looks and round-about remarks, any delicately growing heightening excitement—no—just grind and bang nag nag and then blank exhaustion—wordless, skill-less—no use of charm, retreats, the lovely game of love—pretty games. (*EAP* 342)

Instead of taking this as an interesting, rich take on the day's relation of music to eros, Quinn suggests that this is a note about Bishop's "disaffection with the milieu in which she had suddenly found herself" (341). Keep in mind that this was also a period when Bishop was reeling from her partner Lota de Macedo Soares's suicide; that event alone sponsored the idea of going to San Francisco after a discouraging trip to Brazil. Thus, her approval or disapproval of hippie culture would inevitably get caught in the complex machinery of her shock and her mourning, as well as in the luckiness and ambivalence of her relation to her young companion, Roxanne. "The Fairy Toll-Taker," lumped with other poems of the time, is imagined as extra evidence that Bishop really hated San Francisco, hated the culture that was on the rise with its hippies, its music, its sexual revolution. The poem's attenuated importance and placement in and relation to the volume of *Edgar Allan Poe & the Juke-Box* indicate that "The Fairy Toll-Taker" is hanging on to publication, relevance, or even status as a literary object by its fingernails.

This chapter's goal is twofold: First, I hope to show that this, while not a finished poem, *is* a complete poem; this distinction is discussed further below. But second, I want to suggest that this poem acts as a poem most when presented in its draft form, not necessarily in facsimile, but in a strictly transcribed, unbowdlerized form. Both of these arguments are underpinned by the fundamental poetic notion of closure. Barbara Herrnstein Smith presents closure best in her 1968 tour de force, *Poetic Closure: A Study of How Poems End*. Smith argues that closure isn't just where the ink ends and the white space starts; that is the "end" of the poem. Closure is the feeling the reader has, and has to have, to constitute a poetic unit at all, the feeling that the patterns introduced in the poem have been brought to completion. This particular account of closure is counter to certain poststructuralist approaches to "closure" popular right now where "closure" would shut down multivalence or possibility; "closure," however, as used here, and as I believe it is most compellingly used, is simply an element of a poetic unit. The meaning of a poem's closure may very well be open-ended, but no poetic unit is complete without closure. Usually, this means something like denser rhymes in the final line, a completed chiasmus, or a recurrence of a particular device, or some kind of thickly settled repetition of a gesture important to the piece. It can also be multivalence, chaos, or disorder if the poem has used said for patterning. If the poem ends without closure, you don't have a postmodern paradise, but instead you have a feeling that the unit is incomplete. If a poem produces a sense of closure it can be understood to be complete (even if it is officially "unfinished"). It completes its patterns, and it deserves to be understood as a unit. This is true of "The Fairy Toll-Taker."

Based on the title and its prose form, I initially thought the poem would be a little "fairy tale," probably involving trolls, in a sprawling, obviously fragmentary, incomplete, and unfinished piece. I have since come to understand "The Fairy Toll-Taker" as a fully realized prose poem—which is to say, a poem that has a complete structure fully activated. Its various elements are held in necessary relation to one another in a way that can be parsed across the arc of the poem. A finished poem is one the poet saw to some presentable final version—this, instead, while unfinished, is complete enough to cohere and be read as a poem where the various patterns it introduces are seen through to completion—no matter how rough around the edges.

The only mention of this drafty poem I could find before *Edgar Allan Poe & the Juke-Box* is from a 1993 study, Victoria Harrison's *Elizabeth Bishop's Poetics of Intimacy*. Harrison forthrightly dismisses any value the piece might have as poetry and further suggests that Bishop herself not only abandoned the piece but abandoned it in disgust at its titular subject. Also, keep in mind that the brief material Harrison quotes—the final sentence and a half of the piece—is all that she made available

THE?FAIR?TOLL?TAKER?   THE FAIRY TOLL-TAKER   SF - 1968 ?

We drove back from Berkeley across the Bay Bridge about ten-thirty last night. A thin fog, more a mist, really. Thousands of small lights in lines, arcs, bows and isolted high ones /all// mostly gold but many red and green and that long low line of very fiene ones - I don't know what that is - it seems to exteen across the bay lieke a railway line but I've never had a good look at it. The bridge towering above us - the buildings of Sf - two or three tallest ones - with their heads in fog, pinkish. Sky on/ blending two shdes: pinkish and greenish. The one clock tower that always reminds me of a Klee - not the Ferry Landing tower, another one, dark, not all lit up, just the face which seems too big for the pointed tower and therefore childish. We went along in our slow cautiou
    neck-turning way - not so many cars that time of night but those there are go extra-fast and the mammoth two-car trucks /oat/by/like// overtake like rapid buildings or over-sized freight trains with a new kind of heavy breathing mechanism - smooth and awful as fate.

    The toll booths lit up inside rather dimly. Inside the one we stopped at just long enough

        /nity// sentry sentinel of Sodom -
                                                hears
                    (Stevens letters - one feels the ground bass   of MONEY.
        pink Kleenex   sense constantly - almost unheard

to hand over the quarter, I had one good glimpse of a strange small figure, like a dummy propped up there, really like a ventriloquests doll, because he was chewing gum and his rather long jaw went up and down as if he were trying to speak but couldn't very well.
Or was speaking, without making any sounds. His face was rather large and flat and stranggely
pink& white, enammelled looking.His long eyes seemed to be either pale blue or green, but scarceyey looked at us. He was wearing I suppose the peajacket that is issued to toll-takers, a uniform, but it was much too big for him,a and so was his (navy blue) his navy blue peaked cap - low on his head with a space all around. At the sides were long wisps of thik thick wisps of bright straw-colored hair. A weird little figure, a lay figure?? looking as if tossed into his glass box like a toy and forgotten there at night in the fog, at the beginning of the mighty bridge -   An obvious homosexual. Perhaps he picks up men on his odd job?

Draft of "The Fairy Toll-Taker," recto. (VC 53.1; Courtesy of Vassar College) to her (non-archive adjacent) readers at the time. Harrison uses the poem to make an argument that Bishop didn't like sexual displays of "any" kind. (Although one might note in her assessment of rock and roll music quoted earlier that Bishop doesn't dislike sexual display in the music; she dislikes its lack of play, its lack of lovely games and modulating intensities.) Harrison is sustained and absolute in her dismissal:

> She did not like open display in life any more than she did in writing. Overt homosexuality in San Francisco in the late 1960s, for instance, bothered her enough that she did not finish a prose piece, entitled "The Fairy Toll-taker," [sic] whose description of San Francisco's fog-colored lights is disturbed by the title figure, a diminutive, doll-like San Francisco Bay Bridge toll taker. Though she had lived as a lesbian for the past several decades, this man's display of his sexual identity – "An obvious homosexual. Perhaps he picks men up on his odd job?" [this is the only quotation Harrison provides] – wrenched her out of her fantasy of color and light; this question stopped her half-page description short, and she could not or would not go on. (9)

Harrison reads this poem as stopped in disgust, but I hope to show that the two stanzas aren't really stopped at all but rather carry on a meditation to the poem's closure, a complete chiasmus, completing a circuit of thought.

"The Fairy Toll-Taker" has two large chunks and a kind of intermission, or break, in the middle: two movements with an interruption. The first paragraph, if I may call it that, the first chunk, describes returning to San Francisco from the East Bay over the Bay Bridge on a foggy night. The fog is not just the dominant element (or motif) of the physical scene—Bishop's description is a fog (or mist) of descriptors, continually foregrounding her uncertainty about what she is seeing or saw. Her descriptions start with exact physical detail that then transforms through her ruminations into high, and highly abstract, metaphor.

The poem starts in a firmly declarative mode: "We drove back from Berkeley across the Bay Bridge about ten-thirty last night." She seems to be taking down immediate impressions (last night's); this first sentence has a whiff of a diary or notebook fragment. This is the establishing shot, if you will. She will now, the opening announces, perform the description of a scene from that time and in that place.

The poem, however, quickly moves from fairly vague if not outright abstract description of the lights on the Bay Bridge to pronouncements of what *she does not know* or *never noticed*: "Thousands of small lights in lines, arcs, bows and isolated high ones mostly gold but many red and green and that long low line of very fine ones—I don't know what it is—it seems to extend across the bay like a railway line but I've never had a good look at it." She goes on to make a delightful description of a childish clock tower and the way the tallest buildings of San Francisco pink the fog with their airplane avoidant lights. However, the fairly lacy description doesn't find an organizing principle. It sort of shuffles along until the danger of looking takes over—there are fast cars and giant trucks to look at instead: "We went along in our slow cautious neck-turning way" in order to stare at the design of the cityscape and to stare at a Klee-like clock tower whose clock is so big it seems childish.

But while lost in rapt observation, the speaker and her companion are terrorized by "extra-fast . . . two-car trucks" which overtake them "like rapid buildings or oversized freight trains with a new kind of heavy breathing mechanism." Notice how the imagined or fancied railway line morphs into a very exact metaphor for the trucks. This kind of morphing is central to the poem. Although I won't be able to trace all of its poetic CGI effects, notice how the echoic turns into material for the poem—buildings plus imagined "railway line" turn to hurtling muzzled trucks— truly a kind of fascinating fairy tale or nonsense tale logic. So this first movement places the poet in time and space only to have the time and space she seems foggily enchanted by morph into anxiety and even terror. The lights and grandeur of the bridge-inflected landscape hunch into giant roaring building-like trucks (rapid buildings). It seems as if the landscape does come to life for Bishop here, but not as anticipated, instead as a ferocious car-eating monster.

This first stanza, paragraph, or you might even call it movement, stages or allegorizes the problem of foreground to background, detail to landscape. But also, it literalizes the dangers of looking. If you are in a little conveyance, a car, and are enchanted by the lights and sights of San Francisco, you quite literally risk joining the details ("ending up in the décor") by rubbernecking for beauty when you might need to be attentive to the real and deadly vehicular "details" sharing the road with you.

This first section of the poem is a kind of cautionary tale for the descriptive poet or for anyone, so to speak, "blinded by beauty." One might even, given the title, suggest that a theme is taking shape about the "toll" that attention to detail takes. The final line of the first paragraph seems to recoil from even describing the death-dealing trucks; they go from the gorgeously described "over-sized freight trains with a new kind of heavy breathing mechanism" in the space of one em dash into the impossibly abstract "smooth and awful as fate." This final fillip isn't simply a small bad line; it is a completion of the movement of the first paragraph into atomized abstraction. The second paragraph will snap us back to the scene with its first line and then enact the same kind of movement away from material time and place into vaporous reverie at closure.

Here, before we get to the intermission, I'd like to point out the dominant colors that shroud the scene, and from firsthand knowledge, I can say that they are precisely right. A foggy night on the Bay Bridge is a composition of green and pink. No red is red in mist or fog, and somehow greens seep to a kind of flak jacket color. As Bishop has it, "The bridge towering above us—the buildings of S.F.—two or three tallest ones—with their heads in fog, pinkish. Sky blending two shades: pinkish and greenish." I mention this not only for its delicious accuracy but also to introduce these colors as the elements with which she will paint in the second movement. Just as the majesty of the detail of the landscape turns into the rapid buildings of the death-dealing trucks, so will the landscape of the first stanza seep into and fill the contours of the figure introduced in the second. In a way this reminds me a bit of the exactness of Bishop's watercolors—using the seepiest of mediums to make a kind of preternatural accuracy.

The second stanza starts again with an "establishing shot" only to be interrupted; for all intents and purposes the interruption isn't its own stanza, so let's look at the original.

The second stanza begins, "The toll booths lit up inside rather dimly. Inside the one we stopped at just long enough." It breaks off abruptly into what seems like several possible strands. First and most alliterative is the "sentry sentinel of Sodom—," which is certainly too much for a final poem version but is a fun whimsical blurt. It consolidates in too precious and polished a summation the figure in the box. But this little interruption is, in a sense, a delightful performative isomorph for the moment between pulling up to a toll booth, rolling down the window, winnowing out a quarter, and looking up into the booth where a hand must appear—the brevity of the moment of cognition as well as the brevity and completeness of the exchange, quarter for passage, one gesture, one glance that lasts only as long as that gesture. This break from the stanza, only one full sentence in, creates an interesting effect. It delineates two consciousnesses in the poem: the surface, straightforward, declared speakerly position ("We drove back from Berkeley across the Bay Bridge about ten-thirty last night") and the ruminative position of the crafting poet stepping out of the descriptive thick to "finger the yard goods," if you will. During this intermission, the poet queries the terms "sentry" and/or "sentinel" of "Sodom" just as in the commentary on money, where she places "hears/feels/sense[s]" in a stack before "the ground bass of MONEY." Notice also the way the Klee-like look of the clock tower melts into "pink Kleenex" in the intermission. The descriptive immediacy desired for the finished poem vies with the second-degree consideration of the value and texture of the materials.

The stanza restarts—after the word from our sponsor—unfazed as if never interrupted: "to hand over the quarter, I had one good glimpse of a strange small figure, like a dummy propped up there, really like a ventriloquist's doll, because he was chewing gum and his rather long jaw went up and down as if he were trying

THE?FAIR?TOLL?TAKER?   THE FAIRY TOLL-TAKER   SF - 1968 ?

We drove back from Berkeley across the Bay Bridge about ten-thirty last night. A thin fog, more a mist, really. Thousands of small lights in lines, ares, bows and isolted high ones /all// mostly gold but many red and green and that long low line of very fiene ones - I don't know what that is - it seems to exteen across the bay lieke a railway line but I've never had a good look at it. The bridge towering above us - the buildings of Sf - two or three tallest ones - with their heads in fog, pinkish. Sky an/ blending two shdes: pinkish and greenish. The one clock tower that always reminds me of a Klee - not the Ferry Landing tower, another one, dark, not all lit up, just the face which seems too big for the pointed tower and therefore childish. We went along in our slow cautiou neck-turning way - not so many cars that time of night but those there are go extra-fast and the mammoth two-car trucks that/by/like// overtake like rapid buildings or over-sized freight trains with a new kind of heavy breathing mechanism - smooth and awful as fate.

The toll booths lit up inside rather dimly. Inside the one we stopped at just long enough

/half// sentry   sentinel of Sodom -
                                              hears
             (Stevens letters - one feels the ground bass   of MONEY.
   pink Kleenex   sense constantly - almost unheard

to hand over the quarter, I had one good glimpse of a strange small figure, like a dummy propped up there, really like a ventriloquests doll, because he was chewing gum and his rather long jaw went up and down as if he were trying to speak but couldn't very well.

Or was speaking, without making any sounds. His face was rather large and flat and stranggely pink& white, enammelled looking. His long eyes seemed to be either pale blue or green, but scarceyey looked at us. He was wearing I suppose the peajacket that is issued to toll-takers, a uniform, but it was much too big for him, and so was his (navy blue) his navy blue peaked cap - low on his head with a space all around. At the sides were long wisps of thik thick wisps of bright straw-colored hair. A weird little figure, a lay figure?? looking as if tossed into his glass box like a toy and forgotten there at night in the fog, at the beginning of the mighty bridge -   An obvious homosexual. Perhaps he picks up men on his odd job?

Draft of "The Fairy Toll-Taker," recto. (VC 53.1; Courtesy of Vassar College) to speak but couldn't very well. Or was speaking, without making any sounds." This figure is the foil to the deadly double trucks, who make too much sound and give too little warning. He makes no sound and is all appearance with no apparent substance. Also, Bishop makes it clear that she gets only a glimpse—and a glimpse of this figure is worth his own whole stanza; on the scalepan of this poem, he has equal weight to the entire San Francisco cityscape. He has a strikingly "pink & white" "enameled looking" face with "pale blue or green" eyes. He has morphed out of the image of the clock with the too big face, which looks childish, the sight of tall buildings poking through fog (pink), the entire sky and bay scape, and the fog generally as it sets details like satin in a casket.

The toll taker's hat and coat are too big. The detail of the "peaked cap—low on his head with a space all around" has the tone, arguably, of the ridiculous and also of the carefully and fondly observed. Like the speaker in her little car beside the mighty trucks with their "new kind of heavy breathing mechanism," so is the toll taker dwarfed by the bridge to whose apparatus he is appended. "A weird little figure, a lay figure?" A lay figure, besides being someone not in the priesthood, is one of those little wood figures with movable joints that artists use to model the human form. They are movable but frozen in gesture—"looking as if tossed into his glass box like a toy and forgotten there at night in the fog, at the beginning of the mighty bridge—." The lay figure is useful for the artist by striking and holding a pose. It is exactly that: a device that holds poses *for an artist*.

The concluding gesture of the poem—"An obvious homosexual. Perhaps he picks up men on his odd job?"—is at once the kind of revelation that marks a poetically earned closure of a descriptive poem, that is, a kind of "ta-da!" that gathers the variety of visuals that precede it, familiar from "The Map," "Large Bad Picture," and other Bishop poems. However, this poem suggests that the coding of the figure—his hyperactive silence, his enameled-looking face, his jauntily oversized clothes, his held pose, his wisps of straw-colored hair—becomes consolidated in the obviousness of his homosexuality. These all add up to obviousness, and like the obviousness of the deadly trucks, it is a sudden obviousness. But, unlike the trucks, his obviousness was not the obliteration but instead the proliferation of detail. The result is the poem's final awkward syntax, hedged declaration, and suspended speculation. It is packed in so much rhetorical hesitance and mist as to shout about the interest the speaker has in the figure. You can, after all, see a fairy in a toll booth without associating the depositing of tolls in his hands with cruising. "Perhaps he picks up men on his odd job?" [as his odd job?]. The association of toll-taking with cruising is rich and really dirty—in a fun way.

However, I'd like to shy away from having too much fun and return to the original. First, I want to suggest, given the kind of misspellings, repetitions, and the curious middle section, that this was a first draft of this poem. The neatening up that Quinn gives it doesn't really improve the poem. She removes the ragged middle of the poem without noting that she has except in a footnote that bowdlerizes the middle of the poem as follows: "There is a reference to the letters of Wallace Stevens tucked in this draft, 'one feels (hears) the ground bass of MONEY . . . sense constantly—almost heard'" (*EAP* 215). There are a number of invisible choices made here. I think "hears," "feels," and "sense" in Bishop's draft are a stack meant as possible verbs to fit before "the ground bass of MONEY." Furthermore, Quinn, in perhaps her most egregious lapse of editorial duty, omits "pink Kleenex" without a trace or note. The rawness of the original does carry the charge of the sharply seen scene as well as the second stanza's amazingly dense glance. The effect is one of immediacy and density all at once. What is also missing from Quinn's cleaned-up copy is the first crossed-out title.

Notice that the first title of the piece was "THE FAIR TOLL-TAKER," which is crossed out in a lovely kind of Riddler (in "Batman") gesture with question marks. That title brings together the notion of the toll taker doling out the gorgeous view of the mighty bridge, his fair "bright straw-colored" hair, as well as his pale "enameled looking" pallor. But the title Bishop ends up with serves to undergird the closural effects of the final gesture. As it is, the title "The Fairy Toll-Taker" imbues the poem with a fabulist mien, a fable-feeling, an otherworldliness, which then bends to the more 1960s vernacular use of the term *fairy*. In fairy tales there are many toll takers and many fairies. One's mind, at least mine, first goes to tiny winged creatures rather than to "obvious homosexuals." What Bishop has done with this title "The Fairy Toll-Taker" is make the poem into a recodification of the urban and human landscape. Also, perhaps, she is bemoaning this subsumption of details under a fantasy of unifying identity. Not that gay and lesbian identities weren't already consolidated by terrifying and generative stigma, but maybe what Bishop's poem gives us is a dramatization of the value of this new identity. "The obvious homosexual"—the description gives way to a kind of fantasy of the fairy toll taker using his "odd job" to fulfill his own non-job-related desires. He is an isolated figure in the fog, not entirely dissimilar from the speaker of this poem, and Bishop's speaker runs to ways to mitigate his loneliness. She leaps ahead of the details to start to build a kind of narrative pulsion for this frozen figure with movable joints. She uses him precisely as a lay figure, as a little wooden manikin. He is a kind of symbol of the often-overlooked ingenuity of loneliness.

Fair or fairy, the poem comes down on the side of fairy, but it is important to see the poem deciding what sort of unit it wants to be, where its center of gravity is. It beautifully stages an identification across category modeled by a relation of detail to landscape. The fairy toll taker exceeds the commerce of his job—as mentioned in the intermission quoting Stevens, "the ground bass of MONEY"—and suggests that there is fun to be had past all this mundanity. Becoming picturesque (obvious) for fun is a real option, he materially argues. And that self-created picturesqueness is advertisement against solitude. You might see where I'm going here. The serial surprise and adventure embedded in the fairy toll taker's hypothesized cruising, while not outright simply celebratory, is at least figured through this poem's beautifully staged serial descriptions. Bishop's changing of the title in the original, from fair to fairy, does show her adjudicating modes of pulsion and deciding on the magnetic pole of the poem—the description of hair and physiognomy seemingly ceding to but actually overspilling any simple outright statement of sexual identity into a kind of fairy story. She uses description to come out the other side of denomination—which it turns out is narrative. She retreads ye olde timey fairy to both contain and exceed the contemporary valences of the term.

And what about the lavish attention the speaker pays to that one glance?! And the fact that Bishop titled the piece after the fairy? Titles are often the last element of composition meant to consolidate the whole, a whole that can only be consolidated after it is composed. I have argued that Bishop's gesture at the end, while not a gesture of giving up, is also not a gesture of disgust. It completes the pattern of the poem and offers a gesture beyond the closure of the pattern—the man, isolated as he is, pulled from his isolation by minute detail and also by the speaker's fantasized narrative action of cruising. One might be alone, very alone, in a fog, on a bridge, in a toll booth, in an ill-fitting outfit, in a silent movie almost, but still reach out beyond the "ground bass" of money and instead reach for the hand that proffers it.

The final question mark of the poem is peculiar but also splays the mode of the speaker—is she asking herself a question, the reader a question, or is she asking the figure in the poem a question? In a way, it repeats the interrogative intermission's upshot—essentially asking "How should I proceed?" But the closing gesture asks everyone available at the site of the poem rather than just asking herself—in a way, not to be too cute, she's cruising those crossing the bridge of her piece's arc.[1] I hope it is okay now to call the work a completed, if not a finished, poem.

Furthermore, that final gesture—"An obvious homosexual. Perhaps he picks up men on his odd job?"—does not just speculate about the lurid nature of the toll taker's habits but links the obviousness of his sexuality to his ability to find sexual partners, even in as quick an encounter as the rolling down of a window and the exchange of a quarter. A sentence before he was just a toy tossed in a box. Now, like Pinocchio, he has some real-boy potential. The title "The Fairy Toll-Taker" combined with this final fillip suggests that perhaps the tolls the fairy toll taker takes are not all in coin. As opposed to being a detail endangered by abstraction, "forgotten there in the fog, at the beginning of the mighty bridge" (the dominant theme in the first half of the poem), in some way the toll taker is an abstraction that generates detail, the detail of imaginative flight. How might that happen, this toll taker cruising passing drivers? Would he have to turn off the light in his booth? Would he send them to a quiet place nearby? Would he give men his number? Somehow he has to do it "on," that is, while doing, his "odd job." Or is his job odd because it so sexily metaphorizes and enables his sexual activity based on his visible homosexuality?

What's interesting about all the things that Bishop hated about the rock and roll band practice she went to, and which I quoted her impressions of above, is that she hated the lack of games, "the lovely game of love." By this I don't think she meant flirting that stays only flirting. Cruising is the most distinct corollary to that lovely game of feints and parries. One does not merely identify a willing partner for sex, which is only one potential final result. There is all manner of reading and sorting that goes on before that result is even a possibility. One becomes semiotically promiscuous. Cruising is about cruising first and foremost and not about having sex per se. That too, but one cruises definitionally much, much, much more than one tricks. Some cruisers only cruise to cruise. Details, the kinds of details that Bishop rakes the landscape for, become supercharged. In some sense, her poetic eye is cruising, scanning for language that serves as an assignation of word and vision. She has found for herself a figure of the poet, and he has to cruise in order to be a living member of the landscape, to escape being dwarfed by his scene. Cruising is the definition of "delicately growing heightening excitement" around the reading of signs. The inevitability of rock and roll sex is not at all similar to the misfireable, dangerous, tentative, eye play of cruising. Also, while flirting is what rock drowns out, the mechanical taking of tolls ("the ground bass of MONEY") enables flirting.

As Lee Edelman has elegantly theorized, there is a particular kind of writing that happens around and on the male homosexual body. He calls it *homographesis*, and it is the process of making the gay body legible, both for homophobes and for other homosexuals (Edelman, *Homographesis* 3-23). The homosexual difference from the male heterosexual body has to be written and in being written, Edelman suggests, produces all of the endemic deconstruction of its own bases that writing in general does. Always producing a site of reading, the gay body enables a critique of meaning itself as arbitrary and as multivalent. Bishop's naming of the toll taker as "an obvious homosexual" is interesting after the accumulation of totally gay details about him. He's been presented as a small, skinny ventriloquist's dummy, as a fair, enameled, delicate, baggily dressed, effeminate, broken toy. Why the sudden "reveal" after all the revealing details? It is as if by stating the obviousness of his homosexuality, Bishop were corralling all the details into a single stall. But then, one step further, her poem realizes that there might be some use for obviousness. It could reap rewards. It is as if in the last lines of the poem, Bishop realizes that this little gay figure figures as gay not only from without but also as a broadcasting station of a person.

The final query and the final question mark grant the toll taker more mystery than his fairy status already has. He is opened up coincident with the upturn of a question. It is as if the question were not an epiphany but the spark and uptake of interest and imagination. From its very beginning, this poem struggles to find an organizing principle in a dense mist of detail. And here the poem has found an organizing principle: this figure and the interest he incites. He is a cynosure both for the poet and for figures inside the poem's world. As opposed to the sheer danger of getting snagged in detail, which early in the poem was embodied by the giant trucks whose dangerousness grounds the poet's interest in the landscape—though there is still danger around—the toll taker offers the fantasy of an organizing principle, desire, and all the details in the world for it to organize. The poem has completed a chiastic structure, one of the sturdiest ways to flag a poem's closure, and come to understand its central terms anew, though not, that is to say, with any final certainty.

Paul de Man has suggested that Yeats's famous rhetorical question at the end of "Among School Children"—"How can we know the dancer from the dance?"—stages the coexistence of two irreconcilable meanings. The question is being asked as a question, but it is also being asked precisely because it cannot be answered. Bishop's use of the rhetorical question is even stranger. Since her final sentence begins with "perhaps," the speculation might very well end in a period. But instead of mere speculation, the question becomes also solicitation. A "what do you think?" or "what do I think?" gesture. But it is also an excessive gesture. It is too much to speculate *and also* intone upward. Bishop is playing with a little bit of circus-y audience participation. In a sense, she is testing out the very gesture the fairy toll taker seems expert in.

As opposed to being disgusted by the toll taker, Bishop's interest is piqued, and she seems delighted and imitative. And, best of all, she seems hell-bent on sharing her delight by overdoing her curiosity, such that it reaches out to those reading her report of the scene. The way the toll taker helps shape his own covert plans by obvious signs is imitated with the crash of speculation into rhetorical question to create an excessive rhetorical gesture, raising the voice of the poem from its initial demonstrative tone to almost a giggle of delight. But it is also a wink to the reader. This is a giddy, a naughty, Bishop. She's found a place where the sexiness she misses in rock music might be found: a sexiness she describes as "delicate sex-play—flirtation—a kiss that is led up to by looks and round-about remarks, any delicately growing heightening excitement." In other words, a promiscuity of signs. And no promiscuity of signs is more promiscuous than cruising. For that insight alone, this poem deserves a place in her oeuvre.

I hope that by giving this poem room to be read in its draft form, which requires the reader to be critic, archivist, and theorist, I have not simply made an argument for the value of this poem itself. It is a wonderful poem. But it is also a signal case of queer cross-identification, which would be lost to acid-free folders and Hollister boxes if archives are treated as mere sites of storage and curation. The archives must also be read, not merely evaluated or sorted—read as poems, read as writing—and brought to life on their own material, historical, textual, and literary terms.

NOTES

1. I am not the first to suggest that Bishop "cruises" her readers. Bethany Hicok in *Degrees of Freedom* (2008) has suggested that "[m]uch of Bishop's work can be seen anew if one considers it in the light of the possibility of 'cruising' the reader" (26).

PART II

TRAVELS: SCALE, LOCATION, ARCHITECTURE, ARCHIVE

CHAPTER SEVEN

ELIZABETH BISHOP AND RACE
IN THE ARCHIVE

Marvin Campbell

The questions—or perhaps provocations—that a little known 1969 interview Elizabeth Bishop conducted with Kathleen Cleaver, wife of Black Panther Party member Eldridge Cleaver and significant party member in her own right, raise for Bishop's understanding of race is a subject not sufficiently attended to, leaving a real lacuna in discussions of the poet's work. Critics have begun paying attention in recent years (Camille Roman, Kirstin Hotelling Zona, Steven Axelrod, Tyler Schmidt, and perhaps most significantly, Renée R. Curry), but a thorough investigation of the archive reveals how deeply racial otherness—and blackness in particular—broadly informed Bishop's lyric subjectivity in ways that should re-shape our understanding of her poetry and poetics. Against the tacit homilies permeating criticism that Bishop revered black culture and that her own outsider position made her a useful interlocutor for black subjects on the one hand, and the charge that Bishop—along with Sylvia Plath and H.D.—were "ignorant, but not innocent, perpetuators of colonialism" (Curry 8) on the other, I wish to suggest that there is a more complex portrait of Bishop's racial identification, with both strengths and limitations that hold meaningful lessons for how we read and teach mid-century American poetry.

We don't need to ask, as Axelrod does, "Was Elizabeth Bishop a racist?" Nor do we need to engage in a form of special pleading by asserting she was comfortable with black people because of her own poor white background—in the process, passing over the most problematic passages from letters, notes, and poems. We neither have to rescue Bishop from, nor indict her for, the racial attitudes she held, however retrograde they may appear to us. We need to be honest about them.

Being honest requires a forthright acknowledgment that Bishop's understanding of blackness and of black people, as for many white mid-century liberals, proved complex and ambivalent. However "progressive" in political sympathies, Bishop's moral imagination was inflected by age old ideas governing the other that have existed at least as long as Rousseau's idea of the "noble savage," and the same romantic primitivism that led dissipated white intellectuals and artists to the Mexican Revolution informed her own journey to the Southern hemisphere.[1] Candor also demands recognizing that Bishop's withering, self-surveilling irony; famed modesty; career-long commitment to engaging with the vectors of race, class, and gender; and meaningful contact with the lived realities in Brazil and Key West reveal a poet sufficiently self-critical to subvert the reductive and crude racial logics that operate in the white imaginary. Roxanne Cumming, Bishop's California paramour, may have arranged the interview with Kathleen Cleaver in San Francisco—this single mother closer to the spirit of the radical sixties not to mention the pregnant Cleaver whose husband Eldridge was on the run—but Bishop, for all her gentility and discomfort with the America she had returned to, was the one who stayed, even when the radical Cleaver challenged her liberal innocence.

Before the Black Panther Party emerged and sought out a sympathetic Bishop, the blues of the 1930s and 1940s provided her main access to black culture. Her love of the genre proved so deep that in a letter to Frani Blough Muser she contemplated an article on "modern American ballads," singling out the "Negro ones" (*OA* 72) for especial praise. In a 1958 letter, also to Muser, her appreciation remains undiminished: "I haven't had time yet to play Odetta all through, but she certainly has an extremely beautiful voice. Of course I like Negro voices anyway—have most of Bessie Smith, Billie Holiday, etc. (as you may remember.)" (*OA* 378). While likely sincere, Bishop's enthusiasm depends on a racial essentialism in which black music emerges from an undifferentiated mass—consider the easy shorthand of "Negro ones" and "Negro voices." Such pat generalizations rely on the customary stereotyping of African Americans as fundamentally musical, leading the usually fastidious poet to conflate the wildly divergent Smith, Holiday, and Odetta and, in the process, deny each figure their distinct and remarkable artistry.

At a broader social and cultural level, Bishop's engagement with jazz and blues singers belongs to a context where many "rich white chick[s]" (qtd. in *REB* 86)—the term Holiday used to describe her onetime patron and Bishop's lover Louise Crane—slummed in Harlem.[2] In her role as collector of black music, well attested by friends who observed stacks of records (*REB* 75), Bishop also stands situated within wider studies of reception where white critics of jazz, blues, and folk translated black music for a white audience—frequently, as in the case of the Lomaxes and Leadbelly, exploiting the musicians.[3] The choice of correspondent matters for situating her within this particular framework of expertise, too. Frani Blough Muser had studied music throughout her education at Walnut Hill and Vassar, eventually gaining admittance to the Conservatoire Américain, Fontainebleau (*OA* 8). Bishop's childhood friend stands in a position both to validate Bishop's musical opinions and be impressed by them, dazzled by a Bishop who might know *more*, hence, the anxious "of course" and "as you may remember" in Bishop's letter to Muser—as if her knowledge of black "cool" had been in doubt (*OA* 378).

These twin contexts—white interpretation and appreciation—found poetic expression in the 1944 "Songs for a Colored Singer," a poem singled out for measured praise by Adrienne Rich and Randall Jarrell in their influential reviews. Modern critics, such as C. K. Doreski, Curry, and Axelrod, have been less sympathetic. It is perhaps easy to see why: the stilted vernacular, the lack of any real grounding in African American life, "vaudeville idioms" (Doreski 122) that belong neither to the best popular song of the period nor the blues, the conceit of a rich white woman speaking for the black poor. As even the generally favorable reading by Rich concedes, that position represents a "risky undertaking" (Rich, *Blood* 131).

The poem has its defenders. Jonathan Ellis, perhaps its most persuasive champion, argues that we sidestep the first two songs and their reliance on racial ventriloquism to regard the sequence's more politically charged second half (Ellis, *Art* 137). In Ellis's reading, thoughtfully drawing on Toni Morrison's influential thesis from 1992's *Playing in the Dark*, whiteness mines racial realities that black voices cannot articulate. He argues that these oblique sections—where the two characters depicted, an impoverished couple, disappear—offers a critique of the socioeconomic conditions that constrain their lives in the first place. But the problem seems little changed: troped nobly or shallowly, Le Roy and his unnamed wife are not, strictly speaking, there. Even in Ellis's rendering, they exist purely for Bishop to articulate an argument. In this way, the blues provides the poem with little more than a *donnée* that reduces the blues from song to a literary idea of the genre—ironically, the same criticism Bishop leveled at the samba featured in *Black Orpheus* (*OA* 382). Betsy Erkkila's contention that Bishop's voice "speaks not only *for* but *as* and *through* a black blues-woman" (296) may unwittingly illustrate the problem. The palpable elusiveness of a fixed, single-speaking position that the critic sees as a strength instead underscores the absence of any racial reality, without any apparent self-consciousness on Bishop's part.

But if that ambiguity never becomes a self-critical irony—a more fruitful pose found in Bishop's work elsewhere—a perusal of the archive reveals a more sophisticated engagement with the blues. In what appear to be notes for an article on "modern American ballads," transcriptions of blues lyrics from a wide array of blues and country singers popular during the 1930s and 40s (Blind Boy Fuller,

Peetie Wheatstraw, Big Bill Broonzy, Bill Cox, Red Foley, and Bob Wills) foreground the difficulties imperiling any white encounter with black music and the racial essentialism that governs how aesthetic expression is seen (VC 74.12).

By drawing on figures from across the country (Texas, North Carolina, St. Louis, Chicago, Kentucky), across genres (western swing, country, blues), and, crucially, across racial lines, Bishop reveals what the segregated music industry of the 1930s could not conceal—the blues, while an expression of black culture in the post-Reconstruction and Jim Crow South, were not reducible to any standard racial grammar. White audiences frequently requested the blues from both black and white performers at the same time as black audiences "enjoyed square dances similar to those at white functions" (K. Miller 78, 77). More to the point, the genres themselves are hardly pure musical idioms—the cross-pollination of blues and country, for one, has been well established.[4]

In Wheatstraw's "Kidnapper's Blues" (VC 74.12.2), the Westerners's "If Jesse James Rode Again" (VC 74.12.11), and Fuller's "Evil Hearted Woman" (VC 74.12.1), Bishop's predilection for the periphery emerges to the fore: outlaws, criminals, and "bad" women on full display. Others, such as Foley's "The 1936 Floods" (VC 74.12.9) and Cox's "The Trial of Bruno Richard Hauptmann" (VC 74.12.6) reveal an interest in the lived experience of these same margins, Bishop opting for unusually journalistic examples alongside the more archetypal figures of the kidnapper and the outlaw.

Even as Bishop reveals a deeper knowledge of American blues, folk, and country than her rhapsodizing of "Negro voices" might suggest, her social consciousness for these separate but interconnected musical traditions has its limits. She doesn't seem particularly interested in the black blues of protest that take aim at segregation, as Axelrod pointedly observes. She instead turns her attention to erotically charged selections, such as Fuller's "Evil Hearted Woman" (VC 74.12.1) and "My Brownskin Sugar Plum" (VC 74.12.2) or local colorist sketches of Southern life, such as Wheatstraw's "Froggie Blues." Even those blues focused on the conditions of a black speaker—like Wheatstraw's "Kidnapper's Blues" or Broonzy's "Pneumonia Blues"—do not offer any measure of social critique for the power structure that placed such figures in their desperate straits.

But if Bishop defuses the blues of their political charge, her encounter reveals a useful discomfort—a fundamental untranslatability at white hands. In the rendering of "Evil Hearted Woman" (VC 74.12.1) by Fuller, several question marks betray a halting confidence about words and phrases. Even when Bishop seems more certain, she employs ditto marks over several lines, as if fully reproducing the song is impossible. By the end of the page, scattershot words remain, the white space acknowledging the failure to represent unfamiliar cultural material.

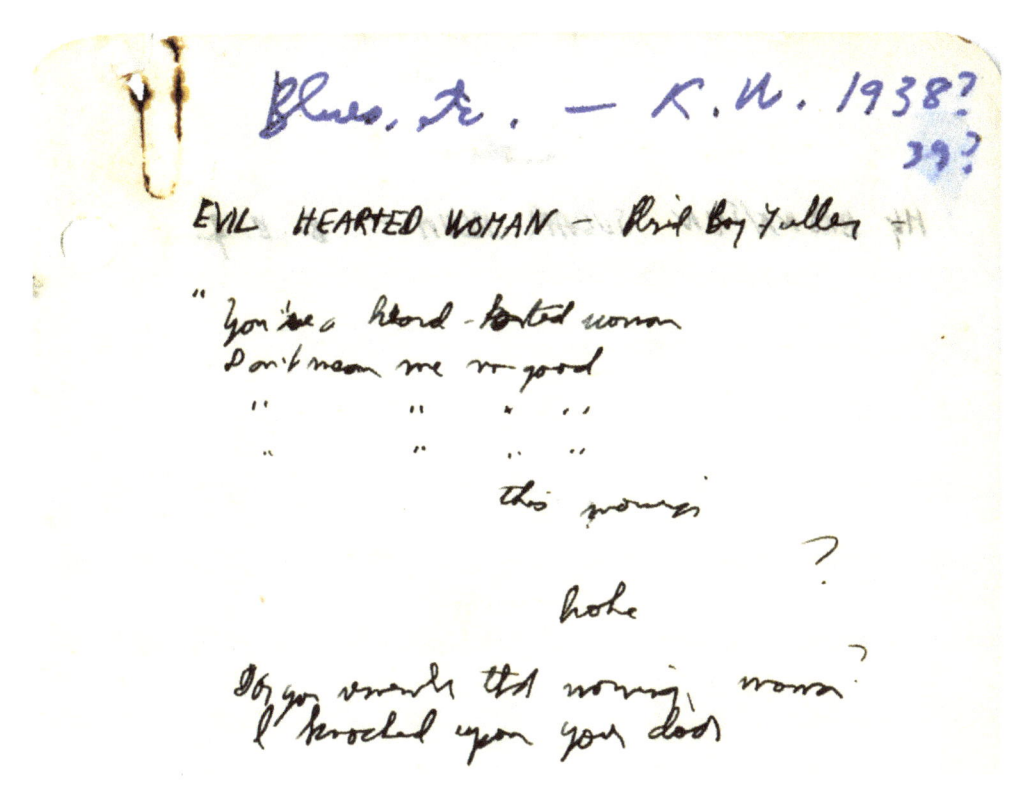

Bishop copied "Evil Hearted Woman" by Blind Boy Fuller into her notebook. (VC 74.12.1; Courtesy of Vassar College)

That increasingly baffled position produces a copy of "Kidnapper's Blues" (VC 74.12.2) with not only the same ditto marks but also irregular lineation and illegible writing. Indeed, under pressure from the former, the blues lyrics lose the shape of stanzaic form entirely—unruly and resistant to her careful domestication. (This formal dissolution does not happen to the songs she copies by any of the white artists.) It is in Bishop's rendering of Fuller's "My Brownskin Sugar Plum" (VC 74.12.1), however, that the challenge of black music reaches a flash point. Perhaps mindful of the song's intimacy—or unable to decipher the song at all—Bishop offers a largely blank page with only the song's title and Fuller's initials. "Froggie Blues" (VC 74.12.3) meets the same fate, perhaps too culturally specific in its blackness, too tied to the rural South. Lest I overdetermine what may have simply been a project taken up and discarded for reasons entirely unrelated to the content—perhaps, for example, she didn't have time—it is still worth asking within the broader context of difficulty why she ran out of time *there*, especially when, first among the numbered pages, these were likely the first attempts at transcription.

Even without these issues of untranslatability, these songs belong to broader Bishop concerns—her translations of samba, her interest in folk culture writ large, her continued attention to the interdependence of music and songs—and therefore merit serious attention. These are not marginal issues to an understanding of Bishop's work. After all, it was "Songs for a Colored Singer" that led to *North & South*'s (1946) publication, as Schmidt has helpfully reminded us (69). When the poem was published in *Partisan Review*, it caught the attention of Jean Pedrick, an editor at Houghton Mifflin, who encouraged Bishop to submit her work to the contest responsible for the publication of *North & South*—a fact, he adds, that has "rarely [been] acknowledged or interrogated" (Schmidt 69). This omission in readings of Bishop appears all the more striking when one considers that "Songs for a Colored Singer" is far from the last mediation of her voice through a black woman, or even black person.

Her relationship to ordinary black people—and black women, in particular—was even more vexed, depending upon a white paternalism and a taste for the exotic that proved quite comfortable mining encounters with "the help" for anecdotal interest. Throughout the letters, individuals like Cootchie, Faustina, and an unnamed Negro cook provide objects for Bishop to pose, tropes to circulate among her monied white peers, lives to aestheticize with high cultural reference points (e.g., George Herbert and Milton). Validating them through an Anglo-American framework made her more comfortable, and, paradoxically, helped emphasize their strangeness through the incongruity of such comparison.

But if Bishop belongs to a nineteenth-century tradition dating back to Harriet Beecher Stowe and Joel Chandler Harris that purloined black life for its sentimentality, she also resisted that impulse in the published poetry, forsaking the picturesque. In "Cootchie" (*PPL* 35) and "Faustina, or Rock Roses" (*PPL* 55), Bishop attended unflinchingly to the grimmer realities of their raced and gendered oppression, reserving her scorn and contempt for their white female masters. Perhaps this is even part of the reason why Bishop had trouble transcribing the blues lyrics black men like Wheatstraw and Fuller addressed to black women: she realized they were not even seen there. Why she did not trust these women to speak for themselves by transcribing the lyrics of, say, Bessie Smith, when she knew them well, is hard to say. It might just be—as Schmidt suggests—that Bishop employed the voices of black women to shore up her own novice poetic voice (Schmidt 70), when someone like Billie Holiday was both more critically lauded and commercially successful. Less cynically, she saw in Lady Day a poetic model to emulate and, perhaps, if we take seriously the poem's aim to provide Holiday with a song, a voice to empower alongside her own.

Whatever the case, black women occupied a central role in Bishop's imaginary—both the ordinary women whose experiences as the help she might elevate into art and the blues singers, who did the work of elevation themselves. "Faustina, or

Rock Roses" and "Cootchie" reflect an arguably richer portrait of such figures. They belong to a Florida triptych—alongside the Afro-Cuban Jerónimo from the eponymous poem "Jerónimo's House"—that focuses on the mechanisms of oppression that constrain their shared lives in the Keys. They also belong to a servant class familiar to Bishop in Brazil that, as Lorrie Goldensohn has persuasively observed, stood in for Bishop's partner Lota de Macedo Soares. Bishop mediated Macedo Soares through images of the servants in her employ to imagine a "darker, more primitive self" (Goldensohn, *Elizabeth Bishop* 76) on her partner's part.

Bishop's archive provides a useful context for these poems of the servant class, suggesting they are not merely challenging American racism but, more precisely, the cultural forms that confine these figures to images that serve white needs and desires. Through a tranche of materials that include the Foster letters and the Methfessel-Bishop correspondence, there is a startling piece of ephemera—an advertising leaflet for Sapolio soap (VC 121.19), an extensively advertised brand popular in the 1930s. To preserve its status as advertisement, Bishop does not paste the leaflet into a notebook, preferring to string the pages together into its own notebook, and she takes enough care with the document that its condition remains pristine, with a few faded water stains visible in the background. The eight-page document depicts eight vignettes—two black servants cleaning pots and pans (1 and 3); a woman standing amazed at the appearance of the white, shining "Modern Household Fairy" bringing Sapolio soap (2); a man standing before a dirty white statue (4); a mother, joined by her son, in a dirty room (5); the same man standing before a gleaming white statue (6); the mother and son presiding over a clean room (7); and a father and son stained by ink spilled from an inkwell at the father's desk (8). Each image is accompanied by doggerel that describes the action in each—the language of the advertising jingle. By virtue of this text, Bishop may have felt a particular obligation and perhaps special power as a poet to engage with this image of mass culture. The visual grammar of blackness/dirt and whiteness/cleanliness unfolds over the first three panels: the black help cannot clean the pots until a "Modern Household Fairy come[s] / With tablet white as snow," and "uncleanliness quick fades away before SAPOLIO"; the black figures cannot, in fact, even see themselves until whiteness has effaced the literal stain of their blackness from the cookware that provides an extension of their personhood. Once the miraculous soap has accomplished its aim, the black woman stares admiringly at her reflection now in the pot. The black woman's purpose achieved, she has been discarded. The subsequent panels from the leaflet depict lily-white tableaus—an art collector who has scrubbed clean an alabaster sculpture and a white woman cleaning a mantel and table as her child plays on the floor—and reveal the prototypical white fantasy Ralph Ellison responded to in "What America Would Be Like without Blacks":

> Her pots and pans, and kettles, too,
>   Were never bright and shining;
> Her servants at the labor hard
>   Were all the while repining.
> Her dishes put away half washed,
>   And scratched with brick dust scouring;
> Her knives—in fact the lady felt
>   Her household cares o'erpowering.

Page one of the advertising leaflet for Sapolio soap, an extensively advertised brand popular in the 1930s, where the visual grammar of blackness/dirt and whiteness/cleanliness unfolds over the panels. The image overlaps with page three of the booklet. (VC121.19; Courtesy of Vassar College)

"a fantasy . . . at least as old as the dream of creating a truly democratic society" (Ellison).

Bishop had her own brand of racial innocence. As Bethany Hicok has observed, "Bishop (with some qualifications) bought into the dominant myth that Brazil was a racial paradise" (71).[5] Popularized by Gilberto Freyre's influential 1933 work, *Masters and Slaves*, and adopted by the Brazilian elite, "racial democracy" held that racial prejudice did not constrain social mobility, a lack of strict racial categories owing to

Pages two and three of the Sapolio soap advertising leaflet. (VC121.19; Courtesy of Vassar College)

the unique historical conditions of the country. Subsequent revisionist historians, led by Thomas E. Skidmore, have taken aim at this consensus view, showing how a predominantly white elite employed the fig leaf of racial democracy to mask actual forms of racial oppression. Afro-Brazilians, then as now, did not suffer the indignities of Jim Crow, but they were consigned to the lowest rungs of Brazilian society.

Here, as elsewhere throughout Bishop's remarks on servants (Macedo Soares's in Brazil as well as Bishop's in Key West), she emphasizes the apparent harmony between black and white Brazilians, choosing images of amity that elide the former's subject position.[6] As Goldensohn observes in an icy aside, "It is worth noting that while Bishop was perennially eager to see the dissolution of racial barriers, her interest in dissolving class barriers was rather less keen" (Goldensohn, *Elizabeth Bishop* 77). On the contrary, Bishop reified them, opting for a white paternalism that routinely chided and condescended to the black underclass in Brazil throughout her letters.

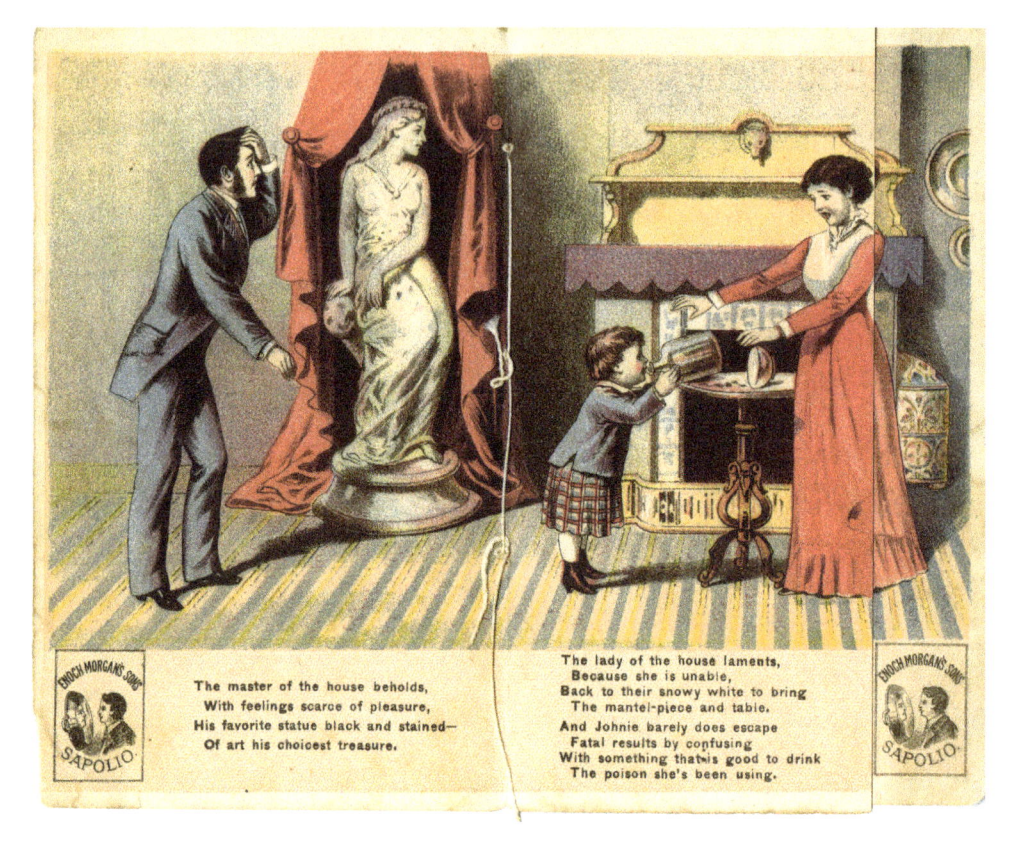

Pages four and five of the Sapolio soap advertising leaflet. (VC121.19; Courtesy of Vassar College)

But this vision of subservient blackness—quite literally domesticated by the Sapolio ad copy—does not hold up ideologically any more than Lincoln's dream of resettlement of slaves to Liberia accomplished the vision of an entirely white America. The last Sapolio ad panel reveals a blackness that has returned in the form of a spilled ink pen to contaminate a horrified patriarch and his mournful son; there included no panel to expunge the overspreading stain, no maid to handle the mess. Whatever Bishop's private feelings, the image here—like Faustina's diseased mistress, like Cootchie's racist one—reveal whiteness as the ultimate stain, unable to cope with the demands of the mess on its hands.

In terms of color, I was also struck by the literal blue that appears throughout the archive, in poem drafts like "The Blue Chairs" (VC 73.4) and "Blue Postman" (VC 75.3). The hue also resonates with other sociopolitical and identitarian valences, occupying a central role in the unusually frank love poem for Alice Methfessel, "Breakfast Song," where the beloved's eyes are "awfully blue" (*PPL* 257); the violent imperialism of "Brazil, January 1, 1502," with the abundant "blue, blue-green, and olive" (*PPL* 72) leaves that anticipate the sexual rapacity of the invading Christians;

Pages six and seven of the Sapolio soap advertising leaflet. (VC121.19; Courtesy of Vassar College)

and the antiwar politics of "Roosters," with its militaristic "gun-metal blue" (*PPL* 27). The color is perhaps nowhere more suggestive in these drafts than when viewed alongside a letter Bishop wrote to Moore during a visit to Cape Cod: "A great many Portuguese Negroes live near me and come around in very high-set, polished Fords selling blueberries and blackberries that go beautifully with their black faces and blue denim clothes" (*OA* 44). Given the black and blue color scheme operative in this image of the "Portuguese Negroes"—and given the fact that a song like Louis Armstrong's 1929 "What Did I Do To Be So Black and Blue" used the melancholy of the blues to signify upon bruising—blue in the Bishopian imaginary evokes not only the blues, with their "blue notes," but also the brutal oppression the musical genre encodes. It is also worth thinking how this imaginative blue deployed elsewhere in Bishop's work might carry the fetishistic charge from this passage, serving to code ostensibly neutral spaces black.

With a throwaway rendering of a black community and their labor in an unexpected space, this letter is important in providing a powerful reminder why a

Papa has overturned his ink,
And soiled his face and fingers;
A strong perfume of nasty tar
Around poor Johnie lingers.

Page eight of the Sapolio soap advertising leaflet. (VC121.19; Courtesy of Vassar College)

Global South Atlantic, drawing on Joseph Slaughter's resonant evocation of the term, operative from Key West, plays an outsize role in dissolving the nation's borders and boundaries for Bishop when she took up residence there in 1936 with Louise Crane. Closer to Havana than Miami, the southernmost point of the United States enabled her to grapple with the intersections of race, history, gender, language, and nation over the next decade. The island, a diverse mixture of Bahamians,

Cubans, Southern whites, and African Americans, provided Bishop's entrée into a polyglot, multicultural space that had its sequel in the almost two decades she spent in Brazil. Moving from a Northern clime, where Bishop identified as "New-Englander-herring-choker-bluenoser" (*WIA* 317), to a tropical space of profusion and decay in "Seascape" (*PPL* 31) and "Florida" (*PPL* 24), respectively, required her to face the "black help" described in "Cootchie" and "Faustina, or Rock Roses," the Afro-Cuban residents of the segregated district of the island in "Jerónimo's House" (*PPL* 26), and the silenced indigenous sediment of "the murdered Indian princess" that gives lie to Florida's designation as "the state with the prettiest name" (*PPL* 24). In all of these poems, Bishop "read the landscape as a possible mirror of culture" ("Becoming a Poet" 113).

Key West—as important as it may be to any complete understanding of Bishop's poetry that critics from Thomas Travisano to Hicok have demonstrated—does not play a singular role, instead belonging to a network of spaces across North and South that informed a "comprehensive island hemisphere" that Wallace Stevens first imagined in his 1922 mock-epic "The Comedian as the Letter C." Bishop took the journey neither Stevens nor the poem's Crispin could, exploring Haiti and Aruba during extended hiatuses from Florida. Likewise, during her time in Brazil, she ventured to Puerto Rico and the Galapagos Islands. It is little wonder that Bishop imagined a valedictory poem, "Goodbye to Brazil" that would be modeled on not only Auden's "Ischia" but also Stevens's "Farewell to Florida" (*WIA* 660), revealing the region's persistence in her imaginary. Nor should it surprise that she would dream of Tierra del Fuego (*OA* 386), the continent's own Key West, betraying her continued hankering for continental extremities. Even the two hemispheres were hardly discrete in her geography: Bishop experienced "total recall" about Nova Scotia while in Brazil (*OA* 249). The Portuguese Negroes of Cape Cod belong to this expansive configuration of the hemisphere, where the Lusophone Brazil—to borrow Bishop's section titles from 1965's *Questions of Travel*—was always here, never elsewhere.

At a more basic level, the passage reflects Bishop's interest in the African dimensions of Brazil. This curiosity is evident throughout the letters, but a more suggestive engagement exists in the archive. There is the constant referral to Bahia, the Afro-Brazilians, and, perhaps most of all, the astonishing "Trip to the Mines" (VC 67.20). In two drafts for an unfinished and undated poem, Bishop offers a searing exploration of slavery in Brazil, registering the deep loss of the Middle Passage "from Angola" (VC 67.20, pp. 1, 2), the brutalization slaves faced in the New World at the hands of the Portuguese, and the cost of the imperial wealth that is purchased through their labor: "the church the slaves built for themselves is still the finest" (VC 67.20.2), "the diamonds [that] are dull and blue / like small blue old blue eyes" (VC 67.20.2), and the "three sedan chairs" (VC 67.20, p. 2) all having led, in some measure, to their disappearance. Against the barbarism of the transatlantic slave trade, Bishop launches a fevered search for the absent bodies, hazarding an attempt at historical recovery by asking at the outset of the poem, "Where could they hide so many graves?" The question already implies that they could not, but its repetition—both in the following lines ("where can their graves be / where can their graves be") and at the poem's terminus ("But where are the two million slaves?") from the second draft—reveals the full extent of the pressure that their absence produces on the speaker. Searching "among the charging rocks" (VC 67.20, p. 2), the "fine green grass [that] / marks . . . the slave encampments" (VC 67.20, p. 2), "the native grasses" (VC 67.20, p. 1), Bishop almost resembles her most famous animal familiar, "The Sandpiper," "looking for something, something, something" (*PPL* 126). In the frantic attempt to reach these murdered black bodies displaced by the "black and broken waves," the "fine green grass," "the old, old blue eyes," she is indeed "obsessed" (*PPL* 125). The color spectrum exploited so effectively throughout her career to map the world—from early poems like "Florida" and "The Map" (*PPL* 3) to the later "Brazil, January 1, 1502" (*PPL* 72)—eventually leads her astray into racist description: "a glinting nigger-brown" preserved across two drafts.

The use of "nigger" and "nigger-brown" takes us out of the historical frame into Bishop's present. The slur recalls not only contemporary American racial discourse at the height of the civil rights movement but also, in its use as a modifier of brown, discourse tied to an early twentieth-century history of American advertising that relied on such depictions, much like the Sapolio advertising leaflet belongs to the visual iconography of minstrelsy. As Hicok has explored at length, Bishop deployed "nigger" in connection with Brazil—namely, her translation of *The Diary of Helena Morley* (1957)—and its minstrel cousin, "pickaniny." In the latter, as well as a racially loaded mistranslation from Life World Library's *Brazil* (1962), where *minha negrinha* (my little nigger) was placed in favor of *minha neguinha* (my little sweetie),[7] we see Bishop's willingness to traffic in the same racialized language deployed here.

The abhorrent rhetoric joins other anachronisms in the poem—"the native grasses . . . fresh as Ireland" and the "plane" the observer sits in—that may indicate the enslaved Angola stands in for the contemporary moment, where the Angolan War of Independence unfolded from 1961-74 within a broader wave of decolonization in Africa. They may also reflect Bishop's growing awareness of political instability through the presidencies of Getúlio Vargas, Juscelino Kubitschek, Jânio Quadros, and João Goulart. Their coups were all orchestrated by Macedo Soares and Bishop intimate, the charismatic politician Carlos Lacerda, whom Skidmore called "the destroyer of presidents" (qtd. in Hicok, *Elizabeth Bishop's Brazil* 98).[8] During this period, she became more vocal in her conversations with Lowell and in her criticisms of North American coverage and more outward facing in her own journalism. Aside from signifying the immediacy of the present, the images might have a more specific valence. The plane where the Bishop observer imagines watching this unfold belongs to what Marit J. MacArthur has called "the poetics of passenger flight" ("One World?" 264). Such poetry, according to MacArthur, is "exceptional in illuminating the perceptual, affective, and ethical confusions of the global perspective" (266). What MacArthur says about 1972's "Night City" (*PPL* 156) from *Geography III* (1976)—namely, that the poem's ethical confusions reside in its "haunting by aerial bombing and [the flight's] possible complicity in the poverty and destruction it allows us to fly over" (270)—has equal relevance to a poem where "the foreign traveler is shocked / straining earnest" (VC 67.20, p. 1).

The perspective provided by the "plane" might help widen the context, imagining another link to the Latin American South specifically. In a letter lamenting Macedo Soares's nephew Flavia's marriage of convenience, Bishop mentions reading an airline hijacking organized by five Brazilians in *The New York Times* (*WIA* 666), where a flight to Rio from Montevideo, Uruguay—with forced stops in Buenos Aires, Argentina, and Antofagasta, Chile—eventually landed in Cuba.[9] Already the presence of the plane speaks to a not only modern but global context, but what the backdrop of this news report—with its account of "well-dressed hijackers"— helps clarify is that the curious international tourist conscripted into Bishop's usual pose of the voyeur might also double in for the wealthy alienated native of the Southern Hemisphere seeking some understanding of his or her past. "A Trip to the Mines" belongs to a series of unpublished poems about Brazil—drafts such as "Suicide of a Moderate Dictator," "Brasil 1959," "Capricorn," "A Baby Found in the Garbage"—with unusually explicit foundations in social and historical reality, representing the culmination of the trend with its investment in enslavement and colonialism.

By the time Bishop met with Kathleen Cleaver in San Francisco at the home of a Black Panther Party supporter, she had grappled with the transatlantic slave trade, the aesthetic dimensions of black bodies, the agency of black female voices, and the character of the blues, only to have her own ideas about race and class—particularly in the context of the Brazil she had just left—further tested by the black radical. In February 1969, Bishop spoke with Cleaver for a lengthy interview (VC 53.12) that Elizabeth Hardwick at *The New York Review of Books* expressed interest in publishing for the magazine. This was an especially fractious time for the Black Panther Party: throughout 1969, the organization saw internal dissension, fomented by J. Edgar Hoover's increasing use of the Counter Intelligence Program, COINTELPRO, that led to sometimes violent purges; periodic skirmishes with a rival group, the Black nationalist U.S. Organization; shoot-outs with police in Chicago and

Los Angeles; the imprisonment of Bobby Seale; and the state-sanctioned execution of Fred Hampton in Chicago at the hands of the city's police department. A year before, a shoot-out between Panthers and police in Oakland—prompted by the assassination of Martin Luther King Jr.—left seventeen-year-old Bobby Sutton dead and Eldridge Cleaver wounded and a fugitive spending time in Cuba and Algeria. Pregnant and soon to join him in Algeria, Kathleen was attempting to raise money for the cause.

Appended to the end of the interview, a note indicates that Cumming, who arranged the meeting, has enclosed a typescript copy of the interview's transcription from an audio recording (Cleaver stipulated that she be given a copy); offers details on publication plans; and expresses a desire on Bishop's part to meet with Cleaver again before she and Cumming depart for Ouro Prêto. Over the course of a document that amounts to twenty-two typescript pages, Bishop asks extensive and searching questions about Cleaver's upbringing, education, ideological commitments, and political aspirations. Cumming interjects several questions of her own—most significantly about the role sympathetic whites can play in the movement—a subject Bishop also seems interested in, although not nearly to the same degree as her partner. The transcript also indicates the presence of two party members who routinely interject jeers at Bishop's and Cumming's remarks and affirmations ("Right on!") in response to several of Cleaver's most acidulous responses.

The gloss that the oral history provides—that Bishop was bemused by Cleaver, that Bishop gained Cleaver's confidence, that Cleaver was very defensive (*REB* 251-52)—do not provide what seems to be a particularly accurate nor meaningful account of the text. A letter to Lowell called the meeting a "weird and wild experience" that left a significant enough impression on both women to warrant plans for another interview (*WIA* 654).[10] We can see that weirdness and wildness in the tenser moments; the cordiality emerges in the fact that the conversation lasted as long as it did.

The first challenge to Bishop's worldview occurs when she suggested racism was not a problem in Brazil, influenced by Freyre's influential "racial democracy" argument. Cleaver bristled against the idea of giving the South American nation any special consideration in comparison to its northern neighbor, however, taking a hard line against its supposed racial tolerance:

> KC: Brazil is an equally racist country as the United States. It's just a different kind of racism.
> EB: But at present the situation there is quite different from here.
> KC: That's what white people say. Black people don't say that. They've had Black people rioting in Brazil. You know, it just so happens that all the

wealth of Brazil is in the hands of white people, and the vast majority of the poor people, the poorest of the poor in Brazil, are black, you know. (12)

When Bishop objected with a biological understanding of race, Cleaver explained its social reality:

EB: No, the poor are mixed – black and white.
KC: No. They're not white.
EB: The poor are mixed.
KC: Of course they're mixed. I'm mixed. He's mixed, you see, but we're Black, you see, so it's a question of whether—
EB: But they don't use that expression there. (12)

After discussing the beauty of the Portuguese language, the history of colonialism and slavery in Brazil, and Portugal's war in Angola, Cleaver returns to finish her point on the meaning of blackness in Brazil:

KC: It [slavery] was less tight. Less tight because of the views of the Catholic Church, that's all. I mean, the details were different; the phenomenon was the same. The phenomenon was racism. And you ask any Black Portuguese if he is aware of discrimination against Blacks and he will tell you "If you're dark." You see, the light black people there, they don't get discriminated against, but the dark black people do, so – so what?
EB: Well, –
KC: So they call you different names. That's like Louisiana. In Louisiana they have five – they have four categories of non-white people. In Alabama they have one. That doesn't mean there's less racism in Louisiana than there is in Alabama. It just means a different variety. (13)

Even as Cleaver insists on the fundamental sameness of anti-black racism across the world, she is thinking in terms of the African diaspora—Brazil, Angola, and the American South—in a way that bears comparison with the Global South Atlantic in Bishop's imaginary that dissolves borders and boundaries. Class and race emerge as another point of contention when Bishop insists that the "problems in Brazil are more economic than racist." Cleaver disagrees forcefully ("Yeah, that's what all racist countries will say"), explaining how anti-black racism—rather than class conditions—have made black people poor (14). There is an eerie echo of contemporary debates among progressives about where the emphasis should reside in discussions of social justice when Cleaver observes, "Communism doesn't even solve the problems of racism. Understand there is economic exploitation and there is a color factor involved." Largely silent, Bishop is forced to confront more complex ideas of hegemony here.

When Cumming describes visiting the all-black neighborhood of Hunter's Point in San Francisco with Bishop, the limits of both race and class in identifying with a place emerge to the fore. Cumming was clearly confused, for example, when the municipal staff person she spoke to told her how much she loved Hunter's Point, even though the health center and mental health clinic had just closed. "How would you deal with a person like that?" Cumming asks incredulously. Cleaver tries to explain why everyone from Hunter's Point loves their neighborhood: "It's their home – their territory, you see. They feel secure. Ain't nobody live there but Black people." Cumming tells Cleaver she got the impression from the conversation that "there was no room for improvement." Cleaver tells her she has the wrong idea:

> That's not what she meant. I love the Fillmore; that doesn't mean I like the way it looks. It has something about it. You like whatever you're accustomed to to a certain extent. That doesn't mean you don't want to improve it, you know. . . . I mean, you love your children whether they're sick or well, you know what I mean? Alive or dead, they love their children. That doesn't mean their children can't stand any additional benefits. (16)

What Cleaver articulates here is an attachment to a space that supersedes its material conditions—namely, the racial composition of the space and a broader sense of home in which that character forms a part. Here, Bishop finally speaks, repeating her earlier objection that the neighborhood was not "entirely black." Cleaver corrects her, but Bishop insists, telling her they saw some white children in the two schools they visited. "Well, they always call it a black ghetto," Cleaver replies. At this point, one of Cleaver's assistants makes Cleaver's point crystal clear: "There are maybe forty white kids in Marin City, but ten million niggers, you know."[11] Cleaver expresses surprise: "They got white people in Marin City? It's a black neighborhood, that's all. Like this is a all white neighborhood" (17). When Bishop attempts to transpose her understanding of race in Brazil to an American context—demonstrating again her transnational thinking, regardless of its merit— Cleaver posits more useful albeit depressing affinities between black neighborhoods in San Francisco, Brazil, and the southern United States. For Cleaver, spaces are racialized not by their literal composition but by a broader social construction. Whatever the number of white children there are in Hunter's Point or Marin City, "they always call it a black ghetto."

If Cleaver's discussion of the slave trade in Brazil leads her to think about contemporary politics in Angola and the urban planning of the Bay Area, it also puts Bishop in mind of another effaced history, moving backward as Cleaver moves forward. To even the radical with revolutionary ambitions, "the slave Republic of Palmares," about which Bishop informed Cleaver, seemed fanciful: "Is that a myth or a fairytale? Is that the truth?" Bishop assures her it existed but that "not many people know about it" (22). Bishop tells Cleaver that "runaway slaves in the North of Brazil" set up a "separate republic," which lasted more than sixty years "against the combined forces of Portugal and Holland" (22). Cleaver is impressed: "That's out of sight," she says. Bishop explains how the republic had "its own government and architecture and social system" and that many of these slaves had been African kings themselves: "They had over 100,000 members—several towns and villages within the quilombo." In response to Cleaver's question about what languages they spoke, Bishop notes that it may have been a combination of Portuguese and African languages. "That's beautiful," Cleaver says.

Bishop was trying to assemble this material for a new book entitled *Black Beans and Diamonds*—a collection of essays, photographs, and poems—that the Rockefeller Foundation agreed to fund for $12,000 from 1966-68. Despite Bishop's wish to avoid being regarded as "some sort of authority on Brazil for the rest of my life" (*WIA* 660), the book had a long gestation. As Jay Prosser has helpfully observed, she drew on a title originally proposed for "The Diary of Helena Morley" and announced plans for such a book in 1960, 1956, and even as early as 1946, before even traveling to Brazil (*Pr* 144). With its shared imagery and subject matter, "A Trip to the Mines" likely belonged to *Black Beans and Diamonds*, and more specifically, to this context of Palmares. By using the term *quilimbo*, which refers to slave communities in Brazil generally, particularly those in the South, Bishop refers to entire pockets of slave resistance that existed throughout the Americas.[12]

One could argue that, in remaining unpublished, these late-breaking investments in the social reality of Brazil remain negligible. It has long been a critical commonplace that Bishop could not write a political poem. Even Prosser, who expends so much valuable work contextualizing *Black Beans and Diamonds* within Bishop's oeuvre, acidly remarks, "'A Trip to the Mines—Brasil' searches out for the graves of slaves now hidden in the obsolete gold mines they worked. Its several unresolved drafts don't unearth them" (156). Bishop's investments in race are no less vulnerable to such reasonable objections. But its sheer diffusion across her archive gives lie to any sense of the subject playing an abortive role in her poetics. The long penumbra that extends from her early interest in blues to her twilit encounter with the Black Panther Kathleen Cleaver should force us to rethink not only poems expressly about race but also her own racial identity.

NOTES

1. See Delpar.
2. Such a group included such figures as Nancy Cunard, Pannonica de Koenigswarter, and Charlotte Osgood Mason; see Kaplan.
3. See Filene.
4. See Pecknold; Hughes.
5. For further discussion of Bishop's racial attitudes in Brazil, see "Bishop's Brazilian Translations," in Hicok, *Elizabeth Bishop's Brazil* 64-72.
6. In the most vivid example, Bishop marveled over an advertisement that depicted a wealthy white mistress kissing her black cook, taking such material seriously for understanding the country's underlying racial reality. See Bishop, "On the Railroad."
7. See "Bishop's Brazilian Translations" in Hicok, *Elizabeth Bishop's Brazil* 68–72 for a complex discussion of Bishop's engagement with racial discourse.
8. See "Bishop's Brazilian Politics" in Hicok, *Elizabeth Bishop's Brazil* for a fuller discussion of Bishop's political entanglements.
9. See "Brazilian Airliner."
10. According to an email with the author, Kathleen Cleaver remembers the exchange as cordial.
11. This individual is referred to only as "BD" in the transcript but is clearly one of Kathleen Cleaver's retinue.
12. For more background on the term, see D. Davis 114.

CHAPTER EIGHT

"I MISS ALL THAT BRIGHT, DETAILED FLATNESS"

Elizabeth Bishop in Brevard

Charla Allyn Hughes

Asheville no longer has a low season. Though its streets and those of several nearby towns currently buzz year-round with bachelor/ette parties waving selfie sticks and assorted throngs of tourists seeking souvenirs and culinary delights, the mountains of western North Carolina have been a popular vacation destination for the better part of the past two centuries. One small town about thirty miles southwest of Asheville, Brevard, is particularly distinctive for its cultural heritage and its accessibility to the Pisgah National Forest, the Blue Ridge Mountains, and the many waterfalls therein. Whereas Asheville's history of attracting writers and artists is well known (among others, F. Scott and Zelda Fitzgerald, Thomas Wolfe, and O. Henry all spent time there), nearby Brevard's is significantly less publicized. In the fall of 1940 and again in 1941, Elizabeth Bishop stopped over in this remote mountain town on her way back to New York City from Key West.

A poet renowned for her depiction of place, Bishop vividly describes the surrounding landscape and its wildlife and also offers a few portraits of local characters in her travel journal and her letters from Brevard. Despite the significant impact of these stopovers on her work, Bishop criticism has very little to say on this segment of Bishop's travels. The Brevard entries in her 1938-42 travel journal and Bishop's contemporaneous correspondence with Vassar classmate Frani Blough Muser and mentor Marianne Moore highlight unsettled moments in which the poet was geographically between her North and South; moreover, these entries and letters speak to Bishop's interest in travel and in-betweens, of here-and-elsewheres.

Bishop's attention to wildlife and geography—and her longings for the landscapes of other places, particularly for Key West's coastal beauty—offer a glimpse into the poet's workshop and, more broadly, suggest a layering of place that transformed the mid-century American poetic landscape. Bishop's landscapes, as depicted in the Brevard journal entries and letters as well as in the poems influenced by this stopover, suggest both a processing of the past—especially of her childhood, shame, poverty, and trauma—and a conception of geography as simultaneously specific and composite, interwoven with multiple memories and times.

Bishop's prose considerations of the mountainous landscape in and around Brevard, a landscape that appears to her at first oppressive but later beautiful, highlight a heightened sensitivity to verticality, flatness, and surface that is also present in her poems, especially in the Florida and New York poems she was working on during this period and shortly after. The first journal entry from her first stay, dated August 7 and August 10, 1940, is about two pages long with several crossed-out words and other assorted marks of self-editing. Bishop concludes the entry with humor and optimism, "I miss all that bright, detailed flatness of K.W.—both the natural & the artificial scenery—all this Nature feels like a big wet sofa-pillow right on the face. I hate masses of things you can't see the shape of, no familiarity anywhere. But when the sun comes out things will be better, I hope" (VC 77.3). With its short, flat line, the underscored "flatness" quite literally emphasizes the contrast between the landscape she just left in Florida and the one she is slowly, albeit seemingly begrudgingly, getting to know. The remote, undeveloped "Nature" seems suffocating and disorienting in its unknown quality, as clouds and fog obscure a clear vista. This initial reaction to the mountain landscape (capital *N* "Nature," seemingly a location of its own) emphasizes Bishop's longing not just for the coast but for a landscape that is "natural *& artificial*"—for a place that is natural and wild yet at the same time distinguishable, mappable. This entry features several juxtapositions, both stated and implied—bright/dark, natural/artificial, flat/mountainous, familiar/unknown—that also appear in *North & South* (1946) and in even later collections. Alongside these recurring juxtapositions, I use these entries from the 1938-42 travel journal and Bishop's letters as intimate renderings of experience and place that are in dialogue with her poetry, representing place and time as qualities both lyrically hyper-specific and multiple, layered in memory.

While the blending effects of memory create their own here-and-elsewheres, Brevard itself is a place of in-betweens, positioned both geographically and culturally between Bishop's North and South. Bishop's explorations of this remote in-between locale, one that is new to her, speak to artistic displacement and alienation. In this change of place, this retreat and isolation, she finds a sense of homesickness for other places as well as the creative possibilities offered by being removed from the familiar. Ernest Hemingway describes this phenomenon in *A Moveable Feast* (1964) when he details the experience of writing about Michigan in Paris: this process of "transplanting [him]self" to find that "in one place [one] could write about it better than in another"—a process he claims "could be as necessary with people as with other sorts of growing things" (17). Bishop shares a similar insight on travel and the creative process in a 1952 letter to Kit and Ilse Barker[1]: "It is funny to come to Brazil to experience total recall about Nova Scotia—geography must be more mysterious than we realize, even" (*OA* 249). Exploring a mysterious geography and removed from New York and Key West—away from her North and South and discovering an elsewhere—Bishop pushed herself to write and revise while in North Carolina. As Bishop confessed to Muser and Moore, she was afraid to return north without work to show for her time away. Brevard seems, then, a place of "transplanting" herself for work as well as a place of geographic convenience and refuge.

One in a series of travel notebooks and datebooks in the Vassar Archives, Bishop's 1938-42 notebook contains entries from both of her stopovers in Brevard as well as notes of travel between New York, Key West, Mexico, and Cuba. This journal is a small—appropriately, travel-sized—beige notebook with a pink binding. The thin pages today exhibit waves of mild water damage, particularly in the copper-colored residues emanating from the rusted staples, a lingering testament to the humidity of the places the journal traveled. These lined pages seem ruled more for ledger-keeping than for composition, and Bishop uses the columns on the far left almost exclusively for dates, in addition to the occasional note or sketch. The verso of the marbled flyleaf includes the dates "March 6, 1938-Sept. 25th, 1942," and the facing recto of the first page jumps right into a story of Key West, that of a twelve-year-old girl taken from a Jacksonville orphanage to spend the summer with a wealthy family on the island. Both the flyleaf and the first page feature an embossed stamp of an owl perched on a leaping rabbit, a playful image that reminds the reader of Bishop's youth at the time—she would have been twenty-seven when she began writing in this notebook—and one that is suggestive of the attention to movement and wildlife that will follow in the journal's pages.

Although she offers no explanation for the image in this travel journal, Bishop would describe its history nearly a decade later in correspondence with Katharine White of *The New Yorker*. The conversation begins in a November 6, 1950, letter, in which Bishop writes, "Here is an old old dream that doesn't seem to want to grow any longer," indicating her submission of "The Owl's Journey" (*EBNY* 52). In a November 14 letter updating Bishop on decisions regarding this poem and several others, White searches for more details on the image: "Is there a picture, say, from Audubon, or from a nursery book, or from an old chromo, or even from Blake, that

The owl and rabbit embossed stamp (in reverse) from the verso of the marbled flyleaf at the front of a travel journal. Bishop notes the date range for the travel journal here: March 6, 1938-Sept. 25, 1942. (VC 77.3; Courtesy of Vassar College)

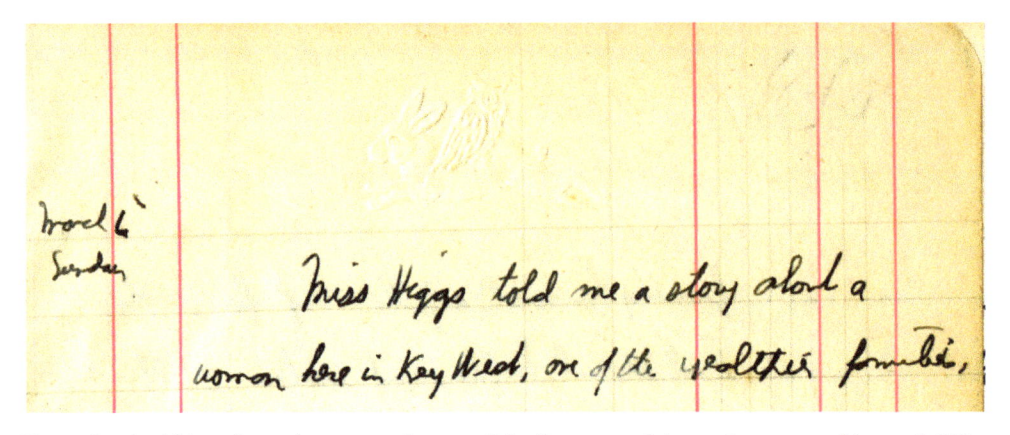

The owl and rabbit embossed stamp at the top of the first page of the 1938-1942 travel journal. (VC 77.3; Courtesy of Vassar College)

was the basis of your dream? If there was, it might be interesting and clarifying to put it in the subtitle. However, it may be purely a dream" (53). Unable to identify a source for the image herself, White muses, "Perhaps this is just something on the fringe of everybody's subconscious and not in an actual picture at all" (53). Whether from a historical, literary, or subconscious source, White's considerations suggest the roots of the dream in shared nostalgia for a real or imagined past.

Bishop's response on November 16, however, offers a specific history. Though she rejects Blake and Audubon as her source, she writes that the image "might have been in a nursery book" (54). Bishop reports that she described the image to an artist friend in college (Margaret Miller), who was unable to produce a satisfactory rendition of it until after graduation, when Miller enrolled in an illuminated manuscript class at New York University. Bishop's account reveals an even older origin story for the owl and rabbit picture than White imagined: "Well, I've forgotten exactly where & how she found it—I think in the British Museum, but I'm not sure, but she'd know—she came across, in the margin of a very early English manuscript—I think 12th century, but again I'm not sure—the exact picture I had had in mind all those years, and she was able to get me a tracing of it" (55). The many pauses and interruptions here highlight the imperfect, uncertain nature of human memory. From Miller's historical find, whatever the details of that find may be, Bishop made the image a part of her life that she could easily reproduce. She writes, "I was so pleased and mystified I decided to use it as a kind of seal, and I even had one of those gadgets made, at great expense, that make an impression in the paper. It's in storage now, or I'd give you a sample" (55). Although this story indicates a clear pleasure in finally finding an accurate rendering of Bishop's "old old dream," the ongoing reproduction of the image suggests the persistence of youthful memories, both good and bad, in its use.

The seal in the journal is the only known evidence of this expensive "gadget." In addition to the seal, Bishop used the image in a pen-and-ink drawing and in the version of "The Owl's Journey" Alice Quinn includes in *Edgar Allan Poe & the Juke-Box* (2006), the third of three drafts dated 1949-50. An echo of the western North Carolina mountain landscape—a place Bishop often observes in moonlight, with its many shades of green and blue—lingers in the first lines of the poem:

> Somewhere the owl rode on the rabbit's back
> down a long slope, over the long, dried grasses,
> through a half-moonlight igniting everything
> with specks of faintest green & blue. (91)

A few lines later in the poem, Bishop describes the owl's journey, "The adventure's miniature and ancient: / collaboration thought up by a child" (91). Here, Bishop also describes the small image of her drawing and her gadget's embossing. The impressions in the 1938-42 journal are prominent on the flyleaf and the first page, but it is impossible to tell if they were made before, during, or after the journal's pages were filled. The presence of these impressions, however, does emphasize the persistence—and processing—of memory and childhood in these pages.

Though the Brevard entries, which start around page 26 of the notebook, contain several explorations of landscape and catalogues of wildlife observed, they begin with a focus on people. The first entry from Brevard lists two dates: "August 7th, 1940," on the first line of the page and "August 10th" on the following line. Bishop rarely includes multiple dates for a single entry and even more rarely includes the year, so this conspicuously placed date suggests an effort at memorializing. Occasionally in this journal, she commemorates her travels or Louise Crane's with a date and a place or other brief note, but the record of this arrival is unique. Bishop begins the entry with a brief note of her and Nora Hasecher's arrival in Brevard and then abruptly states she received a telegram on the seventh informing her of Aunt Maude's death (VC 77.3). Thus, with the news of her Aunt Maude's death, Bishop inscribes the first four days of her time in Brevard with sadness and loss, amplifying a sense of displacement and unease. In letters to her psychoanalyst Ruth Foster, Bishop made clear that the formative years spent with her Aunt Maude and Uncle George Shepherdson were terribly unhappy ones, the result of sexual abuse by her Uncle George, who also physically abused her Aunt Maude. Later entries in the journal featuring chronicles of Appalachian poverty, particularly her fascination with a local woman who lived an isolated life in a cabin in the woods, suggest preoccupations here that Bishop would explore not only in the 1947 letters to Foster but also in her prose and poetry.

Mention of Aunt Maude signals the poet's reflections on her family and her childhood that are a significant part of the Brevard journals. Aside from the mention of her late aunt, these reflections do not specifically address family members but are rather intertwined with the expressions of fascination and shame in her observations of Appalachian poverty. This attraction to and embarrassment regarding poverty points to unresolved childhood struggles that Bishop seems unable to ignore during this stopover. Although Bishop offers only a brief statement about her aunt's death in this first entry, her letters to Foster provide crucial insight into how shame and poverty become inextricably linked in Bishop's life and work. As she confessed to Foster in a February 1947 letter, "It is true that for years I was intensely ashamed of Aunt Maud, all that part of my life. I concealed it pretty much from everyone" (VC 118.33).[2] This "part of [her] life" was as a teenager, when she would hide details of her background from her more affluent friends. Bishop recounts one day when a friend arrived at her aunt's unannounced: "I was so startled and suddenly so painfully aware of the poverty of the place that I lost my head completely and burst into tears and am not sure what I did after that" (VC 118.33). She concludes the letter by acknowledging that she is no longer "quite as troubled by dirt and disorder as [she] was" (VC 118.33). Although by 1947 Bishop's relationship to poverty seems to have changed, it appears as an undercurrent still both immensely absorbing and troubling in these 1940 entries.

Beyond these first lines, Bishop does not offer any other reflection on Maude's death, nor does she mention Nora much in these entries. Instead, in the second paragraph of this first entry, Bishop's focus turns abruptly to her new environment. She makes note of the accommodations—a cabin shared with Charlotte and Charles "Red" Russell, "perched up on the side of a mountain"—that features a cool spring where they store food and that attracts a friendly pink salamander (VC 77.3). In the following paragraph (and in the most frequently referenced line from these entries), Bishop describes herself as "not much of a Thoreau" and goes on to write that "all this <u>leafiness</u> is very depressing particularly in foggy weather. I've never lived in the mts. [mountains] before. They are all around us, big blue shapes, coming & going through the mist—like recurring thoughts—rather depressing. I miss all that bright, detailed <u>flatness</u> of K.W.'" (VC 77.3). Between Bishop's scrawling cursive and scribbled-out lines, some words are difficult to read in this entry. Highlighting the verticality of the mountainous landscape in contrast to the flatness of Key West, Bonnie Costello records "loftiness" in the place of "leafiness" (*Elizabeth Bishop* 89). While either term seems fitting here, Bishop uses "leafiness" in her letter to Marianne Moore on September 11, 1940, when she implores her mentor to visit her in Key West along with the assessment that she "prefer[s] the Florida landscape—all this dampness and leafiness is a little oppressive" (*OA* 95). In this entry and correspondence, Bishop longs for the flat coastal landscape, finding the foggy forest scenery not only obscuring but also uniform and upsetting. Like the fear of repetition in her work expressed to Foster, the sense of recurrence here is (doubly) "depressing."

Although she longs for the flat Florida landscape, earlier works from Florida also address a state of suspension and dilapidation similar to that which she initially found so troubling in Brevard; these states, however, also hold an immense appeal for Bishop, as is evident in her paintings. Bishop's 1937 painting of Charlotte Russell—the Charlotte with whom she "perched up on the side of a mountain" and explored the surrounding western North Carolina landscape—is one of the few known watercolors to represent a human subject.

Floating on an invisible chair, "Sha-Sha" occupies the foreground in a blue, white, and yellow striped shirt paired with what appear to be blue jeans (but in their vagueness may be a blue skirt). With a neutral expression and blank eyes that recall the portraits of Amedeo Modigliani, Charlotte's face is in the center of the painting with green molding running behind her at nose level, a line that divides the wall between wainscot paneling behind Charlotte's body and a grey, green, and white wall with three paintings above her head. The solid wall above the molding seems more composed and yet lacking in detail compared to the worn, mildew-etched wood paneling in the lower third of the canvas. The three paintings at the top vertically segment the canvas into thirds, with Charlotte front and center; the title "SHA-SHA" in red and the signature "E.B. 2/25/37 Naples, Fa." a focus of the lower left; and the odd equation "$1 + 4 = 7$" in burgundy in the center right. The text's and Charlotte's isolation and suspension in the composition parallel Bishop's later response to a disorienting landscape, while the constructed background presents a worn and dirty but still oddly comforting home. Completed three years before the stopover in Brevard, this painting, thus, depicts themes consistent with Bishop's meditations on place and people.

Bishop painted this portrait of her friend "Sha-Sha," Charlotte Russell, in Naples, Florida, three years before she first traveled to Brevard with her. Bishop's composition poses many intriguing questions, from the odd equation ("1 + 4 = 7") to the contrast between Charlotte's impressionistic face and the detailed patterns of her shirt and the wood paneling in the background. (Courtesy of Vassar College)

In the second Brevard journal entry, dated August 26, Bishop further investigates her mountainous setting with a critical, painterly eye, finding points—and characters—of intrigue. With the date in the far-left ledger and top left corner, Bishop begins the entry with a mysterious fragment, "—and all that the woods and mountains have taught them is violence and disorder" (VC 77.3). Like a derailed John Muir aphorism, this fragment further emphasizes the writer's feelings of uncertainty about her new surroundings, where she finds chaos and little redemption for the disarray.[3] Bishop offers no commentary on this statement and starts a new paragraph instead. She continues, "Every time I look at the mountains, I think of the expression, 'at the back of my mind.' This sensation they give is so strong that I feel a physical compulsion to turn my back and then with them *there,* to go on looking at the ferns, roots, etc." (VC 77.3). "At the back of my mind" evokes both her anxiety of repetition and a sense of persistent presence. Thus, the "physical compulsion" the mountains create for Bishop is inescapable and alienating (and frustratingly repetitive), but their constant pull also drives her to the earth, an attention to surface quite like that in "Florida," wherein despite the vertical departures with birds and trees, focus again and again returns to the water's surface.

Rather than the sea level of "Florida," however, Bishop's emphasis in the journal is earthy; Brevard's geography invites her to search not only amongst the dirt and ferns but also amidst those parts of her past that are unpleasant—working below the surface to allow some traumas to rest. She digs into the soil as she examines the ferns and roots, not altogether unlike the imaginings of alligators, turtles, and shells just below the surface of the brackish water on which "the state with the prettiest name" floats (*CP* 32). In the journal, Bishop again transitions quickly, quoting the couplet at the end of W. B. Yeats's "The Circus Animals Desertion," collected in *Last Poems (1938-1939)*. With only quotation marks to set apart these two lines from the other paragraphs, she writes, "I must lie down where all the ladders start / In the foul rag-&-bone shop of the heart" (VC 77.3). Bishop includes these lines but offers more explanation in her 1969 "Efforts of Affection," noting that she admired the poem after reading the copy of *Last Poems* Moore had shared with her in 1940 (*Pr* 134).

Originally titled "Despair," Yeats's poem about the creative process paints this process as both observational and retrospective, ending with a return to heart, body, and earth in these final lines. Along with echoes of death, Yeats also suggests a sense of beginning again, of rebirth that starts within the self and at the ground level; this rebirth serves as a break from the speaker's previous works and from his poetic lineage/tradition, more generally. Paired with Bishop's attentions to visible ferns, roots, and the other living things at the forest floor in the previous paragraph, these lines are one of the first indications of Bishop's commitment to written production—including her observations for new material and perspectives—while in Brevard. Thus, as she considers what lies on and beneath the forest floor, perhaps she is also seeking inspiration for new poems and reflecting upon her past, including bodies of existing work, such as "Florida" with its similar perspective shifts, printed in the *Partisan Review* in 1939.

For the remainder of the August 26 entry, with the impression of the mountains' persistent presence around her, Bishop scans the landscape, and her observations suggest a further change of opinion on Brevard. Describing the "tremendous racket" of the crickets at night, she seems frustrated to be kept awake her first nights but ultimately relieved to have adjusted to the ambient noise (VC 77.3). Between her descriptions of the crickets and mention of a performance of Austen's *Pride and Prejudice*, she determines that Brevard is, after all, a "rather nice little mountain town" (VC 77.3). She goes on to admire how "the 2 main streets are so steep that coming up to where they cross under the one stop-light it looks as though it ended in mid-day-blue-air"—a suspended moment made all the more dramatic when she observes "thousands of swallows" "plunging" low over the intersection one evening (VC 77.3). In this new assessment, Bishop again turns to a sense of verticality and depth, as the swallows dip down over the two roads. Whereas she longs for Key West's "flatness" in the first entry, Bishop delights in the elevation's sharpness in this entry, indicating her focus on such contrasts in geography. The swallows in the journal plunge downward like the smaller population of "Thirty or more buzzards [that] are drifting down, down, down, / over something they have spotted in the swamp" in "Florida," suggesting a layering of place as the journal echoes this earlier poem (*CP* 32). While the plunging swallows again draw attention to the ground, this main street scene also appears in a state of suspension, with the roads and single stoplight poised perfectly in-between earth and clear sky. This suspended state speaks to the poet's own state of suspension and even isolation and refuge—in the pause between her North and South.

The following journal entry, from August 27, further reveals Bishop's shifting outlook on Brevard, and in this entry, she also offers more landscape description, including images and details that become fodder for both letters and poems. Picking up with little space after the previous entry, Bishop begins with the beautifully sensory observation, "The air is threaded with waterfalls" (VC 77.3). Like the main streets, stoplight, and swallows of the August 26 entry, this scene seems in a state of suspension that is marked by the mountains' persistent presence, the geographical forms that produce waterfalls and that likewise surround her. Like the mountains, this scene, too, seems to linger at "the back of [the poet's] mind." Indeed, echoes of Brevard persist in "Questions of Travel," composed many years later in Brazil:

There are too many waterfalls here; the crowded streams
hurry too rapidly down to sea,
and the pressure of so many clouds on the mountaintops
makes them spill over the sides in soft slow-motion,
turning to waterfalls under our very eyes. (*CP* 93)

In language that is certainly descriptive of the "Brazil" of Bishop's categorizations, these lines similarly describe an "Elsewhere" as well—a here-and-elsewhere of Brazil and Brevard, a collage of (North and South) American landscapes.

Following the ubiquitous waterfalls, Bishop includes a catalogue of some of the unique wildlife she encounters. Like the entry that precedes it, and in the style of many of her poems, this entry contains a few descriptions linked together without transitions. Besides a fascinating lizard called a skink, Bishop lists common and unusual birds, even ones she did not see herself. As if in a researcher's field journal, this entry notes, "Black & White Warblers, a Black-Hooded Warbler, Whip-por-wills—Red says he saw a Pileated Wood-pecker (the bird with a big red crest) –very rare" (VC 77.3). These lists of creatures seem part of Bishop's process of familiarizing herself with the landscape and of memorializing this stopover and documenting material for future use. After the birds, however, she details an odd occurrence, "At night when we try to read at the table, with a lamp at one end and a lantern at the other, there are so many moths flying and alighting and flying again that the table-top looks the way [an] air-port is supposed to" (VC 77.3). Like the cacophonous sounds of the crickets, this passage demonstrates a challenge in adapting to mountain life. The comparison of the swarming moths to an airport evokes the "artificial landscape" of a more urban area as well as the increasing military presence on the Key West Bishop would have just departed—a comparison that paints Bishop as still more resolutely fond of Florida, even homesick for its constructed landscape.

Whereas the August entries focus primarily on the landscape, the September entries from this first stay in Brevard turn to the people Bishop encounters. Brett Millier describes Bishop's Brevard letters and notebooks as "filled with details of the appalling poverty of the neighbors and their bare-bones resourcefulness in 'making do' with what they had" (*Elizabeth Bishop* 161). Bishop does find the rural poverty "appalling," and yet, she also finds it oddly, immensely captivating. Although Bishop mentions a few families in the August 31 and September entries, one particularly resourceful woman steals the scene.

Breaking from her usual cursive, Bishop sets apart her August 31 profile of "POOR CORDIE HYCE" with clearly printed capital letters in parentheses at the top of a new page, a label perhaps added upon reviewing the journal. In this portrait of "Poor Cordie" (as both Bishop and Cordie herself refer to her), Bishop also conveys her own lifelong consciousness of economy; however, Appalachian poverty, as exemplified by Cordie's dress, home, and resilience, signifies a different vision of poverty than that with which Bishop was familiar. Cordie's Appalachian poverty brings Bishop both discomfort and fascination. She describes Cordie's home as "much more orderly than any other cabin I've been in, & clean, although still pretty dirty" (VC 77.3). Bishop compares Cordie's cabin to other homes, but, as the framing in her sketch demonstrates, the cabin is individual and unique in the mountains. Bishop finds pleasure in the moment of orderliness while in Cordie's home, particularly as she has found so much disarray in the wilderness around her. Seeing Cordie's economical three dresses and the fruits and vegetables she has grown, Bishop determines, "she is very industrious" (VC 77.3).

Bishop's observations reveal a fascination with isolation and self-reliance, themes clear in "Crusoe in England," among other poems. These observations also reflect her interest in Appalachian mountain life, though her comments offer evidence of the poet's privilege and anxiety about poverty. Bishop's realizations about Cordie echo the startling feeling of being "so painfully aware of the poverty of the place" that she experienced at her Aunt Maude's house as a young woman, though this poverty is not her own (VC 118.33).

In the September 1, 1940, entry, after mention of Louise Crane and Muser (both in New York at the time), Cordie becomes the focus once again. Bishop's curious portrait of Cordie and her sketch of the cabin offer rich material for Southern and Appalachian studies. These descriptions and images not only paint Bishop as an outsider in this community but also suggest a voyeuristic—even a post-/colonial—Bishop; she is shocked by Cordie's poverty but fascinated in the ways that Cordie and so many other people she encounters in rural Appalachia make do with what they have.

On one page of the September 1 entry, Bishop lists names she finds interesting, cataloging material for some future use, whether for her art or personal memory. The names include "Walterine" (a moonshiner's daughter) and "Cordie," followed by "old weaving patterns," including "rattlesnake trail," "the wheels of time," "the rising and setting sun," "Bonaparte's march," and "the snail's trail."[4] These "old weaving patterns" all suggest a circuitousness of place and/or time, reflecting the intertwining of Bishop's geographic travels and her temporal reflections (circuitousness is even imbedded within her notes, as "Rattlesnake" and "Snail's Trail" are, in fact, two different names for the same pattern). As such, these "weaving patterns" are quite like the Sir Kenneth Clark epigraph Bishop chooses for "Brazil, January 1, 1502" years later: "embroidered nature . . . tapestried landscape" (*CP* 91).

On the facing page, she includes a sketch of Cordie's cabin nestled in the mountains with details of a sign posted by the cabin and the note "as if the neighbor wrote the sign for her." The copied sign reads:

>
> POSTED
> I HAVE GOT ALL of my ground Dug up.
> AND my POTATOES PLANTED AND PLEASE
> Stay Out FROM PROULING AROUND
> on my LAND.   CORDIE.
>   POSTED
> PLEASE STAY AWAY FROM
> my House PROWLING AROUND
> WHEN I AM GONE.
>   CORDIE.

Of course, before being invited in, Bishop found Cordie's cabin by doing just what these signs caution against—"prowling around" with Charlotte on an old trail, where they spotted Cordie's corn growing alongside it. While the signs ask for curious wanderers to stay away, especially from her freshly planted potatoes, the signs and the sketch below speak to a preference for isolation, implying a differentiation of alone and lonely that speaks to Bishop's questions of space and solitude, as well as her own fascination with and shame regarding poverty.

The sketch of Cordie's cabin in the notebook appears quite similar to a reproduction of one of Bishop's paintings that William Benton titles "Landscape with Gray Hills" (81). In the 1996 edition of *Exchanging Hats*, he details the painting's history: "This landscape and the sketches ["Fountain" and "Clocks and Stoves"] were discovered recently by Loren MacIver. Where and when they were done is unknown" (80). In the 2011 edition, however, he notes the painting is in private hands, the image courtesy of the Alexandre Gallery in New York.[5] In this later edition, Benton writes of Bishop's landscape, "Colorists excel in grays. These hills, each differing in shade as well as texture, set the mood of the scene. Under a dull and perhaps cold spring sky, blue smoke rises from the farm house, absorbed into the dark hills. The bleached yellow of the field—a color suffused with brightness—is made brighter by being dotted with white flowers" (80). As Benton observes, the bright yellow and white ground surrounding the house forms a sharp contrast to everything behind it. Indeed, this brightness seems to import some sense of the scorching, bleaching sun from flatter locales, like the Florida Keys, but the illuminated foreground gives way to a dark, gloomy background. Though Benton mentions the many grays in the composition, I would argue these mountains are not only gray

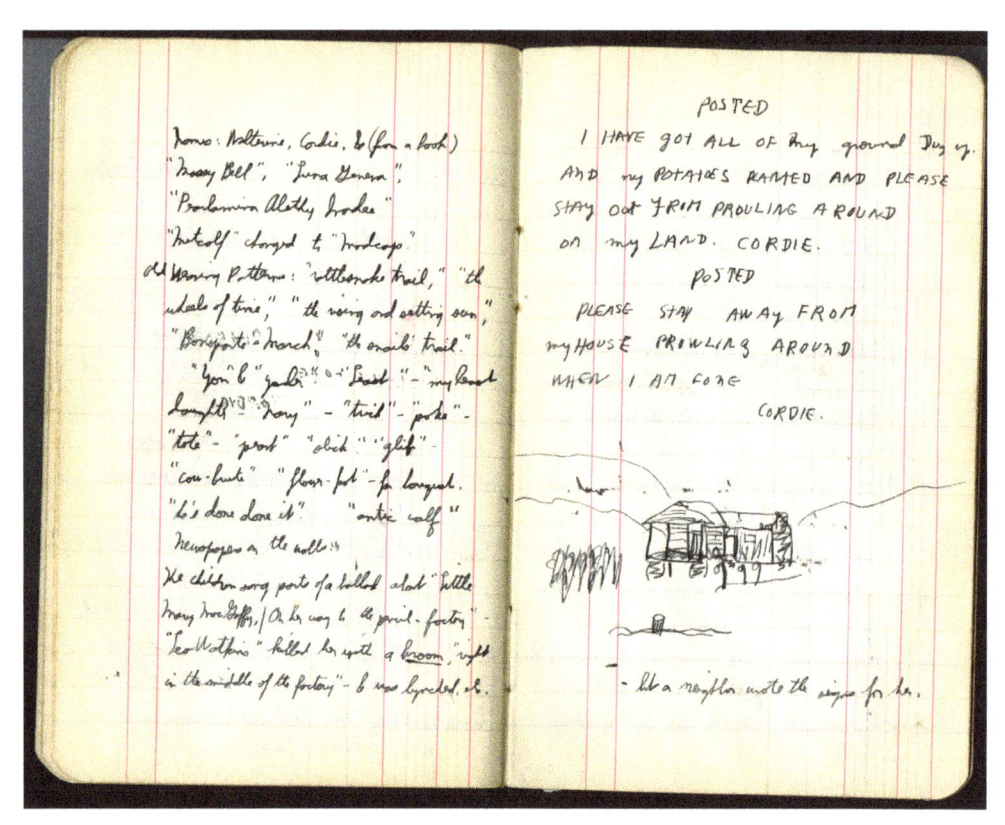

Bishop nestles a sketch of Cordie's cabin amidst a list of names and phrases and the details of a posted sign in the September 1, 1940, entry in her 1938-1942 travel notebook. (VC 77.3; Courtesy of Vassar College)

but also blue—the Blue Ridge Mountains of western North Carolina. The curves of these mountains in the background loosely parallel the curves of the notebook sketch. Like the house in the sketch, too, the house in the painting appears in three distinct segments, the one to the far left significantly larger than the other two and the one to the far right shaded—and perhaps unfinished. The house in the painting has smoke rising from it, however, suggesting a human presence (and even industriousness) inside. Both houses appear secluded in the mountains, suspended on their own from the outside world, capturing in paint and ink the fascination with alienation, poverty, and remote in-betweens, the here-and-elsewheres, that run throughout Bishop's writings.

The notebook sketch and the painting not only address Bishop's consciousness of poverty, but they are also two examples of the many humble and worn-down yet oddly captivating abodes in Bishop's works. Bishop scholars have addressed these recurring images; Jonathan Ellis notes that Bishop's poetry "is full of similar temporary shelters, especially in her writings about Brazil, that seem to be teeming with about-to-collapse structures" (85). These shelters appear in an in-between state of suspension that is unstable yet just barely sufficient for one's needs. Indeed, Cordie's cabin appears similar to that of "Jerónimo's House," a poem categorized as part of a Key West triptych (published in 1941, along with "Seascape" and "Cootchie"). Bishop begins this poem,

> My house, my fairy
>   palace, is
> of perishable
>   clapboards with
> three rooms in all,
>   my gray wasps' nest
> of chewed-up paper
>   glued with spit. (CP 34)

The juxtaposition of high and low, the "palace" and the "perishable," echoes the pairing of Cordie's proud presentation to her guests and Bishop's simultaneous aversion and awe. Later in "Jerónimo's House," the speaker calls this structure a "home" and a "love-nest" but also adds, "At night you'd think / my house abandoned," depicting both a welcoming home and a startlingly isolated, empty shelter (34). This sense of seclusion and precarity further parallels the unique combination of appealing and appalling that Bishop finds in Cordie's situation.

Like the home in "Jerónimo's House," Bishop's written and visual descriptions of Cordie's cabin nestle it in a natural environment that fluctuates between secure and dangerous. Whereas the "fairy palace" is a shelter that may have to be abandoned in a hurricane, Cordie's cabin is its own haven from outside forces (forces that include her curious neighbors). While Bishop expresses her fascination with the retreat the sparse cabin offers Cordie, she also projects her own sense of refuge in the mountains. Millier describes the Russells' homes in Florida and in North Carolina as "refuges for her from time to time" (*Elizabeth Bishop* 113). With this sense of refuge and awareness of poverty, Bishop then seems to recognize some quality of herself in this mountain woman who captivates her attention.

Though there is clearly a gender difference, Cordie also seems an inspiration for the hermit in "Chemin de Fer," which was written around 1945 and published in *The New Yorker* and *North & South* in 1946. While wandering, the speaker in this poem finds the scene "impoverished," a term that suits the cabin in the journal sketch as well. Bishop writes in the second and third stanzas of the poem:

> The scenery was impoverished:
> scrub-pine and oak; beyond
> its mingled gray-green foliage
> I saw the little pond
>
> where the dirty hermit lives,
> like an old tear
> holding onto its injuries
> lucidly year after year. (*CP* 8)

Like Cordie, the hermit in the poem clings to the circumstances of isolation and poverty. Bishop leaves a deliberate vagueness in terms of "scenery"; this description may be of the natural landscape, the artificial one (the hermit's cabin), or some combination of the two.[6] The scenery features details that could be part of a landscape in many parts of the eastern United States: populated by the common oak tree and "gray-green foliage" as well as "scrub-pine," a tree that grows from New York to the Appalachian foothills and was used for railroad ties.

The cry in the final stanza that "Love should be put into action!" has often been read in terms of the stifling societal pressures Bishop faced in expressing—and closeting—same-sex love in the 1940s.[7] These societal pressures seem to contribute to a recurring sense of alienation. James Merrill's reading of this final stanza emphasizes both the social pressure and the subsequent isolation when he notes that, "An Elizabethan poet would have quoted the echoing syllable. Bishop leaves it to the mind's ear: action! . . . shun . . . shun . . . shun. For love's sake, the hermit's cracker-barrel version of an Elizabethan dandy has withdrawn into the wilderness" (253). With the repeated "shun," Merrill emphasizes both society's action and the hermit's resulting withdrawal—a state in which Bishop finds Cordie, both shunned from the people living in the town of Brevard and actively choosing to shun them as well. In both the hermit and Cordie, then, there is some glimpse of the poet herself, as she explores her own feelings of alienation.

Besides the journal entries, Cordie Heiss features in Bishop's September 1 letter to Muser as well. On thin, lightly lined paper, Bishop crossed out the "Woods Hole, Massachusetts" to add her own header of "c/o Charles Russell, Brevard, North Carolina, September 1st, 1940." Perhaps due in part to her audience, the handwritten letter that follows casts Bishop as an outsider in Appalachia, part urban New Yorker and part beach dweller. She writes, "As maybe she [Louise] told you, I've been staying in a <u>very</u> primitive cabin here for about a month now, with my friends Red & Charlotte Russell. The 'Great Smokies' are really beautiful—we are very high up and often see the clouds floating around below us—and the neighboring 'hillbillies' are almost beyond belief, almost like 'Tobacco Road'" (VC 34.8; published with transcription errors in *OA* 93).

Much as she distances the cabin from the rest of the town, suspending the cabin above the clouds (a state similar to the one she would observe in Samambaia years later), she implies a distance between herself and her neighbors, initially describing them with only the Erskine Caldwell reference. Later in the letter, she goes into more detail about selected neighbors, including Cordie. She devotes most of a paragraph to Cordie and expresses her admiration for Cordie's industriousness, describing her routine: "She lives all alone in a little cabin, and <u>walks</u> to town, about 8 miles, once a week to get 50¢ relief money" (VC 34.8; *OA* 94). As in the journals, this description focuses on Cordie's poverty and ability to get by, and her tone, with the underlined "walks"—also conveys a sense of admiration that seems to put Bishop more at ease with her own situation. Millier notes that Bishop was always reluctant to leave Brevard, in part, because "the primitive life there had a deep appeal," and this correspondence with Muser subtly speaks to this attraction, a charm that Bishop develops more fully in the journal passages (*Elizabeth Bishop* 162).

The September 1 letter to Muser overlaps somewhat with the letter Bishop wrote to Marianne Moore on the same day, as this letter also communicates to her audience a growing sense of comfort even in what she sees as the primitiveness of the mountains. While the letter to Muser draws upon her portraits of local characters in the journals, the letter to Moore repeats the catalogues of the surrounding landscape. As in her notebook entry from August 26, Bishop catalogues the local birds: "The woods—we are right in them, almost on the top of a mountain—are filled with Warblers, and Charlotte and I feed them every day—black-and-white Warblers, Black Hooded Warblers—the prettiest—etc., and several varieties of Woodpecker" (*OA* 92-93). As in the letter to Muser, Bishop positions the cabin at elevation in this letter, which offers a kind of bird's eye view of the landscape. Appealing to her mentor's interest in animalia, such reports on bird species also color a slightly different reading of Bishop's letter-poem "Invitation to Miss Marianne Moore" published in *A Cold Spring* (1955), in which the speaker implores, "From Brooklyn, over the Brooklyn Bridge, on this fine morning, / please come flying" (*CP* 82). While the speaker pleads to her subject to "please come flying," Bishop's letter asks Moore to visit Key West, not New York—or Brevard, despite the variety of beautiful birds. In the letter, Bishop reasserts her longing for the tropical environment, "But all this kind of nature seems so unsophisticated compared to Key West. [There] it is much, much better" (*OA* 93). While Muser's letter speaks to Bishop's North/New York identity, Bishop's South/seaside persona reemerges in this letter to Moore. Thus, the letters together further speak to Bishop's moment of in-between and echo the preference, captured in the first Brevard journal entry, for a "natural & artificial scenery"—a desire to encounter both a wild and vibrant yet a mappable and somewhat familiar environment in the interwoven experiences of travel.

Although the letters mention various natural and artificial sceneries along the East Coast, Bishop's last journal entry from this stay is a brief note about Cordie, drawing attention back to Brevard. These lines are in keeping with her poetic style of transition-less collections of images. In a two-line entry for September 18, Bishop seems to write a reminder to herself, "Cordie & the LIFE's posted on her walls—her husband's picture—the Wedding Day" (VC 77.3). In these short phrases, connected by dashes, Bishop's style turns again to that of a field reporter taking down details for future elaboration. Cordie herself is central; the items around her are all images, and they represent the stories of Cordie's past and present. These images combine personal, intimate memorabilia and public, mass media, but they also serve as visual reminders of Cordie's isolation (both willing and unwilling), a curious summation of the poet's first stay in Brevard. Cordie Heiss features prominently in the few paragraphs on Brevard that Fountain and Brazeau include in their collection of oral histories.[8] Charles Russell describes her as the "local crazy woman" who would "sing classical songs at night as she walked through the mountains," a far more dismissive characterization than occurs in Bishop's writings (90). Besides the comments on Cordie's habits, Charles and his wife Charlotte also elaborate on Brevard as a destination (90). Charles states, "Brevard was a resort, but not in a fancy sense of the word" and adds that "it had a sense of remoteness to it" (89). Whereas Fountain and Brazeau suggest part of Brevard's appeal was in its cost effectiveness, especially once military development boomed on Key West, Charles's account designates Brevard as more of a destination than even the journals suggest, describing the area as "the place to go from Florida for vacation, to North Carolina and the mountains" (90). Brevard was, indeed, enough of a destination—or at least a convenience—to lure Bishop back for a second stay, further suggesting the impact of this place and time on her work.

Later in the notebook, Bishop details her return to Brevard the following year, again in the fall and again en route from Key West to New York, traveling by means of bus (up the Keys) and train (from Jacksonville, at least). There are fewer entries from this second trip, which lasted from September 3 to November 15, 1941, but these entries, like the ones from 1940, also offer Bishop's memories of the landscape, including the fog, the sunsets, the trees, and the waterfalls. The language Bishop uses to record these memories in her notebook seems in dialogue with her Florida poems and provide inspiration for later poems, again including "Chemin de Fer." In the first entry from this stay, which begins with her itinerary, "Sept. 3rd Marjorie & I left Key West/ 5th arrived in Brevard, met by Charlotte, staying at 'Holly House,'" Bishop notes that the trip north up the Keys took place in "full moonlight," which offered enough light so that "everything was still colored" (VC 77.3). Illuminated by moon, this journey offers her a last study of coastal Florida's "bright, detailed flatness" before she enters the mountains. Whereas the first entries from 1940 conveyed longing and displacement, the 1941 entries depict a poet who is somewhat more at ease but still seeking material for her art.

Unlike the sofa-pillow-like suffocating presence she found in the early days of her stopover the previous year, Bishop returns to Brevard fond of the mountain scenery. Dated only "October—," Bishop's next entry continues her musings on the moonlight: "The nights of the full moon this month were beautiful. The mountains looked bluish, snowy, & wasted" (VC 77.3). Peggy Samuels describes this passage as exemplary of Bishop's "interest in sparseness, diffusion, varying atmosphere and textures crossing into one another" (*Deep Skin* 75). Indeed, this description of the mountains captures not only an in-between moment for the textures and atmospheres of rapidly changing weather but also an in-between of season and place.

From mention of the effects of the moonlight on the icy nights and descriptions of some of the "many beautiful sunsets" witnessed, Bishop's attention shifts again to Appalachian poverty, a focus of the 1940 entries that resurfaces in 1941. She comments, "On one walk we went by a very poverty stricken mountain cabin, particularly dirty & gloomy. In front was a tall line of pine trees, with down-drooping branches & all the family's hens were roosting in them" (VC 77.3). The physical landscape mirrors the affect Bishop ascribes to this home with the shape of the "down-drooping branches" reflecting the pervasive gloom. She further compares the natural and constructed environments, concluding that "from underneath [the pine trees] it was a scene of wild, disorderly domesticity, just like the cabin itself" (VC 77.3). Much like Cordie's cabin from the 1940 entries (though hers was "orderly" but still "dirty"), this depressed scene also seems an inspiration for the landscape around the hermit's cabin in "Chemin de Fer," most notably as described in the second stanza, where the speaker observes, "The scenery was impoverished: / scrub-pine and oak" (*CP* 8). Both cabins from the journals and the hermit's cabin exist in isolation, surrounded by—and sometimes, pet hens aside, in their own state of—disorder and disarray. This tension of order and chaos runs throughout Bishop's poems as well as throughout Bishop's reflections on her life and her creative process in the Foster letters; although the "mess of life" can be troubling, as Bonnie Costello notes, Bishop also conveys moments of exhilaration and vibrancy in these experiences (*Elizabeth Bishop* 2).

Drawing out these tensions, both the journals and "Chemin de Fer" also comment on Bishop's own anxieties about economy and feelings of alienation. In the October 1941 Brevard notebook entry, Bishop finds a unique beauty in this scene that also exposes a cosmopolitan and artistic perspective on the mountains. Beyond the cabin and its pine and skeletal oak trees, she finds the beautiful with the ugly, discovering, "The same people had a beautiful field of sorg[h]um, which I think is very handsome, anyway" (VC 77.3). In this field, Bishop observes a scarecrow crafted out of a wire coat hanger—another instance of the resourcefulness necessitated by poverty—and compares it to modern art. She writes, "It sounded & looked like a very fine Calder mobile, & was very pretty, flashing in the sunset up above the heavy rich heads of sor[h]gum" (VC 77.3). This sensory scene of high and low art features the verticality of the scarecrow as well as tensions of movement and suspension.[9] Seeing a Calder mobile in the sorghum field scarecrow emphasizes the multilayered nature of Bishop's observations as well as her interest in a variety of art forms and her interpretations of these different media in her own work.

The contrast between the scenic sorghum field and the disorderly cabin nearby offer a moment of chaos and beauty paired with suspension and movement that, much like the unbalanced movement of one of Calder's mobiles, becomes a motif in her poetry. Bishop begins "Seascape," perhaps composed in Brevard during her first stay and published during her second in 1941, with one such moment:

> This celestial seascape, with white herons got up as angels,
> flying high as they want and as far as they want sidewise
> in tiers and tiers of immaculate reflections;
> the whole region, from the highest heron
> down to the weightless mangrove island
> with bright green leaves edged neatly with bird-droppings
> like illumination in silver (*CP* 40)

Although many critics focus on Bishop's commentary on religion, transcendence, and/or secularism here, these lines also convey an approach to artistic perspective.[10] The herons populate a timeless three-dimensional space in the sky above the speaker, while the "weightless mangrove island" suspended along the water's surface draws the gaze down. Along this surface, movements of light make the ugly, bird-dropping-dotted foliage appear beautiful. This "seascape," with its herons and mangroves, evokes Florida or Key West and yet, in its contrasts and its suspensions and movements, seems layered with a glimmer of Brevard.

As my reading of the archival evidence on Bishop's Brevard suggests, in the case of Bishop's North and South, we must not only read a "here" and "there"—or a "here" and "elsewhere," as she categorizes the poems in the 1965 *Questions of Travel*—but instead consider here-and-there-and-elsewheres. The Brevard journals and correspondence offer a unique lens into Bishop's poetic workshop and her layered landscapes. In her study of women walking and composing in various cities, *Flâneuse*, Lauren Elkin quotes French filmmaker Agnès Varda, "By understanding people you understand places better, by understanding places you understand people better" (217). By understanding Bishop's Brevard, we can better understand Bishop, her process, and her poetry.

NOTES

1. Bishop met the Barkers at Yaddo in 1950. Ilse Barker, *nom de plume* Kathrine Talbot, was a German writer of novels, short stories, poems, and many letters to Bishop. Kit Barker was a British painter known for his abstract and landscape works; he created the painting for the poster featuring Bishop's poem "North Haven" in memory of Robert Lowell.
2. In this letter, Bishop omits the *e*, typing "Maud" rather than "Maude," as in the journal. The spelling with the *e* may be a flourish of the handwritten cursive in the journal, but scholars have used both spellings for Bishop's aunt's name.
3. Muir was a nineteenth-century Scottish-American naturalist and environmental philosopher known for statements such as "The mountains are calling and I must go" and "In every walk with nature one receives far more than he seeks."
4. Watercolor drawdowns and drafts of these weaving patterns are available through Western Carolina University's digital collection *Craft Revival: Shaping Western North Carolina Past and Present*.
5. The Alexandre Gallery houses many works by Loren MacIver, including the 1939 "Untitled (Elizabeth Bishop's House)," a watercolor and ink drawing that features a colorful assortment of plants, household objects, and the house's facade.
6. William Logan suggests that the inspiration for the hermit of "Chemin de Fer" was a 1927 visit that Bishop made to "the Hermit," a man who lived a "Thoreau-like" life on Cape Cod. This visit was organized by the staff of Camp Chequesset, where Bishop spent several summers (Logan, "Elizabeth Bishop" 299-300).
7. The poem was first published in *The New Yorker* in 1946, and Millier speculates that White probably "could not see that the cry in 'Chemin de Fer' that 'love should be put into action' speaks eloquently to Elizabeth's struggle to accept her homosexuality" (*Elizabeth Bishop* 178).
8. In the August 31 entry, Bishop spells Cordie's last name "Hyce" in capital letters at the top of the page but opts for "Heiss" in the second line. In the letter to Muser from September 1, she also uses "Heiss," and scholars have generally used this spelling.
9. In "Composing Motions," Samuels discusses Bishop's creative interpretations of Calder's art to conceptualize the lyric, particularly as Bishop establishes distinctive temporal and spatial "motions" attuned to Calder's play of movement, hesitation, and buoyancy.
10. For example, see George S. Lensing's reading of "Seascape" (200). Or see Susan McCabe's reading of this poem, which she pairs with the 1937 "The Sea & Its Shore" (*Elizabeth Bishop* 62).

CHAPTER NINE

"ALL THE UNTIDY ACTIVITY"

Travel & the Picturesque in Elizabeth Bishop's Writings

Yaël Schlick

INTRODUCTION

Each day with so much ceremony begins

—Bishop, "Anaphora"

A 1945 Key West postcard Elizabeth Bishop sent to her friend Lloyd Frankenberg features a Floridian sunrise with swaying palms and a luminous, centered sun, its rays reflected in the sea below.[1] The postcard's caption reads simply, "Sunrise, on the Florida Coast." But the text by Bishop on the back immediately undercuts this pat, transcendent image. Her message reads, "Dear Lloyd: I don't even think this card is funny, but it is the only one I have" (VC 29.8). Here, even in this mundane instance, Bishop is thinking through notions of the beautiful, the sublime, and the picturesque. Her words to Frankenberg intimate her discomfort with what is clearly a clichéd Florida image: with its balanced composition and pleasing colors, the postcard image may qualify as beautiful; with its vast, transcendent (even apocalyptic) feel, it might even qualify as sublime. But as we see again and again in Bishop's poetry, her own aesthetic tends decidedly toward the picturesque, with its characteristic roughness, irregularity, and imperfection.

Bishop's message to Frankenberg on the back of this postcard reveals she does not want to be mistaken as tacitly endorsing the image's aesthetic. It makes clear that she sends it *not even* in jest but for lack of alternatives, and the explicit and

Postcard of a Florida sunrise sent by Bishop to Lloyd Frankenberg in March 1945. She sends it reluctantly, claiming it is the only one she has. (VC 29.8; Courtesy of Vassar College)

immediate disavowal of the image is reinforced when she adds, "I've been in K. W. about a week. The town is looking rather poorly" (VC 29.8). These sentences should remind readers of the image of Key West in many of Bishop's works, from the disheveled scene of "The Bight," to the garbage picker of "The Sea and Its Shore," and, further, to poems that detail the town's charm by referring to its forlorn aspect—like "Full Moon, Key West," "After the Rain," "A Norther-Key West," "Jerónimo's House," and "Little Exercise." Her own Floridian sunrise in "Anaphora," in which our eyes open on "such white-gold skies" (*PPL* 39), quickly descends into something darker and bleaker, despite the speaker's tentative affirmation at the end of the poem that each day ends in "endless assent" (40).

Such ambivalent images belong to what I will call Bishop's aesthetic of the picturesque, her updating and revision of the eighteenth-century notion of the picturesque. It is an aesthetic derived from her travels in Europe and the United States and expressed in her letters, postcards, and published work. In part, her picturesque is a reaction to modernity—both in terms of modernity's increasing influence on touristic practices and in terms of modernity's effects on the places she visits. Her European travels and her experience in Key West in the 1930s—a time when the island was being transformed into a tourist destination—show her partially resisting touristic practices that codify landscapes and forging her own aesthetic. And this aesthetic is everywhere in Bishop's work during the 1930s and beyond: in the offbeat scenes that make travel worthwhile in "Questions of Travel," the run-down (but in its own way attractive) fishing scene in "At the Fishhouses," the travel scenes that make up the large middle section of "Over 2,000 Illustrations and a Complete Concordance," and the dirty yet cared-for locale of the "Filling Station." In these texts, we see that the aesthetic sensibility is always slightly "off," with a predilection for the tattered, dirty, old, careless, crude, stained, pockmarked, gritty, or greasy detail.

Critics William Logan and Roger Gilbert refer to Bishop's use of the picturesque in terms of her tendency toward description of picturesque details. Logan characterizes her "nervousness" with respect to the picturesque as her fear that the accumulation of such details would "turn into solid cuteness" in her poetry ("Unbearable Lightness"), and Gilbert examines "At the Fishhouses" in terms of the way Bishop's penchant for picturesque detail is in tension with the poem's cognitive mode of apprehension (147). Both see in Bishop's work the struggle to find a strategy to bridge the picturesque detail and the contemplative or theoretical aspect of many of her highly descriptive poems. Yet, while the picturesque might appear to be the descriptive foundation of her contemplation in poems like "The Bight" and "At the Fishhouses," Bishop's attentiveness to the picturesque as a concept, discussed with some frequency in her various writings, reveals to us that these details are already theorized. This chapter's exploration of Bishop's understanding of the picturesque—one she developed, as will be shown, in her travels to Europe and in the United States, and apparent in early career Key West writings and correspondence during the 1930s generally—shows that there is no strict division between the "aesthetic and cognitive modes of apprehension" (Gilbert 147) and no definitive divide between detail and argument (Logan, "Unbearable Lightness") in Bishop's verse.

An exploration of Bishop's picturesque involves us in considering how Bishop's aesthetic was formed as part of her views on travel and tourism, themes that are, as Jeffrey Gray has observed in *Mastery's End*, enduring and central to her writing. The picturesque within her discourse on travel shows Bishop's ambivalence about its awkward quotient of beauty and roughness, and, in the context of post-depression Key West, points to the underlying poverty that uncomfortably contributes to the pleasing and evocative aspect of the scenes described. Bishop's avoidance of grandstanding and her attachment to humble details (Gray, *Mastery's End* 59; "Postcards and Sunsets" 27) is forged as a result of Bishop's traveling subjectivity. Just as she questions beauty and sublimity, she avoids typical tourist sights in favor of what Dean MacCannell (following Erving Goffman) has called "back regions": the "putative 'intimate and real' as against 'show,'" the "intimate reality" as opposed to "false fronts" (94, 95). MacCannell is circumspect about this distinction and mindful of the difficulty of distinguishing between front and back regions in all situations, but the division is nonetheless useful both for understanding the kinds of experiences and sites Bishop tends to privilege in her work and her resistance to synthesizing or theorizing picturesque details in her poems lest they coalesce into something grander or masterful. Her insistence on picturesque details is, in other words, a hedge against the tendency to create yet another sight or "front" region through elaboration. It is a poetics that asserts what we should attend to: not to "the Seven Wonders of the world," which "are tired / and a touch familiar" but to "the poppies / splitting the mosaics" at Volubilis ("Over 2,000 lllustrations . . . ," *PPL* 44-45); not to dramatic waterfalls or mountaintops but to the "wooden tune / of disparate wooden clogs / carelessly clacking over / a grease-stained filling-station floor" ("Questions of Travel," *PPL* 75).

This chapter will begin by defining the picturesque and examining Bishop's understanding of it as seen in her postcards, travel journals, and letters, tracing her appreciation of the picturesque as an aesthetic gleaned from her travels and what I see as her self-consciously anti-touristic stance. For in her travels there is, to a certain degree, an avoidance of the typical tourist sights equated with the beautiful and the sublime. Bishop is certainly a typical American traveler some of the time, going to the usual tourist sights, but her letters and postcards reveal also a preference for a different kind of travel experience. In Key West—a place critics have identified as crucial for Bishop's artistic development (Cleghorn 75; Hicok, "Becoming" 113; Travisano, Elizabeth Bishop 19)—Bishop's aesthetic theory is most in evidence, dovetailing with her affinity for the island's landscape and diverse ethnic community. Bishop's initial experience of Key West is at the cusp of this island's transformation. By the time she leaves Key West for good, when it is no longer the charming town she had first come to know, her picturesque aesthetic is firmly established.

The use of archival material in this chapter—of Bishop's ephemera—is not a means to search for origins nor establish context for her final, published work. It is, rather, a pathway to plunge back into the temporal, palpable multiplicity of the travel experience, where we can parse the meanings of Bishop's daily encounters, experiences, responses, and ideas in the moment. Bishop's postcards, especially, offer an intriguing space in which her own experiences and touristic practices combine and collide with codified understandings of places.

POSTCARDS, LETTERS, AND TOURISM: FORGING A PICTURESQUE AESTHETIC

and the careless, corrupt state is all black specks
too far apart, and ugly whites; the poorest
post-card of itself.

—Bishop, "Florida"

The picturesque as formulated by William Gilpin in the eighteenth century is neither beautiful nor sublime but, as applied to nature, "that peculiar kind of beauty, which is agreeable in a picture" (Trott 73). The term *picturesque* never attained the kind of precision in aesthetic debates that the beautiful and the sublime did (Copley and Garside 1), but it is generally understood to be characterized by roughness or irregularity as opposed to the smoothness, neatness, and pleasing uniformity of the beautiful (Gilpin 7-8; Price 85) or the vastness of the sublime (Trott 75). Uvedale Price, another central theorist in eighteenth-century debates on the picturesque, contrasts the sublime and the picturesque, saying that "greatness of dimension is a powerful cause of the sublime; the picturesque has no connection with dimensions of any kind, and is as often found in the smallest as in the largest objects" (94). He also draws distinctions between the beautiful and the picturesque by writing that "[b]eauty and picturesqueness are indeed evidently founded on very opposite qualities; the one on smoothness, the other on roughness; the one on gradual, the other on sudden variation; the one on ideas of youth and freshness, the other on those of age, and even of decay" (90).

These theorists do not necessarily construe this roughness and irregularity, this variation and even decay, negatively. "Roughness adds detail and therefore richness," writes Gilpin (14), and Price insists that the picturesque "requires greater variety" (94). The picturesque could, for example, include scenes that represent manufacturing or industrial activity rather than pristine nature alone (Copley 58). Noting picturesque paintings' frequent use of run-down scenes of poverty or decay, contemporary critics have questioned the degree to which it problematically "translates the political and the social into the decorative," thereby using motifs "for aesthetic effect which in other circumstances are the indicators of poverty or social deprivation" (Copley and Garside, 6). The aestheticization of the scene of decline in "At the Fishhouses" is an example of Bishop's use of the picturesque in this vein—a scene in which the elegiac tone evoked by its distinct aspects (such as the old man, the cracked capstan, the rusted ironwork, and the locale's economic decline) is suffused by the iridescence lent to the landscape by the gloaming's light.

Price and Gilpin attended to these aesthetic categories—the picturesque, the sublime, the beautiful—as part of an interest in landscape and in travel, and it is with respect to her impressions as a traveler that we see the young Elizabeth Bishop (traveling in the 1930s to Newfoundland, Europe, North Africa, and Florida) formulating her own picturesque aesthetic. In these letters and postcards, she uses the word *picturesque* to describe overly attractive scenes or sights that are too touristy. These she tends to reject in favor of something less obviously attractive and more "edgy"—which in fact would qualify as picturesque according to traditional definitions of the word that distinguish it from the beautiful. Examples of this are found in Bishop's 1930s travel writings to Marianne Moore and to Frani Blough Muser, in which she simultaneously engages with and resists standard tourist sights, experiences, landscapes, or scenes that are pleasing or beautiful.

In one example, in 1935, Bishop writes Moore from Douarnenez in Brittany to say, "Douarnenez is too PICTURESQUE for much longer than a month—maybe even for that. The picturesqueness is just like the water in Salt Lake, you simply can't sink in it, it is so strong" (*OA* 33-34). What Bishop dubs the picturesque here is associated with something too typically pleasing and, in a sense, superficial. The following year, she writes Moore from Mallorca to say that she and Louise are tired of being tourists and have opted out of seeing typical tourist sights by electing to stay at a little fishing village: "Until we tired of being 'tourists' we had planned to extend our trip to Burgos, León, etc. but instead we have been staying at this little fishing village in Mallorca. I am afraid I do not mind much missing the Gothic building of those places" (*OA* 42). This Mallorcan village was Soller, a town in northwest Mallorca, a postcard of which she sent to Muser at the same time as the letter to Moore (VC 34.5). The letter to Moore emphasizes the rejection of touristic sightseeing's focus on major cities and public landmarks in favor of staying in a village that is off the beaten path.

The postcard's depiction of this fishing village meets the criteria of the eighteenth-century picturesque rather well in its rough jumble of houses and boats and in the lack of any vast scale, even of the ocean. Of course, the very existence of this postcard indicates that it, too, is a tourist sight. The distinction Bishop creates has therefore more to do with an affirmation of non-urban over urban space, of simple, everyday working life over outstanding and humanmade/cultural structures. But just as Bishop fails to note Soller's codification as a tourist sight through the medium of the postcard, so she neglects to point out the way her own appreciation of this fishing village is touristic. A view, as Geoff Dyer tantalizingly posits, is "the product of a separation of leisure and labour" (Dyer 53). The very appreciation of the view of this fishing town is, in other words, the result of Bishop's leisure. Her affirmation of Soller's picturesqueness and her nominal rejection

Postcard of the town of Soller in Mallorca sent by Bishop to Frani Blough in May 1936. On the back she writes: "I'm sure this was much better than Martha's Vineyard." (VC 34.5; Courtesy of Vassar College)

of touristic practices in the letter to Moore thus highlights her desire to affirm an unconventional aesthetic even as it reveals the conundrum of the tourist—a figure continually in search of new sights and authentic experiences.

Bishop's travel journal as well as her postcards to Muser from her European trip, especially the postcards from the Spanish Steps and from Blarney Castle, detail to varying degrees Bishop's unease with being a tourist. We see Bishop's discussion of touristic practices in her journal entry for November 16, 1937, where she writes, "To-day, a beautiful day, we are most tourist-like. Beginning at the Coliseum, we worked right through, and sank down in the Piazza del Campidoglio, under the statue of Marcus Aurelius. I enjoyed it all much more than I had anticipated" (VC 77.2). While there is a self-conscious ambivalence here about the touristic enterprise, the experience is deemed enjoyable nonetheless. The postcards, however, are more circumspect. As mass produced items on which the purchaser inscribes a private communication (Stewart 138), an item which might be understood, with its reversibility, as a virtual analog of the sign (Schor 237), the postcards become again (as in the Florida sunrise postcard) one of the very subjects of her message. Her commentary on the image of the postcard itself reveals what Mark Simpson has referred to as the postcard's "potential for rupture" given the dissonance created between front and back, between image and message (172).

Bishop's increasing resistance to touristic practices is conveyed in two postcards in particular. The first is a postcard of the Spanish Steps in Rome: The image shows the Spanish Steps leading to the Trinità dei Monti church at the top. Pictured at the bottom is the Fontana della Barcaccia in the shape of a half-sunken ship. The fountain was built slightly below street level because the ancient aqueduct, the source of the fountain's water, had low water pressure. Bishop writes that this tourist sight is "right around the corner from the class 'C' hotel we found in the guide-book, which turned out to be almost too nice. . . . Keats died in the house at the right—and the fountain is supposed to look like a foundering boat, leaking all over—because the water pressure wasn't very high at the spot" (VC 34.6). Phrases like "too nice" or "too PICTURESQUE" can't but remind one of the tourist or traveler's odd complaint at the opening of "Questions of Travel," which foregrounds the speaker's characterization of the landscape as having "too many waterfalls" and streams that "hurry too rapidly" (*PPL* 74). This "too"—in both the postcard and the poem—reveals an evaluative negation on Bishop's part of something most travelers or tourists would delight in. In the Spanish Steps postcard, Bishop represents her engagement in typical tourist activity (visiting a standard Roman sight, consulting a guidebook, relating well-known information about architecture likely gleaned from that same guidebook) while nonetheless distancing herself from a posh tourist by referring to a C-class hotel that is "almost too nice." The mixture of personal and historical information relayed in the message—including her reference to the house in which Keats died nearby—shows both a desire to convey experience of her standard European tour and to distinguish herself from it.

The second is a postcard to Muser that same year proclaiming yet further distance from touristic experience. The postcard depicts Blarney Castle in Ireland, which Bishop visited with Louise Crane. It shows three women looking on as three men help a fourth to kiss the Blarney Stone, purported to bestow the gift of eloquence on the kisser. On the back of the postcard, Bishop responds directly to the postcard's image-message to say, "We did NOT do this—we happened to be the only people on the tour at the time and did not trust each other's grip" (VC 34.6). She does, however, affirm that the castle is a "lovely place" like the rest of Ireland (VC 34.6). The negative response to the activity depicted on the image, like the contradiction between "Whatever one might think" and the assertion that Ireland is "a very lovely place," betrays a general ambivalence toward the touristic enterprise. On the one hand, Bishop resists immersion in the touristic experience; on the other hand, she proclaims her positive appreciation of it. Yet the mocking of the postcard's standardized portrayal of this tourist sight strongly displays Bishop's resistance to tourist experiences and practices. The comments ("man?" "fashion plate," and "ban-shee"), meant to add "sex-interest to the B.S.," make fun

Postcard of the Piazza di Spagna sent by Bishop to Frani Blough in 1937. "Keats died at the house on the right," she tells her friend. (VC 34.6; Courtesy of Vassar College)

Postcard of a group of tourists at Blarney Castle sent to Frani Blough in 1937 by Bishop, who turns the reverential scene of the 'kissing of the stone' into farce with her mocking message. (VC 34.6; Courtesy of Vassar College)

"ALL THE UNTIDY ACTIVITY" 181

Postcard of Newfoundland with Bishop's correction of the angles of the cliffs sent to Frani Blough in August 1932. "This place is far beyond my fondest dreams," she writes. (VC 34.2; Courtesy of Vassar College)

of the figures in the image and take the focus away from the kissing of the stone altogether.

The two postcards selected here highlight Bishop's resistance to a conventional appreciation of European landmarks and locations, but this practice of responding to and altering postcard images is seen in other postcards by Bishop in the 1930s and 1940s and shows her taking issue with the way places are represented in the idealizing genre of the postcard, itself part and parcel of touristic practice and discourse. Her 1932 postcard to Muser of the Narrows in Newfoundland (VC 34.2) corrects the angles of the cliffs on the image and refers to the picture as "really very tame." And her 1949 postcard to Frankenberg picturing Cos-Cob Hub in Connecticut derides the idyllic, small town scene depicted by the postcard by adding at the top, "they have eliminated about 200 cars + sound effects" (VC 29.9).

That Bishop carefully considered the postcard aesthetic and often resisted it, can also be seen in a poem like "Florida," in which we move from "the state with the prettiest name" (*PPL* 24) to a state that is, in fact, "the poorest / post-card of itself" (25). The postcard is taken here as the idealized image, one that the poem, with its emphasis on decay and on Florida's troubled racial history, reveals to be false. Bishop's picturesque is thus a somewhat conflicted terrain, one that acknowledges value and beauty but rejects the pleasing touristic vision in favor of the gritty

Postcard of Cos Cob, a neighborhood in the town of Greenwich, Connecticut, sent by Bishop to Lloyd Frankenberg in May 1949. (VC 29.9; Courtesy of Vassar College)

reality. This gritty quality does not, I think, represent a negative or ambivalent attitude to these places (as at least one critic has suggested—see Millier's discussion of "Florida," *Elizabeth Bishop* 116) but a way of looking below the surface to address what may not be readily apparent or readily appreciated. The sensibility demonstrated in Bishop's travel journal and correspondence during her travels in Europe—which one might characterize as a search for authenticity, an appreciation for the small detail, an attentiveness to so-called back regions and minor features—recurs in her subsequent experiences in the United States. Repeatedly, she does not seek the neatness and uniformity or smoothness that make up the beautiful but is attracted to the rougher, more irregular aspect of the picturesque.

FROM EUROPE TO KEY WEST

Flake on flake
of wood and paint
the buildings faint.

—Bishop, "Full Moon, Key West"

Such moments from Bishop's European travel as are seen in her letters, journal entry, and postcards show her weaving a fine line between pursuing the sort of standard European tour taken by people of her class and distancing herself from touristic practices. She notes major sights and relays standard information about them, yet often conveys her resistance to their charms; she uses a guidebook and knows the typical, major sights one should visit but tires of any slavish touristic practice in favor of simpler pleasures: a small fishing village, a C-class hotel. Her sensibility and her aesthetic resist anything "too nice" or "too PICTURESQUE," and she attends carefully to mundane details. The latter is particularly apparent in her travel journals from this time. For example, in late December 1937, once back in Boston, walking with her uncle in the suburbs, she readjusts to the cold, American northeastern landscape, writing that after Italy, the houses seem "extraordinarily dismal," although "certainly picturesque enough. . . . At night, with all the little stains of color, as from ikons [sic], the intense dark and cold, the hard liquor, the muddy sidewalk, the suburbs are like certain scenes in Dostoyevsky" (VC 77.2).

Having just returned from Europe, Bishop notes walking through the suburbs to the dubious sort of center that marks North American cities. With their peeling paint and sagging porches, the houses are oddly described as both dismal and picturesque. This scene's description is similar to many of those of Florida that Bishop included in her letters at around the same time—1937 and 1938. (Bishop was, at this point in her life, spending time both in Florida and in Europe.) Shortly after her saunter in the Boston suburbs, Bishop is in Florida, writing Moore about eating "on the porch of a little tumbled-down white-washed shanty" (*OA* 58). The following year she describes the view from her verandah: a big tree and the landlady's pink bloomers (*OA* 68). Her poems from this time and place describe "broken sidewalks with weeds in every crack" ("Little Exercise," *PPL* 32), "streets of the tourist-deserted town" ("Florida Deserta," *EAP* 45), tin roofs of ramshackle houses, which, like those of the Boston suburbs, are run-down and marked by some measure of poverty ("Key West," *EAP* 51; "Florida Deserta," *EAP* 45; "Full Moon, Key West," *EAP* 59-60). The following lines from "Full Moon, Key West" indicate, with its shabby subject expressed in regular rhyme and rhythm, an aestheticization of this moonlit, American landscape that also appears in other Key West poems:

> The town is paper-white:
> the moonlight is so bright.
> Flake on flake
> of wood and paint
> the buildings faint.
> The tin roofs break
> into a sweat (*EAP* 59)

Other poems from Key West intimate Bishop's fascination with its multicultural and working-class inhabitants: her devout landlady, Mrs. Pindar; her housekeeper, Hannah Almyda; the impoverished folk artist, Gregorio Valdez; the mixed-race carpenter, Milton Evans; Miss Lula and her African American servant, Cootchie.

Key West at this time jelled perfectly with Bishop's emerging aesthetic. Her delight in and depiction of the island intriguingly coincides with momentous changes to this southernmost point of the United States: its beginnings as a tourist destination through development and promotion initiated by the Federal Emergency Relief Administration (FERA) and the Federal Writers' Project. To some, like John Dos Passos, Wallace Stevens, and Ernest Hemingway, who had begun to visit Key West in the 1920s, the island's transformation was lamentable. By the mid-1930s, Hemingway called the place "this F.E.R.A. Jew administered phony of a town" (Ogle 173) and was no doubt incensed to have his very house on Whitehead Street listed as a tourist sight in the 1939 guide to Florida compiled by the Federal Writers' Project of the Works Progress Administration (WPA) for the State of Florida (201). In a 1935 letter to a friend, Katy Dos Passos declared Key West "a Greenwich Village Nightmare" after the New Dealers' rehabilitation of the island (L. Miller 109), and Wallace Stevens went from thinking the island "a paradise" in 1922 to stating in 1935 that it was "no longer quite the delightful affectation it once was" and decrying unselfconsciously that it had become "rather too literary and artistic" (*Letters* 224, 274, 278). These sentiments echo those expressed in the popular press. In a *Harper's* article that appeared in January of 1929, a year after the opening of the Overseas Highway, Elmer Davis lamented Key West's "annexation" and "assimilation" to the United States. The highway together with the Florida tourist boom of the 1930s and 1940s spelled the end of the Key West many loved: "In another year or two," he predicted, "Key West will no longer be different and exotic" ("Caribbean Conquest" 176). Davis's subsequent 1935 article on the island philosophically reflects that the more Key West succeeds in selling itself as a tourist town, "the more surely it will lose some of the quality that originally attracted tourists" ("New World" 652).

Into this Key West stepped Elizabeth Bishop, first visiting the island in December of 1936. She may well have gone there after seeing the postcards and glossy brochures produced by government-sponsored artists commissioned to promote Key West's charms. And whereas Dos Passos, Hemingway, and Stevens lamented the disappearance of the 1920s Key West, Bishop, who left the island for good in 1949, looked back to the 1930s as a better time, when there were fewer tourists and when the Navy did not so dominate the island and its activities. Clearly, each generation felt their own encounter with Key West to be the authentic one, the one before Key West got ruined, and, likewise, they each saw subsequent visitors to the island as invasive tourists, unlike themselves.

ALONG THE GULF   *Photo by Hamilton Wright, N. Y.*

Few roadways in America can rival the beauty of the Oversea Highway along the palm-fringed shores of the Gulf of Mexico. Eventually this roadway will connect with the mainland of Florida and motorists may then drive from Maine directly into Key West.

The Overseas Highway, a photograph from George Allan England's 1929 article on Key West, titled "America's Island of Felicity."

    Bishop certainly attends to what Davis in his 1929 *Harper's* article pinpoints as Key West's picturesqueness: its run-down shacks, its old, dilapidated structures, its remoteness from the mainland. She is also interested in Key West's exoticism as described by George Allan England in his January 1929 article in *Travel* magazine, one inherent in the presence of its Cuban and African American populations, sponge sellers, cigar factory workers, and seafarers of days past. Bishop's transvaluation of island sights, her celebration of worn, untidy scenes, her focus on what travel writers of the time considered Key West's "local color" indicate her alignment with a wider discourse about the island and reveal the fascinating dialogue between her poetics and the politics of development in Key West.

"THE BIGHT" & "THE SEA AND ITS SHORE"

> *When someone says "beautiful" about Key West you should really take it with a grain of salt until you've seen it for yourself—in general it is really awful & the "beauty" is just the light or something equally perverse.*
>
>   —Elizabeth Bishop to Robert Lowell, 1948

Written respectively at the beginning and at the end of Bishop's time in Key West, "The Sea and Its Shore" and "The Bight" nonetheless have important similarities that link them to the physical realities of the island, to Bishop's evolving aesthetic sensibility, and to her thinking about the picturesque in particular. "The Sea and Its Shore" details the life of Edwin Boomer, appointed to spend his nights keeping the large public beaches free of paper litter. He sifts and organizes these bits of paper, an activity described as his "studies," carried out in an effort to find meaning in the fragments of print. Sadly, no such meaning emerges, and the papers must finally be burned. The effort he makes to read the small type on the bits of paper leads him to see the whole world as "printed too"—even a sandpiper (later to be the subject of another poem about the search for meaning) "rushing distractedly this way and that" looks like a punctuation point, and its speckled feathers have markings "that looked as if they might be letters" (*PPL* 580).

The story shares important aspects with "The Bight," also a seascape, also representing an "untidy" scene, also involving "litter" (though of a metaphorical kind), also entailing the attempt on the part of an individual to make sense of a world hardly inclined to deliver meaning, also playing on the connections between litter and letters, between litter and the literary. In this later poem, the speaker surveys the scene of Garrison Bight in Key West on her birthday, registering "All the untidy activity" (*PPL* 47). Words like *drafts*, *letters*, *correspondences*, and, of course, the name of Baudelaire in the poem signal "The Bight" as the site of a distinctly literary epistemological search and perhaps also of an "aesthetic quarrel" with the Baudelairean perspective on the world (McKendrick 123; qtd. in Ellis, *Art* 96). "The Bight"—which Eleanor Cook humorously refers to as "The Idea of Disorder at Key West" (117)—is also in intertextual conversation with Wallace Stevens's Key West poem. Bishop records being delighted at a copy of Stevens's *Ideas of Order* in a 1936 letter to Moore (*OA* 44-45).

These two works are distinctly located in the Key West of the 1930s and 1940s. In the 1930s, especially, the question of litter would have been uppermost in her mind as the island was being transformed in the post-Depression period into the tourist destination it is known as today. In the fall of 1934, two years prior to Bishop's initial arrival on the island, Julius F. Stone Jr., a Harvard PhD appointed director of FERA's Florida division, began the great Key West cleanup, preparing the island for those hoped-for tourists who would stimulate its economy. Stone "involved everyone in the project to save Key West," writes Maureen Ogle, enlisting local kids to clean up debris and seaweed off the beaches and the unemployed to remove dead foliage, razed shacks, and litter around town (163). Fifty-five thousand cubic yards of garbage were hauled away in the effort to give Key West a face-lift and make it tourist-worthy (Ogle 158-59). Pictures depicting the town's transformation reveal that it was altered largely by such modification rather than complete renovation: beaches were swept clean, palm-thatched cabanas were thrown together, potholes were patched, inhabitants cleaned their backyards and repainted their houses (Kennedy 43-46). In "The Sea and Its Shore," Bishop turns her own litter picker, Edwin Boomer, into a parable, but the connection to Key West's history is palpable. Boomer is "appointed to keep the sand free from papers" (*PPL* 574) and walks about "with his lantern and his stick, and a potato sack on his back to put the papers in" (*PPL* 575). He is humorously said to have a literary life—a "life of letters"—since his primary material is printed matter among the discarded bits of refuse he finds on the seashore that are ultimately burned as so much garbage (*PPL* 575).

"The Bight," too, involves Key West's litter and extends the playful analogies between litter and letter(s). The little white boats "not yet salvaged" from "the last bad storm" are likened to "torn-open, unanswered letters," and the bight as a whole (in this simile and metaphor ridden text) is "littered with old correspondences" (*PPL* 47). The reader is pointed toward a Boomeresque task of making sense, of establishing correspondences between the physical and the spiritual realms in this final reference to Baudelaire. But, ultimately, as in "The Sea and Its Shore," the collection of bits does not add up. In these texts, Bishop literally turns Key West litter to letters, to literature, even as the texts themselves highlight the impossibility of transforming the concrete and physical presence of things into a unified meaning. The analogies between writing and aspects of the landscape in both of these texts raise the problem of constructing a total vision but ultimately reframe that search as subordinate to the fragmented and shifting nature of reality.

That reality is itself linked to the state of Key West at the time Bishop lived there and to Bishop's own choice of modest accommodations. Although cleaned up, the town was not entirely tidied or touristified, and Bishop stayed in rooming houses and, later, in a modest house in Key West on the edge of the Cuban section of town that put her in touch with locals (*REB* 72-73, 365). The watercolor painter Martha Sauer went so far as to suggest that Bishop sought out working-class locales and situations like the Square Roof, a local whorehouse: "It was slumming," as she describes it (*REB* 78). That Bishop herself was aware of the class difference and the difference in surroundings experienced between herself and other literary Key West frequenters like Robert Frost and Wallace Stevens is evident from her letters. A 1940 letter to Moore notes that Stevens was in Key West, too, but "at the 'fancy' hotel" (*OA* 89). The collapse of the sponge and cigar industries in Key West made it a cheap place to live in the 1930s and 1940s, a place Bishop could afford. Thus, these texts are anchored in the physical realities of Key West, which they affirm, aestheticize, but simultaneously refuse to prettify. What value and attraction the picturesque held for Bishop precisely due to its non-unity of meaning will be addressed below.

Certainly, Bishop liked Key West because it was *not* beautiful. In an early letter to Robert Lowell, dated January 15, 1948, she describes her stay in Key West in Jane Dewey's apartment (not a deluxe one like Pauline Hemingway's but rather hideous according to her letter). She refers to this hideous apartment's beautiful view over the harbor but then adds parenthetically: "When somebody says 'beautiful' about Key West you should really take it with a grain of salt until you've seen it for yourself—in general it is really *awful* & the 'beauty' is just the light or something equally perverse" (*WIA* 22). *Awful* is, of course, a word Bishop uses in "The Bight" to summarize the view over Garrison Bight, a poem she composed sometime in late winter or spring of 1948 (White, *Lyric* 73)—that is, shortly after her letter to Lowell. She returns here to the categories of the beautiful and the picturesque that were so prevalent in her 1930s travels and which she used as a means of distinguishing her own predilections as a traveler from those of the typical tourist and to characterize the type of landscape she liked best. The word *awful*, even as it signifies the scene's objectively negative qualities, also gestures at its ability to inspire wonder—a double entendre of which Bishop was surely aware.

The qualities of balance, smoothness, delicacy, and color that Burke associates with the beautiful are entirely absent from "The Bight": the water is colorless, the pelicans crash into the water, the sponge boats are described as "frowsy," and, as if that level of scruffiness were insufficient, they are "bristling with jackstraw gaffs and hooks" (*PPL* 46-47)—yet another reference to a disordered rather than a unified vision. By the time we get to the word *untidy*, it is something we have already deduced from the various elements of the scene, its general disorder. As Jonathan Ellis has noted, this poem's subtitle ("On my birthday") "runs like an insistent dye through our reading of its various images, colouring every detail in an autobiographical hue" (*Art* 96-97). But this autobiographical perspective resists unifying this seashore scene. That the bight reminded Bishop of her own disordered desk—a point she relates in the same 1948 letter to Lowell—further links untidiness to a personal aesthetic of the picturesque: "The water looks like blue gas—the harbor is always a mess, here, junky little boats all piled up, some hung with sponges and always a few half sunk or splintered up from the most recent hurricane. It reminds me a little of my desk" (*WIA* 23). The more expressive and negative diction in this prose description—yet another means through which Bishop conveys that Key West is not beautiful—is made personal and meaningful by likening it to the writer's desk. Bishop may well have been looking out on Garrison Bight on February 8, her birthday, but the personal connection of the poem's subtitle works, more importantly, to signal a connection to the writer's aesthetics more generally.

TRAVEL AND THE PICTURESQUE IN BISHOP'S WRITING

In *The Tourist*, MacCannell explores how sight markers are created, how they form an itinerary for the traveler that is set in advance of their departure, and how duplication of the touristic experience occurs through the mechanical reproduction of these sights, of which the postcard is one example. Although MacCannell tends to view touristic experience as totalizing, it is important to note instances where the letters, journals, and postcards that are meant to convey the tourist's experiences, to chart out and affirm the tourist's "checklist" of sights for the folks back home, also hold the potential to subvert touristic thinking and to work against tourism's unifying logic. In some of the letters she wrote while in Europe, Bishop foregrounds the rejection of aspects of tourism; her travel journals sometimes simply chart out her tourist's itinerary, but often they attend to the small, unusual detail—watching the moon and stars from the round porthole, the sound of water in the radiator at the American hospital (VC 77.2)—and her postcards often display the kind of rupture of the postcard's purported unity of image and message that brings out what Mark Simpson has noted as the medium's "openness to signs of misuse value," its ability to reveal dissonance and incongruity (171-72).

Intermittent with Bishop's writing about her European experiences were her impressions of Key West, as she began to frequent the place in the 1930s. It is in Key West—a locale on the cusp of touristification but that obviously lacks the kind of coherent succession of "must-see" sights so prominent in touristic itineraries through main European cities—that we increasingly see Bishop's attentiveness to the overlooked detail, to the novelty of a terrain not known in advance. In the 1939 guidebook to Florida created by the Federal Writers' Project, there are eighteen "points of interest" in Key West (200-05). Of these, the aquarium (built recently with Civil Works Administration and FERA funds) can be found among Bishop's Key West postcards, but her message on it speaks instead of an apartment she found with the "biggest Poinciana tree in K.W. shading the screened porch. Don't know what I did to deserve it" (VC 29.8). Key West, in the 1930s, as Bishop found it, provided a vast landscape yet to be described or codified. In fact, in her journal she wonders, "Why didn't Stevens do more with it?" (VC 77.2). Key West was both a counterpoint to Europe and a place available for exploration. We see Bishop's attentiveness to the minutiae of Key West life, and it is here that she thought through what such details might add up to. The vision of Key West, I would argue, is not idealized and not synthesized. The aesthetic of the picturesque predominates both in the sense that Bishop tends to focus on scenes that are not typically beautiful or sublime and in the sense that the point of much of the description is the avoidance of unity—whether it be as an overall effect or as an overall meaning offered in the text. Her aesthetic vision emerged as a result of her travels and often reflected on that very activity.

My argument in this chapter has been historical. I have worked to show the development of Bishop's picturesque aesthetic as a function of her experiences as a traveler and also to suggest that the Key West she found in the 1930s (and to a large extent still in the 1940s) dovetailed with this aesthetic. Bishop's anti-visionary and entropic vision (revealed so effectively in Gray's analysis of her attempts to write a poem about revisiting Florida at a later point in her life) echoes, in other words, formulations of the picturesque that characterize it as a "dissatisfaction with a compositional mode that seeks seamless control over all constituent elements" (Copley and Garside 4). The scraps of paper or the various motley elements that appear in "The Sea and Its Shore" or that make up the landscape of "The Bight" remain scattered rather than coalesced into some grand schema of meaning or correspondences. In later poems this aesthetic of entropy is still at work. We do not have a Blakean vision of seeing "a World in a Grain of Sand" in "Sandpiper" but rather the grains themselves at the poem's conclusion: "The millions of grains are black, white, tan, and gray, / mixed with quartz grains, rose and amethyst" (*PPL* 126). The word *millions* warns us that this synthesizing project can never be realized, that even beyond the grains of sand, there are other grains of varying makeup and color. In a temporal version of this same argument, Bishop concludes with the transient nature of any epiphany or understanding in "At the Fishhouses," in which, as in "Sandpiper," she also addresses epistemological questions and insists in the poem's concluding line that knowledge is "historical, flowing, and flown" (*PPL* 52).

What these and other poems in Bishop's oeuvre suggest is that she conceives of this entropic, picturesque state as itself a kind of solution. For the transvaluation of various untidy scenes and various uncoalesceable temporal moments is the only vision available to an observer of the world who wishes neither to abide by pat, touristic images nor to be limited to a touristic itinerary that would make of these a comprehensible world. We can think of this in terms of the experience of the traveler as Dean MacCannell has in *The Tourist*: "Tourist attractions in their natural, unanalyzed state," he writes, "may not appear to have any coherent infrastructure uniting them, and insofar as it is through the attraction that the tourist apprehends society, society may not appear to have coherent structure, either" (56). We can also think of it in terms of the poetic endeavor, characterized in Adam Kirsch's book, *The Modern Element,* in which he writes that only poets "who put themselves genuinely at risk in their work" can fulfill our expectations of modern poetry. This is the risk of acknowledging "that modern experience does not admit of being mastered and interpreted, only of being accurately and passionately shared" (12). In the conclusion of "The Bight," where "[a]ll the untidy activity continues" (*PPL* 47), we find such risk-taking expressed in a picturesque aesthetic that neither unifies (like the beautiful) nor seeks transcendence (like the sublime), but tenuously frames the lyric moment and attends to the task of describing the untidy phenomenal world.

NOTES

1. I am grateful to Bethany Hicok for organizing the 2017 NEH workshop on Bishop's archive, for her invaluable guidance and support, and for her meticulous editing of this essay. Ron Patkus and Dean Rogers of Vassar College made archival research rewarding and fun and were generous with both their time and their expertise. I am also indebted to Glenn Willmott, who read and made so many helpful suggestions on successive drafts of this chapter.

CHAPTER TEN

THE BURGLAR OF THE TOWER OF BABEL

Elizabeth Bishop, Architecture, Translation, Archive

Douglas Basford

FINDING PROJECTS

In a letter to her artist friend Loren MacIver in September 1954, Elizabeth Bishop explained that a bulldozer had been brought up to the ultramodern house she shared with Lota de Macedo Soares in the countryside near Samambaia, with the intention of starting the "immediate landscaping," only to find so much solid rock that Macedo Soares and the crew "had to give up and now the place looks like the beginnings of a Roman fort or something" (VC 29.14). Ongoing construction work was something Bishop had become acclimated to since her arrival three years earlier, when the state of incompletion had meant that the house was excluded from the *Brazil Builds* architecture exhibit at MoMA. This hardly deterred the stream of visitors to the site from around the world, rendering their private space public, in a manner predictably uncomfortable to Bishop, and a "testament to the kind of life," as Bethany Hicok observes in *Elizabeth Bishop's Brazil*, "that education, money, and good taste could buy" (11). "There have been photographs in quite a few of the architectural journals," Bishop beamed in the same letter, "but mostly very bad ones."

The house had benefited because Macedo Soares, drawing on her vast, largely self-taught knowledge of architecture and good taste, had been fighting the architect, Sérgio Bernardes, "every inch of the way" over his inclination to graft on gratuitous features such as, Bishop quipped, "cantilevers, flying buttresses, brise-soleils that look like factories, etc." (*OA* 265). Over the years, a string of improvements was undertaken at the *fazenda*, such as a writing studio for Bishop and a freestanding fireplace.

With a flash of hyperbole fashioning the scene of the building of the latter in

1956 as iconic, Bishop described how Macedo Soares "sat in a safari chair and produced it, with Negro boys streaming past her, each with a rock from the mountainside on his head, just like Cecil B. deMille [sic] directing The Ten Commandments, or the building of the pyramids" (*OA* 329).

Bishop's admiration for Macedo Soares's poise in these scenes can only have been amplified at gatherings of Macedo Soares's circle of friends, which included the country's most famous architects, landscape designers, and mural painters—Bernardes, Oscar Niemeyer, Roberto Burle-Marx, and Cándido Portinari. As she hovered at these cosmopolitan and often polylingual affairs, attended as well by key political figures such as Carlos Lacerda, who lived nearby in another Bernardes house and would become governor of Guanabara (greater Rio de Janeiro) in 1960, Bishop felt both energized by and peripheral to developments heralding a new and distinctively modern nation. Although Bishop told Ashley Brown over a decade later that she was "not interested in big-scale work as such," there is ample evidence to suggest that in some ways Bishop wanted to match Macedo Soares's rising fame and the international visibility of her associates, whose projects—translations, for the most part—of scope, complexity, and durability belied the "translator's invisibility," as Lawrence Venuti calls it (Bishop, *Conversations* 24; Venuti 1-34). Her work on Alice Dayrell Brant's *The Diary of "Helena Morley"* (1957), Henrique E. Mindlin's *Modern Architecture in Brazil* (1956), and twentieth-century Brazilian poetry, limited here to the "poet-engineer" João Cabral de Melo Neto,[1] indicates an ambition to assume the role of "architect" (from the Greek for "master builder"): pursuing mastery, setting forth a vision, marshaling others' contributions, and contending with inadequacy and failure. Traces of each are to be found in the archive and also redefine the archive as the site of becoming.

Jacques Derrida, defining the archive as "at once institutive and conservative. Revolutionary and traditional," ferrets out the archaic origin of the term, as the arkheion, or aristocratic house, where records were held for safekeeping ("Archive Fever" 12). Derrida keeps his sight on authoritative commandment that initially creates and maintains the archive and on the immoderate, impossible desires of the one visiting the archive. But I would like to emphasize a more fluid, generative relation of an author to archive, particularly as the materials involve the traces of projects, some necessarily incomplete. These, too, should be situated against the background of the massive developments in the Brazilian economic and political spheres, what Justin Read identifies as the move of the seat of government from the *casas-grande* (mansions of the Brazilian landed class) to Oscar Niemeyer's modern-style *palácios* in Brasília ("Alternative Functions" 72). This chapter explores how archival materials tell the backstory of on-the-fly and aided autodidacticism—in language acquisition and translation, on one hand, and in architecture and urban

Exterior shot of Bishop's studio at Samambaia, 1955. (VC 24.5; Courtesy of Vassar College)

planning, on the other—as Bishop and Macedo Soares became involved in increasingly public ways in aspects of Brazilian society for which neither had received formal training. "The Burglar of Babylon," one of Bishop's most candidly political poems, is rife from the earliest drafts with language signaling both translation and architecture, implicitly fashioning a Tower of Babel, a figure of ambition and translation—and failure.

Bishop was drawn to architecture early on: she sketched the plans for some baroque churches, with Borromini's name written alongside them, on the back cover of a notebook she filled with notes in the New York Public Library in the 1930s (VC 74.11), and she continually placed herself in relationship to the built environment by marking her places of residence with an "x" on postcards.[2]

But it wasn't until she arrived in Brazil that she undertook actual projects, beginning with houses. In July 1955, she told her friends U.T. and Joe Summers that because of helping a Key West friend remodel her house (by correspondence) and seeing Macedo Soares involved in a third or fourth house, "I know more about houses than I ever dreamed of, and I even dream about them almost every night" (VC 37.3). Housekeeping of this sort preoccupied her, from seeking sources of income to fund renovation of the apartment she and Macedo Soares shared in Rio de Janeiro to purchasing in Ouro Prêto an eighteenth-century house in a state of disrepair. Bishop eventually tapped her friend and occasional lover Lilli de Correia Araújo to manage the work on the latter. With Macedo Soares's example in mind, Bishop likely envisioned an architect as one who was very much on the ground, negotiating with contractors and overseeing progress, rather than setting forth an abstract formal idea at a distance.

A neglected project was the occasion for writing to MacIver. Many months after Bishop had made it clear to her publisher that she wanted her friend to design the cover of her second book, Houghton Mifflin had finally written to MacIver. Bishop comes across as acutely embarrassed by the delay, admitting both here and to Marianne Moore that it had resulted from "my own slowness in making up my mind about 'blurbs,' etc., and the difficulty of arranging the details of a book at such a distance" (OA 304). For four full paragraphs, Bishop skittishly works through her sense of failure in mismanaging the project. Determined to get it back on track, she alternately gives instructions to MacIver about what she wants, spells out her likes and prejudices, and repeatedly vows to write to Austin Olney, the press's main contact, to set things right: "I am going to do my best," she swears, "which is awfully feeble" (VC 29.14). In her estimation, little hope lay in convincing Houghton Mifflin to replicate the specifications of the first printing of *North & South* (1946), larger and on better paper than the second, and to agree to other design demands (e.g., "the same kind of linen, glazed") (VC 29.14). Bishop had even lost interest since the process had dragged on so long. That is, until MacIver's letter arrived. Aware of her own letter's burgeoning length,[3] Bishop relents, "I see I have made it very difficult for you, and very cluttered," striving to distill it all down to "one idea": a two-color pattern, "the kind of thing you do so well," with lettering superimposed. Bishop left everything up to MacIver's judgment, "infinitely better than mine," and hoped she might be able to get a sample of the cloth to be used and a sense of the kind of lettering—gilt, silver, paint—so as to "harmonize with the dust-jacket" (VC 29.14).

Leaving aside the chagrined deference, Bishop is highly attentive to shape and materiality, perhaps more than most writers. What's more, she enclosed an "extra sheet," a piece of lined notebook paper turned upside down and haphazardly ripped to suggest the proportions of the first edition of *North & South*, with the lettering as she wanted it to appear. The mock-up is like an architect's casual rendering—part

Postcard of Hemingway's House, Key West, to Robert Lowell in 1947. (Harvard MS Am 1905; Courtesy of Houghton Library, Harvard University)

Postcard of Seattle, sent by Bishop to Rosinha Leão, 1966. (VC 113.10; Courtesy of Vassar College)

sketch, part blueprint, part three-dimensional model (there is a hard crease, rather than a line in ink or pencil, that distinguishes the front flap from the spine)—and she sent a revised sketch shortly after, supposing she should probably have her name on the front. Bishop would later fuss over *The Diary of "Helena Morley,"* finding the cover's black background worth having words over—Robert Giroux recalled learning that, to her, black "was *always* funereal"—although it was too late in production. From then on, Giroux admitted, he "made sure that on future books Elizabeth approved all production and design matters in advance" (*REB* 154).

BECOMING A TRANSLATOR

Mariana Machova rightly argues that translation was a "recurrent presence" in Bishop's creative life from an early point (3). While still at Vassar, she worked out much of a version of Aristophanes' *The Birds*, a comedy about two elderly Athenians' successful project to convince the birds to build a city to rival Olympus.[4] A month spent on the French poets Arthur Rimbaud, Paul Valéry, and others on her first trip abroad, in northwest France, likewise was an apprenticeship in translation (*OA* 396; VC 54.12). Her first major project awaited her in Brazil, the diary of the pseudonymous "Helena Morley," an adolescent girl in the mining country around the turn of the century. Bishop only began the translation when it had become clear that she and Macedo Soares would not be traveling abroad and that she would, admonishing herself in a letter to Pearl Kazin, have to "really learn the god-damned language" (VC 24.4).[5] Bishop had taken it up at Macedo Soares's suggestion and saw it as not only a chance to render into English a classic of Brazilian letters but also the means by which she could improve her Portuguese. Translating-to-learn is commonplace in second-language pedagogy, but Bishop's drive to publish her translation so soon after arriving in Brazil might raise eyebrows now.

Bishop frequently mentioned her improving competency, such as to Kazin in May 1955 when she writes, "I'm getting a lot better at Portugese"—ironically, Bishop uniformly misspells the English word—"and Helena M writes better as she gets older, too, which helps a lot" (VC 24.5). Yet, even a year after the book comes out, she admits to U.T. and Joe Summers that she still can't distinguish stylistic differences (VC 37.3). As late as an interview with Ashley Brown in 1966, she is given to poking fun at her perpetual struggle with the language: "I'm like a dog: I understand everything that's said to me, but I don't speak it very well" (Bishop, *Conversations* 19).

This wasn't for lack of effort. She purchased multiple textbooks and dictionaries, from Raul d'Eça's *An Outline of Portuguese Grammar* (1947) to M. M. Mickle's *Say It in Portuguese* (1955), and indicated others to consider ordering—James L. Taylor's

A Portuguese-English Dictionary (1958) and Ediçōes LEP's *Enciclopédico Dicionário Inglês-Português* (1951)—on the back cover of a notebook (VC 73.7, discussed below).[6] She knew her shortcomings and also had known since her sojourn in Brittany to look up every word when translating (VC 54.12). In the notebooks containing the *Diary*'s first drafts, Bishop indicated words in all-caps in the margin that she didn't recognize or could not locate in a dictionary at hand—idioms, places, days, plants, food, items of clothing, colors, and stories (VC 72.4 and 73.1). Among these was *coitado*, "poor thing," soon a fixture in Bishop's correspondence, so satisfied was she with its local color, although Kazin as her agent objected to "too many *coitados*" (*OA* 313).[7] The distance to fluency was clear enough: not recognizing *perca* as the third-person singular subjunctive of *perder*, to lose, sent Bishop off to study the subjunctive mood, working from pages she or someone else had typed up from a grammar book (VC 72.4, p. 49; VC 74.13). On one, Bishop scribbled a single word in parentheses, *different*, next to a melancholy sentence illustrating how English and Portuguese diverge sometimes: "Sinto muito que ela não estivesse lá. I am sorry she was not there" (VC 74.13). Anglophone readers would expect the simple past (was), as an expression of regret, which does not require the subjunctive in English.

Bishop dabbled in minor efforts, as well, such as providing the Summerses' daughter with a translation of the Brazilian Bandeirantes (Girl Guides) oath and code of honor (VC 37.4).[8] She took time to laugh at the translationese in a guide to Ouro Prêto (Ruas 8). And she appears, perhaps in frustration, to have aborted an attempt at translating Bernard Malamud's "The Magic Barrel" into Portuguese. The first two paragraphs are in a notebook in which she wrote out verb conjugations and lists of words with long and short vowels and made a distinction between two types of translation, one that would really only have been in circulation in literary circles but which Bishop clearly felt indicated two distinct ontological modes:

<u>verter</u> –   to translate from your own language into another
<u>traduzir</u> – "   "   "   another   "   into your own

(VC 73.7)

To magnify the difference between these was the story's grounding in Jewish-American life, but that may have also been part of the draw for Bishop in working on it, to give Brazilian readers a fuller glimpse of American diversity. The Malamud story is intriguing as well in light of an archive of sorts: the marriage arranger who comes to visit the protagonist, a young rabbi in training living in a tenement, brings a literal binder full of women, that is, prospective wives for him to choose among. Bishop owned the short story collection, of which this was the title story (1958), and this translation may be a late addition to the notebook, possibly upon learning that

Bishop's snide comment on the pages in English in Ruas's *Conhecendo Ouro Prêto*. (Vassar, Grille F2651.O9 R82 1952)

she would be teaching alongside Malamud at Harvard. Bishop clearly struggled with the process, as the extensive set of corrections made by other hands reveals.

Indeed, Bishop sought out native speakers. Rosinha Leão recalled that Bishop "would study so hard to get exactly the [correct] word" for the *Diary*, and Brant's husband, the octogenarian head of the Brazilian national bank, made corrections to her English that Bishop initially found amusing (*REB* 148). She enlisted Macedo Soares to go over every page, few signs of which remain, such as where Macedo Soares's rather emphatic "lard" appears where Bishop struggled with what *banha sem sal* referred to—"(fresh?) lard" or pomade ("pomatum") or, as she finally settled on, the literal "unsalted lard," particularizing the grooming habit (VC 72.4, p. 90).

Years later she continued this practice, writing to Rosinha and Magú Leão for advice on the Brazilian poetry anthology, finding herself "baffled" by names of plants and things, such as *maçaranduba* that one of the translators has as "milk-tree fruits" versus the dictionary "native variety of the West Indian bully tree or cow tree" (VC 113.8).

For Macedo Soares, the assistance extended into helping Bishop to negotiate

Portion of Bishop's partial translation manuscript of Bernard Malamud's "The Magic Barrel," showing corrections in another hand. (VC 73.7; Courtesy of Vassar College)

From the handwritten draft of Bishop's translation of *The Diary of "Helena Morley,"* ms p. 90. (VC 72.4; Courtesy of Vassar College)

with the author and her husband. Now a wealthy dowager, Senhora Brant was in Bishop's telling a strange mix of elite and provincial—a person from the backcountry of the state of Minas Gerais, whose compatriots are "very suspicious, according to L – hospitable but stingy – they have an expression here that Mineiros 'eat out of drawers' – so if anyone comes in while they are eating they can shut the drawer and pretend they weren't" (VC 24.4). Without Macedo Soares's tactful and high-spirited intervention, "me and my Portugese [sic] and my U S idea of getting to the pt. would never have got me anywhere" (VC 24.4). Despite an auspicious start, Bishop became irritated with the Brants' meddling, impatience, and avarice. She found it easier to locate images. Originally intending to visit Diamantina with a photographer in tow, Bishop found that the archive of the Patrimônio Artistico in Rio yielded many pictures of the mining town at around the time the diary was being composed. Heaping praise on the kind, overworked director of the archive, Rodrigo Melo Franco de Andrade, she said, "I am simply amazed at my good luck" (Brant xxxiii; VC 24.4). One of these images she would send to both the Summerses and Robert Lowell, in one case calling it a "picture" for the book, in the other, an "illustration" with quotation marks (VC 37.3; Harvard Houghton MS Am 1905).

In guiding input from authors, family, native informants, photographer, archivist, agent, and publishers, Bishop transcended the conventional portrait of translators as mere conduits for texts. She would not have been "invisible" either because of the name-recognition she brought to translations she saw into print.

Bishop suspended work on the diary to take on another translation, Henrique E. Mindlin's *Modern Architecture in Brazil*, conceived as an update to *Brazil Builds*. Bishop felt a certain obligation to Mindlin, a friend of Macedo Soares who had listed her as an employee for visa purposes (*REB* 148). Writing to Kazin in January 1956, Bishop explained he had wanted her for her facility with language, though she thought herself an odd choice—"me, who couldn't construct a pig pen"—unprepared for the architectural terminology, which proved no end of trouble. She was remarkably aware of her own agency in the venture: "Poor man, I've got him so scared now, and reduced his original after-dinner-speech-Brazilian rhetoric to such simple English prose" (VC 24.6).

She also resisted Mindlin's characterization of the Samambaia house as a gathering place for Macedo Soares's artistic and literary friends, until he finally snapped, "*I know this sounds corny in English, but it's all right in Portugese [sic], really! – this house is really a temple of the arts*" (VC 24.6). Relieved it was almost over, she quipped, "he has been angelic to work with" and might have found Mindlin infuriatingly gracious in his acknowledgments, thanking her for "taking time out of which would have been better used in her own writing" (VC 24.6; Mindlin xiii).

For Bishop, there would always be financial concerns. She complained to Kazin in 1955 that the *Diary* "is so much more than just an assigned translation job," requiring her to have put in a good deal of money, with the likelihood of more still: "I think I shd. be able to get a percentage of the royalties, don't you?" (VC 24.5). She had been thinking of her acquaintance, a major figure in Brazilian letters, Manuel Bandeira, who had translated fifteen "bad" books just for the money, saying she had

Diamantina church photograph. (VC 37.3; photographer unknown; Courtesy of Vassar College)

Seated figure at Samambaia house (Henrique E. Mindlin, *Modern Architecture in Brazil*, p. 56; photograph by Aertsens Michel)

tried to steer him toward at least one worthwhile book, one by Lowell (VC 24.5). She nevertheless planned out projects with such ends in mind, including the visit to the new capital of Brasília, about which she had very little pleasant to say, even taking into account the state of incompleteness in 1958: "if it's still going – in two or three years," she wrote to Bill Maxwell, she could see *The New Yorker* preferring a "full-scale Lewis-Mumford-treatment" (*EBNY* 203).

SAVING THE CITY

In 1961, Lacerda, as governor of greater Rio, appointed Macedo Soares to head the working group for the Parque do Flamengo, a massive multiuse park being constructed along Rio's bay. Bishop visited the site soon after and saw Macedo Soares rising to meet the high-stakes assignment, her comportment "admirable, clear, succinct, quiet, – directives like Napoleon" (VC 24.11). At times Bishop would be less reserved, declaring in a 1963 postcard to Lloyd and Loren Frankenberg that Macedo Soares was "busy saving the city of Rio – simply AMAZING – I am flabbergasted by her" (VC 30.9). A few months later, she's "a wonderful mixture these days of Mumford, Galbraith, and perhaps Mayor La Guardia" (*EBNY* 257). These names rolled off her tongue because she had been reading a good deal in city planning to better assist Macedo Soares and offer ideas. Megan Marshall writes that because Macedo Soares hadn't learned to type, she "conscripted" Bishop into compiling an anthology of brief passages from these texts for the busy Lacerda to shape his thinking on urban reform (*Elizabeth Bishop* 161).

Mumford's social histories of global cities were ubiquitous in periodicals, and Bishop owned several of his books. In *The Condition of Man* (1944), which she liked, Mumford made clear the stakes in establishing a just equilibrium between the West and what is now called the Global South (*OA* 376; Mumford 398). Arguing for "strong regional centers of culture," he promoted the "interchange of ideas, values, and symbols" over goods and travelers for "cultural understanding and harmonization" (403). Surely, as she and Macedo Soares were establishing intellectual networks of international reach, Bishop might have seen herself here: "the leisurely comings and goings of students, artists, scientists, philosophers are more important than the quick journeys of high-pressured executives, coddling their will to power by their speedy appearance in person at distant points" (403-04). She may have warned Anne Stevenson in 1965, "I can't be considered a cultural go-between, *nor do I want to be*," but her protestations seem overstated, if not calculated (*Pr* 444-45). If a decade and a half earlier, as Susan Rosenbaum argues, she was suspicious of the "gigantism" of national institutions, while nevertheless benefitting from them, a sense of herself and Macedo Soares as cultural brokers likely granted a frisson of pride, even if the trappings of fame were unwelcome (63).

Bishop had reservations about the Parque project, some tied into Rio itself, which she tried to forget in her "airconditioned seclusion" (VC 30.9). She complained to her Aunt Grace that Macedo Soares was "getting too damned important for fun" and, worse, that should Lacerda ascend to the presidency, he might appoint her as "an ambassador or something—an awful prospect" (VC 25.11; *OA* xvii). She also was very quick to note the great difficulties Macedo Soares faced, witnessing the working group in action in 1961 and concluding that they were "all so jealous of each other, and of a woman, naturally," worrying about the anti-feminist politics (*OA* xvii; *VC* 24.11). She keenly felt the gender disparities in urban planning, noting in separate letters the year before that of a busload of German architects visiting the Samambaia house only three had been women (*OA* 391; *WIA* 344).

It was in the early 1960s that two exceptional American women fearlessly entered intellectual and public debates in male-dominated fields with books that Bishop owned and admired. She wrote to Katherine White in January 1963 to note items in *The New Yorker* she had liked lately, including Rachel Carson's serialized *Silent Spring* the year before, which had since been subjected to a backlash challenging her credentials, scarcely veiled sexism that Bishop seems to reference when she exclaims, "I am sure she knows what she is talking about!" (*EBNY* 255).[9] Likewise, Jane Jacobs's *The Death and Life of Great American Cities* (1961), a full-on broadside against recent urban planning that took on the dominant Robert Moses, offered a comprehensive vision of what made cities tick, discussing how even after well-intended but clumsy interventions, slums often reconstituted themselves and how city parks needed to be "full of objects" and defined by "ingenious variation" (4, 265, 104). Such ideas decidedly influenced Macedo Soares's pitched battles to include more family- and pedestrian-friendly features in the Parque and Bishop's own contributions to debate about public policy and cultural patrimony.

CITYSCAPE WITH FIGURES

In April 1963, Bishop watched with binoculars as a manhunt unfolded on the hillside north of the apartment in Leme, with soldiers ascending through the *favela* and onto the steep, uninhabited slope to where a notorious criminal, Micuçu, had escaped. The poem she composed, "The Burglar of Babylon," came quickly, hardly requiring revision, she said (*Conversations* 29). The drafts—from the earliest notes in a notebook now at Harvard to the increasingly polished drafts and *New Yorker* proofs at Vassar—suggest a more prolonged gestation and a more complex synthesis than is often acknowledged, particularly for the five-quatrain introit and the shorter refrain-like coda.

Marianne Moore thought it her finest poem, Lowell dutifully reported, perceptibly less sanguine himself about what he called another one of her "peculiar triumphs," but James Merrill enigmatically said the poem "rides to safety on a raft of pastiche" (*WIA* 560; Merrill 252). But a pastiche of what, exactly? Jerome Mazzaro fingers outlaw ballads; Jacqueline Vaught Brogan sees Bishop undermining the "moral" of criminals' confessions just before being executed in "good-night" ballads; Axel Nesme asks whether it's a Wordsworthian lyrical ballad; and Ashley

Brown, Fiona Shaw, and Marit J. MacArthur each suggest some readers would catch notes of an Audenesque ballad. In recent scholarship, it is often compared to a long poem Bishop partially translated for the October/November 1963 issue of *Poetry*. João Cabral de Melo Neto's "Morte e vida Severina" recounts the life and fate of a laborer in the author's native drought-plagued region in the Northeast *sertão* and coast. Nominally a Christmas play and modeled on *literatura de cordel* (popular ballads sung in marketplaces and sold as pamphlets hung on strings, or *cordeis*), the fourteen sections tell a tale that is brutal and de-individuating—every *nordestino* is a "Severino" and subject to the same death—and sympathetic yet distancing, unsentimental, even anti-lyrical, the result of Cabral's formal choices and lexical register (Machova 68; Hicok, *Elizabeth Bishop's Brazil* 86-87; Araújo 137-40).

The focus on the three sections of "Death and Life of a Severino," Bishop's only extant translation of Cabral, has obscured her profound connection to his work, especially the books from mid-1950s and early 1960s, which he felt was his best period. She thought him the most important Brazilian poet of his generation, telling Lowell in 1958 that he was one of the few she liked (*WIA* 278). She defended his sympathy for the poor, recognizing that he was, as Hermide Menquini Braga would later say, the "consciência angariada" (collective conscience) of the landed class, which had been his upbringing (9). She also saw in Cabral a kindred spirit, ensconced in his diplomatic post in Spain, far from his homeland, engaging with another landscape, another language, another literary tradition. Whereas Bishop found tangible difference between Brazil and New England, the train journeys between assignments in Madrid, Barcelona, and Seville saw Cabral connect the "hard plain of Castile" and the harsh *sertão* in Brazil (Campos, "Geometry" 619). He learned from an earlier generation of Spanish writers, Unamuno and Azorín, who had at the turn of the century been seeking to capture the "essence" of Spain in its landscapes (Carvalho 164). In "Pernambuco em Málaga," for instance, he articulates his experience abroad in terms of—or better, *translates*—the conditions of his native state (*Obra completa* 301-02; Brandellero 26).[10] Undoubtedly his *Paisagens com figuras* [Landscapes with Figures] (1956) drew Bishop in because of its play on the beaux arts: the "figures" referring not solely to human figures as in a landscape painting but to *figurations*.

In shifting to a cityscape with figures, "Burglar" references an anything-but-fanciful reality: Pernambuco in Rio. Fleeing their "same Severino death" as Cabral put it, impoverished farmers and laborers took their chances in the *favelas*, some falling into crime and others mustered into the army and police to catch or kill them (*P* 153). This was not lost on Bishop, who depicted the soldiers as scarcely professionalized, one of them letting nerves get the best of him and inadvertently killing his commander, himself an earlier arrival from Pernambuco. Just as Cabral had done with Severino and, in "Festa na casa-grande" (1960), a millworker overcome by the color yellow (suggesting both malaria and the color of dried sugarcane), Bishop cultivates sympathy with the callow youths pressed into service and the dead commander, yielding up his soul to God and his children to the governor (*Obra completa* 279-88; *P* 112-13). Friends though she may have been with Lacerda, there is something rather pointed in an implicit question: Who, or what, are you serving, particularly when you are in a new place?

Before settling on "Severino," Bishop had read Cabral extensively. The introit and conclusion of "Burglar," each set off from the main body of Micuçu's tale, are scenic commentaries that draw on the seven cemetery poems in *Paisagens com figuras* and *Quaderna* [Four-Spot] (1960). In her translator's note in *Poetry*, Bishop noted that cemetery poems are "almost a specialty" for Cabral, "and I think some of his finest short poems are those describing with sympathy and bitterness the sun-baked graveyards of his native state" ("A Note on the Poetry" 18). No one has made anything of her remark to Lowell in May 1963, as she was working on "Burglar," that she had translated one of these poems before settling on the Christmas play (*WIA* 456). Which of them fits Bishop's label, "very Valéry-influenced"? It is tempting to think the poem is on the "translation page" listed in her personal library's card catalog at Vassar as one in the copy of *Quaderna* that made its way to Harvard's Houghton library, no longer among loose pages removed from it and from her other books. Or could it be among the rough—even prose—translations Bishop provided to contributors to the 1972 anthology who didn't know Portuguese? It might have been one of the two cemetery poems finished by Jane Cooper (Machova 52-53; Bishop and Brasil 122-25). In lieu of an identification, even provisional, I want instead to linger on modes of translation not often considered: reading-for-eventual-translation, reading-as-translation, and translating-by-other-means, which point to an interior, evolving archive only partly accessible by inference.

Cabral's cemetery poems ruminate on death and the dead land, the limitless production of corpses, inadequacies of burial, and what Antonio Carlos Secchin calls the "império unânime da morte" (174). Each is geographically located, most in Pernambuco and two in the adjacent states of Paraíbe and Alagoas. The sense that both the final resting places and the poems that describe them are *constructed* spaces is often critical. "Why this great wall?" he asks in one "Cemitério pernambucano," querying the urge to so solidly cordon off and protect the graveyard with a heavy locked iron gate (*Education by Stone* 89). In one poem, the cemetery is a place of residence, too small to be a hotel and "more like a boardinghouse" (*pensão*), and in another, the graves become kilns under the punishing sun (110-11, 118-19). In still another, the cemetery strikes the eye as "a Constantinople / with touches of baroque, / gothic, and opera scenery," its "florid and rhetorical plaster" registering like a politician's grandiloquent language (*palavras esdrúxulas*) contrasted with the backlands "where naked / life does not make speeches / but talks with short sharp words" (*palavras agudas*) (116-17). Bishop said of translating Cabral that "he doesn't come out very well in English, either—too long-winded. Oh these luscious Latin languages and all that assonance and how tempting it seems to be for them to go on and on and on" (*WIA* 341). Although Bishop focused on Cabral's long "Severino" poem in the end, she must have found the pithy, concrete cemetery poems more appealing for their brevity.

Although Cabral was not to publish a poem titled "Cemitérios metropolitanos" until his 1985 collection *Agrestes*, the *paraibano* cemetery poem concludes by alluding to *nordestinos* who never made the move to a city or to the prevalent two-way movement Bishop missed in "The poor who come to Rio / And can't go home again" (*P* 112).

> os poucos que, por aqui
> recusaram o privilégio
> de cemitérios cidades
> em cidades cemitérios.
>
> [those few residents who,
> coming here, refused
> the privilege of city cemeteries
> in cemetery cities.] (*Education by Stone* 110-11)

The introit and coda of "Burglar," I contend, paint the hills of Rio de Janeiro—Chicken, Catacomb, Kerosene, Skeleton, Astonishment, and Babylon, as Bishop lists them—as just so many cemeteries, *cemitérios cariocas*, the cemeteries of Rio where, as Bishop put it in "Capricorn," an undated fragment, "the poor never freeze / they just," or, as she amended it, "merely starve" (VC 65.10).[11] Or, in the case of Micuçu, they are shot dead by the authorities. In the original *New Yorker* version of the ballad,[12] the introit and coda are almost the same length, five and four quatrains apiece; the latter describes how rapidly he had been buried there on the *morro*, with the soldiers already climbing after another two thieves, supposedly less dangerous, less worthy of a ballad but, like the dead *nordestino*, no less likely to meet a similar end.

THE POET-ARCHITECT

Briefly back in Brazil in 1958 to claim a prize in Recife (and presumably when he and Bishop had one or more conversations that so impressed her), Cabral started another poem on graveyards. This one is a satire, Benedito Nunes explains, of the bicameral legislature of Brazil, by then one branch of government not yet comfortably situated in the new capital, as Bishop noted in her travelogue of the same year (81; *Pr* 296). The two serial poems in *Dois parlamentos* (1960) have instructions for voicing cadence and regional accent that confirm the South (Rio, São Paulo, Brasília) as the center of power. The senators in "Congresso no polígono das secas" [Congress in the Polygon of Droughts[13]] speak in lofty tones about *cemitérios gerais* [general or unrestricted cemeteries], admitting to a "rhetorical" interest in them (*Obra completa* 271). The "lower" chamber of deputies in "Festa na casa-grande" fares better in weighing the travails and death of a *cassaco de engenho* [millworker] (279-88).

The *engenho* had a special resonance for Cabral, as his family owned three sugar mills, and he was known as a child for reciting ballads in the *cordel* vein in the company of the *cassacos*. It is the fulcrum for his two enduring images: canefields and buildings. Scholars now refer to Cabral as the "poeta-engenheiro" and, more frequently in recent years, the "poeta-arquiteto."[14] His second collection, *O engenheiro* (1947), marked a lasting stylistic shift, heralded by its epigraph drawn from Le Corbusier, whom Cabral had said was more critical to his development as a writer than anyone: "machine à émouvoir" (*Obra completa* 66). A poem, he said later, is a machine for moving, for causing emotion (Gonçalves 641). Although "poet-architect" was not coined to describe him until much later, Justin Read rightly notes that already in 1958, some of a younger generation of Brazilian writers, the Noigandres group of concrete poets, among them Haroldo de Campos, were already in their manifesto praising his work as having invented the "arquitetura funcional do verso" ("Alternative Functions" 66). Five years later, Campos called him the "geometra engajado" [engaged geometer], declaring that the title poem elucidated the composition of the rest of the poems in the collection, which "seem to be made with ruler and T-square, etched and calculated on paper" (*Metalinguagem* 77; "Geometry" 81).

Overlaying Cabral's arrangement of poems with mathematical proportions shaped by Le Corbusier's dicta, Read takes the architectonic to the macroscopic scale of the book ("Alternative Functions" 73-80). In scaling out still further to his *oeuvre* and yet also maintaining close focus on individual effects, I instead want to call attention to Cabral's quatrain, which, with the exception of the heftier stanzas of *A educação pela pedra* [Education by Stone] (1966) that are the object of Read's study, was the primary formal building block throughout his career. Campos would make out Cabral's *quadras* as "unidade-blocal de composição, elemento geométrico pré-construído" (*Metalinguagem* 70). Set off with white space like mortar, and whether strung together indefinitely or clustered in quartets or series, the quatrain was to Cabral as the *terza rima* was to Dante, not merely a formal scaffold but a condition of possibility. If for Dante the number three suggested divinity, spirituality, and the means to build an inimitable vision, for Cabral the number four carried connotations, Arnaldo Saraíva argues, as a "símbolo da terra, da espacialidade terrestre, do situacional, dos limites externos naturais, da totalidade «mínima» e da organização racional" [symbol of the earth, of terrestrial spatiality, of the situational, of external natural limits, of "minimal" totality, and rational organization] (17). Yet, Sara Brandellero writes of *A educação*, written 1962-65, "Much could be said about Cabral's subversion of the idea of precise construction and order when considered in relation to the social political backdrop" (13). But that doesn't account for the ways in which Cabral's earlier quatrain poems respond to the postcolonial drivers of multigenerational poverty and political instability.

As noted in relation to *Dois parlamentos*, Cabral tended to explore the permutational affordances of his formal choices, yet his preferred quatrain was that of a ballad rhyme, *abxb*, which has built into it both orderly precision and plasticity. Furthermore, with *Paisagens com figuras*, Cabral began working with assonantal rhyme, which preserves the vowel sounds amid shifting consonants and which he would explain in the first poem in *Agrestes* three decades later: "apaga o verso e não soa" [which flattens the line and does not resound] (Brandellero 84). More than confronting readers anticipating the perfect *soante* (consonantal) rhyme with subtle antilyricism, the adoption of *rima toante* serves other ends, he hinted in an interview: *rima toante* is an ancient Iberian tradition, abandoned in Portugal with vestiges remaining in the Brazilian Northeast (Carvalho 166). Recovering an unused form, one with early origins (Galician-Portuguese troubadours) communicated to his home region by imperial expansion, has political undertones. Secchin understood this postcolonial dynamic to be playing out in Cabral's "Paisagens com cupim" [Landscapes with Termites], in that the insects were like the injection of "realidades consideradas não poéticas, ou antipoéticas" into the lyrical (169). In the most telling passages for our purposes, the termites stand in for the Portuguese master builder, who pretends there is robustness to the material eaten by misery (*Obra completa* 238). Look closely enough, and the termites are the "os pais de nosso barroco" [parents of our baroque], the chewed-out hollows elevated to a "gesto pomposo e redondo / na véspera mesma do escombro" [pompous, circular gesture / on the very eve of rubble] (239).[15] But what they attack, little noticed from afar, is not exactly the picturesque:

> Olinda não usa cimento.
> Usa um tijolo farelento.
> Mesmo com tanta geometria

Olinda é já de alvenaria.

Vista de longe (tantos cubos)
ela anuncia un profil duro.
Porém de perto seus sobrados
revelam esse fio gasto

da madeira muito roçada,
das paredes muito caiadas (*Obra completa* 235)

[Olinda does not use cement.
It uses crumbly brick.
Even with so much geometry,
Olinda was once made of masonry.

Seen from afar (so many cubes)
it announces a hard profile.
But from up close its floors
reveal the worn grain

of wood scrubbed a lot,
of walls whitewashed a lot] (my trans.)

Even so, the many cubic structures that comprise the town point to Le Corbusier's interest in that shape and the way in which the eye should respond to shapes brought together: "cubes, cones, spheres, cylinders or pyramids are the great primary forms which light reveals to advantage; the image of these is distinct and tangible within us and without ambiguity." For this reason, we find them "*beautiful forms, the most beautiful forms*" (Costa 242; Le Corbusier 29).

Bishop began writing her own poems in quatrains in greater numbers, from "The Armadillo" to "Going to the Bakery," only upon coming to admire Cabral. Showing greater receptivity to slant rhyming than what she might have found in W. H. Auden's ballads, she nevertheless worked with rhymes preserving the consonants and varying the vowel sounds, a more common pattern of variation in Anglophone verse. The Cabralian *quadra* casts new light on the spare stanzas of "Burglar," allowing us to see the rhyming as anything but "childish" or "childlike," as it has become almost customary to say of the poem, even if with the proviso that it is "deceptively" so (Millier, *Elizabeth Bishop* 345; Spiegelman 155; Page and Oliveira 129). Taking Bishop to have regarded, in no insignificant way, her quatrains as building blocks, particularly in "Burglar," we should be attentive to what is being built.

The poem amplifies interplay between the dizzying vertical and the horizontal. In his flight to the uninhabitable heights of Babylon, Micuçu ascends through what gets called the "vertical slums" in Bishop's 1962 Life World Library *Brazil* (140). Bishop keenly depicted the surprising topography of the city: how a dead-end street suddenly turns into an endless stairway, how upper-class dwellers in high-rises wake to roosters crowing or babies crying in *favelas* a few yards away, details altered or removed entirely by the editors, about whom she complained mightily (*Pr* 198-99; *Brazil* 56). "One story, told as true," she continued in an earlier draft, involved a couple returning to an eighth-floor apartment to the sound of thuds and crashes going on inside. Rather than burglars, a "panic-stricken horse" had somehow fallen from his "minute pasture" right onto their terrace (199). This episode appears to have been recast in "Twelfth Morning, Or What You Will," a poem on her mind in June 1964, when she asked Macedo Soares to locate the draft and send it to her (VC 118.46). In a foggy, rural Illyria-in-Brazil, a young black boy Balthazár looks like he's been crowned "king" by the water bucket on his head, and in mid-poem there stands a big white horse, inside or outside a fence—who can tell? Is perspective "dozing"? (*P* 108).

As Micuçu rests atop the hill, he contemplates the waterfront below, swimmers' heads floating like coconuts. But the disorienting height makes him misperceive the sea: "Flat as a wall," with freighters looking like flies climbing up it (*P* 111). Scarcely visible in this moment is the way in which sea, hill, wall, death, and the dead man walking converge in Portuguese in the form of ontological interchangeability—*mar*, *morro*, *muro*, *morte*, and *morto*—a dynamic that appears in one of Cabral's cemetery poems where boundaries prove porous (*Obra completa* 157). To these we could add the nearly anagrammatic terms in Secchin's observation that, in "Festa na casa-grande," the "noção de 'amarelo'" [notion of "yellow"] is transfigured into the "cor *moral*" [moral color] that defines the inner and outer state of the overworked and dying millhand (193). Perspectival inversions specifically involving water appear elsewhere in Cabral's poems. "Rio e/ou poço" depicts a person standing up from lying down as a horizontal river transformed into the "água vertical" of a well (*Obra completa* 251-52). "Pregão turístico do Recife," the first poem in *Paisagens com figuras*, begins

> Aqui o mar é uma montanha
> regular redonda e azul
> mais alta que os arrecifes
> e os mangues rasos ao sul

[Here the sea is a mountain
smooth and blue and round
taller than the coral reefs
and shallow swamps to the south] (*Education by Stone* 80–81)

Bishop would likely have found her own "travel" poems as kin of the latter. Richard Zenith's title for his translation, "Tourist Pitch for Recife," captures the nimble, sardonic quality, but "pitch" misses the sense of economic desperation, with *pregar* lending "to cry, to clamor," "to inflict something on someone," and even "to collapse" (*Education by Stone* 81). Later, in "Paisagens com cupim," we are told Recife itself "falls" into the sea without contaminating itself (*Obra completa* 235). This precariousness, of the land giving way to industriousness or malaise, points to a confounding of vertical and horizontal that Bishop discusses in the Life book: the demolition of entire hills in Rio (*Brazil* 56). Bishop had been reading into the matter, her copy of Gilberto Freyre's *The Mansion and the Shanties* (1936, translated 1963) underlined where the early nineteenth-century doctor José Maria Bomtempo had been fighting for a Rio de Janeiro more open to the breezes from the sea, or "better ventilation," to offset the dangers of the miasmas from ditches, churches, cemeteries, the ill effects of the dampness of the soil. He even went so far as to hope for the demolition of the hills of San Antônio and Castelo (Freyre 199).

The Morro de Castelo was torn down a full century later, in "one of those scene shifting operations that are so characteristic of the city and astonishing to visitors" (*Brazil* 56)—surprising, too, to a Cariocan returning after some time away to find the cityscape almost unrecognizable. Perhaps nodding to the now-absent Castelo, Bishop places Micuçu on Babylon near "an old fort, falling down," formerly a post for watching for French vessels, but she errs in prefacing the 1968 illustrated version of the poem by saying that the Hill of Kerosene was torn down shortly before Micuçu's death (*P* 111; *The Burglar of Babylon* n.p.). What Bishop conspicuously left out of *Brazil*'s description of the evolving topography of the city was the demolition of the formerly inhabited Morro de Santo Antonio in the early 1950s, for the sake of providing fill for the Parque. At Macedo Soares's insistence, the working group rented a dredge that had seen service in the Panama Canal to add still more to the horizontal expanse of the "Aterro" (fill), as the park was often called, from the Rio bay.

The capstone to the project, one that only adds to the associated vertical-horizontal dynamics, came in 1965, when the exceptionally tall lamps were installed, to much complaining about the lack of visibility below. Even these were ambitious beyond all practicality; the illumination expert, Richard Kelley, brought in to consult wanted them to be twice as tall—90 meters, Bishop exclaimed—as the airport authorities would permit (*OA* 429; VC 23.4).

Photograph of the demolition of the Morro de Santo Antônio, Rio de Janeiro, 1950s (Arquivo Geral da Cidade do Rio de Janeiro)

Rio bay panoramic postcard to U. T. and Joseph Summers in 1963, with the dredge identified in the water and with two X's marking the extreme ends of the Parque do Flamengo. (VC 37.4; Courtesy of Vassar College)

Parque do Flamengo lamps postcard, unused. (VC 78.7; Courtesy of Vassar College)

THE BURGLAR OF THE TOWER OF BABEL

The poor arrive in Rio in increasing numbers, Bishop says in "On the Railroad Named Delight," an essay from a year later, "packed in old buses or in trucks filled with benches called *arraras* ('macaw perches')" (*Pr* 344). An avian metaphor appears early in the drafting of "Burglar" and endures in the final version, where the new arrivals come in a "confused migration," building their shanties like fragile nests that could, with the least hint of wind, come tumbling down (Harvard Houghton MS Am 2115; VC 58.6; *P* 110). Bishop implicitly contrasts what is now dryly called "informal" architecture with the celebrated high-rises of the elite and the new International Style public buildings, their reinforced concrete appearing anything but liable to collapse. Macedo Soares's Parque, too, as a site of deliberate nation-building that was nominally "democratic," stands in contrast to the "general decrepitude" of the city, as Bishop put it, and is "by far the city's best birthday present to its citizens, and although it is only about three-quarters finished, the citizens are embracing it by tens of thousands" (*Pr* 344). What the *favelas* do, however, is remind one of the plight of the poor that persists despite national advances in industry and the arts (*Brazil* 140).

Bishop's striking perception here, encoded in the word *confused*, is to allude to the biblical story of Babel, which Derrida suggested actually should be translated as "confusion." For him the tower "does not merely figure the irreducible multiplicity of tongues: it exhibits an incompletion, the impossibility of finishing, of totalizing, of saturating, of completing something on the order of edification, architectural construction, system and architectonics" ("Des Tours" 165). Sensitive to these resonances three decades earlier, Bishop raises the question about whose ambition and folly it is we should be thinking of. On the one hand, the poor, she notes in *Brazil*, can find little on the hills of Rio, save perhaps sun and breeze, and yet they keep pouring into the city, such that even when a thousand are resettled in stable housing—here Bishop echoes Jacobs on the regeneration of poverty-stricken neighborhoods in the United States—another thousand come from afar to take their places in the vacated shanties (56). In Rio they find relief from rural boredom but not from the poverty that forces them to build with what's at hand. On the other hand, the wealthy aggrandize themselves and aspire to refashion Brazil as an equal to the Western powers without fully recognizing that the city's setting, beautiful as it is, "does not lend itself to city planning" (*Pr* 344). That is to say nothing of the concerns about the enormous expense required to move the government to the newly constructed capital of Brasília. It was not the first time that Bishop had associated government buildings with the Tower of Babel; in 1957, visiting New York and wanting to find the murals painted by Portinari at the new United Nations, she made the connection, suggesting that such international cooperation was foolhardy, if not chimeric (VC 113.8).

To consider the "confusion" of tongues that came from the divine command to knock down the tower is to recognize the belatedness of any allusions to it. On the one hand, in "A Warm and Reasonable People," one of the few chapters the Life editors left largely untouched, Bishop admires the universality of Brazilian Portuguese, claiming that anyone from one region can understand someone from another, although in letters she took pleasure in singling out regionalisms and breakdowns of communication (*Brazil* 12). On the other hand, the cosmopolitan life of the Rio elite involved overseas travel, libraries in four languages, and a reliance on a growing network of global connections frayed by Cold War politics. The Tower of Babel, as the figure of the impossibility of translation, of the endlessly deferred dream of the reunification of human languages and world peace, emerges as a ghostly presence in "Burglar," to register a latent anxiety and ambivalence in Bishop about the roles she had taken up in recent years, to say nothing of her worries about linguistic competence.

Whereas Bishop could point to a longstanding tradition in "Latin countries, old world and new, of poets in the Ministries of Foreign Affairs, vice-consuls or ambassadors," the connection between poetry and politics in the United States was tenuous (*Pr* 225). True, Robert Frost had given the first reading of a poem at a presidential inauguration in January 1961, subsequently spoke publicly about politics, and in attempting to improve Russian-US relations by meeting with Khrushchev in Moscow, drew Kennedy's ire with his remarks afterward (Monteiro, "Frost's Politics" 221, 233; Seale 319-20). After having lost out on the Nobel Prize, Frost warmed to the role of poet-statesman, and his poem "Kitty Hawk," published in its longest version in *In the Clearing* in 1963, more clearly embodied that vision than any other.[16]

Implying that his "skylark" of a poem is a "mixture mechanic," Frost blends multiple genres and influences (41, 57). Of a similarly heterogeneous cast, Bishop's poem, rather than ruminatively spurring humankind onward into space, to see spirit penetrate matter, instead is a record of failure: Micuçu caught multiple times before getting killed, urban planners floundering in the face of persistent inequality, and a gradually dawning understanding, if not a premonition, of the Parque as ultimately unmanageable. Within a few months, at a ceremony inaugurating a space in the Parque where model airplane aficionados could ply their trade, Bishop noted Macedo Soares's incongruous behavior toward the very constituency she was there for. All the speeches praised her "to the skies as a lover of children & a benefactor of humanity," yet there she was, as Bishop wrote to Lowell, "yelling at and kicking at, almost, little boys who were trying to climb up on the platform, cursing photographers, etc." (*WIA* 498). Bishop had tried to intervene, "Try to look *pleasant*! They're all looking at you!" (498). By extension, Bishop felt they were all looking at her.

MASTERING DISASTER

Bishop was encouraged enough about initial reactions to the poem—or at least anticipated reactions, as Lacerda uncharacteristically hadn't responded—that she expressed her desire to see the poem translated and set to an old Brazilian tune (VC 23.4). Her first wish came true, as Macedo Soares's nephew Flávio, a young man with decidedly modern tastes, stepped forward. She had taken him under her wing, helping him apply to Harvard, praising him to Lowell as one whose poems were exceptional among his peers—like Cabral's, she said, but "really 'felt'" (*WIA* 508). Bishop and Flávio collaborated on at least two translations of her work, one being "Burglar," not published until 1968, by which point the poem had generated controversy in Brazil (Monteiro, *Elizabeth Bishop* 62). The other, "O tatú," is as of this writing listed in the Vassar finding aid as by Flávio but is in fact a translation of "The Armadillo" into Portuguese, with Bishop's notes and corrections, a task that he had initially shied away from, citing the far greater degree of difficulty (VC 84.11, 10.1). It is telling that the two of them had worked together on two of her poems among her most Cabralian. "The Armadillo" was written not long after *Paisagens con figuras* was published, a landmark moment for Bishop, as she used quatrains and slant rhymes with far greater frequency thereafter. Both poems also are notably about failure and catastrophe, the armadillo threatened by the popular craze for celebratory fire balloons, and precede, if not presage, a rising number of painful events.[17] For all the support of both Bishop and Lowell, Flávio was not admitted to Harvard. The national political paroxysms that undercut Macedo Soares's authority led to health problems, arguments, infidelity, and Bishop's decisions to go alone to Seattle in 1966 and then New York in 1967.

In a rarely consulted folder at Vassar there is, among newspaper and magazine clippings, a cartoon instantly recognizable as from *The New Yorker* (VC 122.7). In the photocopy, which researchers have been traditionally given at Vassar, it is easy to miss the bittersweet coda this clipping represents, because Macedo Soares's modifications in blue ink almost vanish into Alan Dunn's erratic, loopy pen strokes. Under a looming Earth, an extraterrestrial holds a radio receiver to its ear, listening to broadcasts about the moonscape spurred by photographs from pre-Apollo missions. That figure, clearly unhappy with what's being said, sports both a jaunty, sidewise blue cap and bulbous glasses that Macedo Soares has added, as well as the letter "L" to identify her. Just to the left, also on that bulging hill, another extraterrestrial sits, unadorned, hands on knees in earnest contentment, and declares, "Well, I don't care <u>what</u> they say about it. It's home to me." She is labeled "E."

Much as Normal Rockwell had done earlier in the year for *Look*, Dunn had based the lunar landscape on pictures sent back by the unmanned Ranger orbiters and Surveyor landers. His caption refers to the general consensus about the desolate place, which in the first color photographs taken by Surveyor 3 was "an uninterestingly uniform gray" sharply contrasted with the "spectacular" blue marble. Dunn's depiction of the Earth rise was accurate: one can make out "the cloud cover over areas of Brazil and South American countries" that Evert Clark said scientists discerned in the images (50). Space exploration was far from a national obsession a decade after Sputnik, with only about a third of Americans supporting the continued expense, and bland lunar landscapes didn't change minds (Launius 163). Macedo Soares, perceiving a parallel, indicated that the foreground, punctuated with outcroppings of rock, was "Rio de Janeiro" and that further back, beyond a substantial crater, a flat stretch was "Parque do FLAMENGO."

The resulting adaptation suggests a tender defiance in the face of public opinion, recalling the two women's united efforts in urban planning and translation. Just two years earlier, that intimacy had existed, but the cartoon appeared in the July 29, 1967, issue, less than two months before Macedo Soares would join Bishop

"Well, I don't care <u>what</u> they say about it. It's home to me."

Alan Dunn cartoon, *The New Yorker*, July 29, 1967. (VC 122.7; Courtesy of Vassar College)

in New York, ending a separation originally made on doctor's advice. By then Macedo Soares had lost control of the Parque entirely, and on the eve of departing Rio earlier in the month, Bishop drew up a "proper will," unbeknownst to Macedo Soares (*OA* 465). Discovered folded into a book in Bishop's absence, the will immediately became a flash point in their correspondence, with Macedo Soares cycling from recrimination to, as Bishop put it to the Summerses afterward, "plans for our future together" (VC 118.1-30, 37.5; *OA* 465, 470). Whether subsequently separated from one of these letters (it is folded in half, as though slotted in an envelope), brought by Macedo Soares when she came, or, in the hours before she overdosed on tranquilizers, modified from *The New Yorker* issue Bishop might have had at 61 Perry Street, the modified cartoon also amounts to an attempt to assuage Macedo

Soares's anxieties about Bishop's increasing emotional distance and to persuade Bishop to return to Brazil, by putting words in her mouth that should ring true.

The fitting, cutting irony of this repurposed cartoon is that it sat squarely back-to-back with another cartoon, this one of a long-married heterosexual couple, rather than a pair of genderless aliens; the wife pointedly muses to the husband reposing in an armchair, "You know what's wrong with us? In thirty-seven years we've failed to establish a meaningful dialogue." This living room *aperçu* had echoes in contemporaneous lamentations by UN Secretary General U. Thant and others that there had been no "meaningful dialogue" between the Americans and the Russians since the Cuban Missile Crisis. That last occasion had been so "meaningful"—"rattling everybody's back teeth" and devolving into a shouting match over Berlin, with Khrushchev threatening war—that Kennedy promptly upped the defense budget and sent another division to Europe (Jack 94; Reston 46). But it also registers a marriage-as-cold-war metaphor that suited Bishop's and Macedo Soares's protracted difficulties, in which blowups became more common, one leading Bishop to wish aloud that she had not "wasted fifteen years" with Lota and Macedo Soares returning the favor (Marshall, *Elizabeth Bishop* 197). Macedo Soares's arrival in New York in mid-September 1967, however, lacked such sparks, their one half-day together notably peaceable. We might never know whether Bishop saw this pair of cartoons before she woke early the next morning to the sound of Macedo Soares staggering down the stairs "already almost unconscious," but the pair never returned to Brazil together to initiate the project that Lota's last sketch had set forth (*OA* 471).

CONCLUSION: ARCHIVE FIRE

If there is anything to be learned from this tragedy, it is not a moral lesson about excessive ambition or a lack of caution on any one individual's part. Consider the heightened recognition of the challenges faced by women even now in male-dominated fields, and consider the fire that consumed the national museum in Brazil on September 2, 2018, incinerating perhaps as many as two million irreplaceable cultural and natural artifacts because, it has been reported, improperly maintained fire hydrants ran dry (Andreoni A8). To write at this moment is to be aware not just of the precariousness of the archive but of the broader forces of convention and change. Bishop was keenly aware of the enormous swells of financial, political, and social capital rapidly shaping landscape and cityscape, complaining about, for instance, garish billboards and brand-name signage being erected everywhere. In one such letter about unsightly signboards, to Frani Blough Muser in late 1964, Bishop proudly reported that Lacerda had credited a letter of hers for having persuaded him to block the construction of a skyscraper hotel atop a hill in central Rio (VC 35.1). Building on these concerns in an interview with Léo Gilson Ribeiro published in *Correio da Manhã* on December 13, 1964, three weeks after "Burglar" appeared in *The New Yorker*, Bishop lashed out about the loss of cultural patrimony, ending with the strongest possible words:

> But an even greater crime is to tear down, in Rio, in Minas, in so many places, those venerable edifices of great beauty, which constitute histories and artistic treasures of past epochs. Is there no way to put a stop to such wanton destruction of this nation's heritage? I reiterate that to me it is a crime against nature, against history, even against God! (*Conversations* 17)

Sounding less overtly like Mumford or, for that matter, Jacobs, who promoted saving historic buildings largely for utilitarian ends—namely to maintain economic and demographic diversity—Bishop is uncharacteristically alarmist in a very public venue. But the jeremiad is savvy, her moral indignation meant to be the more persuasive because she was an outsider, a translator.

For *The Diary of "Helena Morley,"* Bishop turned to a photograph of a church to "illustrate" the chronicle of quotidian life from the perspective of a teenage girl and devotes more space in the introduction to the town's architecture, particularly the churches, than to any other subject. Nominally, this was because the young Brant had taken her surroundings for granted (Brant xv). But in casting her eye so fixedly on the undeveloped baroque exteriors and the "disappointing" interiors, Bishop was both translating the spaces for vicarious experience and readying them, even if only in imaginative terms, for what they already were inviting as sites of human engagement and becoming (xvii-xviii). For instance, Bishop stumbles across the Church of the Amparo at the end of an alley, finding it "stricken but dignified, like a person coming towards one whom one expects to beg, who doesn't beg after all" (xix). Perhaps this is one definition of the picturesque, of its affective paradoxes, but it is also an admission that the building, the text to be translated, and the archive are agents, machines for moving, that invite us not only to engage them but to become social within them, to become the engineers and builders that reshape them, to be open to failure and incompleteness.

NOTES

1. A treatment of Bishop and Emmanuel Brasil's 1972 co-edited collection lies beyond the scope of this chapter, though it was "a thoroughly cross-cultural endeavor" (Hicok, *Elizabeth Bishop's Brazil* 64).

2. Most of her postcards depict buildings or cityscapes. In one to Lowell in 1947, she used an "x" to show where she was staying behind Hemingway's Key West house (Harvard Houghton MS Am 1905). In 1966, writing to Rosinha and Magú Leão separately, she located herself topographically in Rosinha's card (gouging the aerial image with her red ballpoint pen to get the ink to sink in) and, unable to do so in the neon-saturated scene of Magú's, geographically ("not sure" where the city is on the flat gray shape of Washington state) (VC 113.10). In an undated card, she dispensed with a mark and just jabbed straight through, telling Magú to hold it the light to see Macedo Soares winking from room 1212 of their hotel behind St. Patrick's (VC 113.10).
3. Although it could not be reprinted here at greater length, the letter is worth reading in full for the tense interplay between Bishop's strong aesthetic preferences and her chagrined deference to MacIver.
4. See Andrew Walker's chapter, "The Archival Aviary: Elizabeth Bishop and Drama," in this volume for a more detailed discussion of this translation project.
5. *One Art* bowdlerizes this to "damned," but Kazin unabashedly quotes the original in her *Partisan Review* memoir (*OA* 288; Bell 45).
6. These titles—with "Lep" mistranscribed for "LEP," perhaps from Bishop having seen the book's all-caps title page somewhere—were jotted down in uncharacteristically large script in pencil, perhaps in a hurry. Below these, in her usual small hand in black ink, are reminders to inquire about the "2nd second volume of the Proust by ?" and the whereabouts of a book on Queen Victoria (published the year before, in 1964) that she had ordered.
7. See Read, "Manners," on Bishop's *non-translations* generally, as well as Machova 41-42 on some in the *Diary*.
8. After the establishment of the Associação das Girl Guides do Brasil in 1919, their leader, Jerônyma Mesquita, solicited the historian Jonathas Serrano for a better name. His suggestion was Bandeirantes, after the roving bands of seventeenth- to eighteenth-century explorers, colonizers, fortune hunters, and enslavers of indigenous peoples, romanticized in popular lore and national sentiment, that he felt suited the Baden-Powell spirit of "aqueles que abrem caminhos" [those who open the way] (Bandeirantes). During the Estado Novo period (1937-45) of Getúlio Vargas's dictatorship, not long before Bishop arrived in Brazil, the mythos of the bandeirantes of old was used to legitimize westward expansion (Dutra e Silva 60-76). Some mid-century Brazilian historians sought to rehabilitate the bandeirantes against charges of "rapacious" (Bishop's own word) greed and violence, painting them as heroes striving against poverty, wilderness, and the Jesuits to create prosperity and the "living substance of democracy" (*Pr* 182; Ricardo 198; see also excerpts by others anthologized by Richard M. Morse). Others were less sanguine, like Vianna Moog, who panned both the "ideal of conquest and swiftly acquired wealth" among the bandeirantes and the Protestant, capitalist, and racist ethos of North American pioneers (169, 59-66).
9. For the harsh reactions to *Silent Spring*, see Michael B. Smith, "'Silence, Miss Carson!'"
10. Cabral once said in an interview that if you take the "ideological structure" of Pernambuco away from him, "eu nada sou" [I am nothing] (Athayde 86).
11. The Tropic of Capricorn bisects the coast between Rio and São Paulo.
12. The poem, covering nearly two pages, shares space with a gallingly inappropriate cartoon, which features an all-male corporate board regaling its chief with a rendition of "Good morning to you! Good morning to you! We're all in our places, with bright shining faces . . ." ("Burglar of Babylon" 57).

13. The semiarid region that includes the states of Pernambuco, Paraíba, Alagoas, Piauí, Ceará, Rio Grande do Norte, Sergipe, Bahia, and northern Minas Gerais and that Nunes calls the "região cemitéria" (78).
14. Joaquim Cardozo had a greater claim to these titles, but Bishop found him less compelling, half-heartedly noting he was a "specialist in calculus" (Bishop and Brasil viii).
15. As Cabral uses it, *redondo*, literally "round" or "curved," is redolent with subtle ironies. For one, although the termites have done their work, rendering all worn out and worse (a connotation of its synonym *acabado*), *redondo* also means "contains abundance," "full," "swollen," "stuffed," "finished," "complete," "perfect." For another, in relation to its close analogue, *rotundo*, it is more in keeping with the human attitude of *pomposo*: decisive, categorical, peremptory, uncontestable (Houaiss and Villar 2408, 34, 2478). It's rarer to hear in English "The very eve of," but "brink" supplants temporal precarity with topographical.
16. Bishop also had received one of Frost's annual Christmas poems in 1956, which was an early, shorter version of "Kitty Hawk" (listed in books to sell, VC 114.5).
17. For a lengthy discussion of Bishop's drafts of this poem, see Heather Bozant Witcher's chapter, "Archival Animals: Polyphonic Movement in Elizabeth Bishop's Drafts," in this volume.

CHAPTER ELEVEN

ELIZABETH BISHOP'S GEOPOETICS

Sarah Giragosian

"EXAMPLES OF HANDWRITING, ILLEGIBLE SIGNATURES"

Even in her juvenilia, Elizabeth Bishop expressed an interest in geology, calling upon geochemical metaphors to inquire into subjective states of internal violence. For her, the "burning, unceasing energy" within the self, like the "rebellious and uncontrolled lava" within the Earth, was aesthetically charged, providing fodder for the content in her high school literary journal *The Blue Pencil*, for which she served as editor (VC 87.3). Geology continued to be a site of investigation and a source of aesthetic material for her into her adulthood, and she developed her interest in the subject with her former student and friend Wesley Wehr, an American paleontologist and artist. In 1967, Bishop wrote a gallery note for Wehr, describing his collections of fossils and stones as an influence on the scale of his paintings:

> Mr. Wehr, works at night, I was told, with his waxes and pigments, while his cat rolls crayons about on the floor. But the observation of nature is always accurate; the beaches, the moonlight nights, look just like this. Some pictures may remind one of agates, the form called "Thunder Egg." Mr. Wehr is also a collector of agates, of all kinds of stones, pebbles, semi-precious jewels, fossilized clams with opals adhering to them, bits of amber, shells, examples of handwriting, illegible signatures—those small things that are occasionally capable of overwhelming with a chilling sensation of time and space. (*Pr* 352)

Bishop's revised draft of "Gallery Note" reflects her efforts to capture a geologically precise analogy for Wehr's artwork (VC 53.8). For Bishop, written into the rock record are stratigraphic signs, "examples of handwriting, illegible signatures,"

Gallery note for Wesley Wehr

I have seen Mr. Wehr open his battered brief-case (with the broken zipper) at a table in a crowded, steamy coffee-shop, and deal out his latest paintings, carefully encased in plastic until they are framed, like a set of magic playing cards. The people at his table would fall silent and stare at these small, beautiful pictures, far off into space and coolness: the coldness of the Pacific Northwest in the winter, its different coldness in the summer. So much space, so much air, such distances and lonelinesses, on those flat little cards. One could almost make out the moon behind the clouds, but not quite; the snow had worn off the low hills, almost showing last year's withered grasses; the white line of surf was visible but quiet, almost a mile away. Then Mr. Wehr would whisk all that space, silence, peace and privacy back into his brief-case again. He once remarked that he would like to be able to carry a whole exhibition in his pockets.

It is a great relief to see a <u>small</u> work of art these days. The Chinese unrolled their precious scroll-paintings to show their friends, bit by bit; the Persians passed their miniatures about from hand to hand; many of Klee's or Bissier's paintings are hand-size. Why shouldn't we, so generally addicted to the gigantic, at last have some small works of art, some <u>short</u> poems, <u>short</u> pieces of music (Mr. Wehr is originally a composer and I think I detect the influence of Webern on his painting), some intimate, low-voiced, and delicate things in our mostly huge and roaring, glaring world? But in spite of their size, no one could say that these pictures are "small-scale."

Mr. Wehr works at night, I was told, with his waxes and pigments, while a cat rolls crayons about on the floor. But the observation of nature is always perfectly accurate; the beaches, the moonlight nights, look exactly like this. Some pictures may remind one of agates, the form called, I think, "fortification agate." Mr. Wehr is also a collector of agates, of all kinds of stones, pebbles, semi-precious jewels, fossilized clams with opals adhering to them, bits of amber, shells, examples of hand-writing, illegible signatures – all those things that are small but occasionally capable of overwhelming with a chilling sensation of time and space.

He once told me that he felt that Rothko had been an influence on him, to which I replied, "Yes, but Rothko in a whisper." And also far away and uninsistent. Who does not feel a sense of release, of calm and quiet, in looking at these little pieces of our vast and ancient world that one can actually hold in the palm of one's hand?

March, 1967

Bishop's revised draft of "Gallery Note" reflects her efforts to capture a geologically precise analogy for Wehr's artwork. (VC 53.8; Courtesy of Vassar College; this note was published as "Wesley Wehr" in Pr352-353 and in PPL469-70; in the archival note, Bishop wrote lonelinesses, which has been incorrectly transcribed as loneliness in both published versions).

possessing information that can be used to identify their age and kind. They are geological *and* archival materials that animate our understanding of and appreciation for a spatiotemporal vastness that can be held in the "palm of one's hand" (353). Blending the linguistic and geological, Bishop becomes almost incantatory as she catalogues the rocks, which can be translated to provide meaning about the geologic record and time itself.

Bishop owned several of Wehr's paintings, which are now in the Vassar archives. Connecting Wehr's paintings to evocations of the sublime in abstract expressionist art, she writes in her gallery note, "[Wehr] once told me that Rothko had been an influence on him, to which I replied, 'Yes, but Rothko in a whisper.' Who does not feel a sense of release of calm and quiet, in looking at these little pieces of our vast and ancient world that one can hold in the palm of one's hand?" (353). In the note, Bishop records multiple levels of observation and scale: the miniature with the sublime, the scientific with the aesthetic, and the human with the posthuman. If we were to read the gallery note as bound up with considerations of Bishop's miniaturist aesthetic, as Susan Rosenbaum suggests,[1] we must concede that the poet's preoccupation with the miniature is in tension with a sophisticated sense of the geohistorical, for her scaling down of Wehr's landscapes to their tangible emblems—agates and stones—folds outwards to epistemological and ontological questions raised by considerations of deep time. As Stephen Jay Gould reminds us, deep time presents a problem of perception and imagination: it is a concept that exists "outside our ordinary experience . . . [and can be] understood only as metaphor" (3). It exceeds human narrative, and metaphor must be summoned to provide meaning. Similarly, Bishop's extended metaphor reminds us that rocks carry information about their history and identity. Wehr's art, and the agates they resemble, provide an opportunity to glimpse the sublime power of deep time. In subordinating historical time to the larger frame of deep time, Bishop evokes the "chill" of ancient time, the chill of an indifferent world that has been and will again be without the human. If the immediate task of the poet is to measure, Bishop reminds the reader that the human is not a baseline for practical or ontological measurement. Indeed, her inquiry into large-scale geological phenomena is an ongoing project that might be overlooked in readings of the poet purely as a miniaturist. Bishop's "Crusoe in England," for example, counterpoises Crusoe's private drama against geological temporalities, such as volcanic eruptions and the birth of islands, whereas "Song for the Rainy Season" anticipates climate change.

This chapter seeks to map Elizabeth Bishop's *geopoetics*, a term that refers to the mutually informing relationship between poetry and science. Harry Hess, who theorized the spreading of the seafloor and continental drift, first introduced the term *geopoetry* in his writing to encourage his readers to inhabit a poetic frame of

Wehr's painting evokes the textural quality of geological formations. (VC 100.31; Courtesy of Vassar College)

mind and suspend their disbelief when considering his hypothesis. Don McKay revives and reimagines the term *geopoetry* to designate the "mental space" shared by creative scientists and poets where "conjecture and imaginative play are needed and legitimate" (47). In turn, geopoetics seeks to reconcile scientific and poetic processes and defers closure or the resolution of scientific analysis into fact. Rather than striving merely for mastery of knowledge, geopoetry understands inquiry as an opportunity to be swept away by wonder's animating currents of possibility while equally valuing intuition and empiricism, affect and materialism.

New materialism, with its critical purchase on projects that address the agency of matter, enables us to conceptualize Bishop's relationship to archival material both planetary and human-made. Her critique of the archive may be read within the context of her geological imagination and understanding of the Earth's vital materiality or—in the words of Jane Bennett—"vibrant matter." Bennett's rejection of the life/matter binary emerges out of the recognition that the study of matter has catalyzed intellectual revolutions and cultural shifts, such as Charles Darwin's study of worms, in which he conceptualized the role the organisms play in refining soil and providing the groundwork for life to take root and flourish. In the same vein, if we were to understand trash heaps as not passive or inert waste but as toxic producers of methane that have concrete effects on the environment, we may be more invested in a sustainable relation to the Earth (Bennett vi). For Bennett, such case studies prove to have political and ontological significance; were we to recognize the "agentic contributions of nonhuman forces," we may appreciate how matter shapes the cultural and environmental conditions around us (xvi). Theorizing the vibrancy of matter is useful in conceptualizing Bishop's geopoetics, which perform the human entanglement with Earth's material processes: both the ways in which vital matter acts upon and transforms human culture and the ways in which culture is conditioned by vital matter. The poem "Verdigris," which Bishop did not publish in her lifetime but appears in Alice Quinn's edited volume *Edgar Allan Poe & the Juke-Box* (2006), imagines ecological processes as forces that both aestheticize and decolonize the archive. "The Mountain," another understudied poem in her oeuvre, may be read as a critical precursor in archival studies and geopoetics, insofar as it casts the mountain into a repository of the past, an archive to be read through the geological "discourse" of vibrant matter. These poems have been considered to be failures or not yet fully realized, either by Bishop's readers at the time or by herself, yet they are significant in the ways they complicate anthropocentric understandings of memory, scale, and agency. Inviting the thrill of apprehension and imaginative play, legitimate geopoetic attitudes, these poems also offer some clues as to how to approach Bishop's own archival materials.

BISHOP'S "STRANGE MUSEUMS"

Before turning to "Verdigris," which dramatizes the intersections of geochemical and cultural processes, this chapter will discuss Bishop's posthumously published draft "The Museum," which is an important precursor to "Verdigris" (*EAP* 72). The draft is significant in introducing readers to Bishop's early preoccupations with museum culture and its archival implications, as well as the didactic function of the modern museum. The twentieth century, according to Sir Frederic Kenyon, was marked by the modern museum's efforts to facilitate what Catherine Paul refers to as a "process of digestion," to educate a diverse public, comprised not merely of the educated but also of the untrained visitor, and thus elevate public taste (17-18). It is this uncritical "process of digestion" that Bishop problematizes in her poem.

Addressed to her beloved, the speaker of "The Museum" asks to return to a museum and attempt again to make meaning of its possessions. Dubious, "worthless," and "unauthenticated," the museum objects are poorly labeled and present a problem of "translat[ion]" (*EAP* 72). The failure of the museum to enlighten or educate its visitors or properly to memorialize cultural artifacts is suggestive of the limitations of institutional memory. It also fails to excite the imagination, which can be necessary for apprehension: "No I can't imagine what / those stone things were ever used for," the speaker concedes to her companion, as she struggles to discern their purpose (*EAP* 72). However, the museum is compromised by what also enlivens it:

> A column of sunlight fell
> clear and thin and alive
> almost like a stream of water—
> alive as a stream of water
> as if it lived there
> commenting fastidiously on lighting— (*EAP* 72)

Despite being housed in a museum, where the regulation of light, temperature, and humidity are essential in preserving collections, the materials are subject to ecological processes that could lead to their eventual deterioration. The poem, however, embraces the light as a source of agency, welcome against the mediating influence of archival technologies.

Bishop's critique of the museum recalls John Dewey's own concerns about museum practices in *Art as Experience* (1934), which she read in the early thirties. Bishop was an admirer of the philosopher and friend of his daughter Jane, relying on him for patronage in her early career (Dewey—along with Marianne Moore—recommended her for the 1944 Houghton Mifflin Poetry Prize Fellowship). In his first chapter, Dewey bemoans the influences of capitalism and imperialism in shaping the modern museum as an institutional power that separates the work of art from "common life" (7). The modern museum represented for Dewey a potential obstacle to aesthetic experience, as it separated cultural material from its original environment:

> Our present museums and galleries to which works of fine art are removed and stored illustrate some of the causes that have operated to segregate art instead of finding it an attendant of temple, forum, and other forms of associated life.... Their segregation from the common life reflects the fact that they are not part of a native and spontaneous culture. (6)

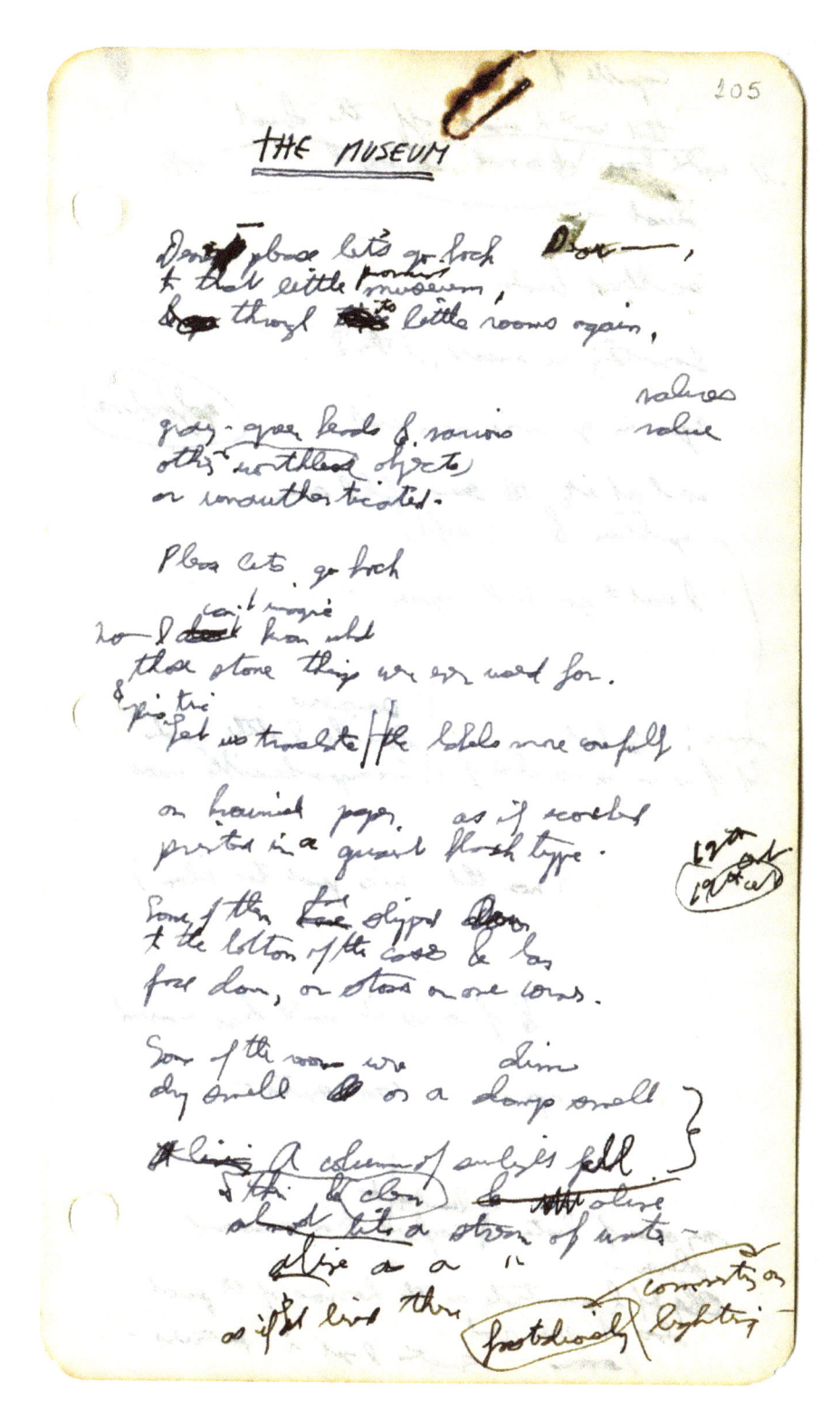

One can see Bishop trying to jimmy her lines into place, but the insistence on the liveliness of the light—its ability to damage materials over time—is worth noting. (VC 75.3; Courtesy of Vassar College; transcribed by Quinn on p. 72 of *EAP*)

Dewey sought to carve out a space for aesthetic experience, which was synonymous for him with the processes of life and antithetical to the encroaching forces of industry and mass production (24). The sunlight that falls in Bishop's museum is vital matter that undermines the museum as an arm of the nation-state: it is a decolonizing force that intervenes in the sequestration of art from "common life." The problem of the museum as a symbol and form of state power is a concern that Bishop would return to throughout her work. When she acted as Consultant in Poetry to the Library of Congress, Bishop began to draft "Verdigris," a poem with similar archival and ecological tensions. At the time, she found herself in the position of archivist, poet, and federal employee, roles that were not always harmonious. Rosenbaum contends that Bishop "was forced to confront her contribution to the national archive, both as a grand symbol of the convergence of poetry and nation, and on a smaller scale as library employee, involved in acquiring and cataloguing poetry and recordings for the library's collection" (75). It was not a position that she would relish, and Rosenbaum argues persuasively that the poet "manipulates scale" to unsettle the "acquisitive perspective and didactic practices associated with the museum" (72). She posits that Bishop's ekphrastic impulse in her later years is a strategy to interrogate value and the modern museum as big business and reads her miniaturism as a means to mediate her own place within such institutions as she faced the end of her life and heightened fame.

Read within the context of Bishop's growing unease in her post as archivist and poet amid the emergence of Cold War culture, "Verdigris" can be viewed as a companion piece to the more explicitly political poem "View of The Capitol from The Library of Congress," which Bishop began to draft on the next page of her journal, seemingly on January 26, 1950 (VC 77.4). Both call upon similar rhetorical strategies that Camille Roman identifies as a hallmark of Bishop's work at the time. Roman aptly traces Bishop's coded dissent and writes that she uses a "strategy of combining physical observation with political commentary" to negotiate her resistance to a Cold War culture (123). Bishop was particularly vulnerable as a lesbian during the Lavender Scare, a time when communism was conflated with homosexuality and the government used surveillance methods and other tactics to conduct private investigations of its employees in order to weed them out of its offices (119).

Against this backdrop, "Verdigris" began to gestate in her mind. She had seen moss growing on the facade of a post office building in Washington and wrote in her journal, "Quite bright green—How wonderful this place would look if all the facades were like that. (Ver de gris-one definition is ver de Greece) (Those green green roses in the Freer) (Time is sometimes green—I want to write a villanelle & that sounds like a possibility)" (VC 77.4). In a train of breathless asides, Bishop was imagining a more earthy, more vibrant Washington, one with facades covered in moss. Such a city would have been in stark contrast to the Washington she observed with "all those piles of granite and marble, like an inflated copy of another capital city somewhere else" (*OA* 194). Her deflationary rhetoric recalls the same strategies she used in such poems as "View of The Capitol from The Library of Congress" and "Roosters," in which she reduces displays of nation-building and militarism to a diminutive scale so as to reveal their "baseness" (*OA* 96).

In her preliminary draft of "Verdigris," recorded in her 1950 diary, Bishop employs images of "stiff, harsh moss" and of "justice on the Dome," lines that would be reprised or cut in later iterations of the poem, becoming instead "Justice an upright leaf upon her dome" in both a fragment and draft (VC 77.4). The draft in her journal began to crystalize into a poem that explores the vitality of matter, the oxidation process by which verdigris forms a patina on objects when copper, brass, or bronze is weathered and exposed to air or seawater over time. Bishop recruits the villanelle, a form associated with repetition, patterning, and memory, as well as the permutations within and among them, to unsettle the museum's aspirations to elucidate its collection, "to tell you what they mean" (VC 64.13). As in "The Museum," "Verdigris" counterpoises the sanitizing and curatorial energies of the museum against a non-human agency, showing that the materials of the archive do not abide by the museum's conservational agendas and are affected—even transformed—by ecological conditions. In turn, they offer up new possibilities for aesthetic appreciation and for affective response. In an understated fashion, Bishop casts matter as an "actant," changing the ancient bronze metalwork to the greenish-blue pigment of verdigris (Bennett 9). The villanelle dramatizes the ways in which culture and nature intersect and the ways in which variously composed materialities, "vibrant matter," can offer an aesthetics that is entirely non-human, independent of human design or meaning.

In both versions of the poem (the only two versions housed in the Vassar archives aside from the sketch in her diary), "Verdigris" is essentially unchanged, and together with the paratext of the diary notes, they suggest that Bishop may have interpreted verdigris as a decolonizing agent against the imperializing culture of Washington at the time. Indeed, in the first three stanzas, the agency of "vibrant matter" is a direct challenge to the modern museum's manipulation of material culture to provide a narrative or meaning for its visitors:

> The catalogues will tell you that they mean
> the Chinese Bronzes were like fresh-turned loam.
> The time to watch for us when Time grows green.

> Some like them green, some still prefer them clean,[2]
> as found in strange museums away from home.
> The catalogues will tell you that they mean
>
> it isn't any old phosphorescent sheen
> confines them to the past; in polychrome
> the time to watch for is when Time grows green. (*EAP* 186)

Despite the documentary drive of the museum, figured in the "catalogues," the bronzes in Bishop's villanelle retain some autonomy from human influence that seems to enable their green(ness), which is derived from the processes of decay that color and enliven them, heightening their status as objects of aesthetic perception. Indeed, Bennett posits that all materials have "thing power;" in other words, all matter possesses a liveliness and meaning that is independent from human projections and associations (6). Similarly, the museum objects are not entirely subject to human possession, and Bishop imagines ecological and chemical processes as interventions in the epistemological and regulatory apparatuses of the museum. "Verdigris" represents the sensuality, the spontaneity, and aesthetics of matter that cannot be entirely structured or determined in advance by human institutions or collective memory.

While the systematizing niceties of the museum space break down in the face of non-human material agency, Bishop exposes the constructedness of human significations in the face of nature's othering/aestheticizing presence. "Verdigris" announces the ascendancy of the ecological, while the museum's artificial ecology (its regulation of air quality, space, lighting, and temperature) is revealed to be ever-contingent upon actual ecological conditions. The rebelliousness of Bishop's poem in the face of an official cultural narrative—exemplified in the museum catalogue that seeks to explicate it—anticipates such postmodern lyric experiments as Jill Magi's *Slot* (2011), which critiques the archival fever of slotting cultural materials into archives to fit a master narrative.

In unsettling the archive as a purely institutional concept or form of state power, Bishop opens a space for agency from within, releasing the archive from its "house arrest," a concept introduced in Jacques Derrida's *Archive Fever* (1995). Her dramatization of the vibrant matter of the archive unsettles the acquisitive impulse or archive fever of which Derrida writes and enables us to rethink his conception of the archives as a site of state power and intractable house arrest. In the aforementioned poems, the archives are above all spaces of action, where fluxes of energy compete against the supposed "arrest" of cultural materials. Moreover, these poems offer a theory of reading that problematizes human conceptions of historical time.

Following the cues of meteorology and geology, Jeffrey Jerome Cohen calls for a "vorticular topology of reading," which reads against linearity and customary reading practices that would uphold human hierarchies or authority (26). Both literary texts and their archives, according to Cohen, "bear unconformities" that mimic the geologic record and resist progress narratives that presume human primacy (33). I suggest that Bishop's poems invite a similar readerly ethos. Reading geopoetically, we read contra-linearly: against the limits of punctuated, linear time and against the archive fever to know and possess the past. Reading instead for temporal and ecological ruptures, and for convolutions in meaning and matter, we may resist the selective and often totalizing nature of the archive, which privileges certain cultural narratives over others.

The archive is selective, but in spatializing time, Bishop's villanelle insists upon an understanding of historical memory as ecological. In other words, memory's verdancy, its contaminating, regenerative, and aestheticizing influence on present and future spaces as much as the past, destabilizes the presumed fixity of the archive. The archive becomes a site of imminence as the verdigris changes archival memory. The poem can be counterpoised against Derrida's articulation of the archive as a site of amnesia, where the institutional and political control over cultural artifacts results in the displacement or elision of alternative or counter-memories. As Derrida contends, "The archive, if this word or this figure can be stabilized so as to take on signification, will never be either memory or anamnesis as spontaneous, alive, and internal experience. . . . the archive takes place at the place of originary and structural breakdown of the said memory" (11). However, in "Verdigris," cultural artifacts are transformed by ecological processes that erode their original significations, and their material agency changes the meaning the catalogues have consigned to them.

As it progresses, "Verdigris" facilitates a geopoetic, counter-memorial reading, one that reinscribes human interdependence on geologic forces and materialities, unsettling any convenient fictions of human primacy:

> The queer complexion of a former Queen,
> Justice an upright leaf upon her Dome,
> the catalogues will tell you that they mean
>
> left in the earth, or out, it is foreseen
> we get like that; also if lost in foam.
> The time to watch for is when Time grows green. (*EAP* 186-87)

Here, the objects of empire are subject to processes of decay, which subsume the state's pretensions to preserve and collect the spoils of its conquests. In the face of ecological processes, the semantics of the catalogue will fail to offer meaning beyond the ideological framework of the culture in which it is situated. In the final stanza, Bishop compares the patina of the statues to the colors of landscape and sea, before returning to the image of the "copper roofs of Rome!" (*EAP* 187). The ecologizing impulse in the poem is figured in the repeated analogies between the cultural objects and their affinities to the material land/seascape and the human body. "The time to watch for," as Bishop writes, punning on the temporal and speculative "watch," is not the historian's or archivist's time but the dynamic processes of the Earth and environment. "Verdigris" announces the breakdown of archival memory, which is identified as synchronous with our own eventual processes of decay: "left in the earth, or out, it is foreseen / we get like that." Such a geopoetics indexes a form of historicity in which flows of matter and energy intervene in linear, human time.

Bishop's poem also anticipates Carolyn Steedman's critique of the Derridean theory of the archives as a site of intractable house arrest and opens a space to re-evaluate "the physical phenomenology of the archive" (81). The archive in her formulation is a site of possibility: "The Archive . . . through cultural activity of history, can become Memory's potential space, one of the few realms of the modern imagination where a hard-won and carefully constructed place, can return to boundless space" (83). In the same vein, "Verdigris" imagines the archive as a site of potential and counter-memory; however, Bishop reminds us that cultural history is necessarily embedded within and dependent upon ecological and geological forces.

Ultimately, the poem remained unpublished in Bishop's lifetime. Katherine White, Bishop's *New Yorker* editor, reported that her colleagues found the poem "to be obscure and not to have quite the simplicity and neatness that a villanelle should have" (*EAP* 186). Bishop replied that she might have to turn it into a double villanelle to make its meaning clear (*EAP* 186). There is a coded politics in the poem that Bishop may have needed more space to realize fully, but it is possible to read the poem's (proto-)politics as a challenge to the museum as prescriber of taste and culture. As in her draft of "The Museum," "Verdigris" teaches us how to read with and against the ideological framework that the museum provides, enabling us to see its objects afresh. Both poems suggest that civic education entails a kind of looking that can resist the authority of the museum's epistemological and theoretical structures. In this way, they anticipate Carol Duncan's critique of the museum's didactic function. She posits that the modern museum trains the visitor in the "political passivity of citizenship" and notes that "visitors to a museum follow a route through a programmed narrative" that "may represent only the interests and self-image of certain powers in that community" (92-94). Mediated by the ecological, the cultural material of Bishop's museum can no longer be read solely as an expression of the supremacy of state power.

READING GEOPOETICALLY

Two years after her stint in Washington, Bishop found herself settling into life in Samambaia, near Petrópolis, with her Brazilian lover Lota de Macedo Soares. This was a productive period for Bishop, one in which she was harvesting memories of Nova Scotia and using the material in her poems and prose. As Brett Millier notes, Bishop "found it odd that she should have 'total recall' about Nova Scotia in its geological mirror image, Brazil; but she did" (*Elizabeth Bishop* 252). For Millier, "The Mountain" is a "poetic exploration of Brazil in her early years there" and is "her weakest published poem" (252). However, "The Mountain" is critically interesting when read in the context of geochronology, or the science of Earth time, whereby the Earth is read as an archive. Perhaps a geopoetic reading also enables a more generous approach to the poem than Millier's.

Read geopoetically, Bishop's lyric becomes an apostrophe for the human, an "other" from the perspective of the speaker-mountain. Her mountain is alive and inspirited, a persona that in the tones of a mentally deteriorating elder, seeks answers about its age and—by extrapolation—its identity. It is a poem about the desire to be read accurately by the "other," a perspective we require in order to access even our own origins. Moreover, in its concerns with deep time and the ways in which humans can operate as readers and interpreters of geologic activity, "The Mountain" may be read as a poem about the Anthropocene.

A term adopted by Nobel Prize–winning geologist Paul Crutzen, the Anthropocene refers to how our current geological era has been shaped by humans. Our influence on the ecosystem is now so far-reaching that we have become a global force of nature, altering geological systems and re-shaping the land. The onset of our age is contested among thinkers, with some citing the Industrial Revolution as its moment of inauguration, whereas others date it back to the beginnings of agriculture. Now, in the midst of the sixth mass extinction, climate change, and ecological crisis, one could reasonably argue that there is a crucial need to be able to think in multiple time scales and intervene in a culture driven by fossil fuel capitalism. As ecopoets and critics have discussed at length, the imaginative work of lyric poetry in the Anthropocene seems to be well suited to help us form a meaningful response to the large-scale temporal and physical phenomena of our age.[3]

However, the Anthropocene is a slippery term, given its uncertain periodization and anachronistic codification, which Cody Marrs addresses directly within the context of Emily Dickinson's poetics:

> Because it is an anachronistic framework, the Anthropocene risks obscuring the ways in which people previously lived in, conceived of, and represented nature. . . . . The term performs a kind of epistemic violence, insofar as it erases the situated practices and knowledges that are indispensable for any literary or cultural historian. Nonetheless, both these issues—the term's amorphousness and anachronism—are put into stark relief by the transformations to biological life that are unfolding before our eyes. (201)

The material effects of the Anthropocene themselves interrupt historical continuity and ask us to re-examine the sociopolitical and cultural conditions that enabled them (201). Extrapolating from Marrs, we may also read Bishop as a poet of the Anthropocene, which helps us to heighten the stakes of her geopoetics and to undertake a critical re-evaluation of our place within deep time. In "The Mountain," we are within the territory of a mountain consciousness, one which destabilizes anthropocentric thinking, reminding us of our place within a pre- and post-human narrative, even while using animistic language.

In two drafts, Bishop titled her poem, "Mountains Complain Continuously," whereas in another, she titled it "The Mountains." Eventually, she seemed to settle on the singular "The Mountain" as her title (VC 57.5). Bishop's movement to the singular, generic mountain endows it with a totemic quality, as if the mountain speaks for the Earth itself. Throughout the poem, Bishop cycles between two refrains that are repeated in the last line of each quatrain, as the mountain declares "I do not know my age" and asks the imploratory "Tell me how old I am" (VC 57.5). There are nine drafts and several fragments of the poem housed at Vassar, in which one can see Bishop attempting to work out the order of the stanzas and lines, indicating that she ran the poem through several permutations before she settled on a sequence that satisfied her.

In all versions of the poem, the mountain is stymied by the limits of myopic, close reading. Even in what appears to be an early draft of "Mountains Complain Continuously," where Bishop had a collage of stanzas but nothing close to the narrative that she would settle on in the version published in *The Complete Poems* (1992), the phrase "by reading" stands alone at the top of the page. The challenges of reading an environment and reading the other are the base notes of the poem, and the trope of misreading is extended throughout the published poem. The inability of the mountain to read itself or its environment is also an existential crisis. In the Anthropocene, one might argue that we share the same ineptitude. In the second and third stanza, we learn that the mountain experiences sensual privation and discontinuity from its environment: "An open book confronts me, / too close to read in comfort" and that "valleys stuff / impenetrable mists / like cotton in my ears" (*CP* 197). In a preliminary draft, "a bland book opens against me," whereas in another "a bright book opens against me" (VC 57.5). In each version, without the context of the human "other," the mountain cannot understand itself or the phenomenological world without a constitutive intersubjective system. In a more ecological idiom, we may read the poem as a dramatization of the first law of ecology; all organisms are interdependent, so much so that introducing change in a system or even a single organism can affect all.[4]

The mountain, elderly, on the edge of senility, complains "I am growing deaf. The birdcalls / dwindle" but is apologetic about its grievances: "I do not mean to complain. / They say it is my fault" (197). A fault, of course, is not only a flaw but also a geological term, meaning the planar fracture in rock that results from the action of plate tectonic forces. Earthquakes are the result of sudden movements of faults, and movement along faults can cause seismic uplift, which contributes to the formation of mountains. Significantly, this was a critical insight for Charles Darwin during his voyage on the HMS *Beagle* when he experienced an earthquake in Chile in 1835. Applying James Hutton's theory of uniformitarianism, the theory that the same geological processes that occurred in the deep past continue to occur in the present, Darwin inferred that the mountain range had been lifted incrementally by many earthquakes over many millennia.

As has been discussed by many readers of Bishop, Darwin was an important influence aesthetically and intellectually on her poetics.[5] Tracing Bishop's reading of Darwin provides a powerful intertext to her poems, and her marked copies of *The Voyage of the Beagle* (1939) and *The Autobiography of Charles Darwin* (1887; housed at Harvard University) reveal that she was aware of the significance of Darwin's geological insights. Moreover, she saw poetic potential in his descriptions and lineated his writing: "In the deep and retired channels of Tierra Del Fuego, // the snow white gander . . ." (qtd. in Rognoni 242). Bishop had brought Darwin's writings with her to Brazil, reading them closely and marking several passages from *The Voyage of the Beagle* (Ellis, "Reading Bishop" 185). One of the marked passages includes Darwin's meditation on the action of geological forces over the span of deep time, which "stupefied the mind in thinking over the long, absolutely necessary, lapse of years" (qtd. in Ellis, "Reading Bishop" 188).

It is important to note here that Darwin's theory of origins was grounded in a conception of deep time that had originally been articulated by John Hutton. In the late eighteenth century, Hutton first conceptualized deep time in his initially maligned, but ultimately revolutionary text *Theory of the Earth* (1788). Unlike the prominent thinkers of his time, Hutton disavowed catastrophism, the widely accepted theory of the day that the Earth was shaped by sudden and short-lived events. Hutton's discovery occurred out of a combination of close reading and inference (Cohen 30). Such inventive reading, however, was perilous. Scorned by the scientific community for his theories, Hutton is nevertheless significant in the story of deep time and Darwin's theory of evolution. Nearly fifty years later, Charles Lyell's *Principles of Geology* (1830) embraced Hutton's worldview and theorized gradualism, the theory that Earth changed by slow, imperceptible increments over time. That vision was later adopted by Darwin, who had read Lyell's book in 1832, bringing it with him on his journey on the *Beagle* and beginning to adopt his worldview, which was iconoclastic in an age when many embraced creationism. Despite having been indoctrinated in creationism, Darwin, seeing the Earth through Lyell's paradigm, saw evidence of gradualism in the Earth's crust.

The lineage that I have traced is critical in understanding the framework for Darwin's theory of origins; he posited that the Earth was not as young as had been thought by creationists and that evolutionary progress happened gradually, over eons. In other words, Darwin's geological understanding was the bedrock of his evolutionary theory. Significantly, what Bishop would later extol in an oft-quoted 1964 letter to Anne Stevenson as "the beautiful solid case being built up out of [Darwin's] endless heroic observations" was predicated on a geopoetic mode of seeing the Earth against the dominant ideology of his time (*Pr* 414).

"The Mountain," read in light of Bishop's knowledge of geological phenomena via Darwin, becomes a scientifically informed text. We can read "The Mountain" geopoetically and see the ways in which Bishop enables us to imagine deep time and hold multiple scales in tension:

> Shadows fall down, lights climb.
> Clambering lights, oh children!
> you never stay long enough.
> Tell me how old I am.
>
> Stone wings have sifted here
> with feather hardening feather.
> The claws are lost somewhere.
> I do not know my age. (*CP* 227)

In these stanzas, Bishop imagines the role of the human against fossilization and the temporal vista of deep time. Given our brief span on the planet, we are akin to children who haven't been able to calibrate the geologic time scale with total accuracy. With older rocks still being discovered, the task of translating the geologic record is still incomplete. As the structural geologist Marcia Bjornerud has written, using the metaphor of reading to describe the challenges of dating the geologic record, "Pages, if not entire chapters, of the Earth manuscript remain undiscovered, and passages from many known sections have not been fully deciphered" (63). The fossil record is fragmentary and still being unearthed, and interestingly, Bishop imagines an Earth that does not have recourse to its record; it requires the human "other" to help translate its meaning. In the final stanza of "The Mountain," Bishop returns to a cosmic framework:

> Let the moon go hang,
> the stars go fly their kites.
> I want to know my age.
> Tell me how old I am. (*CP* 228)

Deferring resolution, "The Mountain" is suspended in doubt. How do we read the appeal of the final stanza? Rhetorically, it is possible to read it as a gesture of despair or an attempt to reconcile the self's own opacity with a cosmic opacity. While ambiguous, the poem's end continues to destabilize the authority of archival memory, not unlike "The Museum" and "Verdigris."

Significantly, this is not the first poem in which Bishop strives to imagine geological time in action. In another geological poem, a love poem entitled "Vague Poem (Vaguely Love Poem)," the speaker tries to read the dynamics of deep time:

> . . . Yes, perhaps
> there was a secret, powerful crystal at work inside.
>
> I *almost* saw it: turning into a rose
> without any of the intervening
> roots, stem, buds, and so on: just
> earth to rose and back again. (*EAP* 152)

In both "Vague Poem" and "The Mountain," there is a desire to see the invisible, to discern the language and temporality of the geological, which moves too slowly for the human eye. However, recall that Darwin, Lyell, and Hutton were able to envision geological time even despite the temporal limitations of their own human scale. Their geopoetic interpretation of the Earth privileged an imaginative and inventive vision. Materializing that vision for us, Bishop's poems invite a process of reading that turns the earthly archive into a sensual experience. Such a reading is epiphanic, even erotic, and can be accessed by the general reader should they enlarge their scale of inquiry beyond the human.

However, Bishop herself called the poem "slight" when she sent it to *The New*

Yorker for consideration. In her letter, Bishop told White that she wanted to send "The Mountain" to *Poetry,* calling it "a little too elliptical for you" (*EBNY* 81-82). The elliptical nature of the text perhaps speaks to some of the difficulties of communicating scientific concepts through lyric poetry, especially when the poem is highly affective and directed to a readership that tends to misread animism merely as folklore.[6]

"The Mountain" is demonstrative of Bishop's geopoetics, which are animated by the continuous process of discovery that art and science might share, as well as the ontological questions they raise. As Tobias Menely and Jesse Oak Taylor note in *Anthropocene Reading: Literary History in Geologic Times*, geologists have often relied upon "imaginative ways of knowing" since the field "deals with scales of space and time unavailable to human experience" (2). Consequently, geology, they contend, "has never altogether transcended its provenance in imaginative narrative forms" (2). Darwin's work, like Bishop's poetry, takes a processual, tentative, and adaptable approach to knowledge, in contrast to any system of knowledge that would seek to dominate or explain nature without recognizing the limitations of its field, its all-too-human perspective. As Zachariah Pickard notes, Bishop was drawn to Darwin's patient, accumulative approach to science; he did not advance his ideas through inductive reasoning but rather determined meaning as he proceeded (65-66).[7] While absolute knowledge suspends science's processes of discovery indefinitely, the methods of geology may have offered a flexible mode of poetic inquiry for Bishop.

Geopoetics also provides a theoretical orientation for reading the materials in Bishop's archives. The question of how to approach archival material, particularly Bishop's own rejected material, is often tantalizingly dubious. In her archives, one happens upon poems slashed out, equivocal squiggles near lines, and her own interrogation into the value of her work. "The Mountain" dramatizes this issue explicitly: "<u>Very Bad</u>?" Bishop asked herself in the margins of one of her drafts (VC 57.5). Watching Bishop enact her own uncertainty about the merits of her work is in some sense illustrative of the dubious nature of the critic's responsibility to a writer's private material in the archives and to her creative process in general. In her own work, Bishop is often adept at performing tentativeness, sometimes at her own expense, as Bonnie Costello and others have discussed at length.[8] Might we read such gestures of indeterminacy in light of her own *ars poetica*? While she doesn't use the word directly, Lorrie Goldensohn gestures to an idea of latency in discussing Bishop's process by way of Alice Quinn's publication of Bishop's uncollected poems, drafts, and fragments: "Bishop's own description of her process as one of waiting for the well to fill up feels right; we could say that the years in which these poems might be finished just ran out on her. But some of them could have been finished, as 'The Moose' in its plus twenty years of gestation proved" ("Elizabeth Bishop's Drafts" 115). As critics, we might ask then what kind of criticism can we imagine that appreciates and does justice to a poetics of recursion, of latent possibility?

Geopoetics, with its accent on imaginative play and conjecture, offers one theoretical direction. Geopoetics extends the conceptual frame for theorizing Bishop's aesthetic processes and concerns and enables us to tease out her own relationship to archives both geological and institutional. With growing critical interest in her posthumous publications, scholars of Bishop will continue to bring attention to the poet's engagement with the cultural and social issues of her day as well as explore the question of how she negotiated her own position as a cultural producer in relation to cultural markets and institutions. If we choose to read Bishop as a poet of the Anthropocene, we can begin to investigate the ways in which her poetics bind historical knowledge and memory to ecological processes and invite us to think through the implications of vital matter interacting with, disrupting, and re-scaling cultural materials and systems.

NOTES

1. See Rosenbaum.
2. In what the archives deemed to be a "fragment," Bishop crossed off the phrase "[Some] like them green" and replaced it with "[Some] prefer patina"; however, Bishop seemed to prefer the original language of the poem and preserved it in her draft. "Odd" she had declared the stanza in her fragment (VC 64.13).
3. See Moe; Ijima.
4. See Barry Commoner's "Four Laws of Ecology," theorized in his *Closing Circle*.
5. Darwin's influence on Bishop's aesthetics and imagination has been a significant theme in Bishop studies, even while interpretations about the scope of his impact are varied. For example, Ellis suggests that Bishop saw Darwin as a "kindred writer" and explores her reading of his major work to trace the ways he may have influenced her *ars poetica* ("Reading Bishop" 188). The most comprehensive study of Darwin's impact on Bishop to date is Zachariah Pickard's study of the aesthetic, intellectual, and empirical methodology that his theories furnished for her poetics. Pickard posits that Bishop was drawn to Darwin's accumulative methodology as a naturalist, in which he patiently collected and studied data, relevant and irrelevant, until synthesizing his findings and forming a hypothesis (65-66). Pickard traces the affinities between the epistemological methods of natural history, which move from "the concrete seen to the abstract imagined," and Romantic poetry, which combines close observation with imaginative synthesis, and explores their mutual influence on Bishop (66).
6. See Allen, in which she argues non-Native readers have often misread the animistic literature of indigenous peoples.
7. Even in her early career, Bishop was thinking through the affinities between art and science. In her first edition of *Art as Experience*, Bishop marked only one passage: "As a Renascence writer

said: 'There is no excellent beauty that hath not some strangeness in the proportion.' The unexpected turn, something which the artist himself definitely does not foresee, is a condition of the felicitous quality of a work of art; it saves it from being mechanical. It gives the spontaneity of the unpremeditated to what would otherwise be a fruit of calculation. The painter and poet like the scientific inquirer know the delights of discovery" (VC 139). The passage anticipates some of Bishop's major concerns as a poet that she would articulate years later when writing that she admired Darwin's "beautiful solid case being built up out of endless heroic observations" that eventually led to discoveries both strange and spontaneous (*Pr* 414). Bishop links Darwin's process as a scientist to the habitude of the artist whose reveries provide the "unexpected turn," in Dewey's words, or the "sudden relaxation, [the] forgetful phrase," in Bishop's, that heralds aesthetic discovery (414). Bishop may have been drawn to Dewey's alliance of art and scientific inquiry and their distinction from a dynamic of power.

8. See Costello, *Elizabeth Bishop*.

PART III

THE WORK IN PROGRESS

CHAPTER TWELVE

THE ARCHIVAL AVIARY
Elizabeth Bishop and Drama

Andrew Walker

In Elizabeth Bishop's 1934 essay "Mechanics of Pretense," her consideration of W. H. Auden, influence, and the possibilities of language, she stakes one of her more enigmatic claims that "much can be done by means of pretense" (*EAP* 183). For a young Bishop writing her way into a life of poetry, pretense functions as a primary means of altering things as they are, as through the use of "imaginary language" we might shape our relationships to real things. Although the nature of this "pretense"—those things "a poet writes to become real"—can take forms as multivariate as poetry itself, it is a theatrical performance that seems to mark Bishop's critical imagination (*EAP* 184). When including specific lines of Auden's work that illustrate such pretense, she notably points to his early play *Paid on Both Sides* (1930) and remarks that pretense is scenic, tangible, and produced: "The play becomes a play on a stage dissolving to leave the ground underneath" (*EAP* 184). Bishop writes these lines at the outset of her poetic career, just after completing her time at Vassar, and it is with her early poetic ambitions in mind, perhaps, that she claims "[i]n his earlier stages, the poet is the verbal actor" (*EAP* 183). Bishop's interest in the poetic nature of feigning, pretense, and personae heighten at a time when she was immersing herself in dramatic works, yet this dramatic context for Bishop's writing has, to its fullest extent, remained scattered in her archive.

Such a shift in focus—from the natural attention given to Bishop's perceptions of lyric subjectivity and toward a kind of dramatic experimentation—has remained a somewhat difficult task given the archival remoteness of her most dramatic compositions. Some studies, such as Peggy Samuels's *Deep Skin*, broach the issue by emphasizing the importance of the visual, performative aspect of Bishop's development of the lyric, seeing verse as a lyric "surface," as a space on which to play the self.[1] Gillian White's reading of Bishop's poetry likewise focuses on the anti-expressive elements of Bishop's corpus by examining the ways Bishop's poems "engage a poetic politics" through their revisions of traditional "lyric reading" conventions.[2] Others, like Kamran Javadizadeh, have sought to more directly engage with Bishop's relationship to the performative or dramatic through a focus on her extreme hesitancy toward public readings and its relationship to perceptions of her personality. He points out from an entry in the Vassar archive that Bishop closed her reading on April 11 of 1973 at the 92nd Street Y with one of her most dramatic poems, "Crusoe in England," a poem which would allow Bishop to stage (from the eminently theatrical stage of the auditorium at the Y) an intricate performance of her own identity as a recently acknowledged cultural celebrity.[3] Yet Bishop's clearest dramatic attempts, her poetic attempts at a poetry perhaps resistant to the expressive excesses of the lyrical mode, have remained largely cloistered in the archive and thus read as modest.

By looking more fully to the journals, unpublished drafts, and letters housed in the Vassar archive, we see more clearly Bishop's extensive engagement with a modulating lyric practice, with dramatic form, theatrical performances, and the intertwining of music and poetry. The Bishop once labeled as "reticent" might thus be thrown into starker relief given her theatrical endeavors. Bishop is, after all, the poet who while at Camp Chequesset writes and performs in a number of skits before famously co-writing with Frani Blough Muser a Christmas miracle play with songs during her senior year at Walnut Hill.[4] Her high school literary journal, *The Blue Pencil*, which includes a number of early Bishop poems, also includes an obscure copy of an early play entitled *The Three Wells*. A dark, death-filled play, and deeply descriptive, the prose work nonetheless announces the clear, poetic tinge that would be more fully articulated in the dramas discussed here. This chapter examines Bishop's cultivation of these interests in performance and drama, her negotiation of dramatic strategies of verse, through an extensive look into her archive. Taking as its title the image of the aviary, the chapter imagines Bishop's archive as a kind of living compendium of poetic endeavors. Particularly, it traces Bishop's engagements with dramatic forms—her critical perspectives of dramatic verse, her crafting of dramatic poems, and her interests in and aim toward performance.

As is shown in her translation of Aristophanes' *The Birds*, as well as two of her own unpublished dramatic pieces, Bishop's experiments with the poetic possibilities of dramatic forms and theatrical performances were central to her early poetics and remain influential to her later development. These dramatic contexts are taken not as mere trivia but as significant symbols of Bishop's poetic archive. Bishop's letters, notes, and drafts housed in her archive allow us to view her explorations of the dramatic voice, to better account for her experiments with the directly communal arts of performance, and to further recognize the ways in which mid-century poetry develops lyric forms, providing a new perspective on Bishop's forms of pretense.

Upon arriving at Vassar, Bishop's schoolgirl interests in drama and acting found a new creative space in the poetic milieu into which she was thrust. In her notebooks located in the Vassar archive, Bishop's handwritten class notes from her drama courses and her class in literary criticism show her repeatedly highlighting the performative nature of poetry and the poetic nature of drama. Clearly writing under the influence of a Vassar faculty who emphasized the classical importance of verse to traditional dramatic form, Bishop's notes include considerations of poetic and verse drama as such. In one example, under a discussion of verse drama she labels "Why Verse?" Bishops writes that it is the "[a]dded pleasure of meter" that justifies the poetic drama—pleasures, she clarifies, of both "similitude and dissimilitude" (VC 69.11).

That there was an ongoing reconsideration of the pleasures of verse and experimental drama is no surprise given the state of the Vassar dramatic scene. During Bishop's time at the college, the Vassar Experimental Theater—led by the indefatigable Hallie Flanagan, the eventual head of the Federal Theatre Project—was ambitious in producing the students' socially conscious and formally inventive plays, including verse drama. Beginning in her sophomore year, Bishop herself took part in on-campus productions, yet she was apathetic about, if not outright dismissive of, the socio-political nature of the more experimental works. Nonetheless, Bishop took an interest in the formally, poetically inclined productions of the experimental theater. Of these, Bishop's attention was particularly drawn to the Vassar Experimental Theater's premiere in the spring of 1933 of T. S. Eliot's *Sweeney Agonistes: Fragments of an Aristophanic Melodrama*, an event that allowed the young Bishop to first meet and interview Eliot. The timing of the production was one of dramatic interest for both individuals, given Eliot's increasing attention to verse drama and Bishop's burgeoning poetic ambitions.

Eliot's dramatic style developed in a moment of profound change, from his early fragmentary work in *Sweeney* to his more religious work *The Rock*, which would premiere in the spring of 1934. The dramatic style in which he would eventually write was ever more driven by an emphasis on modern life and embedded in the speech of his time, yet the production of Sweeney, which was to become influential for Bishop, was deeply experimental, fragmentary, and the clearest example of her exposure to the comedic style that Eliot would call "Aristophanic." After meeting with Eliot, Bishop's study of the form quite clearly accelerates. She carefully scrutinizes Eliot's essays on Greek drama while in the process of her own work translating in the Aristophanic style. Bishop began her translation of *The Birds* as an independent study of Aristophanes' comedy during her senior year at Vassar. Conducted under the direction of Miss McCurdy, the more traditional of her Greek teachers at Vassar, the translation is clearly a response to Eliot, however much the translation may remain an essentially tutelary enterprise. Bishop herself remarks in a letter that her work was to be "half-way between Gilbert Murray and T. S. Eliot, and with nothing 'cheap' in it" (*OA* 10). The comment by Bishop places her work in the midst of a scholarly quibble. Her professor, Miss McCurdy, was a defender of Murray's after Eliot's essay "Euripides and Professor Murray" criticized Murray's translations, saying that rather than allowing the English to be "revitalized" in light of the Greek original, Murray's verses were simply weak imitations of Pre-Raphaelite style. Bishop would even remark upon the spat in a letter to Frani Blough Muser that "Mr. Eliot's vituperous attack on Mr. Murray still rankles in Miss McCurdy's breast" (*OA* 15). Bishop's taking, then, of a "middle path" with her translation and her interests in avoiding the particularly "cheap" seem to place her work at a kind of midpoint between the colloquial approaches of Eliot and the scholarly airs of Murray. The translation and its effects would continue to fascinate her until at least 1950, when she was prodded by Margaret Miller to complete the work.

From the earliest drafts, Bishop's archive reveals that she was interested in the work as much more than an attempt at scholarly translation or an assignment pressed upon undergraduates. Her letters, her friends' reminiscences, and the archival leavings scattered across notebooks and drafts all show that Bishop was carefully considering her translation's dramatic potential and the various possibilities of its performance. In terms of production, Bishop clearly considers the visual and auditory nature of her work—combining a sometimes stilted formal poetry with an ultimately humorous tonal quality—and her drafts include stage notes describing the setting as a "Dante-esque sort of place" and even sketches of a figure in bird costume.

The archival drafts—which include the opening lines and parabasis in typescript as well as a notebook with more extensive manuscript lines—show that Bishop revisited the work on multiple occasions using at least four different writing instruments. In a letter to Donald Stanford, Bishop illustrates her faith in the work's poetic potential, calling her translation "the finest thing I'm doing" (*OA* 10). Stanford would himself remember Bishop's translation, noting how "Elizabeth talked quite a bit in her very first letter and in her later letters about a translation she was doing of Aristophanes' *Birds*. She sent me two or three pages of it in the

Bishop includes a short series of marginal sketches alongside her translated song from *The Birds*, including figures in costume.

early letters. She was getting rather enthusiastic about it by the spring of 1934" (*REB* 56-57). Other friends, like Eleanor Clark Warren, all mentioned the translation as her "most ambitious project," noting that "she was hopeful that it would be performed on campus" (*REB* 55). Bishop had hoped as early as December of 1933 that the translation would be produced in her senior year. She wrote to Donald Stanford at the outset of the winter break that she was "spending part of vacation here ... to work on it, as there is a faint chance of its being given, and I want to get it done" (*OA* 14). Although the student production did not occur, she nonetheless remained insistent on writing toward production, even thinking about composers who might produce an accompanying score.

In the spring of 1934, Bishop would travel to Hartford for *Four Saints in Three Acts*, Gertrude Stein's experimental opera, with the express intent of hearing Virgil Thompson's music. As Bishop herself makes clear, it was this event, along with Eliot's ongoing attempts at shaping a poetic drama, which would drive her own interests: "She was anxious to hear Virgil Thompson's music and had not heard anything by him before. Stein's work, and Bishop's interest in Eliot's *The Rock*, at least temporarily roused Bishop to write her own drama or masque that spring" (*REB* 363). Notably, Bishop's interest in drama was to remain distinctly *poetic* across her experiments, and though she was emboldened by the current enthusiasm for poetic drama, Bishop, in a letter to Muser, shows some initial hesitancy about her ability to succeed:

> Just now I have an unreasonable desire to think about a new drama *in poetry*. Perhaps it isn't so unreasonable after all, as Eliot seems to be working that way. And the Stein opera made me feel cheerful about the return of the masque-like entertainment. Lord, I'd like to attempt that sort of thing. Now I remember that Eliot has just written a masque, too—a liturgical affair for one of his English churches. I suppose it would take years of theatrical training to get anywhere with it—and lots of other things besides. (*OA* 22)[5]

Facing clearly the issue of patronage and the costs of performance, among the many other structural challenges of dramatic staging, Bishop nonetheless focuses on the nature of the project as a poetic endeavor. Upon returning from the Stein opera, Bishop would communicate in a letter to Stanford her mixed sense of the opera's achievement, casting her translation as a possible remedy to or extension of the contemporary practice of the cultural form among Bishop's poetic contemporaries:

> just got back from N.Y.—hearing the Stein opera. It has some beautiful Negro singing and the sets are ravishing. Gertrude had very little to do with its success, however,

the words being mostly unintelligible and then ignored as far as the characters, moods, etc., went. It was awfully nice. Oh dear, I wish Virgil Thompson would begin taking an interest in *The Birds*. (*OA* 19)

Bishop's dramatic ambitions for her translation, of having it accompanied by Thompson's music, appear to heighten her interests in the form and spark an interest in opera that would remain throughout her career. After Thompson's music accompanies Robert Lowell's trio of plays, *The Old Glory*, Bishop would revisit an earlier statement to Lowell, that she had "dreamed of a libretto for years" (*WIA* 316).

While the language of Bishop's translation reveals her intentions for performance and interests in the dramatic, Bishop's emphases also show a clear aptitude for the more lyrical passages of the play. She writes to Muser that she is using varying forms of meter, expressing, further, that she is "letting my fancy run wild on the bird songs themselves" (*OA* 11). Her primary inspiration comes from a highly lyrical poem, Richard Crashaw's "Music's Duell," a long poem about a contest between a lute player and a nightingale. In the parabasis, probably the most polished section of the translation, Bishop reaches for a rather traditional, yet highly lyrical tone. Though the rest of the play follows the comedic type of Aristophanes' comedies, the parabasis serves as the poetic focal point of the play. Here, Bishop uses more regular form, heroic couplets in formal diction. In the typed page of the parabasis, she opens with the invocation:

> Chorus of Birds:
> Dusky bird and bird of gold,
> Of all the birds the one I hold
> Most dear, the one to whom belongs
> The very source of all birds' songs,
> Nightingale, come now and bear
> Delight upon the heavy air.
> Fair-throated, strike the little strings
> Of song till every accent sings.
> As in the spring, the melody
> Begin! Begin the song for me. (VC 72.4; *PPL* 267)

The emphasis on singing and the traditional elements of lyric poetry, even the trope of the nightingale, emanate from this opening invocation and illustrate the comfort a young Bishop would take in the most lyrical passage of the play. Her reference to the nightingale is one marked by its echoes of lyric precedent and pushes toward some of her most heavily revised lines in the manuscript.

In one of her song translations, Bishop clearly signals a lyric mode she would more fully develop in her later work, something akin to an aubade: "Come my mate, stop sleeping / Let loose the strains of the sacred hymn, / The sacred threnody from your divine throat." On the following page is one of the handwritten drafts that Bishop seemed to struggle over, with multiple revisions, strike-throughs, and hazarded changes. Here, she modifies the earlier lines, adding:

(sung formally, as if at a soiree)
Wake, my wife, wake!
Put an end to sleeping;
From thy sweet throat [---]
Sweet notes to end our weeping (VC 72.4)

The revision is more intimate, metrically varied, and ultimately more distinct as a translation. Though Bishop is working from Aristophanes' source text, the lines serve as forerunners to a number of Bishop's original lyrical developments, bringing to mind her poem "It is marvellous to wake up together." In the poem, a slow-waking speaker imagines "dreamily / How the whole house caught in a bird-cage of lightning / Would be quite delightful rather than frightening" (EAP 44). Although *The Birds* was never performed as Bishop had hoped, her ambitions for the play and her continued interest in its completion well into her poetic career establishes *The Birds* as one of Bishop's clearest attempts at a public form of poetry. While still forming her poetic voice, the act of translating was a unique outlet for an ambitious young poet, with the classical work carrying a natural intellectual heft and providing a growing opportunity given the renewed interest in poetic drama.

While Bishop was attempting to have *The Birds* produced in her final semester at Vassar, the director of the Atheneum in Hartford, A. E. Austin, visited Vassar to speak about the Stein opera that Bishop had attended. In the student newspaper account on May 12, Austin was reported as saying that "Gertrude Stein represents the only possibility of opera in English which avoids the pitfalls of the ridiculous. The opera, while amusing, witty and slight is yet more honest than the grand-opera 'shell of pomposity'" (REB 364). Bishop attended the lecture, as well as those by Stein at Vassar in 1934 and in Paris in 1935, and clearly saw the renewed interest in the form among poets like Stein as a model that might be emulated and a potential outlet for her dramatic impulses. During this period, while still working on her translation of Aristophanes, Bishop began to develop her interests more broadly, looking beyond classical forms to the dramatic verse developed by poets in the milieu of Eliot and Stein. A close attention to her archival drafts and notes reveals a seemingly larger dramatic project testing the possibilities of these genres, beginning in earnest in 1934 and 1935, with revisions continuing until as late as the 1950s and 1960s. Previous allusions to these materials and various comments in letters and reminiscences, most markedly the notes in *One Art* (1994), *Remembering Elizabeth Bishop* (1994), and *Edgar Allan Poe & the Juke-box* (2006), have led to some misperceptions as to the project(s) on which Bishop worked and have, as a result, perhaps undervalued the extent to which Bishop was interested in performance, dramatic writing, and the poetic masque.

Particularly, the confusion seems to have arisen over variant readings of Bishop's letters, leading to differing reports as to the work (or works) that Bishop was constructing at the time. The critical confusion seems to have predominantly arisen in response to the curious decision to excerpt Bishop's letters in *One Art*. To take an early, important example, the first letter to broach the subject of dramatic performance in the aftermath of Bishop's translation of *The Birds* occurs at the suggestion of Muser who proposes a collaboration. Muser suggests rather cheekily a project "which is unlikely to be in any way remunerative," a kind of "chamber opera," something "really funny and amusing not heavy" (VC 16.7). Bishop's reaction was overwhelmingly positive:

> WELL, I was so pleased to get your letter, and it really made me feel kind of queer and isn't it STRANGE, because I came away with a large pad of paper, and Ben Jonson's *Masques* to study, with the express purpose of writing something like that. . . . Is your idea to compose it yourself? I think, as you say, an American Pastoral might be excellent. (*OA* 36)

To date, readings of the letters have typically connected Bishop's comments on her dramatic interests with one of two pieces: a dramatic poem that Bishop titles, most consistently, "The Proper Tears: A Masque" or a piece she was simultaneously working on, tentatively entitled "Prince Mannerly." The confusion as to the attribution of these lines seems tied to Bishop's interest in Jonson's masques, the uncertainty as to which drafts she had already begun, and the fact that Bishop's letter in the archive continues (rather than the edited copy in *One Art*). In the complete archival letter, Bishop remarks that she has "two little things like that already started" but emphasizes the more comedic of the pieces, "Prince Mannerly" (VC 34.4). Thus, the editing of the letters in *One Art* might give rise to a faulty perception that Bishop's focus was either singular or simply speculative, erasing Bishop's previously existing interest in composing in the dramatic form.

Considering Bishop's response to Muser's letter, the editors of *Remembering Elizabeth Bishop* note her work's origins this way:

> In the fall of 1935 Bishop was thinking about writing a masque, a stylized dramatic entertainment, in the manner of Ben Jonson: She imagined a Henry James character walking in a garden, talking about manners, attended by a retinue of angels. . . . Muser believed that she and Bishop could write a chamber opera free of Wagner's influence, an opera that would be "a new idea, had by a few select people sitting around after dinner, then polished up." (*REB* 364-65)

In this case, the editors emphasize the second work begun by Bishop—"Prince Mannerly." Bishop's return letter to Muser certainly emphasizes this second masque, accentuating its humor and need for music (VC 34.4). In the existent text of "Prince Mannerly," the drama clearly focuses on the comedic potential of the angels and a narcissistic, singular main character, the titular "Prince." The initial spark for the project looks to have been an essay on James written by Marianne Moore, "Henry James as a Characteristic American," which appears in the Spring 1934 *Hound and Horn*. Originally titled "Prince Winsome Mannerly,"[6] Bishop elides the first name in subsequent drafts and seems to focus the work on the abstract generalities of personality rather than character.

In the manuscript version contained in the notebook, Bishop's initial sketch attempts to harness the possibilities of scene-setting and imagery, imagining the dramatic situation as an essentially comedic one. Bishop describes the stage as set like a hotel terrace with tables, chairs, and umbrellas, ultimately framing a twilight scene featuring two main characters—the Prince and the angels, who are described as "rather like those in the P. Della Francesca 'Nativity'" (VC 72.2). The allusion to Francesca is Bishop's clearest stylistic suggestion. In Francesca's painting, the angels are depicted as observers and musicians, emphasizing their lyric role. On the more detailed and revised typescript included in the Vassar archive, Bishop's notes include suggestions for musical composition, including changes in volume and starting points. Set to have the Angels begin in an opening quatrain, Bishop pens in the right margin "Have the prince begin: —then <u>whispers</u> from angels, interrupt, getting gradually intelligible" (VC 64.4). She also identifies the ways that the varying character lines are to function, identifying the "lines to be played on with*" (VC 64.4). All of these notes suggest that the typescript was to be Bishop's more polished draft for Muser. Given such a context, "Prince Mannerly" functions thus not as closet drama but as Bishop's clearest attempt at a libretto.

As with her translation of *The Birds*, "Prince Mannerly" shows more of a focus on the performative, musical elements than on a coherency of narrative. Yet while the characterization is slight, the James figure is recognizable, and the portrayal of the angels as ironic observers is both apropos and humorous. The Prince's main concern throughout has largely to do with his interest in "confession." Rather than

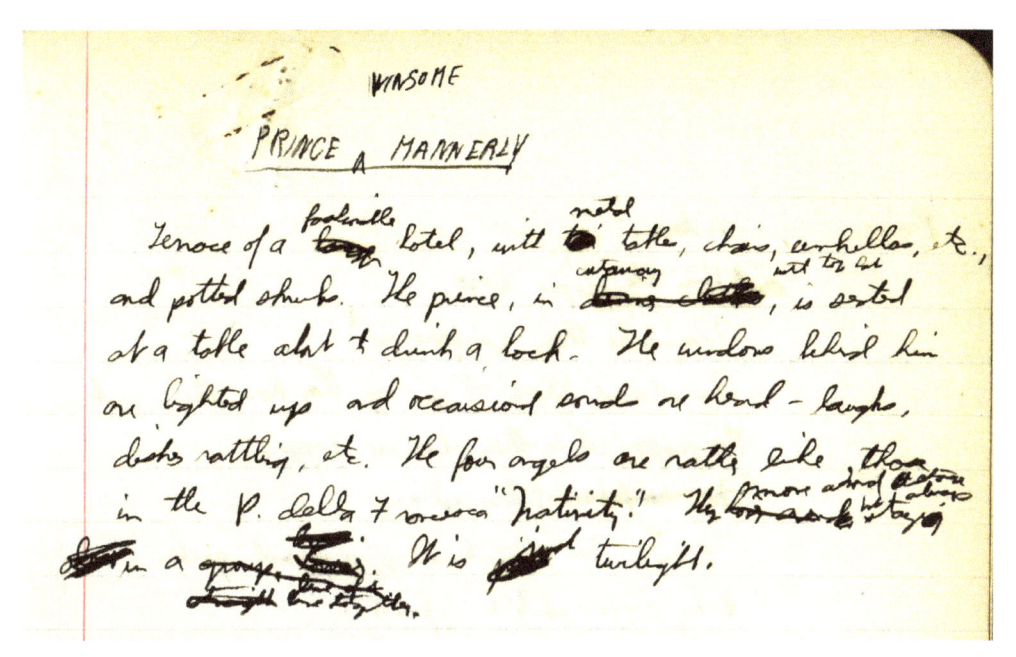

Bishop's manuscript version of "Prince Mannerly" references Francesca's nativity amidst its description and includes suggestions for performance of a work she originally entitled "Winsome."

the direct, psychological mode of the realist novel, the character remains rather playful and pronouncedly shy, with lines exclaiming "Oh dear, how they formulate confessions!" and "Oh pray, no confidences in a formal garden!" Rather than a self-expressive character working in the plain language of confession, Bishop writes Mannerly as endlessly polishing his words in a kind of formal mania. Such attempts at stylization become part of the drama when the Prince's poetic inclinations are described as his "earliest failures" because of the way that he "polished tombstones, blew into the ashes." Yet the Angels' eavesdropping serves to undercut the Prince's lacking confessions by focusing on the variance between the Prince's expressed platitudes and his thoughts:

> Fold wings and float and talk
> In whispers while he takes his walk.
> It's now been some years since
> We've listened to his thoughts. (VC 64.4)

Thus, in crafting such a dramatic irony, Bishop tasks the angels with playing an essentially comic part. The retinue mocks not just his perceived thoughts but also his appearance and demeanor:

THE ARCHIVAL AVIARY   259

> His top hat is just the beginning
> His neat spat may mean standing pat
> Or have no meaning.
> (What can the Prince be driving at?)
> He is leaning
> On the fountain's edge. His hair's been thinning. (VC 64.4)

Clearly alluding to Eliot's "The Love Song of J. Alfred Prufrock," with his thin-growing hair, the angels gently mock the excesses of a character straight out of Henry James.

In the manuscript and typescript pages, the angelic comedic routine does seem occasionally juvenile, repeating couplets and engaging in children's play: "Here's the church and here's the steeple, / Open the door and see all the people." Yet, in one midpoint stanza on the second manuscript page, the angels' chorus becomes much more musical, and they intone the oddest metrical (and formal) part of the poem, again seeming to razz the work of James. The lines stagger along in various repetition, with the angels proclaiming themselves "God's sexless sophisticated angels." That they further allude to their having the "patience of Saints and the tact of / Tact of the Lord" seems a direct nod to Stein's opera. The repetition ends in a repeated refrain, as they note that they are "Never bored, never bored, never bored" (VC 72.2). This stanza, along with the changes that Bishop makes while revising the draft for Muser, suggest a significant effort by Bishop to imbibe the language and style of the comic opera.

While in New York the previous July, Bishop attended *Boris Godunov*, an opera by Modest Mussorgsky. Remarking on the performance, Bishop noted the ways that "[i]t was much more true to life in that way than an ordinary play," further remarking that the operatic form often "seems like marking time," as the vantage point given from a discontinuous form grants the kind of distance one might gain from their own past (VC 72.1). For Bishop, the possibilities of "marking time" in opera might constitute a kind of poetry freeing to the young poet, salving the insistencies and exposure of the more confessional mode dramatized in "Prince Mannerly."

Much of the rest of the journal, in the pages following "Prince Mannerly," are filled with quotations from John Dryden and Alfred Lord Tennyson, with the former setting out many of the formal possibilities Bishop seems to explore. The archival notes show that Bishop was particularly interested in a range of works, including Dryden's "The Secular Masque." Below a quoted portion of "Mars' song" from the masque (which she liked "very much"), she includes further points of reference for her own work in the form, noting particularly the work of Henry

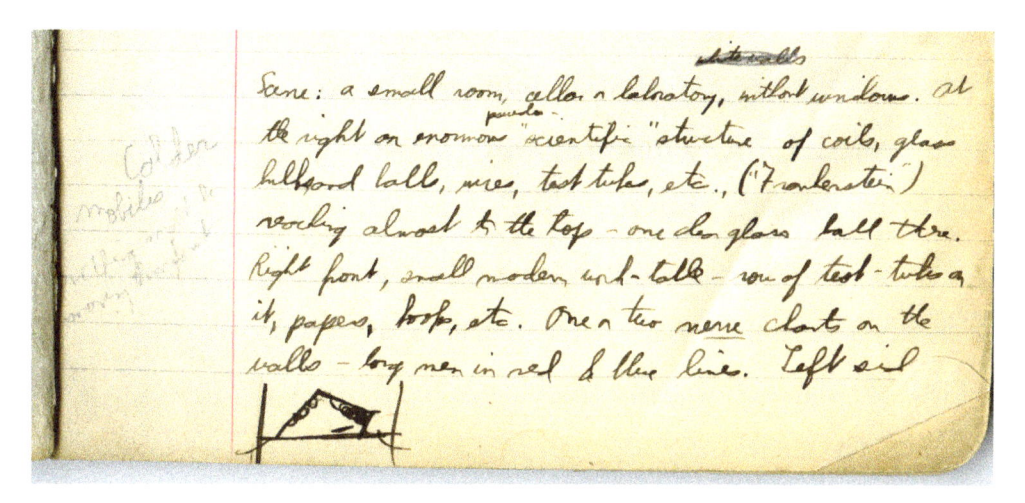

Bishop's earlier draft of "His Proper Tear" shows an opening poem from Fletcher, a penciled revision of the title, and her note regarding Calder's mobiles.

Purcell—who composed music for over forty plays, many of which were Dryden's—and the performance of masques as operas. "Prince Mannerly" clearly remained on Bishop's mind, with both the manuscript and typescript versions showing revisions. Even a few years after beginning work, in 1936, Bishop would write again to Muser wondering if she has moved on to ask Muriel Rukeyser or E. E. Cummings to write some poetry for her instead. Having sent her some work, Bishop remarks, "I am REALLY doing Prince Mannerly, and hope to have it all done for you when I get back" (VC 34.5).

In the same letter to Muser responding to her request for a collaboration, Bishop would ultimately hazard that "if you're really going to try to write some music, I'll send you some of the choruses, scrap, etc. when they're a little more perfected" (VC 34.4). Of the pieces she had already begun, it was chronologically "The Proper Tears" that Bishop first began composing and was still on her mind at the date of Muser's letter. The drama was also the most developed scenario from Bishop, showing repeated attempts at revision, including two manuscript drafts. On the first extant page of Bishop's notebook from this period, she begins the first version, which she titles "His Proper Tear."[7] The scene-setting for this first draft is elaborate and tonally gothic: "Scene: a small room, cellar or laboratory, without window. At the right an enormous 'scientific' structure of coils, glass . . . wires, test tubes, etc., ("Frankenstein")" (VC 72.2). She further includes a description of "One or two nerve charts on the walls—long men in red & blue lines" (VC 72.2). Here, Bishop invokes an essentially Victorian theme while also suggesting something of the modern. In the left margin of the draft, Bishop pencils in a performative and architectural note: "Calders [sic] mobiles something might be moving throughout" (VC 72.2). A

THE ARCHIVAL AVIARY   261

small sketch in pen appears below, suggesting perhaps a stage with mobile atop acting as a kind of gable. The (likely) later pencil marking suggests a more modern setting than the gothic initially seems to suggest—forecasting the kind of dynamism and play that Bishop seeks in the piece. As Samuels has noted, Bishop's drawing on the aesthetics of artists like Calder serves ultimately to reimagine "the structures by which lyric poetry can incorporate event into continuity, unfurl or open toward emotion, [and] orchestrate movements from minimal to abundant" (*Deep Skin* 178). Here, at the outset of the drafting process, the suggestion of the Calder mobile likewise sets the emphasis on movement and event, although sidestepping the essentially lyric surface to which Samuels draws attention.

In the second handwritten draft in the notebook, the work's visual elements have further developed to emphasize the sense of dynamism and visual culture that Bishop seems to invoke with Calder. In this version of the masque, the hero is "chained to the wall, arms and ankles, by massive chromium-plated chains" and "wears ordinary clothes" (VC 72.2). Despite the classical suggestions of the piece, including mythological allusions to Prometheus, the second draft remains a highly modern, dark-comic piece. The shift in scene is made clear in her explicit "Argument." In this drafted opening, the villain (a "Doctor or Magician") has imprisoned the hero (or "Victim") and is attempting to examine the Hero's emotion but must be capable of getting a "'specimen' of the proper tear." To have the Hero produce such a tear, the Doctor introduces a series of figures to "prey on, play on, the sympathies." Bishop also introduces a series of "Tempters"—a dramatic counterbalance and a mirror of Eliot's structure in *Murder in the Cathedral*—who seek to salve the Hero's distress (VC 72.2).

As Bishop herself notes and as the plot further suggests, this work dramatizes what she calls "the problem of sincerity." Not only is Bishop's dramatic work formally addressing the idea of pretense, but the very subject of a chained figure who must produce a "sincere" or "proper" tear suggests that Bishop remains fascinated by the possibilities and perils of a sincere artistic practice. Notably, such a problem was one Bishop ultimately decides to address in verse, believing the form to have the imaginative capacity to engage with the problems of confession, psychology, and feigning. In the second notebook attempt at the masque, Bishop's decision to versify the work was one central to both scene and character, having the Doctor and Hero speak in prose, while it was the tempters who were to speak in "verse." Such a poetic decision seems to throw into relief the focus of the play (lying and sincerity, the polished words of the poet) while also inverting classical poetic drama's tendency to have the hero speaking in prose.

Alice Quinn connects this masque to Bishop's poem "In a cheap hotel," which similarly tells the story of a chained figure.[8] Bishop's notebooks contain a series of other influential texts as well, including the Fletcher poem that begins the first

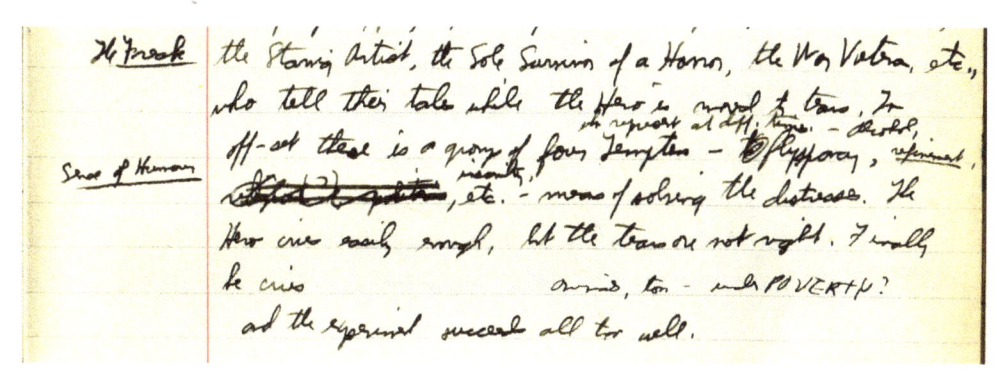

Bishop's later manuscript draft of "The Proper Tear" features an altered setting and a longer list of suggested character types.

draft and the work of St. Ignatius of Loyola, whose spiritual exercises have a clear impact on Bishop's revision. Particularly, Bishop is struck by a quotation from Loyola, one she reproduces in her notebook: "In meditation of the invisible, as here of sins, the composition will be to see with the eye of the imagination and consider my soul imprisoned in this corruptible body, and my whole compound self in this vale of tears as in banishment among brute animals. I mean the whole compound of soul and body" (VC 72.3). The line "this vale of tears" has a direct parallel in the tears and weeping found in the masque. The later allusions to Loyola that Bishop includes in her journal further push the possibilities of the masque beyond the merely comic. In one of Bishop's notes in the second draft, she even writes, "Look up: Anatomy of Tear Ducts, etc. Psychology of Weeping" (VC 72.2). In a masque so thematically concerned with sincerity, Bishop's own poetic crafting likewise focuses on possibilities for shaping the real with the same kind of imaginative pretense she finds in the work of Auden.

In Bishop's famous letter to Lowell in March of 1972, criticizing the memoirish mixing of fact and fiction in his collection *The Dolphin*, she points to a peculiar pair of lines where Lowell writes, "why don't you try to lose yourself / and write a play about the fall of Japan." Bishop wonders, incredibly, if it could "*possibly* be true . . . ?!" (*WIA* 712). The comment is clearly incredulous, amazed at the sheer grandiosity and ridiculousness of Lowell's purportedly autobiographical claim. Yet, in light of the dramatic archival works she herself left, Bishop's incredulity might rather be read as wonder, serving not merely as a reaction to the autobiographical material and Lowell's ego but perhaps the poetic move itself, the very possibility of a poetic pretense. Such a poetic maneuver might further be connected to a note that Quinn mentions finding in an entry (crossed out) in Bishop's notes: "G. Stein's reason for 'concealment' of the 'automatic' nature of her writings = or, is another form of, her 'concealment' of the 'homosexual' nature of her life—False Scents we all give off" (VC 75.4). Bishop's fascination with dramatic forms suggest a kind of poetic concealment similar to that of her operatic influence, offering her another kind of poetic mask to play with.

Bishop's neglecting to have published or performed these pieces might likewise be read as a type of evasion, a hesitancy, or reticence, yet her published poems maintain a dramatic sensibility first captured in these pieces. Bishop finds place for personae in many of her poems, such as "Jerónimo's House," "The Riverman," and her dramatic monologue "Crusoe in England." Likewise, they can be seen in her injection of dialogue and speeches in "The Moose," and "North Haven," not to mention her extended ballad, "The Burglar of Babylon." Even quite late in her poetic career, Bishop was still considering a dramatization she titled "Baby with a Broken Toe," a fragmentary mock-up of the situation covered in Bishop's 1969 interview with Kathleen Cleaver. Although the manuscript initially subtitles the piece an "interview," she definitively labels it a "Play" in the manuscript. Such an impulse, even in Bishop's later life, shows a poet attuned not just to poetic situations but also their dramatic potential, their way of seeing (as in the racially charged context of "Baby with a Broken Toe") into the lives of others. To trace these early dramatic poems, then, is to more fully recognize Bishop's modes of pretense, of acting her way into the poetic world.

NOTES

1. See Samuels, Deep Skin 7.
2. See White, Lyric Shame 96.
3. See Javadizadeh, "Elizabeth Bishop's Closet Drama" 120-21.
4. The play became a regular performance at the school, running for twenty years after her graduation. *The Blue Pencil* also includes a copy of her Nova Scotia play, a dark, death-filled play, deeply descriptive, and though brief, filled with a clear, poetic tinge that would be more fully articulated in the dramas discussed here.
5. To Marianne Moore, Bishop writes of her reaction to verse drama from Eliot and Auden: "I think the W.P.A. . . . production of Murder in the Cathedral must have been much better than the London one—although it . . . was such a success, and ran such a long time. I thought it was AWFUL. . . . The Dog Beneath the Skin was a little better theatrically, I think—but it was very poorly put on, too, and acting brought out the difference between the overprettiness of the in-between 'poems' and the horseplay of the story rather too much" (OA 41-42).
6. The insertion of "Winsome" may have been a joke on Bishop's part, a possible reference to a play within The Little Colonel's Hero by Annie Fellows Johnston.
7. To open, she includes a poem by Phineas Fletcher, "Drop, drop, slow tears," something omitted in the later versions yet revelatory of her larger inspiration.
8. In a note, Bishop would recall a story titled "Chained Love," which features a young man "chained to his bed-post for 25 yrs. by his mother to prevent him from going with a girl she disproved of . . . A very sinister, Bronte-esque tale" (EAP 290).

CHAPTER THIRTEEN

ARCHIVAL ANIMALS

Polyphonic Movement in Elizabeth Bishop's Drafts

Heather Bozant Witcher

In her 1947 letters to her psychoanalyst Ruth Foster, Elizabeth Bishop writes that psychoanalysis illuminated the impact of her "fear of repetition" upon her craft and poetic process: Bishop intimates that she had initially thought of each of her poems as "absolutely new" but is conflicted because she had been told of her own style. Unable to "feel it myself," Bishop asserts that each poetic voice "sound[s] quite different to me."[1] Her insistence on a unique voice or style reveals not only Bishop's supposed "fear of repetition" but also her focus on the poetic usage of different sounding voices—or, what I have taken as an example of polyphony— often within the same poem. To counteract this desire to make every poem "new," Bishop ends her intimation to Foster in this opening paragraph with a firmly stated resolution. Rather than "isolated events," Bishop declares new insight into her poetry as part of a cohesive collection: her poems interweave and overlap and are "all one long poem anyway." This sense of cohesion comes from Bishop's ability to experiment and craft a sense of polyphonic motion within the structure of her poems. To create "one long poem," Bishop's oeuvre relies upon her perfection of poetic craft: a persistent honing of form, style, and voice that is preserved within the cache of rich drafts in the Elizabeth Bishop Papers at Vassar College.

Taking Bishop's own exploration of her poetry as "one long poem" that overlaps or goes "into one another," this chapter investigates one of Bishop's canonical poems, "The Armadillo." "The Armadillo" is notable for its establishment of lyric voice or, as Bishop points out to Foster, several different sounding voices; however, critical attention has not yet explored how this animal-centric poem—in its manuscript form—sheds light on Bishop's creative process with its attention to motion and polyphony. Bishop's careful craft and fastidious revision have long guided representations of her writing style. Most recently, Eleanor Cook's *Elizabeth Bishop at Work*, offers primarily close readings of Bishop's published poems to provide a study of "Bishop at work, at work at her desk, so to speak, reflecting, choosing" (7). Yet Cook leaves aside the numerous drafts and manuscripts that reflect the traces of Bishop's creative process. It is this gap in Bishop scholarship that I draw attention to in this chapter. However, scholarship has yet to embark on a truly critical analysis of this brilliant precision. Such an analysis requires an understanding of Bishop's drafting process as it is revealed in archival materials. I suggest that we can begin to explore the notion of polyphonic blending conveyed by Bishop to Foster with our own form of archival blending: integrating the various textures, materials, and influences upon Bishop's entire oeuvre, composed of poetry, prose, correspondence, and artwork.

In the spirit of genetic criticism, this chapter provides an analysis of the revisionary processes uncovered in the drafts of "The Armadillo." Within the Elizabeth Bishop Papers, there are a total of nine drafts leading to the final form of the poem. Her 1955-56 notebook contains five re-workings of the poem in handwritten form—it is this poem that is the most re-worked in the notebook. Such extensive drafting suggests that "The Armadillo" meant a great deal to Bishop as she moved stanzas around and experimented with different tones and styles. Aside from the notebook, there are three typewritten drafts, with marginal emendations by hand, in a file that has been dated by Vassar archivists as 1957, and there is one final typewritten copy, with Bishop's signature.

In tracing the early revisions, this chapter reveals Bishop's conviction that poetic craft is tied to theories of motion in art and music. While scholarship has begun to document the influence of Alexander Calder's aesthetic theories upon Bishop's poetry and artwork, little attention has been paid to the influence of music and sound.[2] As an undergraduate at Vassar College, Bishop established her conviction of music as a form of literature and honed this belief through epistolary dialogue and poetic experimentation. Juxtaposing Bishop's poetic process, Calder's theories, and her undergraduate notes from an introductory music course during her time at Vassar illuminates her use of motion, temporality, and spatiality in her poems. Foregrounding her emphasis on polyphony and motion—in content, form, and in the various drafts of "The Armadillo"—this chapter prompts scholarship to question how Bishop uses various media to think through her poetry. She not only visualizes her poem, crystallizing images in beautiful verse; she explores aspects of motion and reimagines the aesthetic capacity of mobility to establish multiple and different sounding voices in her creative process. Indeed, the literal moving around of words, stanzas, and rhythm within the archival pages can be read as a training ground for the polyphonic movement ultimately embedded within the structure and tone of the finalized poem. A coda to this chapter briefly discusses how freely available digital tools, such as Scalar, enable accessibility to the Bishop archive and provide an immersive experience that engages student learning and archival methodology.

"HER OWN TUNE": BISHOP'S NOTEBOOK, 1955-56

Sandwiched between draft poems entitled "St. John's Day" and "Poem for a Child," we find Bishop's initial attempt at "The Armadillo" in her notebook from 1955-56 (VC 73.2).[3] Originally entitled "From a Letter," Bishop scratches out this personal biographical context in favor of the title "The Owls' Nest." The poem—in its archival state—looks a mess. Positioned in the center of the notebook, rusted staples hold the collection together; yet, somehow, the reddish stains fit amidst the black ink and pencil scratches, crossed-out stanzas, and squiggly lines. At first glance, "The Owls' Nest" appears to provide evidence for the careful, fastidious process for which Bishop is known: with each crossed-out word, another is chosen; for each eliminated stanza, another is written. This manuscript bears witness to Bishop's deliberate poetic art, an art derived from painstaking syntax and diction. Yet closer examination reveals Bishop's reliance on movement and tone, on the establishment of a multitonal lyric voice.

"I think you never do a poem without your own intuition," wrote Robert Lowell to Bishop on July 12, 1960 (*WIA* 331). "You are about the only poet now who calls her own tune—rather different from Pound or Miss Moore, who built original styles then continue them—but yours ... are all unpredictably different" (331). Such "unpredictably different" styles are, in one way, different due to their emphasis on temporality and motion; in another way, they are derivative from lived experience and thought. In "The Owls' Nest," the first stanza illuminates an active present:

> This is the time of year
> when almost every night
> the frail, illegal fire-balloons appear,
> to &-to climb an the mountain height; (VC 73.2, lines 1-4)

Beginning with a deictic expression—*this* time, rather than any time—Bishop focuses on the Brazilian festival of St. John's Day and carries her sense of present temporality across the verbs stacking the openings of lines four and five—the movement from the first to the second stanza.[4] Eventually, Bishop eliminates "&."

In doing so, she refuses a compound list to favor instead the active, present tense: "to climb" or "to float." Once temporality is established, Bishop begins to consider spatiality: line five demonstrates her hesitance or, perhaps, careful consideration. Still describing the climbing fire balloons, Bishop pauses over their upward movement: "to sail" is excised in favor of a more precise rising motion, providing direction: "to float up." These careful considerations demonstrate Bishop's sense that the poem itself should *do* something—should perform some act of motion within the reader's imagination. Moreover, these revisions provide insight into the "unpredictably different" styles that, for Lowell, characterize Bishop's poetry. Such difference arises from shifting conceptions of time and space that give way, in the poem's published form, to the dynamism characterizing "The Armadillo"—its uncertainty and multiplicity.

In the draft's third stanza, Bishop signals a shift in position by leading with "But," a word noticeably written off in the margins with what appears to be a different pen. This circumstance suggests that Bishop inserted a tonal shift around the same time that she excised the aforementioned ampersands in the first stanza. Linking these revisions establishes the purpose of Bishop's emendations as a means of both clarifying and asserting tension through her insertion of multiplicity. Whereas the first two stanzas provide a distanced and impersonal speaker observing the balloons rising and "fill[ing] with light" (VC 73.2, line 7), the third stanza sets up a division between the balloons and the spectators. This transition suggests both spatial and tonal difference as Bishop moves from the external world of observation to the internal world of reflection: "But once ~~up they're up~~ they're against the sky, ~~we run we run~~ / ~~and~~ we confuse them with the stars,—" (lines 10-11). These lines mark a significant change from the published poem. In its published form, all sense of active, plural spectatorship is deferred until the sixth stanza's emphasis on the second-person plural: "The flame ran down. We saw the pair / of owls who nest there flying up / and up, . . ." (*P* 101-02, lines 24-26).[5]

In the manuscript notebook, Bishop displays a preference for an impersonal but active present that complements the rising motion of the fire balloons. In the first-appearing draft of the poem in the notebook, we witness an earlier shift in tone as spectators confuse the fire balloons with the natural, astronomic world. In its published form, "The Armadillo" surprises readers with its sudden shifts in position as it defers an overt commentary on human culpability in the poem's italicized final stanza. But here, in manuscript, Bishop uses motion to convey a steadily rising, active voice that becomes a communal "we." Inserting the community in the third stanza, therefore, foregrounds human implication in the illegal activity of the fire balloons. Initially, it would seem, Bishop meant for her poem to employ contrast as a means of asserting multiplicity: to present a stark division between the impersonal present and the internalized sense of futurity. Such division suggests a growing conflict between one's self and the wider public concession: the moral concerns felt over the fire balloons and their destruction of existing ecosystems and the spectacle afforded to the public on St. John's Day.

Inherent in "The Armadillo" is a sense of multiplicity and the sensation of circulating motifs, arising from competing events and the uncertainty of reaction and culpability. With each reading of the poem, we gain a different meaning, a finding of some new aspect that leads to closer analysis of a certain poetic theme: influences of astronomy and ecocriticism, biographical context unveiled through the poem's dedication to Robert Lowell, social and political protest. It is precisely this amalgamation that is celebrated within the Bishop archive, which generates a plurality of voices: poetic speakers preserved within manuscript drafts that reverberate with Bishop's daily life as detailed in her correspondence.

To solidify the increased conflict experienced within the draft of her poem, as traced above, scholarship must read these drafts alongside Bishop's entire oeuvre. For it is no coincidence that this tension is played out in her poetic process at the same time as Bishop considers her own experience of St. John's Day in a letter written to her confidant and physician Dr. Anny Baumann on June 24, 1955. Describing the holiday festivity of sending up illegal fire balloons, Bishop writes a prose rephrasing of her poetic lines. Detailing the balloons' drifting mountain ascension, and the "special draught" carrying them into the night, readers find resonance in Bishop's manuscript drafts and the finalized poem. In her correspondence, Bishop draws on the religious connotation of the festival as a means of possible exoneration—the same exoneration provided in the poem's second stanza. At the heart of this life-writing lies Bishop's own internal tension: "too bad" that the rain occurs at the time of fireworks and bonfires in contrast to "very good" for the ecological preservation of the forest; the supposed policing in tension with "everyone send[ing] them up anyway"; aesthetic beauty versus environmental destruction. "One's of two minds about them," Bishop writes, and it is precisely this internal pressure that Bishop publicly works through in the construction of the aptly named manuscript, "From a Letter." Thus, I read these elements of the archive together, as interconnected events, drawing together different sounding voices—from Bishop's personal life and poetic invention—to create an artistic rendering of conflict within the poem's structure and the archival space of the manuscript.

Trapped between these contrasts, Bishop's sense of creative forward motion comes to a halt with a literal space between stanzas four and five in the manuscript notebook, delineated by arrows and a question mark. Knowing the need for a transition between the violent movement of the wind and the stillness of the Southern Cross (which echoes the rapid movement of present action and the stillness of interiority), Bishop leaves a gap in her draft. Interestingly, this gap is filled by experimentation in the margins on the opposite page (f. 8r), discussed here in the next section. Aside from these marginalia, the manuscript draft titled "The Owls' Nest" bears few revisionary marks in its animal-centric stanzas. It appears that the image of owls fleeing from the safety of their nest in the face of an "egg of fire" splattering across the sky was crystallized in Bishop's mind. This clean copy suggests, perhaps, that Bishop remained certain of her poetic depictions of the natural world, further solidified by the shift in title to "The Owls' Nest." Or I propose that, even though this draft is the first in the series of "The Armadillo" reworkings within the notebook, it is the finalized version of the handwritten copy prior to the typewritten drafts dated 1957. This latter supposition will make sense when we consider the unity that underlies Bishop's compositional process: polyphonic motion.

What is certain, however, is that Bishop uses this more or less completed draft to establish tone and movement. In other words, careful consideration of Bishop's drafts establishes a sense of poetic process. Bishop composes this poem in stages, with revisions that draw out specific poetic techniques and formal structures. Later drafts on folios 9v to 10r reveal Bishop at work, instilling a sense of polyphony in the second half of her poem. But here, in the handwritten "The Owls' Nest" draft, Bishop remains intent on overcoming the difficulty of creating a sense of motion that orients the poem's speaker in relation to the present drifting of the fire balloons and the past event of an explosion of fire, creating an emergence of wildlife from their habitats. Curiously, these animal stanzas are written on top of what appears to be, on the left, a penciled list of groceries: "green pepper; orange; peanuts; chutney; currants[?]; [illegible]; 12 apples; onion; raisins."[6] Such palimpsestic writing within the archive again draws attention to Bishop's own sense of temporality: while perfecting her poem, she remains rooted in the present world of physical demands and moral concerns, revealed in her life-writing. Just as the draft poem moves from external observation to the interior reflection of observers, the draft itself witnesses Bishop's participation in, and fluid movement between, both worlds: her craft and reality.

COHERENCE FROM CHAOS: BISHOP'S MOTIONS

Outside of the present, in the liminal space of the margins at top and bottom, Bishop includes trial lines for the absent fifth stanza. These excised lines demonstrate not only Bishop's fastidiousness to get her poem just right but also the centrality of tonal movement within the poem. At top, Bishop suggests:

> ~~A down-draught from the~~   stumble dangerous
> Sometimes a down-draught from the peaks   block
> rising in ~~darkness~~ there   flashes? tumble
> can ~~[illegible] start then~~ start & sway & fall,   [illegible]
> stumbling ~~down~~ _{along} the air.   lock[?]
>
>   (VC 73.2, f. 8r)

In this draft stanza, off to the right, Bishop includes what can be considered a word bank denoting movement—"stumble," "tumble," "block"—presumably in an attempt to create the "stumbling" feeling of the "down-draught from the peaks." Perhaps these isolated words could also represent Bishop's experimentation, or word substitution, with line 4 of this eliminated stanza: "start & sway & fall." As Bishop drafts this stanza, we notice her uncertainty, demonstrated by strike-throughs and marginalized vocabulary. In setting up contrasting positions and tone in the initial stanzas, this gap generates a sense of changeability in terms of the poem's structure. Tracing the revisions allows for insight into how Bishop composes a stanza meant to convey the soft, gentle motion of a gliding fire balloon before it "suddenly turn[s] dangerous" (line 20) and how we might view these motions as vocal performances, preparing us for the published poem's italicized final stanza. At bottom, Bishop continues working through the problematics of conveying motion, utilizing the spacing of two columns. On the left, Bishop appears to work through an initial formulation of her poetic lines, whereas the right column features a series of rewordings and strike-throughs for rhythm and description as Bishop attempts to describe the motion of the fire balloon (VC 73.2, f. 8r).

Part of the difficulty, it seems, lies in positioning, or the orientation of the poetic speaker. Two questions come to light: First, how will the poem transition into commentary on human culpability, returning to the use of "we" in draft stanza five?

> Last night ∧ ^{another} a big one fell.
> It splattered like an egg of fire
> against the cliff behind the house.
> The flame ran down. We saw the pair [of owls] (VC 73.2, f. 7v, lines 18-21)

And, second, is this stanza meant to convey the same distanced spectatorial view as the draft's first stanza? In the option at left, Bishop chooses "also" to link the down-draft to earlier descriptions of the turbulence of the wind or its stillness. In this model, the downdraft maintains agency over the fire balloons: "can make them start & sway." With this option, the destruction of the animal habitat is beyond human control. Yet the incomplete option at right suggests that Bishop remains unsatisfied. By providing partial lines and phrases—"flash invisible air"—Bishop seems to ask herself whether this stanza is meant to be a continuation of interiorized reflection. Is this stanza meant to establish a sense of confusion—or disorientation? Tracing Bishop's uncertainty, demonstrated in the compositional tension derived from, as Lowell put it, the "unpredictably different" voices in the Bishop archive, reveals these questions of creative process, a process that was informed by Bishop's own interest in multimodality and art.

In providing a detailed look at Bishop's 1955-56 draft of "The Owls' Nest," I have been drawing attention to the ways in which the drafting process allows scholarship to substantiate existing interpretations of Bishop's anthologized poem and its movement from distanced, impersonal narration in the opening stanzas to an interiorized sense of poetic protest in the famed italicized final stanza. By privileging the archive, we are provided insight into how Bishop uses language to, as Peggy Samuels argues in *Deep Skin: Elizabeth Bishop and Visual Art*, "compose motion," drawing from Alexander Calder's aesthetic.[7] Additionally, Bishop's multimodal process allows for deeper insight into her poetic use of mobility. As illustrated, Bishop's struggle with the third stanza in her draft indicates an attempt to instill instability, hesitation, and disorientation into her poem. In order to visualize Calder's aesthetic, Bishop combines the suspension of motion in his mobiles with her understanding of musical texture to generate a productive sense of unpredictability that arises from the dynamism of polyphony.

In 1933, while in Pittsfield, Massachusetts, Bishop attended an exhibition of Calder's early small mobiles.[8] In the catalog accompanying the exhibition, Calder described his usage of motion to depict elements in continual relation to other elements, or what he refers to as "variation": "Each element can move, shift, or sway back and forth in a changing relation to each of the other elements in this universe. Thus they reveal not only isolated moments, but a physical law of variation among the elements of life" (qtd. in Samuels, "Composing Motions" 178). Calder's description of the varied continuity between all elements, in contrast to "isolated moments," bears a distinct similarity to Bishop's own description of her poetic process in 1947, when she describes to Foster her initial "effort to make each poem an isolated event" and her newfound recognition that her poems are interconnected, drawn together by different sounding voices that unite to form "one long poem anyway."

In perhaps one of Bishop's widely reproduced watercolors, she includes a Calder-like mobile in one of the rooms in Samambaia, the home she shared with her partner Lota de Macedo Soares in Brazil. By including the mobile, Bishop reinforces "Calder's view that his mobiles captured the cross-rhythms and disparate shapes of parts of the environment" (Samuels, "Composing Motions" 179). In a sort of call-and-response dialogue, Bishop's watercolor incorporates the shapes within the mobile so that they respond accordingly to the arrangement of similar shapes in the room. To demonstrate this response, Samuels provides a detailed analysis of Bishop's watercolor, noticing Bishop's positioning of a black, rectangular stove against the "lightness and openness of the mobile" (179). In particular, Bishop has painted the door opener so that it mimics the mobile's lines and structure: "Positioned so that it is at the same height as the middle of the Calder, the mechanism of the stove pipe, which can move and open, draws attention to the qualities that the stove and the mobile share across their immense differences" (179). In demonstrating the affinity between the mobile and her lived experience of Samambaia, Bishop proves Calder's aesthetic point: the creation of a privileged position for the observer to imagine herself within a continual set of changing relations without feeling the jolt of disruption or chaos. Calder's wire-structured mobiles, with their sketchy lines, "became associated with the human qualities of tentativeness and hesitation" (Samuels, "Composing Motions" 180). Setting this hesitation within a structured three-dimensional space, Calder creates an "organized experience of disparate relations among still and moving objects that ascended and descended, moved out and in, and curved around in different directions [so that he] placed the observer among 'floating motifs'" (180-81). In her creation of the geometric response of the room's environment to the shapes composing the Calder mobile, Bishop likewise instills a sense of balance that allows the randomness or chaos of the environmental elements to feel structured and peaceful without an overwhelming sense of rigidity.

While her watercolor depicts a geometric consideration of peaceful hesitation that suspends the viewer among various motifs, Bishop's poetry reimagines Calder's aesthetic to orient her lyric speaker—as we saw in Bishop's early draft—among variant motions that are posed in relation to others: the rising and hovering of the "frail, illegal fire-balloons" in the midst of a turbulent downdraft. Indeed, the metaphoric influence of Calder's aesthetic was something that Bishop had been musing over for quite awhile. During her time at Vassar, Bishop composed two essays on Gerard Manley Hopkins's prosody, in which she draws attention to the relationship between chaos and order.[9] Unlike Hopkins's reliance on religious hierarchy, Bishop calls on the natural sciences with her metaphor of the moving marksman and moving target. Calder's mobiles, with their "sketchy lines," then, provide Bishop with a materially aesthetic means of translating variation into lyric structure: "lyric images and verse lines, with their disparate weights and trajectories, [can] be arranged as events emerging in responsiveness to other events, arising from and moving into one another" (Samuels, "Composing Motions" 186).

Such a translation occurs not only in "The Armadillo" but also—perhaps even more poignantly—in "The Moose," famously written over a span of some twenty years. Its archival remnants highlight, in colored crayon, the visual orientation of draft stanzas and words circled, moved about, and squeezed into the margins in a way that echoes the movement of the bus. "The Moose" and its many drafts deserve their own space and analysis, pointing toward the ways in which the space of the archive enables—or possibly even enacts—poetic form and structure. In considering Bishop's drafting process of "The Armadillo" and the inclusion of the archive as a whole, we are given a broader picture of Bishop's creative manufacturing of her own hesitation over St. John's Day within the structured space of the poem. Her delicate construction of the whimsical motions of the fire balloons takes center stage as she crafts pace and timing.

The pages in the manuscript notebook immediately following the first instance of "The Owls' Nest" contain drafts of "Poem for a Child" and what appears to be an initial mapping out of "Judy."[10] Turning the page, a draft containing the excision of the title "From a Letter" (without the addition of a replacement title) includes an outline for her stanzas. This outline forms the first poetic draft of the poem, as Bishop works out stanzaic structure, rhythm, and rhyme. Revising the first stanza, rhymed *abab* with variations of iambic trimeter, Bishop settles on what becomes, in its anthologized form, an adaptation of ballad form: trimeter and tetrameter lines rhyming *abcb*, with variants on both meter and rhyme throughout.

Perhaps most striking, however, is Bishop's continuous revision of stanza three, followed by, on the opposite page (f. 10r), arrangements of the first half of the poem. The experimental arrangement of these revisions illuminates the influence of Calder's aesthetic variation in the lyric responses of the manufactured world of the fire balloons against the astronomical, natural world of the cosmos. In stanza three, Bishop suggests an abstractionist or impressionistic description of the confusion between the distant fire balloons and the planets, a confusion also noted by the manuscript's eruption of strike-throughs, additions, and rewritings (VC 73.2, f. 9v). As mentioned, the spectators, in the archival manuscripts, are foregrounded earlier than in the published version: "we confuse them with the stars." The inclusion of "we" suggests an active participation in the distancing effect of the fire balloons and emphasizes the communal error or confusion. In the archive, Bishop juxtaposes the rising flight of the fire balloons with the colors of the cosmos and the falling motion of "Venus, going down, or Mars."

To further the pacing of astronomical descent, Bishop experiments with corresponding actions to convey the dangerous motions of the misperceived manufactured "planet." Tumble—conveying clumsiness—transitions to the metrically expanded, slower, rhythmic motion of "sways & grows dangerous." As the event of blurred or unclear vision gives way to confusion, producing a stanza of reflection on the difference between stars and planets, the manuscript itself—with its three lines of blank space—jerks readers into experiencing another motion: the downdraft. Thus, the lyrical condemnation of the lack of human responsiveness creates, or gives rise to, the "flash" of danger presented by such turbulence.

Configuring the rising and hovering motion of the fire balloons, Bishop composes a balancing act that positions the human world against natural elements, providing motion a sort of voice due to shifting tones and positions: "Calder's mobiles clarify [for Bishop] the role of relative weights of elements and dynamics of pace and timing, a slow drift, followed by a stronger jolt, or vice versa" (Samuels, "Composing Motions" 186). Importantly, these patterns of motion are delivered in response to actions surrounding the spectators: in the drafted lines of folio 10r, Bishop places the flushing of the "paper vessel . . . wobbly, & swaying" against the rapid, consequential movement of the animal wildlife. In the final written stanza on the page, Bishop tersely returns from the cosmos and aesthetic turbulence and their implicit danger to the owls' nest: "The owls' nest must have burned." With this tonal shift toward matter-of-factness, Bishop arranges the present fire balloon's initial motions—and consequent movement away from the spectators—as a reaction against the past destruction of animal life. What is referred to above as a "call-and-response" is often found in poetry (and song) as a refrain, or repetitive echo, and is most apparent in ballad form. It could also be referred to as a form of dialogue in which different voices come together to create a cohesive lyric structure. Although "The Armadillo" carries no overt refrain, the poem does include multiple spectatorial positions that arise from contrasting motions and different temporalities and foregrounds typography as a way of asserting a multiplicity of voices. By paying attention not only to motion but also to sound—and particularly shifting vocal tones—we see how Bishop uses polyphony, to which we now turn to prepare readers for the italicized protest of the armadillo at the end of the poem.

BISHOP'S POLYPHONIC COMPOSITION: OWLS, RABBITS, AND AN ARMADILLO

As an undergraduate at Vassar, Bishop enrolled in an introductory music course entitled "Music as Literature." In the opening pages of her school notebook, Bishop identifies Edmund Gurney's understanding of "ideal motion." She writes in her notes that Gurney measured time both through rhythm and motion, emphasizing that pitch also conveys motion. Moreover, Bishop alludes to "ideal motion" as "an immaterial motion, that can't be measured" but is instead visualized and "disembodied" (VC College Notes 69.9, f. 3). For Gurney, melody is the primary component of music, and "ideal motion" is the "fusion of pitch and rhythm in which neither element has any melodic value apart from the other." Melody, in this view, exhibits a "character of motion, and a motion presenting the character of form. Pitch and rhythm, in consuming 'time,' exemplify movement; there is unity, therefore, of form and motion" (Epperson 42). Bishop calls attention to Gurney's immaterial form and the disembodied quality of rhythm and pitch as it unifies its multiple components into one sound. Linking these initial pages on melodic unity and the visualization of sound in Bishop's college notebook with her later discussion of tonality as a form of motion suggests that, while at Vassar, Bishop was intrigued—and perhaps influenced—by the idea of poetry as a form of motion. Reading music as literature, Bishop focuses on the "psychological & physical" reasons for tone (VC College Notes 69.9, f. 4).

Furthermore, what captures Bishop's attention is, significantly, the ways in which musical theory enables an understanding of literary technique. Melody becomes a "local syntax," with each of the tones participating in syntactical motions, visualized in the composition of notes upon the page. Alongside her understanding of musical motion—or sound in motion—Bishop underscores the texture of musical composition. The notes are not only heard but also felt. Bishop likens texture in music to the "condition of a fabric," the interweaving of various threads to create a whole. This tapestry is not dissimilar to Bishop's own methodology, composing poetry by weaving together vocal fragments from her lived experience, preserved within her life-writing.

Melody, according to the notebook, contributes to the texture of music, and out of this texture, Bishop singles out three styles of music: monodic, polyphonic, and monophonic. Of particular interest is Bishop's focus on polyphony. Her notebook outlines polyphonic music as both "concurrent" and "integrations of individual melodies" (VC College Notes 69.9, f. 6). Viewing polyphony as "<u>concurrent relationships</u>" that supply a prevailing sense of harmony and, later in her outline, as a "recombination of materials" provides an interesting approach to reading the different sounding voices in Bishop's poetry. Just as polyphony is a means of unity that uses "familiar material" to develop something new, Bishop's drafting process can be seen as a form of polyphonic motion: the movement of various concurrent elements—correspondence, artwork, and aesthetic theory—to formulate a new sense of poetic creation (VC College Notes 69.9, f. 6). In other words, in the archival drafts we witness the visualization of polyphony as a coming together of concurrent poetic and archival voices that are unified through Bishop's aesthetic of composing motion. Bishop's experimental marginalia can be viewed as disembodied lines and words that are unified into a finalized stanza, occurring not in the notebooks but handwritten into the typewritten draft of 1957. Supplying an

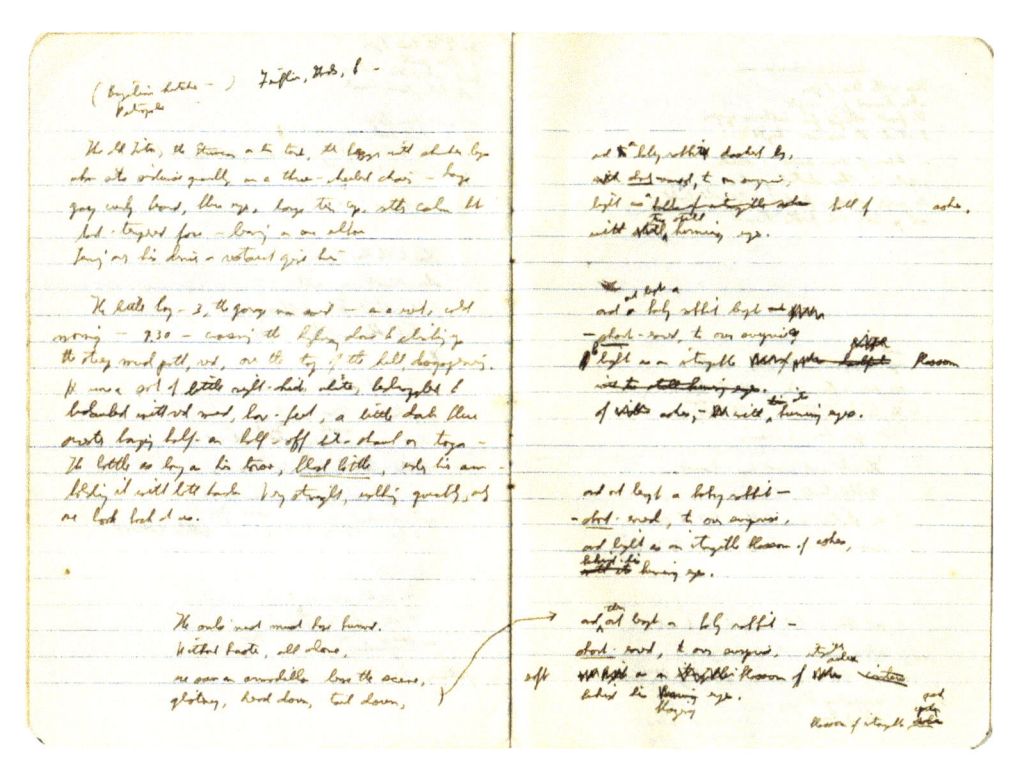

At the top of this notebook page, Bishop includes what appears to be a translation of a Brazilian sketch. The prose translation is followed by revision of the final stanzas of "The Armadillo." (VC 73.2; Courtesy of Vassar College)

underlying texture to her poems through tonal contrasts that complement mobile action, Bishop utilizes the dynamism of polyphony and its generation of a productive sense of unpredictability via a recombination of familiar material found in her experimental drafts and archival ephemera.

Turning, in the notebook, to the corresponding flights of the animal wildlife as a reaction to fiery destruction, Bishop isolates her animal performers on their own notebook pages away from the flight of the fire balloons.

At the bottom of folio 10v, following what appears to be a translation of Brazilian sketches, Bishop configures what becomes, in its published form, the eighth stanza:

The owls' nest must have burned.
Without haste, all alone,
we saw an armadillo leave the scene,
glistening, head down, tail down, (VC 73.2, f.10v)

ARCHIVAL ANIMALS   277

The animals appear out of, seemingly, nowhere—both in the poem and within the manuscript itself, following, as it does, an apparently unrelated Brazilian sketch. The animals' jarring appearance jolts the speaker from the downward drift of the fire balloons to the danger imposed upon the innocent wildlife, depicting Bishop's own "two minds" regarding St. John's Day. And yet, within the context of the archive, it seems that Bishop had been storing up these images, littering her correspondence with detailed prose descriptions. In a letter dated June 15, 1956, to poet and mentor Marianne Moore, Bishop writes of her discovery of armadillos and a small owl in the Brazilian landscape:

> After all this time, I've just found out we have armadillos here—I see one crossing the road in the headlights at night, with his head and tail down very lonely and glisteny. There's also a kind of small owl that sits in the road at night—I had to get out and shoo one away from the front of the car last night. They have large eyes; when they fly off [they] look exactly like pin-wheels—black and white. (Qtd. in Millier, *Elizabeth Bishop* 275)

As in her 1955 letter to Baumann, Bishop uses her correspondence as an initial framing—an initial voicing—of her poetic lines. The animals in the letter reappear in the poem with their same posturing, echoing the same diction, in what appears to be an exact description.

Reframing and rewriting the final stanza in the draft notebook (the penultimate stanza in the published poem), Bishop settles on a pattern of chaotic motion: rising fire balloons; fire flaming down; the ascending flight of the owls; the slow, lonely, ashamed departure of the armadillo; and the surprised leap of a baby rabbit:

> and ^then^ out leapt a baby rabbit—
> short-eared, to our surprise.
> ~soft~ [illegible] as an ~intangible~ blossom of [illegible]^intangible ashes^
> behind his ~burning~ ~blazing~ eyes. (VC 73.2, f. 11r)

And yet, underlying this chaos—perhaps drawing a Calder-like "sketchy line" enabling a reactive sense of motion—there lies unity in polyphony. For, after all, when taking the notebook as a whole, we are given a sense of Bishop's crafting of recombinant materials, and we can return to folios 7v and 8r to consider, in its structuring and poetic creation, the coming together of concurrent poetic and archival voices. Transposing the above stanza from folio 11r with the revisions on folio 8r, we can make sense of the inclusion of parenthesis and the offset "Brazil" in the right column. In this iteration, Bishop draws from variations in the poetic lines

Elizabeth Bishop
Caixa Postal 279, Petrópolis
Estado do Rio de Janeiro
Brasil

THE OWLS' NEST

This is the time of year
when almost every night
the frail, illegal fire-balloons appear,
to climb the mountain height

and float towards a saint
still honored in these parts.
The paper chambers flush and fill with light
that comes and goes, like hearts.

Once they're against the sky even
confuse them with the stars, –
the planets, that is, – the tinted ones,
Venus going down, or Mars,

or the pale green one. With a wind
they flare and falter, wobble and toss;
but if it's still they steer between
the kite-sticks of the Southern Cross,

dwindling, dwindling, solemnly
and steadily escaping us,
unless a down-draught from the peaks
turns them quickly dangerous.

Last night another big one fell.
It splattered like an egg of fire
against the cliff behind the house.
The flame ran down. We saw the pair

of owls who nest there flying up
and up, their whirling black-and-white
stained bright pink underneath until
they circled out of sight.

The ancient owls' nest must have burned.
Without haste, and alone,
a glistening armadillo left,
rose-flecked, head down, tail down;

and then a baby rabbit jumped out,
short-eared, to our surprise.
So soft! A handful of intangible ash
with fixed, ignited eyes.

Typewritten partial draft of "The Owls' Nest," dated by Vassar archivists as 1957. This is the first in the typewritten series, and includes Bishop's handwritten draft of what will become the final, italicized stanza of the poem. (VC 57.13; Courtesy of Vassar College) and the drifting motions that came before, as well as the descriptions depicted in her correspondence relating to the discovery of Brazilian wildlife.

Linking the supposed accuracy of scenic description with the "intangible ash" from the destruction of the animal habitat, Bishop uses polyphony to draw attention to the inaccuracies related in the poem. The fragility, beauty, and ascension of the fire balloons in the first half of the poem correspond with the apparent delight of spotting the baby animal at the close. This parallel is heightened by typographical intervention: the underlining of short and the exclamatory parenthetical: "short-eared, to our surprise. / ?(So soft!)—a handful of intangible [illegible] ash" (VC 73.2, f. 8r). Marring the experience of aesthetic delight, a different sounding tone and temporality registers the destruction of the downdraft, recalling the strong contrast from "Last night." The destruction—unlike the confusion inspired by the ascending fire balloons—is depicted with painstaking accuracy: the marked flight of the owls, stained pink by the glowing flames; the glistening, "rose-flecked" armor of the armadillo; and the "fixed, ignited eyes" of the baby rabbit, which the manuscript revises over seven lines.

In taking apart Bishop's creative process—the separate revisions of the fire balloons from the animal-centric stanzas—the manuscript notebook provides a polyphonic composition, integrating various textures of lived experience, with contrasting voices and temporalities, to constitute a poetic whole that asserts Bishop's own internal conflict over the perceptions of the artificial and natural world. Bishop reimagines the musical texture of polyphony to insert not only differing spectatorial positions but also different sounding voices—the present spectator misperceiving the danger of the fire balloon and the past spectator witnessing the devastation of the animal life as they escape for survival. In the notebook, Bishop inscribes her draft with a recombination of the intangible ash from the illegal balloons alongside a sordid delight in the animals' flight.

Bishop continues to work through the interconnected events of past and present, orienting her speaker amidst disparate motions and events, culminating in a series of typewritten drafts, including the handwritten insertion of the final stanza.

In the first typewritten draft, still titled "The Owls' Nest," Bishop adds a final speaker in the form of a "mailed fist, clenched ignorantly against the night." In doing so, she rewrites the passivity of the escaping animals, lending them a voice of protest. Bishop's drafting process actually prepares us for the shift in perception and condemnation of the "falling fire and piercing cry" in this revelatory stanza—for the descending motions and piercing tonal shifts have prefaced this final, most violent of turbulent shifts, underscored by italics. Intriguingly, tracing the series of drafts reveals this addition as a kind of afterthought that provides unity to the entire poem. As a final voice, this tonal shift asserts no longer the hesitancy and uncertainty that dominate the majority of the poem. Bishop, by 1957, is no longer of "two minds." Instead, in an upward motion that parallels the climbing illegal fire balloons, the "weak" armadillo, ignorant of human folly, raises his fist against the natural world. Such ignorance is juxtaposed with the earlier ignorance of the spectators, with a twist: the armadillo signals revolution or at least a dawning awareness on the part of the poetic speaker of the impact of humanity on the natural world. Using polyphony and motion, Bishop ties together the undercurrents of condemnation and human culpability to assert productive tension arising from the dynamism of differing voices, unveiled in the archive.

CODA: ARCHIVAL IMMERSION AND DIGITAL ENGAGEMENT

Taking Bishop's exploration of her poetry as "really all one long poem" that overlaps or goes "into one another" is an important insight into the archival methodology used in Bishop's poetry and creative process. An integral aspect of this process is the establishment of several different sounding voices within the poems, which generate cohesive unity. To uncover such a process, we must turn to the archive. For what, after all, is an archive? Taking a necessarily broad approach to the archive as an accumulation of materials, we can begin to explore this notion of voice and blending and arrive at new conclusions that bend the boundaries of canonical and archival formation. In tracing the compositional process involved in "The Armadillo," a digital approach that visualizes and enhances the multiple archival elements seems necessary not only for scholarly engagement but also for pedagogical use.

By curating a digital exhibition in Scalar, an open-source platform that enables users to assemble media and juxtapose them with their own annotations and writing in a visually exciting and immersive way, students and scholars can explore the various influences on Bishop's poetry.[11] Indeed, such a platform can visually and sonically bring to life the various voices within the Bishop archive and, in doing so, represent the lived experience of Elizabeth Bishop. Juxtaposing related archival material with poetic drafts, Scalar provides an immersive and accessible archival experience to further questions of how Bishop uses various media to think through her poetry. A clear outcome of curating a digital exhibition is the ability to provide access to archival elements for students to receive archival experience and follow the threads of connection or association. In so doing, students no longer see Bishop's poetry as "isolated events" but as fluid, interconnecting "events" that lead into "one long poem." In other words, we can provide a more nuanced contextualization of individual poems and of the Bishop archive itself. Exploring these interconnections, therefore, provides insight into Bishop's process and its reliance upon dialogue, whether between modes of composition or between individuals within her circle.

NOTES

1. The series contains a set of typewritten letters and a chronology written by Bishop. Throughout the typescript, Bishop's handwriting appears in marginalia. It remains unclear whether Bishop sent the letters to Foster, but archival evidence suggests they were not sent. The letters were acquired by Vassar College after the death of Bishop's literary executor, Alice Methfessel (Elizabeth Bishop Papers, f. 118.33). All subsequent archival material referenced can be found in the Elizabeth Bishop Papers at the Archives and Special Collections Library at Vassar College.
2. For scholarship on Calder's influence, see Samuels, Deep Skin.
3. Alice Quinn has published both "St. John's Day" and "Poem for a Child" in her edition of *Edgar Allan Poe & the Juke-Box*.
4. In a draft of the initial stanzas found in later pages within the notebook, Bishop experiments with a non-specific temporality, changing "This is the time of year" to "About the time of year / in these parts / frail, illegal fire-balloons appear— / rather like glowing hearts" (VC 73.2, f. 101). This is the only instance in which Bishop wavers from specificity, quickly reverting, on the same manuscript page, to the deictic expression in her next iteration of the stanza.
5. All references to "The Armadillo" in its published form come from this edition.
6. In transcribing, I have noted my own uncertainty of Bishop's hand with [?] and [illegible]. Other question marks, without brackets, throughout my transcriptions are Bishop's own.
7. I am indebted to Samuels's insightful study, which includes chapters linking Bishop's craft with Alexander Calder's aesthetics of motion.
8. Additionally, as Samuels points out, Macedo Soares owned three of Calder's mobiles, and, in 1959, Bishop met Calder personally during his visit to Samambaia.
9. See Bishop, "Time's Andromedas" and "Gerard Manley Hopkins: Notes on Timing in His Poetry" (Pr 10). I am grateful to the reader at Lever Press for drawing attention to this resemblance.
10. Jeffrey Westover discusses this poem in chapter 3.
11. I suggest using Scalar, rather than Omeka, as an open-source platform for copyright reasons.

CHAPTER FOURTEEN

"HUGE CROWD PLEASED BY NEW MODELS"

Elizabeth Bishop's Cuttyhunk Notebook as Multimodal and Multimedia Artifact

Laura Sloan Patterson

From 1934 to 1937, Elizabeth Bishop kept an extraordinary journal and scrapbook in a black-and-white composition book that she began while on a month-long, post-college vacation on Cuttyhunk Island, Massachusetts. Full of handwritten observations and pasted-in clippings of all kinds, the journal is known to Bishop scholars as the Cuttyhunk notebook. In it, Bishop makes notes on the improvised nature of island life; observes the culture around her both on Cuttyhunk and in other locations; and sketches out ideas that seem to have led to poems such as "The Map," "The Fish," and "Crusoe in England." Alice Quinn notes Bishop's tendency to record possible poem titles "with marvelous descriptive tags" in the Cuttyhunk notebook in particular (*EAP* ix), and these descriptive moments and the window into Bishop's composition process that the journal provides make it an essential document for Bishop archival studies. This chapter, however, examines aspects of the journal that have received less attention: its multimedia and multimodal facets. The Cuttyhunk notebook uses a collage or scrapbook methodology, combining handwritten notes, newspaper articles, photographs, captions, and headlines as well as programs from concerts and art shows, advertisements, and even product labels.

Although the notebook contains many elements of a journal, including personal observations and notes toward future poems, its dominant mode is that of a scrapbook. Scrapbooks became popular in the United States in the nineteenth century in response to a rapid increase in the availability of printed material, such as newspapers and color advertisements. One-cent newspapers became available in

1833, and by the mid- to late nineteenth century, some readers felt overwhelmed by the amount of daily reading material in their lives. Scrapbooking became a way to control the chaos by retaining the most personally relevant information (Thompson). The trend expanded in the twentieth century, serving wider purposes: the documentation of social and political change, the creation of personalized domestic manuals, the expression of a hidden or private self, and the more common autobiographical function of storing personal mementos (Tucker et al. 2-4). Girls and women were encouraged to create scrapbooks in order to promote basic literacy, to document friendships, to fight "idleness," and, of course, to sell more stationery supplies (Tucker et al. 8-9). Current academic research on scrapbooking likens it to the cutting and pasting practices of contemporary social media, where many users curate collections from favorite sources (Good). Bishop's Cuttyhunk notebook can be situated within the broader context of American scrapbooking in its traditional and less traditional uses of the form; she uses her pages to juxtapose unusual ideas, to record her own participation in cultural activities, to examine political change, and to gather material for her writing.

Bishop encountered a form of scrapbooking in the attic room of her grandparents' Nova Scotia home. As Sandra Barry writes, "At one time, newspaper would have covered the walls of this room – insulation. I have no doubt that Bishop spent time playing in this room covered with text (quite literally 'writing on the wall')" ("Lifting Yesterday"). Barry also notes that the topics of the newspaper clippings on the walls emerge as themes in Bishop's poetry. For instance, a newspaper photo of an erupting Vesuvius is still visible on the attic walls of the Elizabeth Bishop House and may have been Bishop's earliest exposure to the volcanoes that emerge in "Crusoe in England" and "In the Waiting Room" (Barry, "Lifting Yesterday"). A collage or scrapbook technique has been noted in Bishop's poetry as well: Theodore Colson uses Marshall McLuhan's concepts of texture, tactility, and mosaic configuration as an entry point into Bishop's "philosophical" poems, such as "Over 2,000 Illustrations and a Complete Concordance" (217-18), which was based on the Bulmer family's heavily illustrated family Bible (Barry, *Elizabeth Bishop: Novia Scotia's* 54), an early multimedia text Bishop encountered frequently. With its wide range of materials used and the diverse content represented, the Cuttyhunk notebook's scrapbook pages often appear to be an effort to catalogue, capture, and juxtapose extremes of human experience and consciousness. Bishop uses multiple technologies, such as images and words, and even kinetic effects (because the viewer has to unfold documents on some pages) in her collage work, making the journal a multimodal point of entry into Bishop's creative imaginary.

In order to examine the journal through these lenses, it is important to understand both the differentiation and the overlap between the terms *multimodal* and *multimedia*. The term *multimodal* is often associated with academic discourse, particularly with the composition classroom and its twenty-first-century focus on composing many types of texts—traditional print essays but also digital texts and creative hybrid projects that incorporate writing or the spoken word, often in combination with visuals, sounds, or motion. *Multimedia*, however, is a term more frequently used outside of academia within commercial enterprises to indicate the nature of the final product. In her analysis of these terms, Claire Lauer removes the "multi" prefix to focus on *modes* versus *media*. Modes refer to how information is represented (moving images, still images, sound), whereas media refers to the tools and technologies used (books, film, paint, and paintbrush) (227). Another way to frame this distinction involves *process*, which is more strongly associated with multimodal, versus *product*, which is more strongly associated with multimedia (Lauer 225). In order to analyze Bishop's process of composing the journal, as well as the physical product in the archive, both terms are needed for this analysis. This chapter's first section will focus on the multimedia nature of the scrapbook pages in the Cuttyhunk notebook, and the second section will reveal a hidden, secondary multimodal function of the journal. Because Bishop had different aims and an alternate process with the journal's secondary function, the Cuttyhunk notebook can be said to be a truly multimodal artifact, offering multiple visible compositional processes as well as multiple spatial and temporal pathways of navigation.

POLITICS, ABSURDITY, HORROR: COLLAGED JOURNAL PAGES

Throughout the scrapbooked pages of the journal, Bishop creates multimedia collages from newspapers, cartoons, drawings, and other materials, pairing images with captions and headlines that do not appear to match the visual content. Many pages feature newspaper clippings that show close-ups of human faces caught in extreme expressions: shock, sadness, amusement. Other clippings depict oddities, such as two women in costumes covered in spoons and other metal objects, one holding a gun and another holding a ukulele. These images appear to have been advertisements for a hardware store and are combined on the page with a botanical drawing, a "Footnote on Modern Art," and a headshot of a woman with a distressed facial expression.

Little thematic content unites the clippings, and Bishop provides no commentary. The women in costumes partially frame the botanical drawing, which is of a tobacco plant and bears the description "DAS FREMDE KRAUT NICOTIANA," or "the foreign herb nicotine" (VC 72.3).[1] To the left of the plant in the drawing is a tiny human head, upturned, blowing smoke from a large cornucopia-shaped pipe. The

Bishop juxtaposes an art bulletin clipping, a botanical drawing, images of two women in dark dresses, and a headshot of a woman with a distressed facial expression in the 1937 section of the 1934-1937 Cuttyhunk notebook. (VC 72.3; Courtesy of Vassar College)

smaller illustration of the smoking head appears to be an icon to explain the plant's purpose. Beneath the plant, Bishop has pasted a clipping of a newspaper article about a boy in Lyon, France, who was stoned to death by his peers because they did not like his long hair. The headshot of the distressed woman is placed to the left of this clipping, and a pasted clipping beneath her picture reads, "The lady is the wife of a just-killed night-club owner." It is possible that this caption was not originally paired with the photo because it has been cut out and pasted separately, although it is positioned as if to caption the photo. In other places throughout the journal, captions that seem unrelated to the photos have been cut out and placed beneath them. As Gillian White writes, commenting on the 1935-37 journals, Bishop often "courted the accidental as an aesthetic possibility" and wanted to "find a way, as an author, to arrange for a fluid, open text" ("Readerly Contingency" 327). Although White refers to Bishop's journal writing about accident and coincidence, the scrapbook pages take this idea one step further as they actively demonstrate Bishop's exploration of the accidental and the coincidental as ways of making meaning and crafting a personal aesthetic.

Here and elsewhere, Bishop's scrapbooked juxtapositions border on the surreal. Although the pages are primarily composed of newspaper clippings, the combinations of bizarre imagery and seemingly mismatched captions lend a sense of fantasy to the overall multimodal experience of the Cuttyhunk notebook. During this period, Bishop made a study of French surrealism but ultimately rejected it—at least as a conscious, formal aesthetic—for her own poetry. But as Megan Marshall notes, Bishop did hope to convey a "surrealism of everyday life," as she wrote in a letter to Anne Stevenson in 1964 (*Elizabeth Bishop* 58-59). Marshall links the idea of an everyday surrealism to Bishop's poem "The Fish," which was inspired by a late 1930s Gulf fishing trip in Florida (66). To Marshall's assessment of the poem as an exercise in growing empathy, one could add an explicit focus on the speaker's changing vision, which turns from the external nature of the fish's "brown skin hung in strips" (10) to a vision more aligned with the fish's perspective—its "aching jaw" (64). Here I want to focus primarily on the materiality of the fish and its surreal nature—the "five big hooks / grown firmly in its mouth" (54-55)—which is a blend of the non-human natural world and technological objects, of an animal surviving human intervention and even human intent to kill.

This imagery aligns with that of the hardware store advertisement of the women covered in spoons, tools, and other metal objects, one of them holding a gun. Like the fish, the women are trapped and burdened by their hanging metal objects, yet they are also agents, holding a gun and playing a ukulele. Both the women and the fish are objects and subjects, triumphing in their own ways—the fish perhaps even achieving dominance when "everything / was rainbow, rainbow,

rainbow!" (74-75). Bishop's diction in the repeated phrase suggests a tipping point where visual imagery overwhelms not only the other senses but also the ability to process an entire experience. The Cuttyhunk notebook acts as a staging space for moments of what we might term *productive visual overload*—moments when visual sensory processing is primary, moments that lead to new insights and new ways of perceiving the world.

Another clipping on the page showing the wife of the just-killed nightclub owner has a handwritten date of June 23, 1937, and the title "Footnote on Modern Art." Although the publication's title is cut off, it appears to be from *The Bulletin of the Brooklyn Institute of Arts and Sciences* (based on comparison to other issues of the bulletin), and it contains an excerpt from *Stravinsky, An Autobiography*, which details Stravinsky's trouble convincing border control that the painting he carried with him was a portrait (of him) drawn by Picasso. The written piece contains a line drawing at its center: two stylized, cartoon men hold their heads together in friendly conversation.

This page creates an effect of both chaos and order. The visual images veer toward the outrageous, especially the women in costumes covered with metal objects, one with a gun pointed toward the viewer. The collection of images also suggests a sense of irony, with tobacco at the center of things, a plant to be revered, and a public unlikely to understand modernist art (and perhaps modernist writing as well?) to one side. The viewer is invited into Bishop's inner world, to be in on the joke with her. It is difficult to determine if the distressed woman is a part of the ironic tone or if she is a serious footnote, a reminder of the depths of human pain in grief, a lesson Bishop certainly understood from a young age. Bishop tempers the emotional chaos with a sense of visual order: the clippings are arranged at approximate right angles to one another, with little or no blank space between them, creating the effect of a remediated, personalized newspaper or yearbook.

A page labeled November 1936 is similarly formatted. On the left side of the page is a large newspaper clipping featuring a photo of a man with dark hair and mustache, in a bathing costume, being propelled out of water, almost as if he is being shot out of a cannon. A caption (attached to the photo itself, so not one of Bishop's inventions) reads "B-r-r, the water's cold. Or maybe the bather has just seen a shark. Or maybe he is high-jumping to coolness. A guess here is as good as fact." The caption refers to the bather's expression of surprise, an emotion that seems to have been particularly important to Bishop. Barbara Comins has noted Bishop's reliance on surprise as an essential element in poetry, using poems such as "The Fish," "The Man-Moth," and "In the Waiting Room" to make her case (177-81). Perhaps this image of shock and surprise, and even the caption's guesses at its cause, serve as a visual method for Bishop to work through her relationship to this

In the November 1936 section of the 1934-1937 Cuttyhunk notebook, Bishop combines her journal entries with a collaged image of a mustachioed bather and an image of "Woody" Hockaday, who was known for throwing bags of feathers on public figures. (VC 72.3; Courtesy of Vassar College)

"HUGE CROWD PLEASED BY NEW MODELS" 289

emotion and its possible uses in her writing. It is interesting to note that Bishop does more than catalogue surprise. She is also interested in the reason for the emotional surprise, as indicated by her choice to include the caption that questions and guesses at the reasons behind the bather's expression.

In the scrapbooked pages, Bishop seems to be questioning the world around her, as if to say "How can all of these objects and events exist and occur simultaneously?" Her notebook full of multimedia and multimodal compositions celebrates surprise, coincidence, and accident, even as collaged pages question potential connective threads and themes. Readers of Bishop's poetry will recognize this questioning impulse in her work from this period. "The Map," begun in December 1934, opens with a series of descriptions followed by questions. Some are subtle: "Shadows, or are they shallows, at its edges" (*P* 5, line 2) does not even merit a question mark from the poet, but the first stanza ends in a series of two longer, more formal questions:

> Or does the land lean down to lift the sea from under,
> drawing it unperturbed around itself?
> Along the fine tan sandy shelf
> is the land tugging at the sea from under? (lines 5-8)

Here Bishop subtly and perhaps self-consciously questions her own descriptive powers, but she also aims the questions outward. What do maps mean? What do borders mean? What does nationality mean in the context of a natural world constantly making and remaking itself? And, perhaps most important, how do words and images work together to convey or not convey these meanings? How does the multimodal nature of a map represent (and fail to represent) topography, nationality, and culture itself? In the journal and in her poetry of this time period, Bishop explores an aesthetic of the accidental and probes the larger questions that seemingly random juxtapositions invoke.

A second seemingly unrelated caption is pasted below this one: "King Edward VIII in his royal robes— a composite photograph. His bride-to-be is pictured above." The photograph, which is mentioned but not included in the journal, would have been a composite, as Edward VIII never took the throne (having given it up to marry Wallis Simpson), and the only image of him in robes is said to be an unpublished coronation portrait (Buckland). To the right of the surprised bather is a photo of Woody Hockaday. Hockaday originally gained fame as the inventor of the highway mile marker system. Later in life, he began staging protests for peace that involved throwing bags of feathers on speakers at public events. The caption beneath his photo reads, "He sneaked up on a platform, hurled a bag of feathers upon a surprised Father Couglin and got what you see." The "what you see" appears to be an injury to the face, possibly a black eye and bloodied chin. Here, Bishop takes the atypical step of annotating her collage. Her note reads, "He then feathers several times—he says for 'PEACE.' Some association with the Dove?"—a clear attempt to understand Hockaday's motivation. Hockaday may have been suffering from mental illness, as he was eventually institutionalized. Yet here we see another theme from Bishop's life: the attempt to understand behaviors that may defy understanding because they are rooted in disorder.

In the lower right quadrant of the collage, directly below Bishop's annotation, is a newspaper article describing a Nazi-ordered adoption of "new old" dress. Because East Prussia supposedly had no traditional costumes, Nazis declared an invented outfit as the province's official costume. Directly beneath the article is a clipping that has been torn mid-sentence, which is unusual in the Cuttyhunk notebook. It reads, "air is excellent for steadying the nerves. A formula for a lotion for perspiring hands may be had for a stamped, addressed envelope." This piece seems almost torn and pasted at random, but this partial advertisement may serve as a commentary on the anxiety produced by Hitler's increasing power prior to World War II. Was Bishop commenting that there were now more perspiring/nerves with a dictator on the rise? The man in the bathing costume wears a toothbrush mustache like Hitler and has the same dark hair. Is the entire collage page a political commentary? A protester for peace buries public figures in feathers, a dictator on the rise creates national costumes out of thin air, a king gives up his throne for love: perhaps the mustachioed bather's expression, his face frozen into a scream, can be read as an emotional response to the political chaos of November 1936, another moment of productive visual overload.

Two pages away, the headline "Huge Crowd Pleased by New Models" appears in the upper right corner of a collaged layout. The headline is detached and seemingly unrelated to the three contiguous photos. Left of the headline is a photo of a man and a woman leaning over a young boy in bed, possibly in a hospital. The viewer can easily imagine the adults in the photo as the mother and father of the young boy because of their concerned expressions and postures. In another photo directly beneath this one, a man in a tie, vest, and coat, bearing a serious expression, is followed by two boys. Both boys' mouths are invisible, blocked by the shoulder of someone in front of them, so their expressions are difficult to read, but their body postures seem to indicate shame or doubt. They look as if they would like to hide. The caption attached to the photo (original to the photo, not added by Bishop) reads "Freedom was denied to Alfred Papiano, 13 (right), murder [torn paper where caption is cut off] when his mother pleaded she feared gangland threats [torn paper] Spiterleri, 14 (left), was also a witness against gang [sic]." These photos share a theme of children in perilous situations resulting in separation from their families and/or institutionalization in hospitals and jails. The page opposite this one in the journal also highlights children in danger, with headlines (attached to short articles) reading "2 Farm Boys Killed By Cold" and "Boy Falls Through Glass Dome" (p. 40). Bishop seems to be contemplating and documenting the fragility of boys in her contemporary world.

Bishop layers a series of newspaper clippings from 1936, including stories about suicide, accidental death, and imprisonment of men and boys, as well as an image of man-made lightning at an Electrical Age Exposition in an entry in the 1934-1937 Cuttyhunk notebook. (VC 72.3; Courtesy of Vassar College)

The third and final photo on this page depicts a man surrounded by machinery and bolts of electric charge in lightning-like formations. The attached caption reads, "Man-made lightning from Boulder Dam. [illegible] ---eth Strickfaden surrounded by a discharge of high-frequency electricity at the Electrical Age Exposition in Los Angeles which coincided with the inauguration of the current from the dam." In this photo, Strickfaden stands in a powerful pose, with legs apart, arms parallel and extending straight out from his shoulders, with bolts of electricity running between his hands and to the machinery behind him. In many ways, he is the polar opposite of the vulnerable boys, commanding technology to create what is typically a natural phenomenon, mastering his universe like a superhero. Did Bishop create this two-page collage spread to suggest that powerlessness and danger can be overcome? That humans can (re)create their worlds? Was she working through her own past vulnerabilities to envision a more powerful creative future? While it is impossible to know for sure, the multimodal nature of these pages provides a different point of entry for examining Bishop's creative imaginary during these formative post-college years.

Female power receives a nod from this collaged page as well. In the lower left quadrant lie two news stories from Spain documenting the Spanish Civil War (1936-39), a war in which women served as combatants. The first piece refers to soldiers who allegedly threw the remains of kings and queens out of royal tombs and replaced them with their own fallen soldiers. The second piece discusses evidence of female soldiers fighting in the trenches against Nationalists, who wanted to overthrow the democratic government. The article reports that the trenches "were littered with all sorts of feminine belongings. Some of the women had worn high-heeled shoes to the battlefronts and had left them behind. There were also vanity cases." While it is possible to argue that Bishop was merely recording interesting events of November 1936, the process of selection cannot be overlooked. Gender, power, vulnerability, and the instinct to recreate one's world emerge as themes within this multimedia artifact.

The same instinct to recreate one's world, as well as to document the extremes of human emotion, emerges in Bishop's "A Miracle for Breakfast," which depicts a fantasy-laced breadline scenario. A Depression-era desperation reverberates through this sestina, amplified by the patterned repetition of the end words, particularly "coffee" and "crumb," which represent both scarcity and the hope of plenty throughout the poem. "River" and "sun" nod to the natural world, to its ability to appear as a part of a boiled-down reality or as part of a fantastical world. "Balcony" and "miracle" both add to the poem's sense of surreal fantasy, especially in the imagery near the end of the poem: "I sit up on my balcony / with my feet up, and drink gallons of coffee" (*P* 20, lines 35-36). Here, with "one eye close to the crumb" (line 30), Bishop's speaker recreates the world of poverty into a mansion, "made for me by a miracle" (line 32). Bishop promotes the idea that the "miraculous" goods of a rich material culture have the power to transform one's vision of the world, an idea she alludes to visually throughout the Cuttyhunk notebook.

Other pages throughout the journal bear a closer resemblance to a commonplace book variety of scrapbook. We find programs for art gallery shows, plays, and concerts (on two of these Bishop has written "very dull," underlining the penciled words once above a Mahler piece). On a two-page spread, Christmas stickers and stamps are arranged in a group of three, and a label from a maple sugar package is included with the following note penciled beneath it:

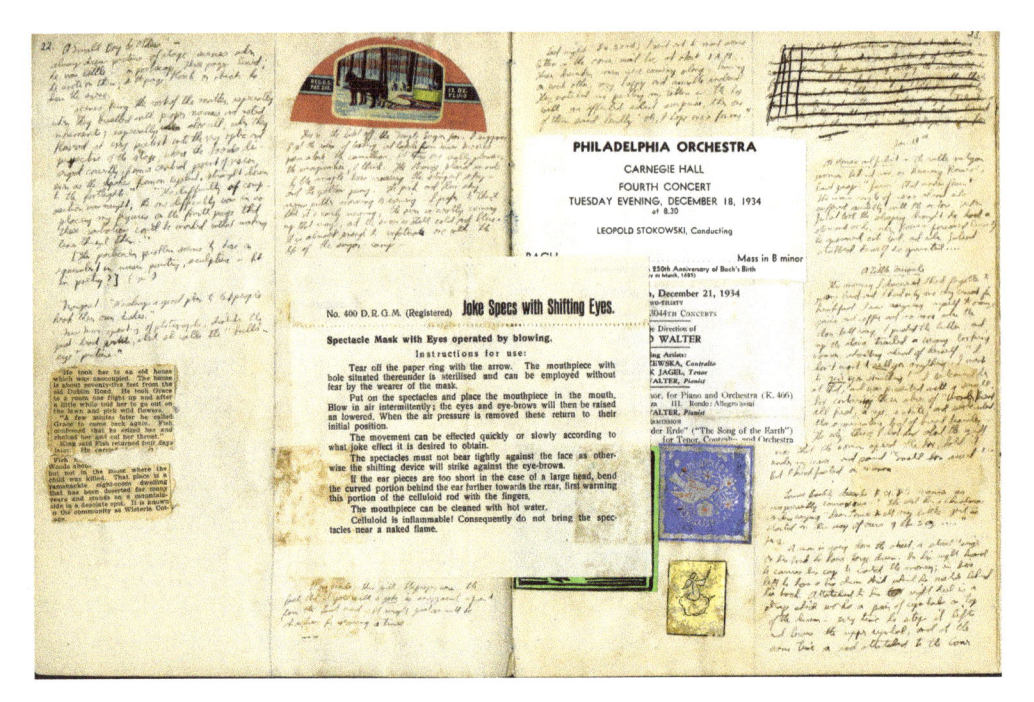

Bishop creates a collage of a red maple sugar label, a Joke Specs label, a Philadelphia Orchestra program, and several smaller images along with journal entries in the 1934-1937 Cuttyhunk notebook. (VC 72.3; Courtesy of Vassar College)

> This is the label off the maple sugar jar. I suppose I got the idea of looking at labels from Miss Moore's poem about the camellias, but this one really [places?] the inauguration, I think. The strange plaid made by the maple trees crossing the striped sky—and the yellow pung.[2] The pink and blue sky means either morning or evening—I prefer to think that it's early morning, the sun is [mostly?] coming up that way, and the snow is still cold and blue. It is almost enough to infatuate one with the life of the sugar-camp— (P. 22)

The Marianne Moore poem Bishop references is "Camellia Sabina," with its conjoined praise and fear of natural objects under glass and its opening examination of the label on a jar of Bordeaux plums. In her journaled notes, Bishop disappears into the maple sugar label's tiny picture, losing herself in the romance of the sugar camp. This commentary speaks to the importance of the images she pasted into her journal and their connection to her reading and her poetic process. Even an advertisement is not merely decorative nor just a catalogue of memory; it is indicative of Bishop's way of seeing the world, of her creative vision and the influences on her creative processes.

On the facing page, next to the program from a Philadelphia Orchestra concert at Carnegie Hall, is a set of instructions for using "Joke Specs with Shifting Eyes," which worked by blowing air into a mouthpiece. According to the instruction, blown air raised and lowered the eyes and eyebrows of the mask. It seems possible that the addition of the joke specs instructions is a commentary on vision and ways of altering one's vision as well as one's projected image. The physical placement of the "joke specs" piece is somewhat unusual in that the instructions are folded into the journal, slightly offset from the notebook's binding. In order to read everything on the right side of the two-page spread, the joke specs instructions must be folded over to the left. Here we find alternate kinetic pathways through the text: we have the choice of leaving this clipping folded or unfolded, and the visible content of the two-page spread changes depending on our choice. The idea of multiple pathways through the text underscores the journal's multimodality in addition to its multimedia composition. Similar to the page containing an image of a woman whose husband, the nightclub owner, had just been killed, this layout uses the lower left quadrant as a space for horror, pain, or perhaps a space for the return of the repressed. Here, Bishop pasted in a clipping detailing a man luring a young girl into a deserted house and killing her. Again, the absurd and the horrific share close quarters on the page, giving us insight into Bishop's reactions to the world around her.

GHOST IN THE MACHINE: GHOST WRITING AND MULTIMODALITY

While the kinetic experience of pages that unfold into various layout configurations provides one type of multimodal experience of the journal, other multimodalities lurk beneath the journal's surface. The opening four pages of the journal contain text only and are therefore not multimodal. In fact, these pages give the impression of a more traditional journal with no scrapbook or commonplace book elements. However, closer examination of pages two, three, and four (using Bishop's hand-numbered scheme), reveals writing behind the central writing.

This ghostwriting appears to have been penciled in as a first layer of text underneath the more visible journaling. It looks as though it either faded with time or possibly was lightly but not completely erased, then written over with the more visible content of the journal. When I first examined the original journal pages in Vassar College's archives, I did not notice the ghostwriting at all. I was only able to view the ghostwriting after taking digital photos of each page of the journal and zooming in on them on a laptop. Interestingly, I was not looking for any writing of this type; I was hoping that the larger image would help me decipher Bishop's infamously illegible scrawl.

The ghostwriting appears to be a layout for some other kind of manuscript. The

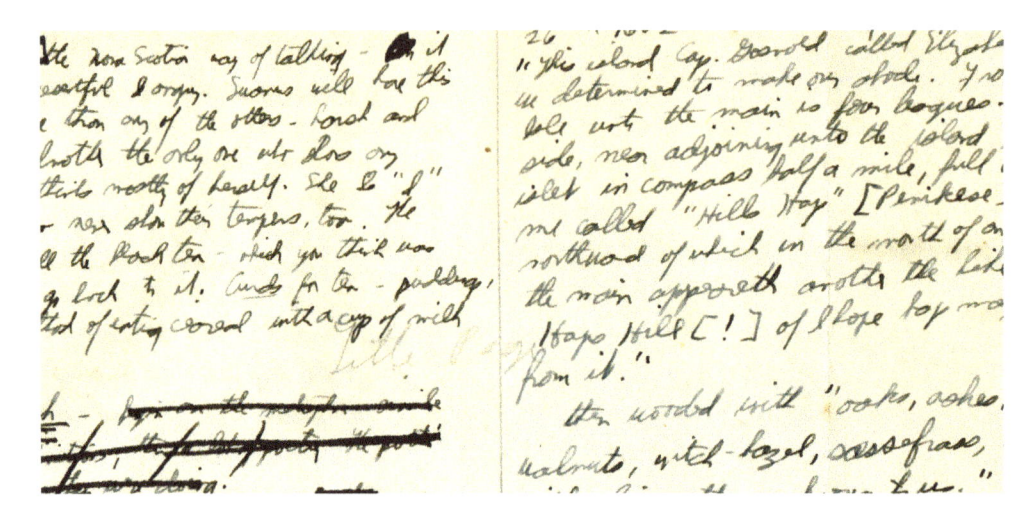

Across the column break on the right side of journal pages from the 1934 section of the 1934-1937 Cuttyhunk notebook, Bishop's faint handwriting reads "Title Page." (VC 72.3; Courtesy of Vassar College)

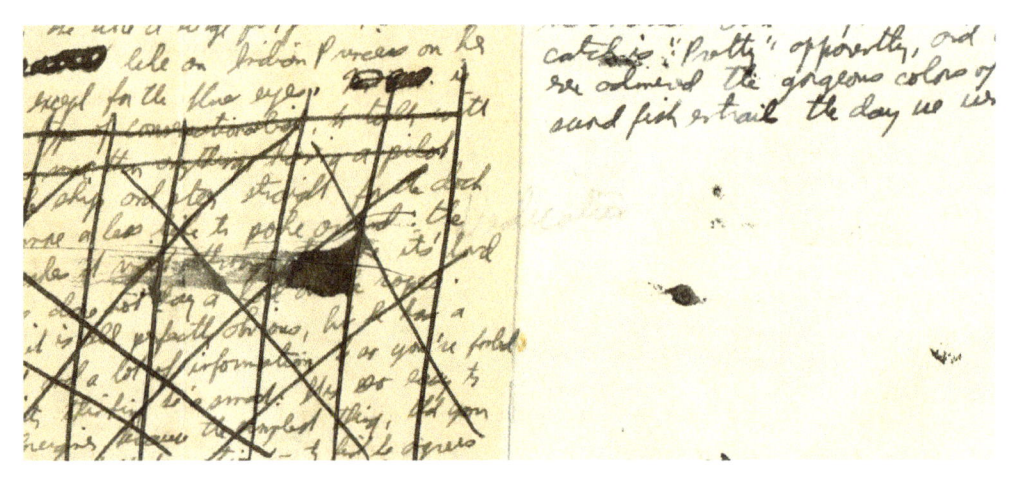

Across the column break on the left side of journal pages from the early pages of the 1934-1937 Cuttyhunk notebook, Bishop's faint handwriting reads "Dedication." (VC 72.3; Courtesy of Vassar College)

most prominent lines on the second page contain the phrases "Copyright 1934" and "Elizabeth Bishop, Editor-in-Chief." The third page contains ghostwriting centered on the page, across the hand-penciled column line. Because this writing appears between the two columns of darker writing, it is easier to decipher; it reads "Title Page." Similarly, the fourth page bears the centered ghostwriting text "Dedication." On the fifth page, collaging begins and covers more than half the page, making it impossible to determine if there is more ghostwriting centered on the page beneath the pasted newspaper clipping.

At first, the ghostwriting seems a mystery. Why would Bishop create a masthead and a copyright page in her own journal? If she were in the planning stages for another publication before she began using this notebook as a journal, which publication was it? The answer to this question was found beyond the archives, in the Vassar College stacks. We know that Bishop served as the editor-in-chief of the *Vassarion* during her senior year, and a copy of the 1934 college yearbook reveals an opening layout and masthead identical to the ghostwriting in the journal. The full masthead reads "Copyright, 1934, by Elizabeth Bishop, Editor-in-Chief / Eleanor Dunning, Business Manager."

Close inspection of the second page of the journal reveals a complete match. Likewise, the next page of the *Vassarion* is the title page, which reads "The Nineteen Thirty-Four Vassarion, Published by the Senior Class, Vassar College, Poughkeepsie, New York." The following page of the yearbook's front matter also follows the layout sketched into the journal. It is a dedication to Helen Kenyon, a trustee who had donated generously for a new gymnasium, Kenyon Hall.

Given the exact match of the ghostwriting and the structure of the 1934 *Vassarion*, it seems reasonable to assume that Bishop used her composition notebook to complete a mockup of the first pages of the yearbook. Perhaps she needed to sketch it out to share it with other staff members. Or perhaps she looked at yearbooks from prior years and noted the layout in her notebook in order to reproduce the same in the *Vassarion* she was to edit. It is possible that a previous editor gave her notes on how the yearbook layout worked. In any of these scenarios, it seems likely that Bishop used the notebook for one purpose, then made a decision to repurpose the same notebook as a journal.

So why is this discovery important? On the one hand, we see an intimate literal and physical connection between Bishop's public and private writing personae. On the other, it could be argued that this notebook was simply on hand when she needed to begin a journal, or that she did not wish to waste money purchasing a separate notebook for her journal after only using a few pages of this one to lay out the opening of the yearbook. Because of the time frame of the 1930s, it is likely that thrift was a motivator. Materials would have been scarce and expensive. Yet the willingness to reuse materials in this particular way indicates that, for Bishop, a public, convention-bound format such as a yearbook can share space with an intimate inner world of private observations and dream-like collages, a kind of personal yearbook. This finding would seem to indicate that Bishop viewed her writing personae as integrated—or at least integrated enough to share the same space. The primary and secondary purposes of this journal also create a truly multimodal experience for the reader. If we are able to see both modes of writing—the journal and the yearbook layout—we literally experience two modes at once, layered as a

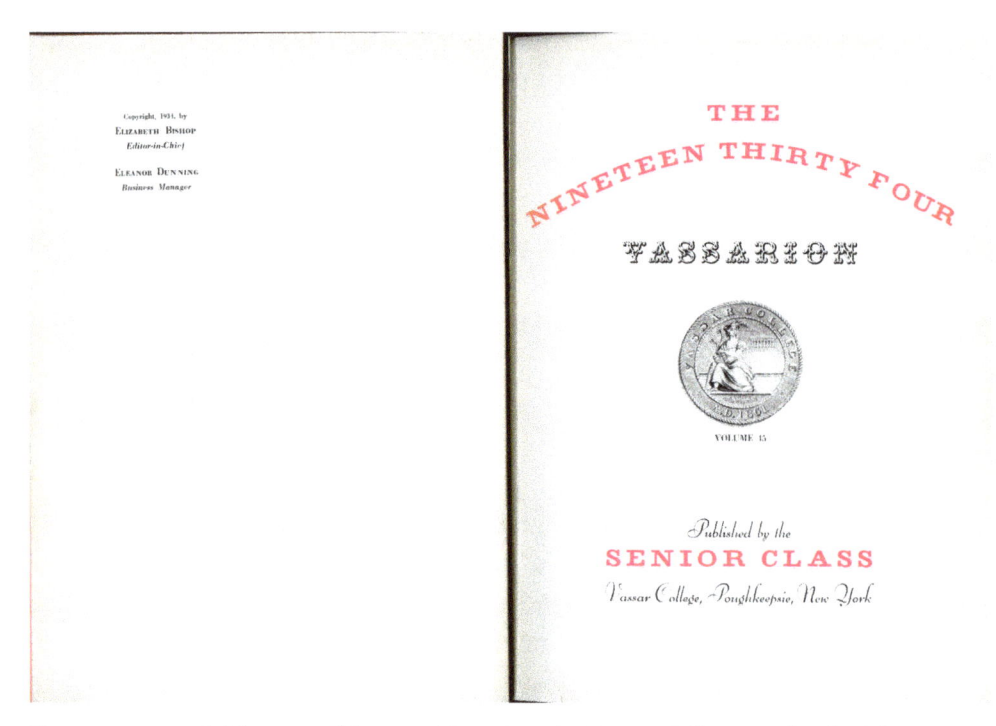

Front matter and title page of the 1934 *Vassarion*, the Vassar College yearbook Bishop edited. (VC 72.3; Courtesy of Vassar College)

Dedication to Helen Kenyon, a trustee and donor for Kenyon Hall, the college gymnasium, in the 1934 *Vassarion*, the Vassar College yearbook Bishop edited. (VC 72.3; Courtesy of Vassar College)

palimpsest. Similarly, the layering of two modes of writing provides multiple temporal and spatial pathways through the text. We may choose to flip through, trying only to decode the yearbook editorial process, or we may ignore the ghostwriting entirely, focusing only on the top layer of the palimpsest. Other pathways include combined reading experiences—those that blend both methods of making one's way through the text. One might read a few lines of Bishop's journal, then focus on the ghostwriting, allowing the foregrounded darker journal writing to blur into the background, then refocus to reverse the layers. This type of multimodal experience is not unlike the navigation of hyperlinks through websites or apps where readers craft their own path through the text.

Reading the Cuttyhunk notebook in this way makes the journal seem less an artifact and more of an immersive experience, much like reading multiple drafts of her poems in the archives provides an immersive experience into Bishop's creative process. Furthermore, there are other ways in which Bishop crafts particular temporal and spatial pathways through her journal, including page divisions and pre-numbered pages. Throughout the journal, Bishop has created a space for two columns of writing per page by way of a penciled vertical line dividing each page. On many pages, this line works in the expected way, guiding the reader to read the left column, then the right column, as one would with a newspaper, and it might seem so commonplace as not to merit notice. But for Bishop, the visual line was deeply significant. Writing about Bishop's paintings, Lorrie Goldensohn notes that "in drawing and painting, Bishop's line is both an instrument of representation and a subject: her pictures think about line and its contradictory properties as both a limiting, as well as a ceaselessly connective element" ("Elizabeth Bishop's Written Pictures" 170). We find these contradictions of line in the journal as well: the line as columnar divider does not always hold because on many pages the collaged photos and clippings violate the integrity of the columns (see fig. 74). In these instances, the reader, although trained to read in a particular way by the typical presence of columns, must choose alternate pathways for navigating pages that are primarily images. Goldensohn notes a similar property of the line in Bishop's paintings as well: "line hesitates expressively between serving as writing or as representation, probing the continuities between letters, pictographs, and likeness in varying assemblies of coded meaning" (171). Far from being insignificant or merely functional, the lines in Bishop's journal offer ideological connections and dividers and may be working as primary subjects in their own right.

It is important to acknowledge that the journal contains many more pages of both scrapbook and journal type than can be discussed in the space available here. Approximately half of all the journal's fifty-two pages contain items other than Bishop's handwritten notes, and many items have been inserted after the final pages of the journal and are loose within the binding. My focus here is on the multimodal and multimedia nature of Bishop's work, primarily in identifying it as such so that Bishop's scrapbooking can be examined through a new framework. More work remains to be done on the connections between Bishop's multimodal compositions and her poetic practice.

The study of Bishop as a multimodal and multimedia collage artist has implications for Bishop studies overall. This framework provides more evidence of Bishop as a curator, a collector, and a miniaturist, as Susan Rosenbaum has argued (61-62)—qualities that appear in her poetry as well. Because of these qualities, it is essential to teach and research Bishop within multimedia and multimodal frameworks to avoid flattening the experience of her creative process. A focus on both the visual and the textual composition processes highlights Bishop's aesthetic collecting and selecting of information from current events, popular culture, and the arts. Having students read and view artifacts—such as Bishop's journals, paintings, photographs, in addition to archival material, such as her drafts and letters—fleshes out their sense of the poet as a human being and provides a fuller picture of the ways in which Bishop saw and mirrored back her world.

Many of Bishop's readers already respond to her poetry multimodally, in YouTube vlogs, in blogs, and in quotations and memes posted on Instagram. Even without knowledge of Bishop's multimodal notebooks, it makes sense to encourage students to voice responses to her poetry within contemporary digital modes. Viewing Bishop's journal/scrapbook as a multimodal and multimedia artifact can enrich this process and add a new twist to multimodal Bishop pedagogy. We can show students the connection between the virtual scrapbooking they do every day through social media and the very similar kinds of scrapbooking Bishop undertook in her twenties: her frequent desire to shock, to be silly, to express her wonder and outrage at the world around her and the way she expressed those desires through what she cut and pasted. We can also help students make the connection between scrapbooking (both physical and digital) and the poetic composition process. It would be interesting to ask them how Bishop would have used social media for her scrapbook content if she had access to our digital world. Another exercise might ask students to create a social media account that functions as a Bishopesque scrapbook of ideas for their own poems. Ideally, students could view Bishop's scrapbooked pages and comment on how they see Bishop using the medium. Because not every student and every professor can venture to the Vassar archive, embracing this kind of pedagogy creates a demand for the archive to be digitized, as many other archives have been. Digital archives allow students to conduct the same kind of research that their professors do, creating an early sense of authentic intellectual inquiry and academic professionalism.

Because Bishop is composing in multimodal ways, we should ask our students to respond to both her poetry and her journals and scrapbooks in their own collages, scrapbooks, videos, artwork, sound recordings, or multimodal reading journals. Bishop's journals and her creative process more generally are multidimensional; our study of Bishop should be multidimensional as well. Recognizing Bishop's journals/scrapbooks as significant to her multimedia and multimodal creative process enriches our experience of her poetry and opens up a new framework for reading and teaching Bishop.

NOTES

1. All subsequent references to the Cuttyhunk notebook can be found in this folder. Page numbers are Bishop's own.
2. Short for tompung, a one- or two-horse sled with a storage box on it, often used for carrying goods to market.

CHAPTER FIFTEEN

THE MATTER OF ELIZABETH
BISHOP'S PROFESSIONALISM

Claire Seiler

Series II of the Elizabeth Bishop Papers at Vassar College houses the poet's "Professional Correspondence, Contracts, and Financial Statements." What is one to make of this series? More to the point: Why would one make anything of it at all, beyond taking its contents as corroborating documents, no longer if ever necessary, for lines on Bishop's curriculum vitae? When I told the NEH Summer Seminar of my curiosity about Bishop's professional self-fashioning, and thus of my plan to read through the professional materials, one colleague remarked, "That'll get old real quick." Titters all around, including from me. We were laughing knowingly about the blandness of professional documentation in general, about the foregone boredom of literary contracts, grant applications, statements of purpose, royalties reports, notifications of prizes, professional chronologies and CVs, and the like. But we were also laughing specifically about the idea of such things in relation to the study of Elizabeth Bishop, where they hardly seem to belong.

Perhaps the least fully told story of Bishop's career is, in fact, the story of her career. From the warm reception of her first book, *North & South* (1946), through the chorus of appreciation that has greeted the six new editions of her work published since 2006, literary critics, scholars, editors, and readers have often envisioned Bishop as a kind of antidote to whatever is or was wrong with modern poetry. (Saying what's "wrong" with modern poetry never goes out of style.) By the late 1940s, when Bishop began her professional career, ills commonly said to plague poetry included its "difficulty" and "obscurity"—charges that Randall Jarrell rebutted in his memorable essay "The Obscurity of the Poet" (1951)—and a creeping professionalization. Reviewers of *North & South* already understood Bishop's distinctive "modesty" (Marianne Moore) and "restraint" (Jarrell) in opposition to both. Despite the gendered implications of such praise, *modesty* and like terms still rank as keywords in the Bishop scholarship.[1]

An associated idea of the poet's anti-professionalism has long worked as something of an operating principle in Bishop studies. As Bonnie Costello, Gillian White, and others have observed, in this authorial subfield, select aspects of the poet's character, personality, and lived experience—what White dubs "the Bishop biographical paratext"—often provide not simply explicatory, but reductive or over-determined, grounds for understanding her poetics (White, *Lyric Shame* 45; Costello "Elizabeth Bishop's Impersonal Personal" 334-36). My initial curiosity about Bishop's professional self-fashioning stemmed, in part, from how seamlessly the biographical-psychological iconography of Bishop studies seems to accord with a critical vision of the poet as sustaining a principled near-abstention from the demands of "Poetry as Big Business," as she put it in a 1950 letter to Jarrell (*OA* 202).[2] On the face of it, Bishop's oft-quoted quip squares with ready impressions of her admirable disdain toward the postwar professionalization of poetry. Less remarked, however, are the thoroughly professional contexts in which Bishop made it. She wrote to Jarrell from her office at the Library of Congress, on her official letterhead, and principally to break the news of two professional disappointments for him: he had been passed over as the next Consultant in Poetry and Houghton Mifflin was not interested in publishing his next book.

To read the whole of Bishop's professional correspondence on-site at Vassar is, at the very least, to see its store of professionally requisite documents continuously interspersed both with materials long invaluable to Bishop scholars—meticulous drafts, dazzling letters, travel notebooks, precocious college writing, photographs—and with newer and more obviously revelatory additions to the Elizabeth Bishop Papers, especially the poet's "letters" to Dr. Ruth Foster (1947), to which I will return. It is also to recognize that the filing system projects a fiction across the Bishop archive, a fiction that organizes, to a significant degree, the study of Bishop's work as well. The standard curatorial heading of Series II suggests a clean separation of professional correspondence from the letters that comprise Series I: Correspondence. This latter unmodified heading implies the more personal and substantive character of the hundreds of letters filed in Series I. But even a cursory reading of the letters of just about any writer of Bishop's era shows that no such clear divide existed; moreover, epistolary writing among members of professional sets or networks often trades in an idiom of familiarity that signals the letter writer's belonging, or aspiring to belong, within said set or network, as the peer-to-peer jocularity of "Poetry as Big Business" attests.

For her part, Bishop was also something of a professional correspondent

(Hammer; Phillips, "Bishop's Correspondence"), and evidence of the porous line between her personal and professional correspondence surfaces everywhere in it—notably at the very start of two of the new editions of her letters that have prompted reconsideration of her work, if not of her professional life. The development of Bishop's professional relationship-turned-friendship with editor Katharine White of *The New Yorker* is among the moving histories to emerge from Joelle Biele's edition of Bishop's correspondence with the magazine (*EBNY*). Readers of *Words in Air* (2008), Thomas Travisano and Saskia Hamilton's edition of the Bishop-Lowell correspondence, will recall the career occasions for Bishop's first few letters to her most storied correspondent. Bishop wrote the very first, dated May 12, 1947, and addressed to "Mr. Lowell" care of Harcourt Brace, to congratulate him on winning the Pulitzer Prize for *Lord Weary's Castle* (1946) and fellowships from the Guggenheim Foundation and the American Academy of Arts and Letters. Her letter quickly slides from the formality of "Mr. Lowell" to a sprightly, ironic, among-peers tone to congratulate him on all "the awards—I guess I'll just call them 1, 2, & 3" (*WIA* 3). Bishop had also just won a Guggenheim but makes no mention of it.

Still, in recent years, the vision of Bishop as exception to the professionalizing rule of postwar American poetry has proven its durability. Even as scholars in the broader fields of modernist and post-1945 US literature have revalued the assumption that professionalization in its various guises exerted mostly deadening effects on American letters (McGurl, Emre, Kindley), it seems to have become only more important for some Bishop scholars to protect, even to promote, the story of the poet's deliberate remove from professional concerns. For example, the first concerted, collaborative effort to take stock of the six new editions of Bishop's work, *Elizabeth Bishop in the 21st Century: Reading the New Editions* (2012), does not simply replay "the deep ambivalence and reluctance with which Bishop confronted the public role of 'major poet' in midcentury American society" (Cleghorn et al. 7). The editors of the collection also romanticize that reluctance: "This was a role her talent may have entitled her to claim, but it was also a role from which she always shied away" (7). Cataloging recent emphases in Bishop scholarship, the volume's introduction presents a "poet crucially engaged with such vital cultural and political issues as outsiderhood, gender, sexuality, national identity, social class, war, the environment, power relations, and family intimacy and conflict" (7)—but not, it would seem, with professional life, much less with what it meant to navigate professional life as a poet "crucially engaged" with these issues.

Although typically promulgated in the celebratory terms of artistic vocation, the story of Bishop's professional abstention or reluctance lines up uncomfortably well with dated, gendered notions of what constitutes truly professional or, for that matter, truly artistic life. Consider, to this point, the ease with which standard comparison of Bishop's pursuit of her career, as if in spite of herself, to Lowell's famously fervent pursuit of his own reproduces those notions, implying that there exists no middle ground between admirable remove from professional concerns on the one hand and maniacal careerism on the other—does a disservice to both poets to boot. But, the stakes of the reigning disinclination to investigate Bishop's professional self-fashioning extend across and well beyond the scholarship on her singular work and that of her peers. For Bishop's career not only synchronized with the increasingly institutional patronage and management of literature and the arts in the postwar United States but also participated in the movement of hundreds of thousands of women into professional and professionalizing fields in the latter half of the twentieth century.[3] Like many of her women peers and contemporaries, Bishop could not—and, contra the mythology, did not wholly seek to—deflect the demands and opportunities of postwar professional life. Nor, in turn, can Bishop's critical readers responsibly ignore the question of how she fashioned herself as poet amid various professional expectations, pressures, and occasions, least of all in the service of protecting her vocational purity.

This is not to propose remaking Bishop as a consummate "professional" poet or a second-wave workplace heroine too long hidden behind the screen of her legendary modesty. Bishop *was* ambivalent about the bureaucratic, institutional, and commercial contours of poetry over career and had a well-documented discomfort with and career-long distaste for many of poetry's professional trappings, including public readings, recordings for posterity, and teaching jobs. One might persist in wrapping her evident ambition in a language of feminine demurral, but it is precisely Bishop's ambivalence that necessitates an accounting of and for her professional self-fashioning. I use the phrase *professional self-fashioning* for two reasons. First, it denotes Bishop's ongoing practices of engagement—neither enthusiastic nor consistent, sometimes deliberate, sometimes not—with the professional field of poetry. Second, the phrase distinguishes between the need to attend to these critically neglected but, for Bishop, necessary practices and the more accustomed habit of measuring her career by a yardstick marked out with fixed professional "roles." Against such a yardstick, Bishop can only succeed by having failed or refused to conduct her career like her male peers or caricatures of them.

Borrowing the terms of Pierre Bourdieu's classic account of the relational constitution of the field of cultural production, it is fair to say Bishop's "disposition" occupies disproportionately more space in accounts of her life and work than either her "positions" or, more to the point in the present context, her "position-takings."[4] To begin to address this disproportion, this chapter turns to that outwardly unpromising array of documents in the Elizabeth Bishop Papers, Series II: Professional Correspondence, Contracts, Financial Statements. Dispersed across more than a dozen boxes in the archive, this series houses material records of the poet's position-takings—that is, those sites at which whom Bishop was or was becoming ran into the positions, themselves malleable, that she sought out or was offered, accepted, or reimagined over the course of her thirty-plus-year professional career. Since it lies beyond the scope of any one chapter to tell the whole history of Bishop's professional self-fashioning or even fully to describe Series II, this concluding chapter focuses on a representative pair of unpublished documents filed there: Bishop's two successful applications for fellowships from the John Simon Guggenheim Memorial Foundation. For both, Vassar holds typescript and autograph drafts as well as fair copies of Bishop's final application.

Let me acknowledge that applications for grant funding are, at root, utilitarian documents, means to a necessary or desired end rather than an end in themselves. Such applications are all but required of artists who, like Bishop, lack ample private means and are not otherwise consistently employed; at the same time, to win a fellowship is also to accrue capital in an economy of prestige. In all these senses, grant and fellowship applications are the opposite of poems yet sponsor the writing of them. But long after their immediate utility, when they are filed away in unassuming archival series, grant applications and like "professional correspondence" also record instances of professional self-fashioning. They record occasions on which the artist presents her record, references, and project to try to win time and money to make her art. Bishop's first application for a Guggenheim, submitted in the fall of 1946, was one of several marks of her arrival in the poetry world; her second, prepared in the fall of 1977, bespeaks her late-career ascendance within it.[5] Read together, and given their situations at the chronological and reputational poles of Bishop's career, these documents can begin to restore a sense of the texture of Bishop's professional self-fashioning. The Guggenheim applications recast some of Bishop's vaunted modesty as also effective professional strategy, show Bishop's savvy about the centers of literary prestige as they moved into the academy over the course of her career, and point to why it matters to consider how Bishop navigated her professional life over three decades.

A PAIR OF GUGGENHEIMS

Bishop's career was bookended not only by the name-making and valedictory successes of *North & South* and *Geography III* (1976), respectively, but also by the two fellowships from the Guggenheim Foundation that followed quickly on the publication of these volumes. No-strings-attached Guggenheim grants supported Bishop's writing for two calendar years, from July 1947 and from September 1978. The latter supported her until within two months of her death, on October 6,

1979. Bishop had just published *North & South* when she applied for and won a Guggenheim in the fall of 1946. The $2,500 award was one of many marks of her establishment as a professional poet. Others included the commencement of her friendships with Jarrell and Lowell, *The New Yorker*'s offer of a first-reading agreement and steady financial retainer, and the welcoming reception of *North & South*. By the fall of 1977, when Bishop applied for a second Guggenheim, she had won the major US literary prizes and several international awards, and *Geography III* had been published the previous winter to sterling reviews. To put all of this more schematically, what changed for Bishop between 1946 and 1977 was as much her professional stature as it was her person or poetics. In the late 1940s, Elizabeth Bishop was a promising new poet; by the late 1970s, among poets and literary scholars and critics, *Elizabeth Bishop* was a signifier whose meaning was perhaps best crystallized by John Ashbery, in an indelible aside from his review of her National Book Award-winning *Complete Poems* (1969): "Miss Bishop is somehow an establishment poet herself, and the establishment ought to give thanks; she is proof that it can't be all bad" (201). Here again is Bishop as exception or antidote. But as Ashbery's "somehow" suggests, such a delicate balance between the "establishment" and its discontents can neither be struck nor maintained by accident.

If Bishop's reputation among poets, writers, critics, and scholars preceded her by the time she applied for her second Guggenheim, the force of her achievement was lost on Stephen L. Schlesinger, the Secretary of the Guggenheim Foundation. In an unpublished letter to Bishop dated September 1, 1977, he cautioned her "that the proportion of second Fellowships has declined in recent years because of the pressure on us from applicants who have not previously held one of our awards" (VC 40.7). From this note in the archival file, several incongruities follow. First, only two months after receiving Schlesinger's letter, Bishop served as an evaluator of other artists' applications for Guggenheim support. Of the group she assessed in November 1977, Bishop found Ashbery's application by far the most deserving but noted that he had already had two Guggenheims. (He won both within a decade, no less, in 1967 and 1973.) A bit of barb laces her invocation of and quotation from the stated priorities of the Guggenheim Foundation: "I know that the Committee's opinion of granting three Fellowships is unfavorable. However, 'on the basis of accomplishments of the highest merit' as your letter says, John Ashbery would ~~certainly~~ qualify[.]" Next, and adding another link in a chain of deference Guggenheim officials alternately withheld from or afforded to Bishop, along with "the formal notice" of her $21,000 award on March 15, 1978, the President of the Foundation, Gordon N. Ray, sent a letter of his "personal congratulations" and asked Bishop to lunch with him in New York (VC 40.7).

Unlike Bishop's professional stature, neither the cover sheet nor the components of the Guggenheim application changed much in thirty years. Minor updates to the application form itself do reflect gradual shifts in normative cultural assumptions about the gender and sexuality of grant applicants between 1946 and 1977, if not much real change in the recipients of such grants. In fact, Bishop's pair of Guggenheim Fellowships speaks to how little access to funding improved for professional-creative women over the three decades of her career: of the thirty-two fellowships awarded in the "Creative Arts, U.S. and Canada" in 1947, six went to women (18.7%); of the seventy-six winners of the same competition for 1978, seventeen (22.4%) were women.[6] Still, at the end of the 1946 form, an FAQ-style section called "Suggestions Concerning Applications" makes a not entirely successful effort to avoid assuming that the artist-, scientist-, or scholar-applicant is a man. Suggestion 4 reads, "Whenever the space provided in the form is not suitable for an applicant to present fully the facts of his or her case, it is requested that they be stated in a separate document." Suggestion 5 reverts to masculine default, directing the applicant to send one copy of the application to the Guggenheim Foundation, while "the other may be retained by him for his files." With Suggestion 7, the form realizes that the second-person pronoun "you" will do the trick: "If you do not get a receipt for your application within a reasonable time, please notify the Foundation." The 1977 form addresses the applicant throughout as "you" (VC 40.7). Regardless, Bishop's family, romantic, and kinship bonds never could—or would—align with the governing social assumptions always manifest on bureaucratic forms, even as those assumptions began slowly to shift. One poignant point of comparison between Bishop's two Guggenheim forms arises out of her answers to a standard-issue application question. Asked in 1946 for "Name and address of nearest kin, if unmarried," Bishop listed her aunt, "Mrs. William W. Bowers" of Great Village, Nova Scotia; asked in 1977 for "Name and address of spouse or nearest kin," she wrote, in her favored affectionate code, "Alice Methfessel (friend)" (VC 40.7).

The dossiers for Bishop's first application and her bid "for further assistance" from the Guggenheim Foundation alike required a statement of accomplishments, a list of publications, references, and—the core of the application—a plan for work to be carried out during the fellowship term. This is standard grant application fare but Bishop's submissions, especially her plans for work, defy application norms. Reading her Guggenheim applications, one is struck, first, by their tonal and rhetorical echoes of her poems. Rather than the self-promotion and confident projection invited from, if not necessitated of, grant applicants across disciplines, Bishop's Guggenheim materials resonate with the celebrated modesty and reticence of her (early) poetics, the related hesitancies and self-qualifications or self-corrections in her work. Even bracketing the ladylike connotations of modesty, restraint, and similar lingering terms in the Bishop scholarship, the Guggenheim

On her first Guggenheim application form, in 1946, Bishop wrote as little as possible about her proposed project but listed as many impressive references as she could fit in the space provided. (VC 40.7; Courtesy of Vassar College)

applications document how these characteristics—or the performance of a certain uncertainty—worked as a part of her professional self-fashioning rather than exclusively as a laudable mark of the poet's holding herself apart from professional demands or opportunities. Bishop won the funds and prestige with which to support her writing in no small part by declining, at least rhetorically, to play the game of self-aggrandizement or to treat poetry like a research project with expected worthwhile outcomes. Her application statements disdain to elaborate much on her proposed work, instead claiming for poetry an ineffable value that defies the bureaucratic forms, material or metaphorical, that would seek to contain them.

On the 1946 application, especially, Bishop's concision might seem easily—or only—to burnish her reputation for modesty. What is certain, however, is the effect of her brevity. Like a person whose whisper makes everyone lean in to hear what she has to say, Bishop's concision proved a winning strategy. Before even asking for the applicant's name, the 1946 application form requested a "Concise statement of project" and provided six lines for a paragraph-long response. Bishop typed only "Creative work in poetry."

The same concision applies to the "Accomplishments" section of the application. Bishop left the first two questions—"Positions held" and memberships in "learned, scientific or artistic societies"—blank. She had to: she had held no positions, joined no societies. The third question requested a "full account of the advanced work, research, or creative work you have already done" and the fourth "a *list* of your publications." On a separate half-sheet of typescript, Bishop drafted a single answer to both questions: "In 1946 I published NORTH & SOUTH a book of poems that received the Houghton Mifflin Poetry Fellowship for 1945. I have contribute [sic] poems and stories to most of the better 'little' magazines including Partisan Review and Life & Letters To-day, New Directions, also to The New Yorker, The New Republic, Forum, etc." (VC 40.7). That "etc." is an uncharacteristically vague throwaway and intriguing for being so. The offhand indication of unspecified work affects a casual confidence that Bishop did not in fact feel about her early career achievements.

What should have been the most thorough and compelling section of the 1946 application was "*PLANS FOR WORK*," equivalent to today's "statement of purpose." In Bishop's case, the Guggenheim's boilerplate description of what these plans must include runs almost as long (113 words) as Bishop's "plan" (148 words). The application prompt reads in full:

> Submit a statement giving detailed plans for the work you would pursue during your tenure of a Fellowship. This statement should include, *inter alia*: a description of the project, including its character and scope, and the significance of its presumable contribution to knowledge, or to art; the present state of the project, time of commencement, progress to date, and expectation as to completion; the place or places where the work would be carried on, and the authorities, if any, with whom it would be done; your expectation as to publication of the results of your work; and your ultimate purpose as a scholar or artist. *This statement should be complete and carefully prepared.* (VC 40.7)

For readers familiar with Bishop's correspondence of the late 1940s—or, for that matter, with her letters to poet-friends and others at just about any point in her career—this typical grant application fodder about plans for work reads as if designed to stir up the poet's professional anxieties. They did not need stirring up in late 1946. In the early wake of *North & South*, Bishop's embarrassment about how long it had taken her to finish the book and doubt as to the seriousness and depth of her work became painful refrains in her correspondence. Far from allaying these concerns, the encouraging reception of *North & South* exacerbated them. Some of the reviews remarked unnecessarily on how long it had taken her to write and publish the book. In *The New Yorker*, for example, Louise Bogan concluded her favorable review by chiding the poet, as if she were a student handing in a school assignment after the deadline: "Miss Bishop has evidently put in eleven years" into "these thirty poems," she wrote. "It is to be hoped that we shall get thirty more . . . in rather less than another decade" (183). Even as Bishop received compliments on *North & South*, "she apologized to everyone for its thinness" (Millier, *Elizabeth Bishop* 180).

Bishop's statement in response to the application instructions is neither "*complete*" nor very "*carefully prepared*" nor does it pretend to self-confidence. Her brief outline of plans never addresses many of the points specified in the application form: Bishop makes no presumption as to the "contribution to knowledge, or to art" her work will make and no proclamation as to her "ultimate purpose as a scholar or artist." Making quick work of the obligation to make and state plans, Bishop first claims the difficulty of giving "an exact idea of what poetry may turn out to be like, while it is yet in progress," then gestures toward the new, "more serious" book that she has "quite well in mind," and concludes by reiterating that "it is almost impossible to give a definite plan or estimate of poetry in advance." Instead of trying to make such an estimate, she directs the selection committee back to *North & South* as an indication of her promise (VC 40.7).

Bishop's description of her new book trades in vague phrasing: the book is only "tentatively called 'Faustina and Other Poems,'" its "emphasis" only "seems to be more directly on real people[,]" and Bishop can only "hope [it] will prove to be more serious" than *North & South*. The plan, such as it is, also escalates over the brief statement from "It is difficult to give an exact idea of what poetry may turn out to be like" to "it is almost impossible to give a definite plan or estimate of poetry." These refusals are categorical—about poetry per se rather than restrictively about Bishop's own. Along with the sheer brevity and vagueness of Bishop's plan, these outward marks of uncertainty also suggest, to my ear, a certain refusal to speak in accordance with the application prompt's evident orientation toward scholarship and scientific research, as witness the syntactical afterthought of "or to art." In other words, if this application statement seems to evince Bishop's modesty, then it also leverages the comparative mystique of poetry.

At the end of her "plans for work," Bishop directs her references and the Guggenheim selection committee back to her first book. Two of her references knew *North & South* well and had their own professional stake in the continued success of the book and the poet. Ferris Greenslet was Bishop's editor at Houghton Mifflin; Katharine White was one of the judges who awarded Bishop the inaugural Houghton Mifflin Poetry Prize for *North & South*. Later in the fall of 1946, she offered Bishop her initial first-read contract with *The New Yorker*. But these small-literary-world alignments—or conflicts of professional interest—come to look almost negligible when compared to the academic-institutional consolidation of prestige and opportunity recorded in Bishop's 1977 Guggenheim application.

In 1946, Bishop provided seven references in support of her application for a Guggenheim fellowship. Two, "Mr. John Dewey" and "Mr. Horace Gregory," were professors, but Bishop gave their "Position[s]" as "philosopher" and "poet & critic," respectively, rather than listing their academic titles and home institutions. Her other references in 1946 were the "poet" "Miss Marianne Moore"; editors "Mrs. E.B. [Katharine] White," "Mr. Ferris Greenslet," and "Mr. Philip Rahv"; and the "critic & novelist" "Mr. Edmund Wilson." Thirty years later, the updated Guggenheim application form provided space for four references and requested "Position (Full Title)." Under "Name of Reference," Bishop listed three professors—Harold Bloom (Yale), Helen Vendler (then at Boston University), Robert Fitzgerald (Harvard)—and Robert Giroux, "Editor-in-Chief" at Farrar, Straus and Giroux. Given that the academy exerted ever stronger gravitational pull on US poetry over the course of Bishop's career, this shift from literary and intellectual types in 1946 to mostly prominent academic literary scholars and critics in 1977 is not surprising. It is, however, significant. Bishop's list of references registers both the esteem in which academics held her—Bloom and Vendler had also both reviewed *Geography III*—and her sense that these recommenders would have the most pull with the Guggenheim Foundation. She could certainly have asked instead poet-friends such as Ashbery or James Merrill, both of whom had already won their first National Book Awards by 1977.

The archival file also contains a handwritten letter from Bloom that crystallizes this signal difference between Bishop's two Guggenheim applications. Dated October 6, 1977, the letter is at once sincere in its "homage" to Bishop and testament to the in-crowd power that coursed through such prestige competitions. In it, Bloom expresses himself "greatly honored to write a Guggenheim Fellowship on your behalf" and certain that "you will receive the Fellowship." He goes on to assert that "there is no poet now alive," writing in any language, "whose achievement is as beyond dispute" as Bishop's and encourages her to apply for still more fellowships than the Guggenheim. For "what matters is that you write more books of poems" (VC 40.7). As far as I know, Bishop had not asked Bloom for further patronage or advocacy, but the professor saw fit to offer it, and Bishop kept his affirmative letter.

The academic support of Bishop's second Guggenheim application lines up, albeit paradoxically, with the central strategy of the statements Bishop prepared for the application. Whereas the 1946 application embraces concision and preserves a kind of aura around poet and poetry, the 1977 application materials assert nothing so plainly as how burdensome Bishop found one aspect of her sometime imbrication in the academy: teaching.[7] The two key documents of the later application

In 1977, the instruction to provide "Full Title" for each reference enabled doing away with the once customary notation of gender and marital status by mode of address (Mr., Mrs., Miss). The instruction also reflected a new expectation that references would be of significant academic or institutional standing. (VC 40.7; Courtesy of Vassar College)

start with teaching jobs Bishop has held. Not least because the first, a "statement of accomplishments" since the previous award, amounted to a summary of almost Bishop's entire career, it might well have begun with books published or awards won. Instead, she fashions herself first as a professor seeking a well-deserved break from teaching and in need of "enough money to live on." "Since 1947, I have had the following jobs" (VC 40.7), her statement of accomplishments begins. Except for her poetry consultancy at the Library of Congress, all are teaching jobs—at the University of Washington, Harvard, and New York University. At Harvard, where Bishop did most of her teaching, her position was lecturer; Washington and NYU honored her with the grander titles of Visiting Professor and Henry W. and Albert A. Berg Professor, respectively. After academic positions, the statement of accomplishments enumerates books published, with the list padded a bit to look as impressive as possible. *A Cold Spring* (1955) is listed as a standalone volume, though it was never published as such; and the Life World Library volume *Brazil* (1962) appears without any of Bishop's customary qualification of her compromised authorship of it (Millier, *Elizabeth Bishop* 327-28). From books, the statement of accomplishments runs, orderly enough, through "fellowships and awards," memberships in honorific professional organizations, and honorary degrees. It concludes with this

314   ELIZABETH BISHOP AND THE LITERARY ARCHIVE

putatively uncharacteristic and refreshingly immodest note: "I have given readings and appeared in anthologies too numerous to mention" (VC 40.7). This is a matter of fact nod to Bishop's prominence and the earned equivalent of "etc." in the 1946 application.

The second key document of Bishop's 1977 Guggenheim application, the statement of plans for the fellowship year, also begins with a recounting of the academic labor from which the fellowship would exempt her. She gives over the first half of her two-paragraph statement to what she frames as the burdensome distraction of teaching and flags with scare quotes what she regarded as a particularly contrived aspect of it: the teaching of "creative writing." While teaching, which Bishop writes has occupied most of her time since the early 1970s, "I find I can do almost no work of my own." Freedom from teaching and "enough money to live on" would, she explains, afford her the freedom "to concentrate for long periods of time on my writing" (VC 40.7). When Bishop won the Guggenheim, the $21,000 award did allow her to bow out of teaching at Brandeis for the 1977-78 academic year.

For only one pained paragraph does Bishop's statement of plans look forward to the fellowship and the writing it would allow her to do. Once again, she breaks customary rules of competitive applications for funding. *Possibly*s and *tentatively*s occupy crucial grant proposal real estate in what amounts to a brief, prospective bibliography of books Bishop means to write. She has two book-length poetry projects "tentatively" in mind and has had "ten pages or so" of one of them "in rough draft for five or six years." She also means to supplement a handful of her published short stories with "a few more and possibly two or three travel sketches," so as to make a book of prose. But Bishop is clear that her "immediate and most pressing interest is in" writing poems (VC 40.7).

Obvious tragedy resides in this projection of work, in that Bishop never would finish these books. But there is another, slower-burning sadness to this statement of plans, too. By the time she applied for "further assistance" from the Guggenheim Foundation, Bishop probably didn't have to say much about the promise of her future work; she was as much a shoo-in as an applicant could be. Yet throughout her career, right up to her death, Bishop could never promise *enough* work, even to herself. In this instance, only after she piles on more promises—a half-dozen short stories, "possibly two or three travel sketches," maybe to "make" another book—does she allow herself to return to her "pressing interest in completing the two books of poems."

Like many readers and probably most scholars of Bishop's work, I wish she had completed these books and that there were more of her poems. These wishes have run through much of the reception of Bishop in the twenty-first century. It is there in Ashbery's blurb for *Edgar Allan Poe & The Juke-Box: Uncollected Poems, Drafts, and*

Fragments (2006), which begins, "For those who love Bishop, there can never be enough of her writing." The wish for more Bishop is there, too, in early scholarly treatments of newer additions to the poet's archive.

This last note points back especially to Bishop's "letters" to Dr. Ruth Foster. So does the phrase "one long poem," which echoes across those "letters" and her Guggenheim application of thirty years later. The Foster "letters" are, more accurately, a therapeutic assignment and chronology that Bishop wrote over one drunken weekend in February 1947; the "letters" are rhetorically addressed to Bishop's psychiatrist, but material details suggest she might never have sent them. The letters describe, among other experiences, the trauma of Bishop's childhood sexual abuse by an uncle, the wonder of some of her first erotic encounters with women, and the emergence of the dream-germ of "At the Fishhouses," which she completed in February 1947. I noted at the outset of this chapter that my curiosity about how the Vassar archive might help us to revalue Bishop's professional self-fashioning derived in part from a sense that accustomed psycho-biographical readings of Bishop tend to occlude her conduct of her career. The strangely eager reception of the Foster letters—they were one impetus for the NEH Seminar—only sharpened my curiosity. "Strangely eager" not because early readings of the letters proceed according to the entrenched biographical imperatives of a good share of Bishop scholarship. How else could readings of such letters proceed? Rather, I mean to flag the eagerness, in the first published account of them, to use the letters as a kind of master key (Goldensohn, "Approaching") or, in Heather Treseler's more circumspect account, the positing of the Foster letters as "something of an *ars poetica*" for Bishop ("One Long Poem"). It is neither to indulge in contrarianism nor to minimize Bishop's—or anyone's—trauma nor to weigh in on the endless debate about what Bishop did or didn't mean to keep "private" that I suggest an ethos of proportion with respect to critical use of the Foster letters. The question, to my mind, is less *whether* than *how* to use the letters, or how much interpretive weight to make them bear with respect to Bishop's poetics writ large.

Alongside stories about Bishop's life that such new, compelling archival materials can deepen—or, one would hope, complicate—there remain untold and undervalued stories to be found in materials that have been there all along. One is the story of Bishop's professional self-fashioning, which began in earnest right around the time of the Foster letters but cannot be wholly subsumed into their revelatory force. Put more evocatively, in reading through Series II: Professional Correspondence, Contracts, Financial Statements on-site at Vassar, one is reminded at every turn that the promise of the archival sublime—the major discovery, the boldface revelation—rests on and is conditioned by the presence of the archival mundane. If Bishop's professional life continues to loom small in the study of her work, or if we continue to fashion her romantically as a kind of miraculous anti-professional legible primarily according to often reductive psychological diagnostics or characteristics, then we miss a crucial historical instance—messy, textured, unscripted—of a woman gaining access to literary authority, public discourse, and professional life in the latter half of the twentieth century. If we skip over the outwardly unremarkable, ostensibly boring documents in her archive, then we also dodge the chance—the imperative—to do what Bishop's poems, from "At the Fishhouses" to "Poem," teach us to do: attend to the apparently unremarkable thing and discover what knowledge it holds.

NOTES

1. Six reviews of *North & South*, including those cited in the main text, are collected in Schwartz and Estess 177-93.
2. Rosenbaum notes that Bishop's phrase "was partially ironic, given the small income generated by sales of poetry, but nevertheless indicated her discomfort with the commercial and institutional aspects of the profession" (63).
3. Bishop's career also lined up with the concomitant devaluation of some professional fields as women moved into them and with widespread wage and salary discrimination against working women in the United States. A recent report by feminist historian Heidi Hartmann for the Institute for Women's Policy Research includes relevant longer trend lines on women's work and pay in relation to men's, as well as the correlation of work and pay with level of education. In a related vein, Bethany Hicok tracks Bishop's undergraduate education at Vassar, in the early 1930s, amid the backlash against women's education that followed on women's suffrage (Degrees of Freedom). Finally, my emphasis on women's professional history does not mean to downplay the specific history of gay women—or of queer people broadly—in postwar workplaces in the United States. Margot Canaday unearths this history in her book-in-progress, Pink Precariat: LGBT Workers in the Shadow of Civil Rights, 1945-2000.
4. Bourdieu writes, "To understand the practices of writers and artists, and not least their products, entails understanding that they are the result of the meeting of two histories: the history of the positions they occupy and the history of their dispositions. Although position helps to shape dispositions, the latter, in so far as they are the product of independent conditions, have an existence and efficacy of their own and can help to shape positions. In no field is the confrontation between positions and dispositions more continuous and uncertain than in the literary and artistic field" (61). Only one "position," Consultant in Poetry to the Library of Congress, has much traction in the Bishop scholarship. See, for two examples, Roman 115-40; Javadizadeh, "Institutionalization" 130-39.
5. On Bishop's professional arrival, and for a reliable biographical chronicle of milestones in Bishop's professional career, see Millier, Elizabeth Bishop 187-88 and passim.
6. Statistics are tallied from the website of the Guggenheim Foundation, which provides a searchable database of fellows. In 2018, 50.4% of Guggenheim Fellows in the Creative Arts (US & Canada) identified as women, https://www.gf.org/fellows/all-fellows/, accessed 30 Apr. 2019.
7. Several of Bishop's drafts and notes toward revising her 1977 Guggenheim application indicate

that she had clerical help in preparing the materials, likely from Methfessel. At one point, on a mostly typescript sheet mapping out the various elements of the application, Bishop noted that the required list of publications "seems to be taken care of by the section called 'Books'" in the statement of accomplishments. Methfessel dutifully prepared a separate list of publications anyway. At another point on the same page, Bishop asked "you" to compile her statement of accomplishments out of "<u>everything</u> on that curriculum vitae (?) you have so kindly made out for me, that comes after my birth and 'Vassar College 1934'" (VC 40.7). Judging by its dating and the document format, this "curriculum vitae (?)" likely refers to a clean typescript chronology of Bishop's personal and professional life in VC 122.5.

Works Cited

Allen, Paula Gunn. "The Sacred Hoop: A Contemporary Perspective." *The Ecocriticism Reader: Landmarks in Literary Ecology,* edited by Cheryll Glotfelty and Harold Fromm, U of Georgia P, 1996, pp. 241-62.
Anderson, Linda R. *Elizabeth Bishop: Lines of Connection.* Edinburgh UP, 2013.
Andreoni, Manuela. "Chronic Neglect Made Museum Fire 'Bound to Happen.'" *The New York Times,* 4 Sept. 2018, p. A8.
Andrews, Malcolm. "The Metropolitan Picturesque." *The Politics of the Picturesque,* edited by Stephen Copley and Peter Garside, Cambridge UP, 1994, pp. 282-98.
Araújo, Homero José Vizeu. *O poema no sistema: A peculiaridade do antilírico João Cabral na poesia brasileira.* Porto Alegre: UFRGS, 2002.
Ashbery, John. "The Complete Poems." *Elizabeth Bishop and Her Art,* edited by Lloyd Schwartz and Sybil P. Estess, U of Michigan P, 1983, pp. 201-05.
Athayde, Félix de. *Idéias fixas de João Cabral de Melo Neto.* Rio de Janeiro: Editora Nova Fronteira, 1998.
Axelrod, Steven G. "Was Elizabeth a Racist?" *"In Worcester, Massachusetts": Essays on Elizabeth Bishop: From the 1997 Elizabeth Bishop Conference at WPI,* edited by Laura Jehn Menides and Angela G. Dorenkamp, Peter Lang, 1999, pp. 345-56.
Bailey, Iain. "Allusion and Exogenesis: The Labouring Heart of Samuel Beckett's *Ill Seen Ill Said.*" *The Boundaries of the Literary Archive: Reclamation and Representation,* edited by Carrie Smith and Lisa Stead, Ashgate, 2013, pp. 31-43.
Bandeirantes. "História." bandeirantes.org.br/historia.
Barry, Sandra. *Elizabeth Bishop: An Archival Guide to Her Life in Nova Scotia.* The Elizabeth Bishop Society of Nova Scotia, 1996.
---. *Elizabeth Bishop: Nova Scotia's "Home-made" Poet.* Nimbus, 2011.
---. "Lifting Yesterday—Supplement—Chapters 9 and 10: Old Volcanoes." *The Elizabeth Bishop Centenary,* 2 Aug. 2015, http://elizabethbishopcentenary.blogspot.com.
Bell, Pearl K. "Dona Elizabetchy: A Memoir of Elizabeth Bishop." *Partisan Review,* vol. 58, no. 1, 1991, pp. 29-52.
Bennett, Jane. *Vibrant Matter: A Political Ecology of Things.* Duke UP, 2010.
Biele, Joelle. "'Like Working without Really Doing It': Elizabeth Bishop's Brazil Letters and Poems." *The Antioch Review,* vol. 67, no. 1, 2009, pp. 90-98.

Bishop, Elizabeth. *The Ballad of the Burglar of Babylon*. Farrar, Straus and Giroux, 1968.

---. "The Burglar of Bablyon." *The New Yorker*, 21 Nov. 1964, pp. 56-57.

---. *The Collected Prose*. Farrar, Straus and Giroux, 1984.

---. *The Complete Poems*. Farrar, Straus and Giroux, 1992.

---. *The Complete Poems, 1927-1979*. Farrar, Straus and Giroux, 1983.

---. *Conversations with Elizabeth Bishop*. Edited by George Monteiro, UP of Mississippi, 1996.

---. *Edgar Allan Poe & the Juke-Box: Uncollected Poems, Drafts, and Fragments*. Edited by Alice Quinn, Farrar, Straus and Giroux, 2006.

---. *Elizabeth Bishop and* The New Yorker: *The Complete Correspondence*. Edited by Joelle Biele, Farrar, Straus and Giroux, 2011.

---. Elizabeth Bishop Papers. Archives and Special Collections Library, Vassar College Libraries, Poughkeepsie, New York. https://bit.ly/2NPRRNx.

---. *Exchanging Hats*. Edited by William Benton, Farrar, Straus and Giroux, 1996.

---. *Exchanging Hats*. Edited by William Benton, Farrar, Straus and Giroux, 2011

---. *North & South*. Houghton Mifflin, 1946.

---. "A Note on the Poetry." *Poetry*, vol. 103, nos. 1/2, 1963, p. 18.

---. *One Art: Letters*. Edited by Robert Giroux, Farrar, Straus and Giroux, 1994.

---. "On the Railroad Named Delight." *The New York Times Magazine*, 7 Mar. 1965, pp. 30-31, 84-86.

---. *Poems*. Farrar, Straus and Giroux, 2011.

---. *Poems, Prose, and Letters*. Edited by Robert Giroux and Lloyd Schwartz, Library of America, 2008.

---. *Prose*. Edited by Lloyd Schwartz, Farrar, Straus and Giroux, 2011.

Bishop, Elizabeth, and Emanuel Brasil, editors. *An Anthology of Twentieth-Century Brazilian Poetry*. Wesleyan UP, 1972.

Bishop, Elizabeth, and the Editors of *Life*. *Brazil*. Life World Library, Time Incorporated, 1962.

Bishop, Elizabeth, and Robert Lowell. *Words in Air: The Complete Correspondence between Elizabeth Bishop and Robert Lowell*. Edited by Thomas Travisano with Saskia Hamilton, Farrar, Straus and Giroux, 2008.

Bjornerud, Marcia. *Reading the Rocks: The Autobiography of the Earth*. Westview Press, 2005.

Bogan, Louise. "On *North & South*." *Elizabeth Bishop and Her Art*, edited by Lloyd Schwartz and Sybil P. Estess, U of Michigan P, 1983, pp. 182-83.

Bossis, Mireille, and Karen McPherson. "Methodological Journeys through Correspondence." *Men/Women of Letters*, special issue of *Yale French Studies*, no. 71, 1986, pp. 63-75.

Bourdieu, Pierre. *The Field of Cultural Production: Essays on Art and Literature*. Edited by Randal Johnson, Columbia UP, 1993.

Braga, Hermide Menquini. *O sagrado e o profano em* Morte e vida Severina. São Paulo: Zouk, 2002.

Brandellero, Sara. *On a Knife-edge: The Poetry of João Cabral de Melo Neto*. Oxford UP, 2011.

Brant, Alice Dayrell. *The Diary of "Helena Morley."* 1957. Translated by Elizabeth Bishop, Farrar, Straus and Giroux, 1995.

"Brazilian Airliner Is Hijacked by Five." *The New York Times*, 2 Jan. 1970, www.nytimes.com/1970/01/02/archives/brazilian-airliner-is-hijacked-by-five.html.

Brinnin, John Malcolm, and Bill Read, editors. *The Modern Poets: An American-British Anthology*. 2nd ed., photographs by Rollie McKenna, McGraw-Hill, 1970.

Brown, Ashley. "Elizabeth Bishop in Brazil." *Elizabeth Bishop and Her Art*, edited by Lloyd Schwartz and Sybil P. Estess, U of Michigan P, 1983, pp. 223-40.

Buckland, Lucy. "All Dressed Up with No Place to Reign: Unseen Portrait of Edward VIII in Royal

Robes after the Coronation That Never Was." *Daily Mail*, 10 Dec. 2011, http://www.dailymail.com.uk/news/article-2072480/Unseen-portrait-Edward-VIII-royal-robes-Coronation-was.html. Accessed Feb. 2018.

Bystrom, Kerry, and Joseph R. Slaughter. *The Global South Atlantic*. Fordham UP, 2018.

Cabral de Melo Neto, João. *Education by Stone: Selected Poems*. Translated by Richard Zenith, Archipelago, 2005.

---. *Obra completa*. Edited by Marly de Oliveira, Rio de Janeiro: Editora Nova Aguilar, 1994.

Campos, Haroldo de. "The Geometry of Commitment." *The Rigors of Necessity: João Cabral de Melo Neto, 1992 Neustadt Prize Laureate*, special issue of *World Literature Today*, vol. 66, no. 4, 1992, pp. 617-21.

---. *Metalinguagem e outras metas*. 4th ed., São Paulo: Perspectiva, 1992.

Carlyle, Jane Welsh. *I Too Am Here: Selections from the Letters of Jane Welsh Carlyle*. Edited by Alan and Mary Simpson, Cambridge UP, 1977.

Carvalho, Ricardo Souza de. *A Espanha de João Cabral e Murilo Mendes*. São Paulo: Editora 34, 2011.

Clark, Evert. "Eclipse Depicted in Moon Photos." *The New York Times*, 24 May 1967, p. 50.

Cleghorn, Angus. "Bishop's 'Wiring Fused': 'Bone Key' and 'Pleasure Seas.'" *Elizabeth Bishop in the 21st Century: Reading the New Editions*, edited by Angus Cleghorn et al., U of Virginia P, 2012, pp. 69-87.

Cleghorn, Angus, et al., editors. *Elizabeth Bishop in the 21st Century: Reading the New Editions*. U of Virginia P, 2012.

Cohen, Jeffrey Jerome. "Anarky." *Anthropocene Reading: Literary History in Geologic Times*, edited by Tobias Menely and Jesse Oak Taylor, The Pennsylvania State UP, 2017, pp. 25-42.

Colebrook, Claire. "The Anthropocene and the Archive." *Durham University Memory Network*, the memorynetwork.net/the-anthropocene-and-the-archive/. Accessed 17 Oct. 2018.

Colson, Theodore. "'Over 2,000 Illustrations and a Complete Concordance': A McLuhan Mosaic." *Divisions of the Heart: Elizabeth Bishop and the Art of Memory and Place*, edited by Sandra Barry et al., Gaspereau Press, 2001.

Comins, Barbara. "'Shuddering Insights: Bishop and Surprise.'" *"In Worcester Massachusetts": Essays on Elizabeth Bishop*, 1997 Elizabeth Bishop Conference at WPI, edited by Laura Jehn Menides and Angela G. Dorenkamp, Peter Lang, 1999, pp. 177-86.

Commoner, Barry. *The Closing Circle: Nature, Man, and Technology*. Knopf, 1971.

Cook, Eleanor. *Elizabeth Bishop at Work*. Harvard UP, 2016.

Copley, Stephen. "William Gilpin and the Black-Lead Mine." *The Politics of the Picturesque*, edited by Stephen Copley and Peter Garside, Cambridge UP, 1994, pp. 42-61.

Copley, Stephen, and Peter Garside. Introduction. *The Politics of the Picturesque*, edited by Stephen Copley and Peter Garside, Cambridge UP, 1994, pp. 1-12.

Costa, Cristina Henrique da. *Imaginando João Cabral imaginando*. Campinas, São Paulo: Editora Unicamp, 2014.

Costello, Bonnie. *Elizabeth Bishop: Questions of Mastery*. Harvard UP, 1991.

---. "Elizabeth Bishop's Impersonal Personal." *American Literary History*, vol. 15, no. 2, 2003, pp. 334-66.

Craft Revival: Shaping Western North Carolina Past and Present. Hunter Library Digital Initiatives at Western North Carolina University, www.wcu.edu/library/DigitalCollections/CraftRevival/index.htm. Accessed 23 May 2019.

Craven, Louise. "From the Archivist's Cardigan to the Very Dead Sheep: What Are Archives? What Are Archivists? What Do They do?" *What Are Archives?: Cultural and Theoretical Perspectives: A Reader*, edited by Louise Craven, Routledge, 2008, pp. 7-30.

Crowley, Ralph M., and Maurice R. Green. "Revolution within Psychoanalysis: A History of the William Alanson White Institute." Unpublished typescript, *Erich Fromm Online,* opus4.kobv.de/opus4-Fromm/frontdoor/index/index/start/0/rows/10/sortfield/score/sortorder/desc/searchtype/simple/query/revolution+white+institute/docId/24509. Accessed 29 Aug. 2018.

Crumbley, Paul, and Patricia M. Gantt, editors. *Body My House: May Swenson's Work and Life*. Utah State UP, 2006.

Csikszentmihalyi, Mihaly. "Why We Need Things." *History from Things: Essays on Material Culture,* edited by Steven Lubar and W. David Kingery, Smithsonian Institution P, 1993, pp. 20-29.

Curry, Renée R. *White Women Writing White: H.D., Elizabeth Bishop, Sylvia Plath, and Whiteness*. Greenwood Press, 2000.

Cushman, Philip. *Constructing the Self, Constructing America: A Cultural History of Psychotherapy*. Addison-Wesley, 1995.

Davis, Darién J., editor. *Beyond Slavery: The Multilayered Legacy of Africans in Latin America and the Caribbean*. Rowman & Littlefield, 2006.

Davis, Elmer. "Another Caribbean Conquest." *Harper's,* vol. 158, January 1929, pp. 168-76.

---. "New World Symphony with a Few Sour Notes." *Harper's,* vol. 170, May 1935, pp. 641-52.

Delpar, Helen. *The Enormous Vogue of Things Mexican: Cultural Relations between the United States and Mexico, 1920-1935*. U of Alabama P, 1992.

De Man, Paul. "Semiology and Rhetoric." *Diacritics,* vol. 3, no. 3, 1973, pp. 27-33.

Deppman, Jed, Daniel Ferrer, and Michael Groden, editors. *Genetic Criticism: Texts and Avant-textes*. U of Pennsylvania P, 2004.

Derrida, Jacques. "Archive Fever: A Freudian Impression." *Diacritics,* vol. 25, no. 2, 1995, pp. 9-63.

---. "Des Tours de Babel." Translated by Joseph F. Graham, *Difference in Translation,* edited by Joseph F. Graham, Cornell UP, 1985, pp. 165-207.

Dewey, John. *Art as Experience*. Penguin, 2005.

Dickie, Margaret. "Elizabeth Bishop: Text and Subtext." *South Atlantic Review,* vol. 59, no. 4, Nov. 1994, pp. 1-19.

Dickinson, Emily. *Open Me Carefully: Emily Dickinson's Intimate Letters to Susan Huntington Dickinson*. Edited by Martha Nell Smith and Ellen Louise Hart, Paris Press, 1998.

Doreski, C. K. *Elizabeth Bishop: The Restraints of Language*. Oxford UP, 1993.

Duncan, Carol. "Art Museums and the Ritual of Citizenship." *Exhibiting Cultures: The Poetics and Politics of Museum Display,* edited by Ivan Karp and Steven D. Lavine, Smithsonian Institution P, 1991, pp. 88-103.

Dutra e Silva, Sandro. "'Heroes' of the *Sertão*: The *Bandeirantes* as a Symbolic Category for the Study of Brazilian West Colonization." *Revista Territórios & Fronteiras, Cuiabá,* vol. 11, no. 1, 2018, pp. 60-76.

Dyer, Geoff. *Yoga for People Who Can't Be Bothered to Do It*. Canongate, 2003.

Edelman, Lee. "The Geography of Gender: Elizabeth Bishop's 'In the Waiting Room.'" *Contemporary Literature,* vol. 26, no. 2, Summer 1985, pp. 179-96.

---. *Homographesis: Essays in Gay Literary and Cultural History*. Routledge, 1994.

Eliot, T. S. "The Love Song of J. Alfred Prufrock." *Poetry,* vol. vi, no. iii, June 1915, pp. 130-35.

Elkin, Lauren. *Flâneuse: Women Walk the City in Paris, New York, Tokyo, Venice and London*. Chatto and Windus, 2016.

Ellis, Jonathan. *Art and Memory in the Work of Elizabeth Bishop*. Ashgate, 2006.

---, editor. *Letter Writing Among Poets: From William Wordsworth to Elizabeth Bishop*. Edinburgh UP, 2016.

---. "Reading Bishop Reading Darwin." *Science in Modern Poetry: New Directions,* edited by J. Holmes, Liverpool UP, 2012, pp. 181-93.

Ellison, Ralph. "What America Would Be Like Without Blacks." *Time,* vol. 95, no. 14, 6 Apr. 1970.

Emre, Merve. *Paraliterary: The Making of Bad Readers in Postwar America.* U of Chicago P, 2017.

England, George Allan. "America's Island of Felicity." *Travel,* vol. 50, no. 3, January 1929, pp. 3-17, 43-44.

Epperson, Gordon. *The Mind of Edmund Gurney.* Fairleigh Dickinson UP, 1997.

Erkkila, Betsy. "Elizabeth Bishop, Modernism, and the Left." *American Literary History,* vol. 8, no. 2, Summer 1996, pp. 284-310.

Evans, F. Barton III. *Harry Stack Sullivan: Interpersonal Theory and Psychotherapy.* Routledge, 1996.

Faderman, Lillian. "Who Hid Lesbian History?" *Frontiers,* vol. 4, no. 3, 1979, pp. 74-76.

Filene, Benjamin. *Romancing the Folk: Public Memory & American Roots Music.* U of North Carolina P, 2000.

Florida: A Guide to the Southernmost State. Compiled and written by the Federal Writers' Project of the Work Projects Administration for the State of Florida, Oxford UP, 1939.

Foote, Kenneth E. "To Remember and Forget: Archives, Memory, and Culture." *American Archivist,* vol. 53, no. 3, Summer 1990, pp. 378-92.

Fountain, Gary, and Peter Brazeau. *Remembering Elizabeth Bishop: An Oral Biography.* U of Massachusetts P, 1994.

Frankenberg, Lloyd. "Our Complex Complexes." Review of *Psychoanalysis: Its Evolution and Development,* by Clara Thompson, *The New York Times,* 23 Apr. 1950, www.nytimes.com/1950/04/23/archives/our-complex-complexes.html. Accessed 29 Aug. 2018 (subscription required).

---. "Theories of Analysis." Review of *Oedipus—Myth and Complex: A Review of Psychoanalytic Theory,* by Patrick Mullahy, Introduction by Erich Fromm, *The New York Times,* 13 Mar. 1949, www.nytimes.com/1949/03/13/archives/theories-of-analysis-oedipus-myth-and-complex-by-patrick-mullahy.html. Accessed 29 Aug. 2018 (subscription required).

---. "A Theory of 'Interpersonal Relations.'" Review of *Conceptions of Modern Psychiatry,* by Harry Stack Sullivan, with a Critical Appraisal of the Theory by Patrick Mullahy, *The New York Times,* 3 Aug. 1947, www.nytimes.com/1947/08/03/archives/a-theory-of-interpersonal-relations-concep|tions-of-modern.html. Accessed 29 Aug. 2018 (subscription required).

Freedman, Estelle B. "'The Burning of Letters Continues': Elusive Identities and the Historical Construction of Sexuality." *Journal of Women's History,* vol. 9, no. 4, 1998, pp. 181-200.

Freyre, Gilberto. *The Mansions and the Shanties: The Making of Modern Brazil.* Translated by Harriet de Onís, Knopf, 1963. Vassar College Special Collections.

Friedel, Robert. "Some Matters of Substance." *History from Things: Essays on Material Culture,* edited by Steven Lubar and W. David Kingery, Smithsonian Institution P, 1993, pp. 41-50.

Frost, Robert. *In the Clearing.* Holt, Rinehart and Winston, 1962.

Fuss, Diana. "How to Lose Things: Elizabeth Bishop's Child Mourning." *Post 45,* 23 Sept. 2013, http://post45.research.yale.edu/2013/09/how-to-lose-things-elizabeth-bishops-child-mourning/. Accessed 29 Aug. 2018.

Gilbert, Roger. "Framing Water: Historical Knowledge in Elizabeth Bishop and Adrienne Rich." *Twentieth Century Literature,* vol. 43, no. 2, Summer 1997, pp. 144-61.

Gilman, Charlotte Perkins. *Charlotte Perkins Gilman's* In This Our World *& Uncollected Poems.* Edited by Gary Scharnhorst and Denise D. Knight, Syracuse UP, 2012.

Gilpin, William. "Three Essays and a Poem." *The Picturesque: Literary Sources and Documents,* edited by Malcolm Andrews, vol. 2, Helm Information, 1994, pp. 5-60.

Goldberg, Susan. "For Decades, Our Coverage Was Racist: To Rise above Our Past, We Must Acknowledge It." *National Geographic Magazine*, vol. 233, no. 4, Apr. 2018, www.nationalgeographic.com/magazine/2018/04/from-the-editor-race-racism-history/. Accessed 5 Apr. 2019.

Goldensohn, Lorrie. "Approaching Elizabeth Bishop's Letters to Ruth Foster." *Yale Review*, vol. 103, no. 1, January 2015, pp. 1-19.

---. "The Body's Roses: Race, Sex, and Gender in Elizabeth Bishop's Representations of the Self." *Elizabeth Bishop: The Geography of Gender*, edited by Marilyn May Lombardi, U of Virginia P, 1993, pp. 70-90.

---. *Elizabeth Bishop: The Biography of a Poetry*. Columbia UP, 1992.

---. "Elizabeth Bishop's Drafts: 'That Sense of Constant Readjustment.'" *Elizabeth Bishop in the 21st Century: Reading the New Editions*, edited by Angus Cleghorn et al., U of Virginia P, 2012, pp. 104-16.

---. "Elizabeth Bishop's Written Pictures, Painted Poems." *"In Worcester, Massachusetts": Essays on Elizabeth Bishop*, from the 1997 Elizabeth Bishop Conference at WPI, edited by Laura Jehn Menides and Angela G. Dorenkamp, Peter Lang, 1999, pp. 167-75.

---. "In the Footsteps of Elizabeth Bishop '34 in Brazil." *Vassar Quarterly*, vol. 88, no. 1, Winter 1991, pp. 22-27. vq.vassar.edu/docs/pdf-archives/vq_19911201PascalStGerard.pdf.

Goldman, David L. "Dorothea Dix and Her Two Missions of Mercy in Nova Scotia." *Canadian Journal of Psychiatry. Revue canadienne de psychiatrie*, vol. 35, no. 2, March 1990, pp. 139-43.

Gonçalves, Aguinaldo José. "João Cabral de Melo Neto and Modernity." *The Rigors of Necessity: João Cabral de Melo Neto, 1992 Neustadt Prize Laureate*, special issue of *World Literature Today*, vol. 66, no. 4, 1992, pp. 639-43.

Good, Katie Day. "From Scrapbook to Facebook: A History of Personal Media Assemblage and Archives." *New Media & Society*, vol. 15, no. 4, 2012, pp. 557-73.

Gould, Stephen Jay. *Time's Arrow, Times Cycle: Myth and Metaphor in the Discovery of Geological Time*. Harvard UP, 1987.

Graves, Ralph. "Helping to Solve Our Allies' Food Problem: America Calls for a Million Young Soldiers of the Commissary to Volunteer for Service in 1918." *National Geographic Magazine*, vol. 33, no. 2, February 1918, pp. 170-94.

Gray, Jeffrey. *Mastery's End: Travel and Postwar American Poetry*. U of Georgia P, 2005.

---. "Postcards and Sunsets: Bishop's Revision and the Problem of Excess." *Elizabeth Bishop in the 21st Century: Reading the New Editions*, edited by Angus Cleghorn et al., U of Virginia P, 2012, pp. 26-40.

Greenberg, Jay R., and Stephen A. Mitchell. *Object Relations in Psychoanalytic Theory*. Harvard UP, 1983-.

Halberstam, Jack (as Judith). *Female Masculinity*. Duke UP, 1998.

Hammer, Langdon. "Useless Concentration: Life and Work in Elizabeth Bishop's Letters and Poems." *American Literary History*, vol. 9, no. 1, 1997, pp. 162-80.

Harrison, Victoria. *Elizabeth Bishop's Poetics of Intimacy*. Cambridge UP, 1993.

Hartmann, Heidi. "The Economic Status of Women in the U.S.: What Has Changed in the Last 20-40 Years." Institute for Women's Policy Research, 28 Mar. 2018, iwpr.org/wp-content/uploads/2018/04/GAO-Research-Presentation-March-2018_Heidi-Hartmann.pdf. Accessed 3 Sept. 2018.

Helle, Anita. "Lessons from the Archive: Sylvia Plath and the Politics of Memory." *Feminist Studies*, vol. 31, no 3, Fall 2005, pp. 631-52.

---, editor. *The Unraveling Archive: Essays on Sylvia Plath*. U of Michigan P, 2007.

Hemingway, Ernest. *A Moveable Feast*. 1964. Scribner, 2009.

Hicok, Bethany. "Becoming a Poet: From North to South." *The Cambridge Companion to Elizabeth Bishop,* edited by Angus Cleghorn and Jonathan Ellis, Cambridge UP, 2014, pp. 111-23.

---. *Degrees of Freedom: American Women Poets and the Women's College, 1905–1955.* Bucknell UP, 2008.

---. *Elizabeth Bishop's Brazil.* U of Virginia P, 2016.

---. Unpublished essay on the Foster letters.

Horney, Karen. *The Neurotic Personality of Our Time.* Norton, 1937.

Houaiss, Antônio, and Mauro de Salles Villar. *Dicionário Houaiss de Língua Portuguesa.* Rio de Janeiro: Objetiva, 2001.

Howard, Richard. "Comment on 'In the Waiting Room' and Herbert's 'Love Unknown.'" *Elizabeth Bishop and Her Art,* edited by Lloyd Schwartz and Sybil Estess, U of Michigan P, 1983, pp. 208-09.

Hughes, Charles L. *Country Soul: Making Music and Making Race in the American South.* U of North Carolina P, 2015.

Ijima, Brenda. *Eco Language Reader.* Nightboat Books, 2010.

Jack, Homer A. "When Joe and Ivan Sit Down to Talk: Is It Hopeless?" *The New York Times,* 16 Sept. 1962, pp. 29, 94, 95.

Jacobs, Jane. *The Death and Life of Great American Cities.* Random House, 1961.

Jacobus, Mary. *Psychoanalysis and the Scene of Reading.* Oxford UP, 1999.

Jarrell, Randall. "On *North & South.*" *Elizabeth Bishop and Her Art,* edited by Lloyd Schwartz and Sybil P. Estess, U of Michigan P, 1983, pp. 180-81.

Javadizadeh, Kamran. "Elizabeth Bishop's Closet Drama." *Arizona Quarterly,* vol. 67, no. 3, 2011, pp. 119-50.

---. "The Institutionalization of the Postwar Poet," *Modernism/modernity,* vol. 23, no. 1, 2016, pp. 113-39.

Jimerson, Randall C., editor. *American Archival Studies: Readings in Theory and Practice.* Society of American Archivists, 2000.

Johnson, Osa. *I Married Adventure.* 1940. Kodansha, 1997.

Kalstone, David. *Becoming a Poet: Elizabeth Bishop with Marianne Moore and Robert Lowell.* Farrar, Straus and Giroux, 1989.

Kansas Historical Society. "Martin and Osa Johnson." www.kshs.org/kansapedia/martin-and-osa-johnson/12102. Modified Dec. 2012. Accessed 14 Mar. 2018.

Kaplan, Carla. *Miss Anne in Harlem: The White Women of the Black Renaissance.* Harper, 2013.

Kennedy, Stetson. *Grits & Grunts: Folkloric Key West.* Pineapple Press, 2008.

Kindley, Evan. *Poet-Critics and the Administration of Culture.* Harvard UP, 2017.

Kirsch, Adam. *The Modern Element: Essays on Contemporary Poetry.* Norton, 2008.

Klein, Melanie, and Joan Riviere. *Love, Hate and Reparation: Two Lectures.* Hogarth Press, 1937.

Knudson, R. R., and Suzzanne Bigelow. *May Swenson: A Poet's Life in Photos.* Utah State UP, 1996.

Kwawer, Jay S. "Origins, Theory, and Practice: 1943–Present." *William Alanson White Institute of Psychiatry, Psychoanalysis, and Psychology,* www.wawhite.org/index.php?page=our-history. Accessed 29 Aug. 2018.

Labio, Catherine. "Woman Viewing a Letter." *L'Esprit Créateur,* vol. 40, no. 4, 2000, pp. 7-12.

Lauer, Claire. "Contending with Terms: 'Multimodal' and 'Multimedia' in the Academic and Public Spheres." *Computers and Composition,* vol. 26, no. 4, 2009, pp. 225-39.

Launius, Roger D. "Public Opinion Polls and Perceptions of US Human Spaceflight." *Space Policy,* vol. 19, no. 3, 2003, pp. 163-75.

Le Corbusier. *Towards a New Architecture.* Translated by Frederick Etchells, Dover, 1986.

Lensing, George S. "Elizabeth Bishop and Flannery O'Connor: Minding and Mending in a Fallen World." *Elizabeth Bishop in the 21st Century: Reading the New Editions*, edited by Angus Cleghorn et al., U of Virginia P, 2012, pp. 186-203.

Logan, William. "Elizabeth Bishop at Summer Camp." *Guilty Knowledge, Guilty Pleasure: The Dirty Art of Poetry*, Columbia UP, 2014, pp. 250-302.

---. "'I Write Entirely for You.'" *The New York Times*, 31 Oct. 2008.

---. "The Unbearable Lightness of Elizabeth Bishop." *Southwest Review*, vol. 79, no. 1, Winter 1994, pp. 120-38.

Lombardi, Marilyn May. *The Body and the Song; Elizabeth Bishop's Poetics*. Southern Illinois UP, 1995.

---, editor. Elizabeth Bishop: The Geography of Gender. U of Virginia P, 1993.

MacArthur, Marit J. *The American Landscape in the Poetry of Frost, Bishop, and Ashbery: The House Abandoned*. Palgrave, 2008.

---. "One World? The Poetics of Passenger Flight and the Perception of the Global." *PMLA*, vol. 127, no. 2, 2012, pp. 264-82.

MacCannell, Dean. *The Tourist: A New Theory of the Leisure Class*. Rev. ed., Schocken, 1989.

Machova, Mariana. *Elizabeth Bishop and Translation*. Lexington Books, 2017.

Macksey, Richard, and Eugenio Donato, editors. *The Languages of Criticism and the Sciences of Man: The Structuralist Controversy*. Johns Hopkins UP, 1970.

Malamud, Bernard. *The Magic Barrel*. Farrar, Straus and Cudahy, 1958.

Maquet, Jacques. "Objects as Instruments, Objects as Signs." *History from Things: Essays on Material Culture*, edited by Steven Lubar and W. David Kingery, Smithsonian Institution P, 1993, pp. 30-40.

Markowitz, Gerald, and David Rosner. *Children, Race, and Power: Kenneth and Mamie Clark's Northside Center*. U of Virginia P, 1996.

Marrs, Cody. "Dickinson in the Anthropocene." *ESQ: A Journal of Nineteenth-Century American Literature and Culture*, vol. 63, no. 2, 2017, pp. 201-25.

Marshall, Daniel, et al. "Editors' Introduction: Queering Archives: Historical Unravelings." *Radical History Review*, vol. 2014, no. 120, Fall 2014, pp. 1-11.

Marshall, Megan. "Elizabeth and Alice: The Last Love Affair of Elizabeth Bishop, and the Losses Behind 'One Art.'" *The New Yorker*, 27 Oct. 2016.

---. *Elizabeth Bishop: A Miracle for Breakfast*. Houghton Mifflin Harcourt, 2017.

Mazzaro, Jerome. "Elizabeth Bishop and the Poetics of Impediment." *Salmagundi*, no. 27, 1974, pp. 118-44.

McCabe, Susan. *Elizabeth Bishop: Her Poetics of Loss*. Pennsylvania State UP, 1994.

---. "Survival of the Queerly Fit: Darwin, Marianne Moore, and Elizabeth Bishop." *Twentieth Century Literature*, vol. 55, no. 4, 2009, pp. 547-71.

McClay, B. D. "'This Suffering Business': The Lives of Robert Lowell & Elizabeth Bishop." *Commonweal*, vol. 144, no. 8, 2017, pp. 23-25.

McGurl, Mark. *The Program Era: Postwar Fiction and the Rise of Creative Writing*. Harvard UP, 2011.

McIntosh, Hugh. "Conventions of Closeness: Realism and the Creative Friendship of Elizabeth Bishop and Robert Lowell." *PMLA*, vol. 127, no. 2, 2012, pp. 231-47.

McKay, Don. "Ediacaran and Anthropocene: Poetry as a Reader of Deep Time." *Making the Geologic Now: Responses to Material Conditions of Contemporary Life*, edited by Elizabeth Ellsworth and Jamie Kruse, Punctum Books, 2013, pp. 46-54.

McKendrick, Jamie. "Bishop's Birds." *Elizabeth Bishop: Poet of the Periphery*, edited by Linda Anderson and Jo Shapcott, Bloodaxe Books, 2002, pp. 123-42.

Menely, Tobias, and Jesse Oak Taylor, editors. *Anthropocene Reading: Literary History in Geologic Times*. Pennsylvania State UP, 2017.

Merrill, James. Afterword. *Becoming a Poet: Elizabeth Bishop with Marianne Moore and Robert Lowell*, by David Kalstone, Farrar, Straus and Giroux, 1989, pp. 251-62.

---. "Elizabeth Bishop (1911-1979)." *The New York Review of Books*, vol. 26, no. 19, 6 Dec. 1979, reprinted in *Elizabeth Bishop and Her Art*, edited by Lloyd Schwartz and Sybil P. Estess, U of Michigan P, 1983, pp. 259-62.

Miller, Karl Hagstrom. *Segregating Sound: Inventing Folk and Pop Music in the Age of Jim Crow*. Duke UP, 2010.

Miller, Linda Patterson, editor. *Letters from the Lost Generation: Gerald and Sara Murphy and Friends*. Rutgers UP, 1991.

Millier, Brett C. *Elizabeth Bishop: Life and the Memory of It*. U of California P, 1993.

---. "Elusive Mastery: The Drafts of Elizabeth Bishop's 'One Art.'" *New England Review*, vol. 13, no. 2, 1990, pp. 121-29.

Mindlin, Henrique E. *Modern Architecture in Brazil*. Reinhold Publishing, 1956.

Mitchell, Stephen A., and Margaret J. Black. *Freud and Beyond: A History of Modern Psychoanalytic Thought*. BasicBooks, 1995.

Moe, Aaron M. *Zoopoetics: Animals and the Making of Poetry*. Lexington Books, 2014.

Monteiro, George. *Elizabeth Bishop in Brazil and After: A Poetic Career Transformed*. McFarland, 2012.

---. "Frost's Politics and the Cold War." *The Cambridge Companion to Robert Frost*, edited by Robert Faggen, Cambridge UP, 2001, pp. 221-39.

Moog, Vianna. *Bandeirantes and Pioneers*. Translated by L. L. Barrett, George Braziller, 1964.

Moore, Marianne. "A Modest Expert: *North & South*." *Elizabeth Bishop and Her Art*, edited by Lloyd Schwartz and Sybil P. Estess, U of Michigan P, 1983, pp. 177-79.

---. *New Collected Poems*. Edited by Heather Cass White, Farrar, Straus and Giroux, 2017.

---. *The Selected Letters of Marianne Moore*. Edited by Bonnie Costello et al., Knopf, 1997.

Morra, Linda M. *Unarrested Archives: Case Studies in Twentieth-Century Canadian Women's Authorship*. U of Toronto P, 2014.

Morse, Richard M., editor. *The Bandeirantes: The Historical Role of the Brazilian Pathfinders*. Knopf, 1965.

Moss, Howard. "All Praise." Review of *Questions of Travel*, by Elizabeth Bishop, *Kenyon Review*, vol. 28, no. 2, March 1966, pp. 255-62.

Mumford, Lewis. *The Condition of Man*. Harcourt, Brace, 1944.

Neely, Elizabeth. "*Cadela Carioca*: Bishop's 'Pink Dog' in Its Brasilian Cultural Context." *South Central Review*, vol. 31, no. 1, 2014, pp. 99-113.

Nesme, Axel. "The Ballad Revisited: Elizabeth Bishop's 'The Burglar of Babylon.'" *Cercles*, vol. 12, 2005, pp. 94-107.

Newman, Sally. "The Archival Traces of Desire: Vernon Lee's Failed Sexuality and the Interpretation of Letters in Lesbian History." *Journal of the History of Sexuality*, vol. 14, nos. 1/2, 2005, pp. 51-75.

Nunes, Benedito. *João Cabral: a máquina do poema*. Edited by Adalberto Müller. Brasília: Editora Universidade de Brasília, 2007.

Ogle, Maureen. *Key West: History of an Island of Dreams*. UP of Florida, 2003.

Page, Barbara, and Carmen L. Oliveira. "Foreign-Domestic: Elizabeth Bishop at Home/Not at Home in Brazil." *Elizabeth Bishop in the 21st Century: Reading the New Editions*, edited by Angus Cleghorn et al., U of Virginia P, 2012, pp. 117-32.

Patkus, Ronald. *From the Archive: Discovering Elizabeth Bishop*. Vassar College, 2011.

Paul, Catherine E. *Poetry in the Museums of Modernism: Yeats, Pound, Moore, Stein*. U of Michigan P, 2002.

Pecknold, Diane. *Hidden in the Mix: The African American Presence in Country Music*. Duke UP, 2013.

Phillips, Siobhan. "Bishop's Correspondence." *The Cambridge Companion to Elizabeth Bishop*, edited by Angus Cleghorn and Jonathan Ellis, Cambridge UP, 2014, 155-68.

---. "Elizabeth Bishop and the Ethics of Correspondence." *Modernism/modernity*, vol. 19, no. 2, 2012, pp. 343-63.

Pickard, Zachariah. *Elizabeth Bishop's Poetics of Description*. McGill-Queen's UP, 2009.

Pollak, Vivian R. *Our Emily Dickinsons: American Women Poets and the Intimacies of Difference*. U of Pennsylvania P, 2017.

Poulet, George. "Criticism and the Experience of Interiority." *The Languages of Criticism and the Sciences of Man: The Structuralist Controversy*, edited by Richard Macksey and Eugenio Donato, Johns Hopkins UP, 1970.

Price, Uvedale. *An Essay on the Picturesque: As Compared with the Sublime and the Beautiful; and on the Use of Studying Pictures, for the Purpose of Improving Real Landscape. The Picturesque: Literary Sources and Documents*. Edited by Malcolm Andrews, Vol. II, Helm Information, 1994, pp. 72-141.

Prosser, Jay. *Light in the Dark Room: Photography and Loss*. U of Minnesota P, 2005.

Przybycien, Regina. "Elizabeth Bishop in Brazil: Traveler, Ethnographer, and Castaway." *The Art of Elizabeth Bishop*, edited by Sandra Regina Goulart Almedia et al., Belo Horizonte: Editora UFMG, 2002, pp. 62-73.

Quinn, Alice. Introduction. *Edgar Allan Poe and the Juke-Box: Uncollected Poems, Drafts, and Fragments*, edited by Alice Quinn, Farrar, Straus and Giroux, 2006, pp. ix-xv.

Ravinthiran, Vidyan. *Elizabeth Bishop's Prosaic*. Bucknell UP, 2015.

Read, Justin. "Alternative Functions: João Cabral de Melo Neto and the Architectonics of Modernity." *Luso-Brazilian Review*, vol. 43, no. 1, 2006, pp. 65-93.

---. "Manners of Mistranslation: The *Antropofagismo* in Elizabeth Bishop's Prose and Poetry." *CR: The New Centennial Review*, vol. 3, no. 1, 2003, pp. 297-327.

Reston, James. "United Nations: U Thant's Gloomy Conclusions." *The New York Times*, 21 Sept. 1966, p. 46.

Ricardo, Cassiano. "Westward March." *The Bandeirantes: The Historical Role of the Pathfinders*, edited by Richard M. Morse, Knopf, 1965, pp. 191-211.

Rich, Adrienne. *Blood, Bread, and Poetry: Selected Prose, 1979-1985*. Norton, 1986.

---. "The Eye of the Outsider: The Poetry of Elizabeth Bishop." *Boston Review*, vol. 8, no. 2, 1983, pp. 15-17.

Rockwell, Norman. "Man on the Moon." *Look*, 10 Jan. 1967, front cover.

Rognoni, Francesco. "Reading Darwin: On Elizabeth Bishop's Marked Copies of *The Voyage of the Beagle* and *The Autobiography of Charles Darwin*." *Jarrell, Bishop, Lowell, & Co.*, edited by Suzanne Ferguson, U of Tennessee P, 2003, pp. 239-48.

Roman, Camille. *Elizabeth Bishop's World War II-Cold War View*. Palgrave, 2001.

Rosenbaum, Susan. "Elizabeth Bishop and the Miniature Museum." *Journal of Modern Literature*, vol. 28, no. 2, 2005, pp. 61-99.

Ruas, Eponina. *Conhecendo Ouro Prêto*. 4th ed., Belo Horizonte, 1952.

Ruhl, Sarah. *Dear Elizabeth: A Play in Letters from Elizabeth Bishop to Robert Lowell and Back Again*. Farrar, Straus and Giroux, 2014.

Sackville-West, Vita. *The Letters of Vita Sackville-West to Virginia Woolf*. Edited by Louise DeSalvo and Mitchell Leaska. Cleis Press, 2001.

Samuels, Peggy. "'Composing Motions': Elizabeth Bishop and Alexander Calder." *Elizabeth Bishop in the 21st Century: Reading the New Editions*, edited by Angus Cleghorn et al., U of Virginia P, 2012, pp. 153-69.

---. *Deep Skin: Elizabeth Bishop and Visual Art*. Cornell UP, 2010.

Saraíva, Arnaldo. *Dar a ver e a se ver no extremo – O poeta e a poesia de João Cabral de Melo Neto*. Porto: Centro de Investigação Transdisciplinar Cultura, Espaço e Memória, 2014.

Schmidt, Tyler T. *Desegregating Desire: Race and Sexuality in Cold War American Literature*. UP of Mississippi, 2013.

Schor, Naomi. "'Cartes Postales': Representing Paris 1900." *Critical Inquiry*, vol. 18, no. 2, Winter 1992, pp. 188-244.

Schwartz, Lloyd. "Back to Boston: *Geography III* and Other Late Poems." *The Cambridge Companion to Elizabeth Bishop*, edited by Angus Cleghorn and Jonathan Ellis, Cambridge UP, 2014, pp. 141-54.

Schwartz, Lloyd, and Sybil P. Estess, editors. *Elizabeth Bishop and Her Art*. U of Michigan P, 1983.

Seale, Lisa. "Meet the Press: Robert Frost as Pundit." *Robert Frost in Context*, edited by Mark Richardson, Cambridge UP, 2014, pp. 317-23.

Secchin, Antonio Carlos. *João Cabral de Melo Neto: uma fala só lâmina*. São Paulo: Cosac Naify, 2014.

Shaw, Fiona. *One Art: A Study of the Life and Writing of Elizabeth Bishop*. 1991. U of York, PhD dissertation.

Simpson, Mark. "Postcard Culture in America: The Traffic in Traffic." *The Oxford History of Popular Print Culture, Vol. 6: US Popular Print Culture 1860-1920*, edited by Christine Bold, Oxford UP, 2012, pp. 169-89.

Skidmore, Thomas E. *Brazil: Five Centuries of Change*. Oxford UP, 1999.

Smith, Barbara Herrnstein. *Poetic Closure: A Study of How Poems End*. U of Chicago P, 1968.

Smith, Carrie, and Lisa Stead, editors. *The Boundaries of the Literary Archive: Reclamation and Representation*. Ashgate, 2013.

Smith, Michael B. "'Silence, Miss Carson!': Science, Gender, and the Reception of *Silent Spring*." *Feminist Studies*, vol. 27, no. 3, Autumn 2001, pp. 733-52.

Spiegelman, Willard. "Elizabeth Bishop's 'Natural Heroism.'" *Elizabeth Bishop and Her Art*, edited by Lloyd Schwartz and Sybil P. Estess, U of Michigan P, 1983, pp. 154-71.

Steedman, Carolyn. *Dust: The Archive and Cultural Memory*. Manchester UP, 2001; Rutgers UP, 2002.

Stern, Donnel B. "Interpersonal Psychoanalysis: History and Current Status." *Contemporary Psychoanalysis*, vol. 53, no. 1, 2017, pp. 69-94.

Stevens, Wallace. *Collected Poetry and Prose*. Edited by Frank Kermode and Joan Richardson, Library of America, 1997.

---. *Letters of Wallace Stevens*. Edited by Holly Stevens, U of California P, 1996.

Stewart, Susan. *On Longing: Narratives of the Miniature, the Gigantic, the Souvenir, the Collection*. Johns Hopkins UP, 1984.

Sullivan, Harry Stack. *Conceptions in Modern Psychiatry*. With a critical appraisal of the theory by Patrick Mullahy, William Alanson White Psychiatric Foundation, 1947.

Swenson, May. *Collected Poems*. Edited by Langdon Hammer, Library of America, 2013.

---. *Dear Elizabeth: Five Poems & Three Letters to Elizabeth Bishop*. Utah State UP, 2000.

---. *Made with Words*. Edited by Gardner McFall, U of Michigan P, 1998.

---. *To Mix with Time*. Charles Scribner's Sons, 1963.

Theodor, Erwin. *Tradução: ofício e arte*. Editora Cultrix, Editora da Universidade de São Paulo, 1976.

Thompson, Clara. *Psychoanalysis: Evolution and Development*. Introduction by Patrick Mullahy, Hermitage House, 1950.

Thompson, Clive. "When Copy and Paste Reigned in the Age of Scrapbooking." *Smithsonian*, July 2014, https://www.smithsonianmag.com/history/when-copy-and-paste-reigned-age-scrapbooking-180951844/?all.

Tiffany, Francis. *Life of Dorothea Lynde Dix*. Houghton Mifflin, 1891. archive.org/details/lifeofdorothealy00tiffuoft. Accessed 29 Aug. 2018.

Travisano, Thomas. *Elizabeth Bishop: Her Artistic Development*. U of Virginia P, 1988.

---. "The Elizabeth Bishop Phenomenon." *New Literary History*, vol. 26, no. 4, 1995, pp. 903-30.

---. "Emerging Genius: Elizabeth Bishop and *The Blue Pencil*, 1927-1930." *Gettysburg Review*, vol. 5, no. 1, Winter 1992, pp. 32-47.

Treseler, Heather. "Dreaming in Color: Bishop's Notebook Letter-Poems." *Elizabeth Bishop in the 21st Century: Reading the New Editions*, edited by Angus Cleghorn et al., U of Virginia P, 2012, pp. 88-103.

---. *Lyric Letters: Elizabeth Bishop's Epistolary Poems*. 2010. U of Notre Dame, PhD dissertation. ProQuest Dissertations Publishing, 2010. 3436245.

---. "One Long Poem." *Boston Review*, 17 Aug. 2016.

Trott, Nicola. "The Picturesque, the Beautiful and the Sublime." *A Companion to Romanticism*, edited by Duncan Wu, Blackwell, 1998, pp. 72-90.

Tucker, Susan, et al. *The Scrapbook in American Life*. Temple UP, 2006.

Van Mierlo, Wim. "The Archaeology of the Manuscript: Towards Modern Palaeography." *The Boundaries of the Literary Archive: Reclamation and Representation*, edited by Carrie Smith and Lisa Stead, Ashgate, 2013, pp. 15-29.

Vassar College. *The Vassarion, 1934*. Graduating Class of 1934, Vassar College Library.

Vaught Brogan, Jacqueline. "Naming the Thief in 'Babylon': Elizabeth Bishop and 'The Moral of the Story.'" *Contemporary Literature*, vol. 42, no. 3, 2001, pp. 514-34.

Vendler, Helen. "The Art of Losing." Review of *Edgar Allan Poe & the Juke-Box: Uncollected Poems, Drafts, and Fragments*, by Elizabeth Bishop. *The New Republic*, 3 Apr. 2006, pp. 33-37.

Venuti, Lawrence. *The Translator's Invisibility: A History of Translation*. 3rd ed., Routledge, 2018.

Vider, Stephen. "Lesbian and Gay Marriage and Romantic Adjustment in the 1950s and 1960s United States." *Gender & History*, vol. 29, no. 3, 2017, pp. 693-715.

Wake, Naoko. *Private Practices: Harry Stack Sullivan, the Science of Homosexuality, and American Liberalism*. Rutgers UP, 2011.

White, Gillian. *Lyric Shame: The "Lyric" Subject of Contemporary American Poetry*. Harvard UP, 2014.

---. "Readerly Contingency in Bishop's Journals and Early Prose." *Twentieth Century Literature*, vol. 55, no. 3, Fall 2009, pp. 322-56.

Wilde, Oscar. *The Portable Oscar Wilde*. Edited by Richard Aldington and Stanley Weintraub, Viking Penguin, 1981.

Zona, Kirstin Hotelling. "Bishop: Race, Class, and Gender." *The Cambridge Companion to Elizabeth Bishop*, edited by Angus Cleghorn and Jonathan Ellis, Cambridge UP, 2014, pp. 49-61.

---. *Marianne Moore, Elizabeth Bishop & May Swenson: The Feminist Poetics of Self-Restraint*. U of Michigan P, 2002.

Contributors

Douglas Basford is Assistant Director of the Academic and Professional Writing Program at the University at Buffalo, SUNY. His critical prose, translations, and poetry have appeared in such places as *The FSG Book of Twentieth-Century Italian Poetry, Poetry, Two Lines, The National Poetry Review, Literary Matters, Metamorphoses, SubStance, Western Humanities Review*, and *Words without Borders*. He has received a National Endowment for the Arts Literature Translation Fellowship, two National Endowment for the Humanities summer program stipends, and scholarships from the Summer Literary Seminars, Bread Loaf, and Sewanee conferences.

Marvin Campbell is Assistant Professor of English at Fisk College, where he teaches African American literature. He has an essay in *The Wallace Stevens Journal* as well as contributions to edited volumes on Elizabeth Bishop from University of Edinburgh Press and Cambridge University Press.

Richard Flynn is Professor of English at Georgia Southern University in Statesboro, Georgia, where he teaches modern and contemporary poetry and literature for children and young adults. He is the author of a critical book, *Randall Jarrell and the Lost World of Childhood* (U of Georgia P, 1990), and a collection of poetry, *The Age of Reason* (Hawkhead Press, 1993). His articles and book chapters about contemporary poets include work about Randall Jarrell, Elizabeth Bishop, Robert Lowell, June Jordan, Gwendolyn Brooks, Muriel Rukeyser, Marilyn Nelson, and Jacqueline Woodson.

Sarah Giragosian is a poet and critic living in Schenectady, New York. She is the author of the poetry collections *Queer Fish* (Dream Horse Press, 2017), winner of the American Poetry Journal Book Prize, and *The Death Spiral* (Black Lawrence Press, forthcoming). Her criticism has appeared in several peer-reviewed journals, including *Interdisciplinary Literary Studies: A Journal of Criticism and Theory, Association for the Study of Evolutionary Biology and Ethical Behavior in Literature Journal,* and *TAB: The Journal of Poetry & Poetics.* She teaches in the Writing and Critical Inquiry program at the University at Albany-SUNY.

Bethany Hicok is Lecturer in English at Williams College. She is the author of *Elizabeth Bishop's Brazil* (U of Virginia P, 2016) and *Degrees of Freedom: American Women Poets and the Women's College, 1905-1955* (Bucknell UP, 2008) and co-editor of *Elizabeth Bishop in the 21st Century: Reading the New Editions* (U Virginia P, 2012). Her articles and book chapters on modern and contemporary poetry and literary history and archives have appeared in the *Journal of Modern Literature, Contemporary Literature, The Wallace Stevens Journal,* with Cambridge, and elsewhere. She is currently writing a book on feminist poetry and second wave feminism.

David Hoak is an independent scholar and the recipient of a 2019 Franklin Research Grant. His most recent work is centered on Bishop's significant correspondence, especially with May Swenson, Dorothee Bowie and Ruth Foster. He also transcribed and annotated the last letters of Lota de Macedo Soares to Bishop. This work is available to scholars in the Bishop archive at Vassar College and was the subject of a paper published in *PN Review*. In addition to his archival focus, Hoak is a vocalist for the online spoken poetry archive *Voetica*, for which he has recorded all of Bishop's published poetry.

Charla Allyn Hughes, like Elizabeth Bishop, graduated from Vassar College and used to call Florida-North Carolina-New York home. Charla recently defended her dissertation, *Fragments and Flânerie: Modernity, Cosmopolitanism, and the Art of Wandering,* earning her PhD in English with a graduate minor in Women's & Gender Studies from Louisiana State University, where she is currently a Post-doctoral Instructor in English. Her writing and photography can be found in travel journals such as *South East Asia Backpacker* and *Blacktop Passages*.

Alyse Knorr is Assistant Professor of English at Regis University and, since 2017, co-editor of Switchback Books. She is the author of the poetry collections *Mega-City Redux* (Green Mountains Review, 2017), *Copper Mother* (Switchback Books, 2016), and *Annotated Glass* (Furniture Press Books, 2013); the non-fiction book *Super Mario Bros. 3* (Boss Fight Books, 2016); and three poetry chapbooks. Her work has appeared in *Alaska Quarterly Review, Denver Quarterly, The Cincinnati Review,*

The Greensboro Review, and *ZYZZYVA*, among others. She received her MFA from George Mason University, where she co-founded Gazing Grain Press.

Laura Sloan Patterson is Professor of English at Seton Hill University in Greensburg, Pennsylvania, where she teaches American literature, southern literature, composition, and creative writing. She is the author of *Stirring the Pot: Domesticity and the Kitchen in the Fiction of Southern Women* (MacFarland, 2008), and she has published articles and essays in *Mississippi Quarterly, Southern Quarterly, Feminist Media Studies,* and *The Chronicle of Higher Education.* Her poetry has appeared in *Lines + Stars, Spry, Pittsburgh Poetry Review,* and other journals. She was a finalist for the James Applewhite Poetry Prize awarded by the *North Carolina Literary Review.*

Yaël Schlick is Professor of English at Queen's University, where she teaches courses on travel writing, autobiography, and contemporary American literature. Her work on polar explorer Richard Byrd, feminism and travel, autobiography, and Elizabeth Bishop has been published by *The Polar Journal*, Bucknell University Press, the University of Mississippi Press, and *Environmental Ethics*. She has co-edited, with Shelley King, a volume of essays on the female coquette and has translated Victor Segalen's *Essay on Exoticism* for Duke University Press (2002). Her contribution for this collection is part of her ongoing interest in the literary culture of Key West.

Claire Seiler is Associate Professor of English at Dickinson College. She is the author of *Midcentury Suspension: Literature and Feeling in the Wake of World War II* (Columbia UP, 2020). Her work has appeared in *Modernism/modernity, Contemporary Literature, Twentieth-Century Literature,* and elsewhere.

Heather Treseler is Associate Professor of English and Presidential Fellow for Art, Education, and Community at Worcester State University and a visiting scholar at the Brandeis Women's Studies Research Center. Her poems appear in *PN Review, Harvard Review, Iowa Review, Missouri Review, Cincinnati Review,* and *Frontier Poetry,* among other journals, and her chapbook, *Parturition* (2020), won the Munster Literature Centre's International Chapbook Award in 2019. Her essays appear in the *Los Angeles Review of Books, Consequence, Boston Review,* and in six books about American poetry. Her work has received fellowship support from the American Academy of Arts and Sciences and the Boston Athenaeum.

John Emil Vincent is an archivist, critic, and poet living in Montreal. His critical books include *Queer Lyrics: Difficulty and Closure in American Poetry* (Palgrave

Macmillan, 2002) and *John Ashbery and You: His Later Books* (U of Georgia P, 2007). He has published a first book of poems, *Excitement Tax* (DC Books, 2017), and his second, *Ganymede's Dog*, appeared in fall 2019 from McGill-Queen's University Press.

Andrew Walker is Assistant Professor of English at Liberty University. He has recently published essays on rural modernity in Britain and Sylvia Plath's relationship to radio drama. He is currently working on a book-length study of twentieth-century drama in verse, focusing on works by T. S. Eliot, Gertrude Stein, Djuna Barnes, and others.

Jeffrey Westover is Professor of English at Boise State University. He is the author of *The Colonial Moment: Discoveries and Settlements in Modern American Poetry* (Northern Illinois UP, 2004), which was designated an Outstanding Academic Title by *Choice* magazine in 2005. Recent publications include articles about W. S. Merwin, H.D., Thylias Moss, and Maxine Hong Kingston.

Heather Bozant Witcher is Assistant Professor at Auburn University at Montgomery. Her research focuses on archival studies, collaboration, and sociability in the eighteenth and nineteenth centuries. Her first monograph, *Sympathetic Texts*, explores sympathetic collaboration in the long nineteenth century. The book argues that the nineteenth-century collaborative process is a form of communal self-identification, indebted to the imaginative power of sympathy, as well as a mode of writing that is steeped in the liberal tradition. In addition, her research on Pre-Raphaelite poetics has resulted in a co-edited collection, *Defining Pre-Raphaelite Poetics*, forthcoming from Palgrave Macmillan.

Acknowledgments

I would like to thank the National Endowment for the Humanities (NEH) for funding the NEH Summer Seminar for College and University Professors, Elizabeth Bishop and the Literary Archive, that I taught at Vassar College in June 2017. Without that funding, which allowed sixteen scholars to join me for three weeks of intensive study of the Elizabeth Bishop Papers, this book would not have been possible. Ron Patkus, Associate Director of the Libraries for Special Collections at Vassar College, proved to be a great collaborator and colleague on-site at Vassar leading up to and during the seminar and remained an invaluable source of support and knowledge about the archives throughout the writing of this book. Dean Rogers was gracious as always in supporting all the NEH scholars and making sure that everyone had equal time in Archives and Special Collections throughout the seminar. He also created most of the high-resolution images featured here. I am indebted to Thomas Travisano, Barbara Page, and Alice Quinn for sharing the experience and insight they have gained from many years of working in the Bishop archives. And to all the scholars who joined me for three incredible weeks in the archives and contributed to this volume, thank you for one of the most productive and stimulating intellectual experiences of my career.

Index

Note: italicized page numbers indicate images

abuse, childhood, 39, 46, 47, 48, 152
Africa, 27, 29, 34–35, 37, 43n1, 144
Afro-Brazilians, 143–144
agency of matter, 230–231, 232, 235–238
Agrestes (Cabral), 210, 212
alcoholism, Bishop's, 38, 41, 42, 46, 49, 59, 61n4
    Bowie and, 57
    Methfessel on, 89
Alcott, Louisa May, 76–77
Alexandre Gallery, New York, 163, 171n5
alienation, 166, 167, 170
American Poetry Review, 4
"America's Island of Felicity" (England), 186, *186*
"Among School Children" (Yeats), 127
"Anaphora" (Bishop), 173, 174
Androcles and the Lion (Shaw), 61n4
Anthropocene, the, 239–240, 244, 245
Anthropocene Reading: Literary History in Geologic Times (Menely, Taylor), 244
anti-professionalism, idea of Bishop's, 304, 305
"anyone lived in a pretty how town" (Cummings), 72
"Approaching Elizabeth Bishop's Letters to Ruth Foster" (Goldensohn), 13n11
Araújo, Lilli de Correia, 196
architecture, 193–198, 217

Archive Fever (Derrida), 13n3, 236
archive of Bishop's writing and effects, 7–8, 128
    at Harvard, 1, 207, 209, 241
    at Indiana University, 4
    Methfessel and, 91
    at Pousada do Chico Rei, 2
    reformatting and, 5–6, 13n10
    scholarship gap on, 2
    at Washington University, 114n7
    See also Vassar College Archives and Special Collections Library, Elizabeth Bishop Papers
archives, 11
    archival memory, 238, 281
    Archive Fever (Derrida), 13n3, 236
    as arrested, 2, 4, 236, 238
    Bishop's (*See* archive of Bishop's writing and effects)
    Derrida on, 13n3, 194, 236, 237
    digitization of, 6–9, 98, 281–282, 282n11, 300
    geopoetic approach to, 244
    importance of, 8, 12, 79n7
    Magi on, 236
    Patrimonio Artistico, 203
    precariousness of, 222–223
    private materials in, 79n6, 244
    self-archiving, 91

Aristophanes, 198, 250, 252–256, *253*, 258
Aristophanic style, 251–252
"Armadillo, The" (Bishop)
   Calder and, 278
   chaos and order in, 278
   dedication to Lowell, 269
   drafts of, 267–271, 274–275, *277*, 277–278, 282n4
   environmental destruction in, 269, 281
   form of, 269–271, 274–275
   "From a Letter," 267, 269, 274
   human impact on environment and, 269, 281
   letter to Baumann and, 278
   Lowell, dedication to, 269
   motion in, 268, 269, 270–271, 274–275
   multiple voices in, 265–266, 275
   multiplicity and circulating motifs within, 269
   "O tatú," 219–220
   "Owl's Nest, The," 267–268, 270, 272, 274, *279*, 280–281
   polyphony and, 276, 280
   St. John's Day festival and, 267, 269, 274, 278
   titles of, 267
   tonal shifts in, 268, 270
   translation of, 219–220
Armstrong, Louis, 141
arrested, archive as, 2, 4, 236, 238
Art and Memory in the Work of Elizabeth Bishop (Ellis), 52–54
Art as Experience (Dewey), 232, 234, 245n7
artwork, Bishop's
   paintings, 157–*158*, 163–164, 272–273
   sketches, 163, *163, 164*, 165, *253*
Ashbery, John, 308, 315–316
Asheville, North Carolina, 151
Associação das Girl Guides do Brasil, 199, 224n8
Association for the Advancement of Psychoanalysis, 50
"At the Fishhouses" (Bishop), 34, 49, 191
   dreams and, 54
   in Foster letters, 316
   Gilbert on, 175
   picturesque aesthetic and, 177

"River Rat, The" and, 71
Swenson on, 110
Auden, W. H., 249, 263, 264n5
Austin, A. E., 256
Axelrod, Steven, 131, 134

Bandierantes, 199, 224n8
Barker, Ilse, 153, 171n1
Barker, Kit, 153, 171n1
Barry, Sandra, 284
Baumann, Anny, 61n2, 84, 269, 278
Bell, Alexander Graham, 36
Bell, Pearl Kazin, 76–77
Bennett, Jane, 230–231, 236
Benton, William, 163
Bernardes, Sérgio, 193
Best, William, 54, 63n14
Bidart, Frank, 42
   on Bishop's lesbianism, 65
   Bishop's letters to, 21, 33, 79n9, 79n12
   on "In the Waiting Room," 17, *18*
   letters to Bishop, 17, *18*, 19
Biele, Joelle, 70–71
"Bight, The" (Bishop), 104, 111, 187, 188, 189, 191, 192
Birds, The (Aristophanes, trans. Bishop), 198, 250, 252–256, *253*, 258
Bishop, Gertrude Bulmer, 36, 41, 49, 57–58, 61n1
Bishop, John W., 61n1
Bishop, William Thomas, 61n1
"Bishop: Race, Class, and Gender" (Zona), 32
Bjornerud, Marcia, 242–243
Black, Margaret, 51
Black Beans and Diamonds (Bishop), 149
black music, 132–135, 136, 141
blackness, 131, 132, *138*, 140, 141, 147
   See also race; racism
Black Panther Party, 131, 132, 145
black women, Bishop speaking as, 133, 135, 136
Blarney Castle postcard, 181
Bloom, Harold, 313
Blough, Frani. See Muser, Frani Blough
Blue Pencil, The, 227, 250, 264n4
"Blue Postman," 52–54, *53*, 62n11–12
blues music, 132–135, 136, 141
Body and the Song, The (Lombardi), 58–59

Bogan, Louise, 311-312
Bomtempo, José Maria, 215
book cover of Diary of "Helena Morley," The (Brant, trans. Bishop), 196, 198
Boris Godunov (Mussorgsky), 260
Bowers, Grace Bulmer, 61, 87-88, 206
Bowie, Dorothee, 47, 57-59, 58
Bradley, Louise, 2, 4, 178
Brandellero, Sara, 212
Brant, Alice Dayrell Caldeira, 202-203
Brasília, Brazil, 205
Brazeau, Peter, 257-258
Brazil
   Afro-Brazilians, 143-144
   Brasília, 205
   Brazil, Life World Library, 144, 214, 215, 218
   "Brazil, January 1, 1502," 112-113, 140, 144, 163
   Cleaver on slave trade in, 148-149
   Lacerda and, 86, 144, 206, 219, 222-223
   national museum fire, 222-223
   Ouro Prêto, 57-60, 82
   political instability in, 144, 208-209
   poverty in, 218
   "Questions of Travel" and, 160-161
   race in, 138, 139, 143-144, 146-147
   Read on, 194
   Rio, *216,* 218
   Samambaia, 193-194, *195,* 203, *205,* 239, 272-273, 282n8
   "Trip to the Mines, A" and, 143-144, 145, 149
   unpublished poems about, 145
Brazil, Life World Library (Bishop), 144, 214, 215, 218
"Brazil, January 1, 1502" (Bishop), 112-113, 140, 144, 163
"Breakfast Song" (Bishop), 94, 140
breasts, descriptions of, 32, 33-34, 36, 54, 88
Brevard, North Carolina, 10-11, 151-171
   Appalachian poverty, 156, 161-168, 169
   "Chemin de Fer" and, 168-169
   correspondence with Muser while in, 151, 153, 167
   Heiss in, 161-168, *163,* 169, 171n8
   juxtapositions in travel journals from, 152
   landscape of, 157, 159-161, 168, 169
   lists in travel journals from, 163, *164*
   Moore, Bishop's correspondence with, 151, 153, 157, 167
   outsiderhood, Bishop's, 152-153, 159, 163
   people-focused travel journal entries from, 155, 156, 161-168
   "Questions of Travel" and, 160-161
   Samuels on travel journals from, 169
   wildlife in, 161, 167
Brinnin, John Malcolm, 45-46
Brown, Ashley, 194, 198
Buber, Martin, 65
"Burglar of Babylon, The" (Bishop), 195, 207-210, 213-215, 217-219, 223, 224n12
Burns, Katherine (Bishop's pseudonym), 71, 75

Cabral de Melo Neto, João, 208-213, 214-215, 220, 224n10, 224n13
Cage of Spines, A (Swenson), 103-105
Calder, Alexander, 170, 171n9, 261-262, 266, 272-273, 275, 278, 282n7-8
"Camellia Sabina" (Moore), 294
Campbell, Marvin, 13n5
Camp Chequesset, 171n6, 250
cannibalism, 27, 29
"Capricorn" (Bishop), 210
Cardozo, Joaquim, 224n14
Carson, Rachel, 207
cartoons, *The New Yorker,* 220-222, *221*
cemetery poems, 209-211
"Cemitérios metropolitanos" (Cabral), 210
chaos and order, relationship between, 169-170, 273, 278, 288
"Chemin de Fer" (Bishop), 165-166, 168-169, 170, 171n6-7
Chequesset, Camp, 171n6, 250
childhood, Bishop's, 6, 36, 38-39, 48, 57, 156
   trauma in, 46, 47, 152
child narrator, 17, 19, 24, 30, 37
Churchill, Winston, 30, *31*
"Circus Animals' Desertion, The" (Yeats), 159
Clark, Evert, 220
Clark, Kenneth, 163
class, Bishop and, 48, 137, 138, 139, 185, 188
Cleaver, Eldridge, 131, 132, 146

Cleaver, Kathleen, 49, 131–132, 145–146, 148, 150n10–11, 264
Cleghorn, Angus, 5, 305
closure, 117
Cohen, Jeffrey Jerome, 227
Cold Spring, A (Bishop), 110–111, 167–168, 314
Cold War culture, 18, 218, 222, 234
Cole, Nat King, 63n14
collages in Cuttyhunk notebook, 285–288, *286,* 290–295, *292, 294,* 300
colonialism/imperialism, 24, 37, 131
    "In the Waiting Room" and, 30, 32–33, 37, 42
    National Geographic Magazine and, 30, 35, 36–37, 42, 43n2
color, 198, 209
    in Bishop's paintings, 163–164
    in Bishop's writing, 120–121, 140–142, 144, 155, 234–235
    in Cabral's poetry, 214
    in Methfessel-Bishop correspondence, 93–94
Colson, Theodore, 284
"Comedian as the Letter C, The" (Stevens), 143
Comins, Barbara, 288
"Commonplace, The" (Gilman), 74
Complete Poems, The (Bishop), 240, 308
"Composing Motions" (Samuels), 171n9
"Compulsory Heterosexuality and Lesbian Existence" (Rich), 68
Conceptions of Modern Psychiatry (Sullivan), 50
Condition of Man, The (Mumford), 206
"Congresso no polígono das secas" [Congress in the Polygon of Droughts] (Cabral), 211, 224n13
Conhecendo Ouro Prêto (Ruas), 200
Constructing the Self, Constructing America: A Cultural History of Psychotherapy (Cushman), 49–50
Consultant in Poetry to Library of Congress, Bishop as, 59, 234, 304, 317n4
Cook, Eleanor, 187, 266
Cooper, Jane, 209
"Cootchie" (Bishop), 135, 136, 137, 143
copyrights, FSG and, 6–8
Correio da Manhã, 223
Cos-Cob Hub postcard, 182–*183*

Costello, Bonnie, 157, 169, 244, 304
"Country Mouse, The" (Bishop), 48, 61n1
Crane, Louise, 51–52, 61n3, 132, 142, 155, 163, 180
Crashaw, Richard, 255
Croll, M. W., 19
Crowley, Ralph, 50
cruising, 123, 125, 126, 128, 128n1
"Crusoe in England" (Bishop), 1, 20, 57, 58, 59, 163
    dramatic reading of, 250
    geopoetics and, 229
    Moss and, 63n15
    queer reading of, 90–91
    self-archiving process and, 91
    Swenson on, 113–114
Crutzen, Paul, 239
Csikszentmihalyi, Mihaly, 93
cultural-interpersonal school of psychoanalysis, 50, 51, 62n6
Cumming, Roxanne, 47, 57, 59, 132, 146, 148
Cummings, E. E., 72
Cushman, Philip, 49–50
Cuttyhunk notebook (Bishop), 283–301
    collages, 285–288, *286,* 290–295, *292, 294,* 300
    digital media and, 300
    ghost writing in, *295,* 295–301
    Hockaday image in, *289,* 290–291
    loose inserts, 300
    "Miracle for Breakfast, A" and, 293
    newspaper clippings in, 285, *292*
    pathways through, 299
    poems that arose from, 283
    productive visual overload and, 288
    programs in, 293–294, *294,* 295
    scope of, 299–300
    as scrapbook, 283–284, 293
    surrealism in, 287
    White on, 287

Darwin, Charles, 231, 241–244, 245n5, 245n7
Davis, Elmer, 185–186
de Andrade, Rodrigo Melo Franco, 203
de Araújo, Lilli Correia, 2
Dear Elizabeth: A Play in Letters from Elizabeth Bishop to Robert Lowell and Back Again (Ruhl), 81

Dear Elizabeth: Five Poems & Three Letters to Elizabeth Bishop (Swenson), 114n1
"Death and Life of a Severino" (Cabral, trans. Bishop), 208–210
Death and Life of Great American Cities, The (Jacobs), 207
de Campos, Haroldo, 211
decolonization, 231, 234, 235
Deep Skin: Elizabeth Bishop and Visual Art (Samuels), 249–250, 272
deep time, 227, 229, 240, 241–242, 243
Degas, Edgar, 41
Degrees of Freedom (Hicok), 128n1
de Man, Paul, 127
depression, Bishop's, 38, 92
Derrida, Jacques, 2, 13n3, 194, 218, 236, 238, 327
Dewey, Jane, 189
Dewey, John, 41, 232, 234, 245n7
Diagnostic and Statistical Manual of Mental Disorders, 73
Diamantina church, *204*, 223
Diary of "Helena Morley," The (Brant, trans. Bishop), 149, 199, 200–204, *202*, *204*, 223
  book cover, 196, 198
  racism in language of, 144
Dickinson, Emily, 86, 239–240
digital media, 2, 6–9, 98, 281–282, 282n11, 299, 300
digitization of Bishop's archives, 6–8, 98, 281–282, 282n11, 295, 300
Dix, Dorothea, 58–59
Dois parlamentos (Cabral), 211, 212
Dolphin, The (Lowell), 263
Dos Passos, Katy, 185
drafts and manuscripts, 266
drama, Bishop and, 249–264
  Aristophanic style, 251–252
  Birds, The, 198, 250, 252–256, *253*, 258
  in *The Blue Pencil*, 250, 264n4
  Camp Chequesset and, 250
  Christmas miracle play (Bishop, Muser), 250, 264n4
  Cleaver interview and, 264
  "Crusoe in England" reading, 250
  influences on, 251–252, 254–258, 260–261
  Javadizadeh on, 250
  poetry, links to, 249–250, 251, 264
  "Prince Mannerly," *258*, 258–259, *259*, 260, 264n6
  "Proper Tears, a Masque, The," 257, *261*, 261–263, *263*, 264n7
  Three Wells, The, 250, 264n4
  Vassar and, 251
  at Walnut Hill, 250, 264n4
  White on, 250
"Dreaming in Color: Bishop's Notebook Letter-Poems" (Treseler), 52
dreams, 34, 40–41, 52, 54, 62n6, 89, 154–155
Dryden, John, 260–261
DSM, 73
Duncan, Carol, 238
Dunn, Alan, 220–222, *221*
Dyer, Geoff, 178

Eberhart, Richard, 111
Edelman, Lee, 27, 29, 35, 126
Edgar Allan Poe & the Juke-Box: Uncollected Poems, Drafts, and Fragments (Bishop, ed. Quinn), 5, 33, 67, 114n2, 155, 231, 244, 282n3
  Ashbery's blurb for, 315–316
  "Fairy Toll-Taker, The" in, 115, 116, 124
  transcription errors in, 7, 124
educação pela pedra, A [Education by Stone] (Cabral), 211–212
"Effort at Speech Between Two People" (Rukeyser), 45–46
"Efforts of Affection: A Memoir of Marianne Moore" (Bishop), 50–51, 159
Eliot, T.S., 251–252, 254, 256–257, 260, 262, 264n5
Elizabeth Bishop: A Miracle for Breakfast (Marshall), 69, 81
Elizabeth Bishop and the Literary Archive (ed. Hicok), 3, 7, 9–12, 13n5
Elizabeth Bishop at Work (Cook), 266
Elizabeth Bishop House, 284
Elizabeth Bishop in the 21st Century: Reading the New Editions (ed. Cleghorn et al.), 5, 305

Elizabeth Bishop Papers. *See* Vassar College Archives and Special Collections Library, Elizabeth Bishop Papers
Elizabeth Bishop's Brazil (Hicok), 86, 193
Elizabeth Bishop's Poetics of Intimacy (Harrison), 117, 119
Elizabeth Bishop: The Biography of a Poetry (Goldensohn), 4
Elizabeth Bishop: The Geography of Gender (Lombardi), 4
Elkin, Lauren, 171
Ellis, Jonathan, 52-54, 133, 164-165, 189, 245n5
Ellison, Ralph, 137-138
"Elusive Mastery" (Millier), 84
England, George Allan, 186, 186
ephemera in archive
   in Methfessel-Bishop correspondence, 95-96, 97
   New Yorker cartoon, 220-222, *221*
   programs, 293-294, *294*, 295
   Sapolio soap leaflet, 137, *138-142*, 140, 144
   travel and, 176
   See also Cuttyhunk notebook (Bishop)
Erkkila, Betsy, 133
"Eula Wiggle" (Bishop, Hemingway), 66, 68-70, 71, 74-76, 79n9
"Euripides and Professor Murray" (Eliot), 252
European travel, Bishop and, 183-186, 190
Evans, E. Barton, 62n7
"Evil Hearted Woman" (Fuller), 134, *136*
Exchanging Hats (Ed. Benton), 163

"Fairy Toll-Taker, The" (Bishop), 115-128
   as complete poem, 117
   cruising and, 123, 125, 126, 128, 128n1
   descriptions within, 119-121, 123, 125-126
   as draft, 117, *118, 122*, 123-124
   in *Edgar Allan Poe & the Juke-Box*, 115, 116, 124
   Elizabeth Bishop's Poetics of Intimacy on, 117, 119
   form of, 119, 120-123
   Harrison on, 117, 119
   homosexuality and, 123, 124, 125, 126-127
   music's sexuality and, 115
   queer cross-identification and, 128
   Quinn's mistranscription of, 124
   title of, 124, 125
family of origin, Bishop's, 36, 61, 61n1, 206
   Bishop, Gertrude Bulmer (mother), 36, 41, 49, 57-58, 61n1
   Bishop, John W. (grandfather), 61n1
   Bishop, William Thomas (father), 61n1
   Bowers, Grace Bulmer, 61, 87-88, 206
   Hutchinson, Robert (great grandfather), 59
   Shepherdson, George (uncle), 38-39, 46, 48, 59-60, 61n1, 156
   Shepherdson, Maud (Maude) (aunt), 38, 48, 59, 61n1, 62n10, 156, 163, 171n2
   violence in, 38-39, 42
Farnham, Marynia F., 62n6
Farrar, Straus and Giroux (FSG), 6-8
"Faustina, or Rock Roses" (Bishop), 136-137, 140, 143
Federal Emergency Relief Administration (FERA), 185, 187, 190
Federal Writers' Project, 185, 190
female bodies, 32, 33-34, 36, 54, 88
female friendship, 60-61, 72
FERA (Federal Emergency Relief Administration), 185, 187, 190
"Festa na casa-grande" (Cabral), 209, 211
Field, Edward, 107, 114n5
fiend persona, Bishop's, 102, 104
"Fish, The" (Bishop), 287-288
"Five Flights Up" (Bishop), 88
Flâneuse (Elkin), 171
Flávio, 219-220
Fletcher, Phineas, 261, 262, 264n7
flirtation, Bishop on, 126, 127-128
"Florida" (Bishop), 143, 159, 160, 177, 182-183
Flynn, Judy, 48, 67, 73-74, 274
Foote, Kenneth E., 73
"(I Love You) For Sentimental Reasons" (Best, Watson), 54, 63n14
Foster, Ruth, 19, 38, 46
   as analyst, 47, 49, 50, 61n2, 61n3
   dreams of, Bishop's, 34, 40-41
   in "Efforts of Affection: A Memoir of Marianne Moore," 50-51

Goldensohn on, 50
Northside Child Development Center and, 61n3
seals and, 54–55
Thompson and, 50
transference to, Bishop's, 51, 52–54
See also Foster letters
Foster letters, 4, 36, 42, 46–47, 61, 87–88, 104
"Approaching Elizabeth Bishop's Letters to Ruth Foster," 13n11
childhood in, 156
dreams in, 62n6
Flynn in, 73
Frankenberg in, 50
Goldensohn on, 13n11
MacIver in, 50
marriage discussed in, 66–67
and NEH Seminar, 316
order and chaos, tension between, 169–170
physical descriptions of, 59–60, 282n1
poems and, 1, 21–22, 34, 40–41, 81, 265, 272, 316
as possibly unsent, 316
poverty discussed in, 156
reading, portrayal of in, 37, 40
reception of, 316
repetition, fear of in, 265
sexuality in, 40, 41, 66
shame discussed in, 156
"Sunday morning" [February 9, 1947] letter, 49, 62n6
as therapeutic assignment, 316
transcription of, 157
transference and, 52, 54
Treseler on, 316
Vassar's acquisition of, 38, 81, 282n1
Fountain, Gary, 257–258
"Four Poems" (Bishop), 111–112
Four Saints in Three Acts (Stein), 254–255, 260
Francesca, P. Della, 258, *259*
Frankenberg, Lloyd, 50, 61n4, 62n6-7, *174*, 182, 206
Frankenberg, Loren, 206
Freud, Sigmund, 19, 21, 51, 60
Freyre, Gilberto, 138–139, 215

Friedel, Robert, 93
"Froggie Blues" (Wheatstraw), 135
"From a Letter" (Bishop), 267, 269, 274
See also "Armadillo, The" (Bishop)
Fromm, Erich, 50, 62n7
"From the History of an Infantile Neurosis" (Freud), 19
"From Trollope's Journal" (Bishop), 29
Frost, Robert, 219, 225n16
FSG (Farrar, Straus and Giroux), 6–8
Fuller, Blind Boy, 133, *135*
"Full Moon, Key West" (Bishop), 183, 184

"Gallery Note" (Bishop), 227, *228*
gender
Elizabeth Bishop: The Geography of Gender, 4
female bodies, 32, 33–34, 36, 54, 88
female friendship, Klein and Riviere on, 60–61
Guggenheim fellowships and, 309, 317n6
Institute for Women's Policy Research, 317n3
Modern Woman: The Lost Sex (Farnham), 62n6
professionalism and, 305–306
women, discrimination against, 207, 317n3
"Gentleman of Shalott, The" (Bishop), 12
Geography III (Bishop), 20, 37, 45, 82, 145
See also "In the Waiting Room"
geological time, 227, 229, 240, 241–242, 243
geology, 227, 230, 239–244
geopoetics, 227–246
agency of matter and, 230–231, 232, 235, 236
archival approach and, 244
"Crusoe in England" and, 229
Darwin and, 241
deep time and, 227, 229, 240, 241–242, 243
Hess and, 229–230
"Song for the Rainy Season" and, 229
term, 229–230
"The Mountain" and, 231, 239, 240, 244
vibrant matter and, 230–231, 235–236
ghost writing, 295, 295–301
Gilbert, Roger, 175
Gilman, Charlotte Perkins, 74
Gilpin, William, 177–178

Ginsberg, Allen, 83
Giroux, Robert, 7, 114n1, 198, 224n5, 257
Goffman, Erving, 175-176
Goldberg, Susan, 36-37, 43n2
Goldensohn, Lorrie, 4, 13n11, 244-245
    on Bishop's paintings, 299
    on Bishop's relationship with servant class, 137, 139
    on Foster, 50
    on "The Thumb," 68
Gould, Stephen Jay, 229
Graves, Ralph, 23-24, *25, 26*
Gray, Jeffrey, 175, 191
Green, Maurice, 50
Grifalconi, Ann, 114n5
Griggs, Robert, 24, *25, 28,* 35
Guggenheim fellowships, Bishop's applications for, 316
    application forms, 308-309, *309,* 314
    Bloom on, 313
    clerical help with application, 317n7
    first application, 307, 310-312
    gender and, 309, 317n6
    North & South in, 311
    published books list, 314
    Ray and, 308
    references in, 312-313
    reserve in, 309-310
    Schlesinger on, 308
    second application, 307, 315
    teaching, and burden of, 313-314, 315
Gurney, Edmund
    motion and, 275-276

Halberstam, Jack (Judith), 86
handwriting, qualities of, 94, 295
Hardwick, Elizabeth, 145
Harlem, New York, 38, 50, 61n3, 62n3, 132
Harper's, 185-186
Harrison, Victoria, 63n17, 117, 119
Hart, Ellen Louise, 86
Hartmann, Heidi, 317n3
Harvard, Bishop's archive at, 1, 207, 209, 241
Hasecher, Nora, 155
Heiss, Cordie, 161-168, *163,* 169, 171n8
Helle, Anita, 8
"Helping to Solve Our Allies' Food Problem" (Graves), 23-24, *25*
Hemingway, Ernest, 153, 185, *197*
Hemingway, Pauline, 65, 66, 68-70, 71, 74-76, 79n8-9, 189
"Henry James as a Characteristic American" (Moore), 258
"Her Early Work" (Swenson), 101
Hess, Harry, 229-230
Hicok, Bethany, 21, 86, 128n1, 138, 144, 193, 317n3
"His Proper Tear" (Bishop, Muser). *See* "Proper Tears, A Masque, The" (Bishop, Muser)
historical material culture theory, 93
Hockaday, Frank Woodville "Woody," *289,* 290-291
Holiday, Billie, 132, 136
homographesis, 126
homosexuality, 73, 123-127
    lesbianism, 65, 66, 68, 79n3, 86, 88, 263
    Love, Hate and Reparation on, 63n18
    in San Francisco, 119
    See also "Fairy Toll-Taker, The" (Bishop); queer poet, Bishop as
Hopkins, Gerard Manley, 19, 273
Horizon, 50
Horney, Karen, 21, 50, 51, 62n7
Houghton Mifflin, 136, 196
Hound and Horn, 258
"House Guest" (Bishop), 66
Hubbard, Gardiner, 36
Hughes, Charla Allyn, 13n5
Hunter's Point neighborhood, 148
Hutchinson, Robert, 59
Hutton, James, 241-242, 243

"Idea of Order at Key West, The" (Stevens), 187
Ideas of Order (Stevens), 187
I Married Adventure (Johnson), 27
imperialism/colonialism, 24, 131
    "In the Waiting Room" and, 30, 32-33, 37, 42
    National Geographic Magazine and, 30, 35, 36-37, 42, 43n2
"In a cheap hotel" (Bishop), 262
Indiana University, Bishop's archive at, 4

344   INDEX

Institute for Women's Policy Research, 317n3
International Style architecture, 217
"In the Bodies of Words" (Swenson), 110
In the Clearing (Frost), 219
"In the Waiting Room" (Bishop), 17–43, 45, 57, 58
   Africa in, 27, 34–35
   Bidart on, 17, *18*
   breasts, descriptions of, 32, 33–34, 36
   child narrator, 17, 19, 24, 30, 37
   colonialism/imperialism and, 30, 32–33, 37, 42
   "Country Mouse, The" and, 48
   drafts, 21–24, *23,* 29, 30, 33, 35
   female bodies in, 32, 33–34, 35–36
   Foster letters and, 40–41
   imperialism/colonialism and, 30, 32–33, 37, 42
   National Geographic Magazine and, 17, 19, 21, 33, 34–35 (See also *National Geographic Magazine*)
   The New Yorker, in, 36
   pigs and, 24, *26,* 27, 29
   pith helmet imagery in, 30
   published version, 29, 35
   punctuation and, 22
   queer subtext in, 30, 33, 34, 41
   race and, 30, 43n2
   reading portrayed in, 33, 36, 39–40
   stereotyping and, 27, 29, 35
   "Time's Andromedas" and, 35
   Zona on, 32, 33
"Invitation to Miss Marianne Moore" (Bishop), 110–111, 167–168
isolation, 163, 166, 168
"It is marvellous to wake up together" (Bishop), 4

Jacobs, Jane, 207, 218, 223
Jacobus, Mary, 18, 19, 20, 37, 42
James, Henry, 258, 260
Jarrell, Randall, 49, 133, 303–304
Javadizadeh, Kamran, 250
"Jerónimo's House" (Bishop), 137, 143, 165
John Simon Guggenheim Memorial Foundation fellowships. *See* Guggenheim fellowships, Bishop's applications for
Johnson, Martin, 27, 29, 30, 37, 40, 43n1

Johnson, Osa, 27, 29, 30, 37, 40, 43n1
Jonson, Ben, 257, 258
journals, travel, 54, 153–156, 159, 161–168, *164, 169*
"Judy" (Bishop), 73–74, 79n7, 274
juxtapositions, 152

Kansas Historical Society, 43n1
Kazin, Pearl, 198, 199, 203, 224n5
Kelley, Richard, 215
Kenyon, Frederic, 231
Kenyon, Helen *296, 297, 298*
Kenyon Review, 45, 47
Key West, Florida
   accommodations on, 188, 189
   "America's Island of Felicity" (England), 186, 186
   Davis on, 185–186
   Dos Passos on, 185
   economy, 175, 188
   Federal Emergency Relief Administration (FERA) and, 185, 187, 190
   Federal Writers' Project and, 185, 190
   Hemingway and, 185, 189, 197
   "Idea of Order at Key West, The," 187
   landscape of, 152
   Lowell-Bishop correspondence and, 186, 189, 197
   Moore-Bishop correspondence and, 188
   in notebooks, Bishop's, 54
   picturesque aesthetic and, 174, 176, 185, 186, 189–191
   poems, Bishop's and, 183, 184, 187, 188, 189, 191
   race and, 142–143
   slumming in, 188
   Stevens and, 187
   Stone in, 187
   "The Overseas Highway," 186
   tourism, 185
   working-class in, 185
   Works Progress Administration (WPA) and, 185
Kirsch, Adam, 191
"Kitty Hawk" (Frost), 219, 225n16

Klein, Melanie, 60–61, 63n17–18
Knudson, Rozanne, 107, 110, 113

Labio, Catharine, 97
Lacerda, Carlos, 86, 144, 206, 219, 222–223
"Landscape with Gray Hills" (Bishop), 163
Last Poems (Yeats), 159
Lauer, Claire, 285
Leão, Magú, 200, 224n2
Leão, Rosinha, *197*, 200, 224n2
Le Corbusier, 211, 213
lesbianism, 65, 66, 68, 79n3, 86
  See also homosexuality
Letters of Vita Sackville-West to Virginia Woolf, The (Sackville-West), 86
Lever Press, 7
Library of Congress, Consultant in Poetry to, Bishop as, 59, 234, 304, 317n4
"Lifecycle of an Interperson" (Frankenberg), 50
Life World Library, *Brazil* (Bishop), 144, 214, 215, 218
Little Women (Alcott), 76–77
Logan, William, 49, 81, 171n6, 175
Lombardi, Marilyn May, 4, 58–59
long pig, 27, 29
Love, Hate and Reparation (Klein, Riviere), 63n18
"Love, Guilt and Reparation" (Klein), 60
"Love Song of J. Alfred Prufrock, The" (Eliot), 260
Lowell, Robert, 59, 65, 205
  "Armadillo, The" dedicated to, 269
  Bishop, correspondence with (See Lowell-Bishop correspondence)
  Bishop, relationship with, 49, 78n1, 81
  on Bishop, 112
  on breasts, Bishop's descriptions of, 34
  career, pursuit of, 306
  Dolphin, The, 263
  Flávio, support of, 220
  "North Haven" and, 171n1
  Old Glory, The, 255
  on polyphony in Bishop archive, 272
  on "The Burglar of Babylon," 207
Lowell-Bishop correspondence, 34, 57, 66, 84, 91, 209

Cabral in, 208
Cleaver interview and, 49
"*Diary of "Helena Morley," The*" images and, 203
Dolphin, The, Bishop's criticism of, 263
Hemingway house, postcard of, *197*
Key West and, 186, 189, *197*
Parque ceremony and, 219
political instability and, 144–145
on Swenson, 100
on "The Burger of Babylon," 207
Lyell, Charles, 242, 243

MacArthur, Marit J., 145
MacCannell, Dean, 175–176, 190, 191
Macedo Soares, Lota de, 59, 98n5, 109, 195, 224n2, 239
  architecture and, 193–194, 196
  Bishop, relationship with, 76, 77, 78, 221, 222
  Bishop after death of, 57, 58, 90, 116
  and Bishop's relationship with servant class, 137, 138
  Calder mobiles and, 282n8
  as cultural go-between, 206
  death of, 221
  Diary of "Helena Morley, The" and, 200, 202–203
  friends and acquaintances, 144, 194, 203
  New Yorker cartoon, modification of, 220–222, *221*
  Parque do Flamengo and, 206–207, 215, *216–217*, 219, 221, *221*
  political unrest and, 220
  Portuguese, encouragement of Bishop to learn, 198
  Samambaia construction projects and, 193–194
  in Swenson-Bishop correspondence, 101
  translations and, 220
Machova, Mariana, 198
MacIver, Loren, 49, 50, 61n4
  artwork, Bishop's, and, 163
  book cover design and, 196, 224n3
  correspondence with Bishop, 62n6, 193
  "Untitled (Elizabeth Bishop's House)", 171n5

Made with Words (Swenson), 114n1
Magi, Jill, 236
"Magic Barrel, The" (Malamud, trans. Bishop), 199–200, *201*
Malamud, Bernard, 199–200
Mallorca, 178, *179*
Mansion and the Shanties, The (Freyre), 215
"Map, The" (Bishop), 290
Maquet, Jacques, 93
Marianne Moore, Elizabeth Bishop & May Swenson: The Feminist Poetics of Self-Restraint (Zona), 99
marriage, Bishop's perspectives on, 65–79
    Cold War culture and, 222
    comic treatment, 67–68
    in "Eula Wiggle," 66, 68–69, 75–76
    Flynn and, 67, 74
    in letters, 66–67, 79n10, 79n12
    negative views of marriage, 66–69, 72–77, 79n12
    in poems, 66–68, 76, 77–78
    pragmatism and, 78, 79n11
    social pressure and, 66
    in "The River Rat," 66, 68–69, 72–73, 74
    in "The Thumb," 66, 68, 76
    Vider and, 65–66
    in "Was It in His Hand?", 66
Marrs, Cody, 239–240
Marshall, Daniel, 98
Marshall, Megan, 38, 69, 79n7, 81–82, 206, 287
Mason, John Edwin, 43n2
Masques (Jonson), 257
Masters and Slaves (Freyre), 138–139
Mastery's End (Gray), 175
material culture theory, 93
matter, agency of, 230–231, 232, 235, 236
Maxwell, William (Bill), 70, 71, 79n9, 205
Mayhall, Jane, 106–107
McCabe, Susan, 88, 90
McFall, Gardner, 106–107
McIntosh, Hugh, 78n1
McKay, Don, 230
McLuhan, Marshall, 284
"Mechanics of Pretense" (Bishop), 249
Menely, Tobias, 244

Merrill, James, 47, 166, 207
Mesquita, Jerônyma, 224n8
Methfessel, Alice, 60–61, 282n1
    age difference with Bishop, 88–90, 91
    on alcoholism, Bishop's, 89
    as archivist, 91
    Bishop, correspondence with (*See* Methfessel-Bishop correspondence)
    Bishop's papers purchased from, 3
    "Breakfast Song" and, 140
    and Guggenheim application, Bishop's, 309, 317n7
    Marshall on, 81–82
    New Yorker profile, 81–82
    relationship with Bishop, 81, *83,* 87–90, 91, 94–95
Methfessel-Bishop correspondence, 4, 5, 60–61, 282n1
    age difference and, 88–90, 96, 98n4
    Bishop's works discussed in, 83–84
    color in, 93–94
    emotions expressed in, 86, 90, 91, 92, *97*
    ephemera and clippings in, 95–96, *97*
    Geography III and, 82
    handwriting in, 94, 295
    historical material culture theory and, 93
    letterhead and envelopes used, 94–95, 96
    letters as physical artifacts, 82, 91–98
    news shared through, 83
    openness in, 84, *95*
    original letters, benefits of studying, 94–95, 96–97
    Ouro Prêto described in, 82
    photos in, 96
    publishing of, 81
    as queer archival recovery, 82, 86–91
    Russier in, 89
    separation and, 87
    spontaneity in, 84–85, *95*
    as technology of intimacy, 91–98
    transcriptions, drawbacks of, 94–95, 97, *97*
    transcriptions, recommendations for, 97–98
    and writer's block, 83–84
Micuçu, 207, 209, 210, 214, 215, 219
Miller, Margaret, 41, 52, 153–155, *154,* 252

Millier, Brett, 37, 49, 57, 69
    on Bishop as queer poet, 171n7
    on Bishop in Brevard, 161, 167
    on "Chemin de Fer," 171n7
    on "Crusoe in England" dates, 63n15
    "Elusive Mastery," 84
    on "Florida," 183
    on "One Art," 84
    on "Sestina" influences, 63n17
    on "The Mountain," 239
Mindlin, Henrique E., 203
miniaturist aesthetic, Bishop's, 96, *97*, 229, 300
"Miracle for Breakfast, A" (Bishop), 293
mistranscription, 7, 53, 79n7
Mitchell, Stephen, 51
mobiles, Calder's, 272–273, 275
Modern Architecture in Brazil (Mindlin), 203
Modern Element, The (Kirsch), 191
Modern Poets, The (Brinnin, Read), 45–46
Modern Woman: The Lost Sex (Farnham), 62n6
modesty, Bishop's. *See* reserve, Bishop's
Moog, Vianna, 224n8
Moore, Marianne, 4, 103, 232
    Bishop, correspondence with (*see* Moore-Bishop correspondence)
    on Bishop's mental state, 62n10
    "Camellia Sabina," 294
    digital humanities and, 8
    in "Efforts of Affection: A Memoir of Marianne Moore," 50–51, 159
    "Henry James as a Characteristic American," 258
    Last Poems and, 159
    in *Marianne Moore, Elizabeth Bishop & May Swenson: The Feminist Poetics of Self-Restraint*, 99
    on marriage, 66
    "Prince Mannerly" and, 258
    on psychotherapy, 50–51
    on "The Burglar of Babylon," 207
Moore-Bishop correspondence, 38, 47, 141–142, 187, 196, 264n5
    animals in, 278
    Brevard and, 151, 153, 157, 167
    Key West and, 188
    picturesque and, 178, 184
"Moose, The" (Bishop), 49, 61, 87–88, 245, 274–275
Morrison, Toni, 133
Morro de Santo Antônio, Rio de Janeiro, *216*
"Morte e vida Severina" (Cabral), 208–210
Moss, Howard, 45, 47, 63n15, 78
motion, 266
    Calder and, 272–273, 278
    Gurney and, 275–276
    poetry as, 276
    Samuels on, 272
    in "The Armadillo," 268, 269, 270–271, 274–275
    in "The Moose," 274–275
"Mountain, The" (Bishop), 231, 239, 240, 242–243, 244
Moveable Feast, A (Hemingway), 153
"Mr. and Mrs. Carlyle" (Bishop), 67, 76, 77–78, 79n11
Muir, John, 171n3
Mullahy, Patrick, 62n6
multimedia artifacts, 285, 300–301
    Cuttyhunk notebook as (*see* Cuttyhunk notebook (Bishop))
multimodal artifacts, 284–285, 295, 297, 299, 300–301
    Cuttyhunk notebook as (*see* Cuttyhunk notebook (Bishop))
Mumford, Lewis, 206, 223
Murder in the Cathedral (Eliot), 262
Murphy, Kevin, 98
Murray, Gilbert, 252
Muser, Frani Blough, 66, 163, *179*, *181–182*, 182, 250, 264n4
    "Proper Tears, a Masque, The," 257, *261*, 261–263, *263*, 264n7
    See also Muser-Bishop correspondence
Muser-Bishop correspondence, 66, 222–223, 254, 255
    blues in, 132–133
    Brevard and, 151, 153, 166, 167
    collaboration and, 257, 261
    on Eliot, 252

on Mr. Carlyle, 78
on Murray, 252
picturesque in, 178
postcards sent to Muser, *179*, 179-180, *181-182*, *182*
"Museum, The" (Bishop), 231-235, *233*, 238
museums, 133, 135, 237
    in *Art as Experience*, 232, 234
    Dewey on, 232, 234
    Duncan's critique of, 238
    Kenyon and, 231
    national museum fire in Brazil, 222-223
    "Verdigris" and, 238
music, Bishop and
    Birds, The song translations, 256
    blues music, 132, 133-34, *135*, 136, 141
    "Burglar of Babylon" and, 219
    "(I Love You) For Sentimental Reasons", 54, 63n14
    "Music as Literature" course notes, 275-276
    music theory and understanding of literary technique, 276
    "Prince Mannerly" music suggestions for, 256
    rock-and-roll, 115, 126, 127
    sexuality in music, 115
    Thompson and, 254-255
    Vassar College and, 256
musicians, black, exploitation of by whites, 132
"Music's Duell" (Crashaw), 255
Mussorgsky, Modest, 260
"My Brownskin Sugar Plum" (Fuller), 135

Nation, The, 42
National Endowment for the Humanities (NEH) Summer Seminar, 3, 6, 303, 316
National Geographic Magazine, 21-22, 27, 32
    colonialism/imperialism and, 30, 35, 36-37, 42, 43n2
    Goldberg and, 36-37, 43n2
    "Helping to Solve Our Allies' Food Problem," 23-24, *25-26*
    National Geographic Society, 36
    "Race Issue, The," 43n2
    racism and, 36-37, 43n2
    "Valley of Ten Thousand Smokes, The," 24, *25*, *28*, 35
    See also "In the Waiting Room" (Bishop)
National Geographic Society, 36
"Nativity" (Francesca), 258, *259*
Nemer, Linda, 4
Neurotic Personality of Our Time, The (Horney), 51
New and Selected Things Taking Place (Swenson), 105
Newfoundland postcard, 182, *182*
New materialism, 230-231
newspaper clippings, 284, 285, 291
New Yorker, The, 36, 69, 83, 100, 205
    "At the Fishhouses" and, 49
    Biele and, 70-71
    Bishop, profile of, 81-82
    Bogan in, 311-312
    "Burglar of Babylon, The" in, 207, 210, 223, 224n12
    cartoons, 220-222, *221*
    "Chemin de Fer" in, 165, 171n7
    files of, 70-71
    "In the Waiting Room" in, 36
    Marshall in, 81-82
    Methfessel, profile of, 81-82
    North & South review, 311-312
    "Owl's Journey, The" and, 153
    "Pink Dog" in, 114
    "Riverman, The" in, 113
    Silent Spring in, 207
    "Vague Poem (Vaguely Love Poem)" in, 243-244
    White as editor, 238
New York Review of Books, The, 145
New York Times, 50, 62n6, 145
"Night City" (Bishop), 145
Noigandres group, 211
"North Haven" (Bishop), 171n1
Northside Child Development Center, 61n3
North & South (Bishop), 49, 165
    juxtapositions in, 152
    physical specifications of, 196, 198
    reviews of, 311-312, 317n1
    "Songs for a Colored Singer" and, 136
    Swenson and, 107

notebooks, travel, 54, 153–156, 159, 161–168, *164*, 169
Nova Scotia, 49–56, 61
Nunes, Benedito, 211, 224n13

object-relations psychoanalysis, 60
"Objects as Instruments, Objects as Signs" (Maquet), 93
"Obscurity of the Poet, The" (Jarrell), 303–304
O'Casey, Sean, 62n4
OED (*Oxford English Dictionary*), 27
Oedipus—Myth and Complex: A Review of Psychoanalytic Theory (Mullahy), 62n6
O engenheiro (Cabral), 211
Ogle, Maureen, 187
Old Glory, The (Lowell), 255
"One Art" (Bishop), 84, 91
One Art: Letters (Bishop, ed. Giroux), 7, 114n1, 224n5, 257
"On the Railroad Named Delight" (Bishop), 217
Open Me Carefully: Emily Dickinson's Intimate Letters to Susan Huntington Dickinson (Dickinson, ed. Hart, Smith), 86
order and chaos, relationship between, 169–170, 273, 278, 288
"O tatú" (Flávio), 219
Ouro Prêto, Brazil, 2, 57–60, 82
outsiderhood, 4, 85, 152–153, 159, 163
"Over 2,000 Illustrations and a Complete Concordance" (Bishop), 176, 284
Overseas Highway, The (Wright), *186*
owl and rabbit image (Miller), 153–155, *154*
"Owl's Journey, The" (Bishop), 153–155
"Owl's Nest, The," 267–268, 270, 272, 274, *279*, 280–281
See also "Armadillo, The" (Bishop)
Oxford English Dictionary (OED), 27

Paid on Both Sides (Auden), 249
paintings, Bishop's, 157–*158*, 163–164, 272–273, 299
"Paisagens com cupim" [Landscapes with Termites] (Cabral), 212–213, 215, 225n14
Paisagens com figuras [Landscapes with Figures] (Cabral), 208, 209, 212, 214–215, 220

Palmares, 149
para-literary text, 17–19, 27, 37, 42
Parque do Flamengo, 206–207, 215, *216–217*, 217, 219–221, *221*
Partisan Review, 136, 160, 224n5
Patkus, Ron, 13n1
Patrimonio Artistico archive, 203
Paul, Catherine, 231
Pedrick, Jean, 136
"Penelope Gwin" (Bishop), 66, 67–68, 76
"Pernambuco em Málaga" (Cabral), 208, 224n10
pets, 109–110
Pfeiffer, Virginia ("Jinny"), 79n8
Phillips, Siobhan, 77–78
photocopies, preservation, 6, 13n10
photographs, Bishop's insecurities about, 108
Pickard, Zachariah, 244, 245n5
picturesque aesthetic, Bishop's, 173–192, 223
    Davis and, 186
    Gilbert on, 175
    Gilpin on, 177–178
    Key West and, 174, 176, 185, 186, 189, 190–191
    in letters, 178, 184
    Logan on, 175
    modernity, as reaction to, 174
    picturesque defined, 177, 178
    in poems, 176, 177, 180, 182–183, 184, 187
    postcards and, 173, *174,* 178, *179,* 179–180
    poverty and, 184
    Price on, 177–178
    race and, 135–136
    risk-taking and, 191–192
    Soller and, 178, *179*
    tourism, resistance to, 174–176, 179
    travel and, 175–176, 178, 190–192
"Pink Dog" (Bishop), 85–86, 90, 114
pith helmets, 30, *31*
Plath, Sylvia, 8
Playing in the Dark (Morrison), 133
plays. *See* drama, Bishop and
"Poem" (Bishop), 96
"Poem for a Child" (Bishop), 274, 282n3
Poetic Closure: A Study of How Poems End (Smith), 117
Poetry, 208–210

350   INDEX

political unrest, 144–145, 220, 292
polyphony, 265–282
    "Armadillo, The" drafts and, 276, 280
    Calder and, 272
    as concurrent relationships, 276
    drafting process as form of, 276, 280–281
    Lowell on, 272
    motion in poetry and, 268
    polyphony defined, 265
    tonal shifts and, 280–281
    unpredictability and, 277
Poor Cordie, 161–168, *163*, 169, 171n8
Portinari family, 4, 6
Portuguese language, 198–199, 218, 224n6
postcards, 190, 195
    Blarney Castle, 179, *180–181*
    Cos-Cob Hub, *182–183*
    Florida sunrise, 173, *174*
    to Frankenberg, *174*, 182
    Hemingway's house, Key West, *197*
    to Leão, Magu, 224n2
    to Leão, Rosinha, *197*
    to Lowell, *197*
    to Muser, *179*, 179–180, *181–182*, 182
    Newfoundland, 182, *182*
    Piazza di Spagna, 179–180, *181*
    picturesque aesthetic, 173, *174*, 178, *179*, 179–180
    Rio bay, *216*
    Seattle, *197*
    Simpson on, 179
    Soller, 178, *179*
Poulet, George, 24
Pound on Demand, A (O'Casey), 62n4
Pousada do Chico Rei, Bishop's archive at, 2
poverty
    Appalachian poverty, 156, 161–168, 169
    in artwork, Bishop's, 163–164
    Bishop's attitudes toward, 48, 156, 163, 170
    in Brevard, 156, 161–168, 169
    in "Chemin de Fer," 166
    Gray on, 175
    Heiss and, 161–168, 169
    in Key West, 175
    in landscapes, 152

    and picturesque aesthetic, 184
    in Rio, Brazil, 218
    shame and, 48, 156
    Shepherdson and, 163
"Pregão turístico do Recife" (Cabral), 214–215
preservation photocopies, 6, 13n10
Price, Uvedale, 177–178
"Prince Mannerly" (Bishop, Muser), *258*, 258–259, *259*, 260, 264n6
Principles of Geology (Lyell), 242
professionalism, Bishop's, 303–318
    Ashbery on, 308
    as Consultant in Poetry to the Library of Congress, 59, 234, 304, 317n4
    correspondence, porous boundary between personal and professional, 304–305
    disposition *vs.* position/position taking in scholarship on, 306–307, 317n4
    establishment as professional poet, marks of, 308
    gender and, 305–306
    and Guggenheim fellowship applications (*See* Guggenheim fellowships, Bishop's applications for)
    Jarrell on, 303–304
    Library of Congress position, 59, 234, 304
    "Obscurity of the Poet, The" and, 303–304
    and professional self-fashioning, 306, 316
    professional tasks, Bishop's ambivalence about, 306
    scholarship gap on, 303
"Proper Tears, a Masque, The" (Bishop, Muser), 257, *261*, 261–263, *263*, 264n7
Prosser, Jay, 149
psychoanalysis, 19, 21, 34, 37, 47–51, 60, 61n2–3, 62n6
Psychoanalysis and the Scene of Reading (Jacobus), 37
Psychoanalysis: Its Evolution and Development (Thompson), 51
Purcell, Henry, 260–261

Quaderna (Cabral), 209
quatrains, 211–212, 213
queer archival recovery, 86–91

queer poet, Bishop as, 9–10, 32, 59, 74
   "Chemin de Fer" and, 166
   closetedness and, 79n3
   "Crusoe in England" and, 90–91
   "Fairy Toll-Taker, The" and, 123, 124, 125, 126–127, 128
   "In the Waiting Room," queer subtext in, 30, 33, 34, 41
   Lavender Scare and, 234
   love poetry and, 79n3
   McCabe on, 88
   McIntosh on Bishop's relationship with Lowell, 78n1
   Methfessel-Bishop correspondence and, 82, 86–91
   Millier on, 171n7
   "Moose, The" and, 87
   queer readings of late poems, 87–88
   resistance to pathologizing of homosexuality, 73
   Rich on, 4, 73
   and Stein's sexuality, comments on, 263
   "Survival of the Queerly Fit: Darwin, Marianne Moore, and Elizabeth Bishop," 88
   "Thumb, The" and, 68
   "View of the Capitol from The Library of Congress," queer subtext in, 35
Questions of Travel (Bishop), 45, 47, 160–161, 171
   picturesque aesthetic in, 176, 180
   Swenson on, 112–113
Quinn, Alice, 263
   on Bishop's draft dates, 63n13
   on Bishop's poems, 67, 115, 155, 262
   "Blue Postman" reproduction, 63n12
   Edgar Allan Poe & the Juke-Box (See *Edgar Allan Poe & the Juke-Box: Uncollected Poems, Drafts, and Fragments* (Bishop, ed. Quinn))
   on poem titles in Cuttyhunk notebook, 283
   on "The Proper Tears: a Masque," 262

rabbit and owl image (Miller), 153–155, *154*
race
   in advertising, 137, *138–142*, 140, 144

   in Bishop's archive (See race in Bishop's archive)
   blackness, 131, 132, *138*, 140, 141, 147
   Ellison on, 137–138
   Key West and, 142–143
   "Race Issue, The ," *National Geographic Magazine*, 43n2
   "What America Would Be Like without Blacks," 137–138
   See also racism
race in Bishop's archive, 32, 37, 131–150
   Axelrod and, 131
   Bishop as self-critical, 132
   black music and, 133–134
   black women, Bishop speaking as, 133, 135, 136
   blues music and, 132–136
   Cleaver and, 49, 131–132, 145–146, 148, 150n10–11, 264
   "Cootchie" and, 136, 137, 143
   Erkkila on, 133
   essentialism and, 134
   "Faustina, or Rock Roses," 135, 136–137, 140, 143
   Hicok on, 138, 144
   Holiday and, 136
   Hunter's Point neighborhood, 148
   innocence/ignorance, Bishop's, 138
   in "In the Waiting Room," 27, 29, 35, 43n2
   picturesque and, 135–136
   Schmidt on, 136
   and sentimentality, resistance of, 135–136
   servant class and, 137, 139
   social consciousness, limits of, 134
   "Songs for a Colored Singer," 66, 133, 136
   transcriptions of blues lyrics, 133–135
   white paternalism and, 136, 139
   See also race; racism
"Race Issue, The," *National Geographic Magazine*, 43n2
racism
   in advertising, 137, *138–142*, 140, 144
   black musicians, exploitation of, 132
   in Brazil, 139, 146–147
   in "Brazil, January 1, 1502" drafts, 144
   in *Brazil* translation, 144

Cleaver on, 146–147
in *The Diary of "Helena Morley,"* 144
"In the Waiting Room" and, 27, 29, 35, 43n2
National Geographic Magazine and, 36–37, 43n2
in Sapolio soap leaflet, 137, *138–142*, 140, 144
Skidmore on, 139
white paternalism, 136, 139
See also race; race in Bishop's archive
"Rain Towards Morning" (Bishop), 112
Ray, Gordon N., 308
Read, Bill, 45–46
Read, Justin, 194, 211
reading, Bishop's portrayal of, 19–20, 21, 33, 36, 37, 39–40, 42
reading, Jacobus on, 20, 37
Remembering Elizabeth Bishop: An Oral Biography (Brazeau, Fountain), 257–258
repetition, 144–145, 157, 159, 235, 260, 288
reserve, Bishop's, 86, 99, 101, 107, 304
  Costello on, 244
  and Guggenheim application, 309–310
  as performative, 244
  shyness and, 21, 22, 36, 39, 42
  theatrical involvement and, 250
restraint, Bishop's. *See* reserve, Bishop's
rhetorical strategies, 234–235
Ribeiro, Léo Gilson, 223
Rich, Adrienne, 4, 68, 73, 133
Rio, Brazil, *216*, 218
"Riverman, The" (Bishop), 113
"River Rat, The" (Bishop, Hemingway), 66, 68–74, *70*, 75, 76, 79n5, 79n9
Riviere, Joan, 60–61, 63n18
Rock, The (Eliot), 251–252, 254
rock-and-roll music, Bishop on, 115, 126, 127
Rockefeller Foundation, 149
Roman, Camille, 234
"Roosters" (Bishop), 141
Rosenbaum, Susan, 96, *97*, 206, 229, 234, 300, 317n2
Ruas, Eponina, *200*
Ruhl, Sarah, 81
Rukeyser, Muriel, 45–46
Russell, Charles "Red," 156, 166, 168

Russell, Charlotte, 156–*158*, 163, 166, 167, 168, 169

Sable Island drafts (Bishop), 59
Sackville-West, Vita, 86
Samambaia, 193–194, *195*, 203, *205*, 239, 272–273, 282n8
Samuels, Peggy, 169, 171n9, 249–250, 262, 272, 282n7–8
"Sandpiper, The" (Bishop), 144, 191
San Francisco, 116, 119, 148
  See also "Fairy Toll-Taker, The" (Bishop)
"Santarém" (Bishop), 90
Sapolio soap leaflet, 137, *138–142*, 140, 144
Saraíva, Arnaldo, 212
Sarton, May, 106
Sauer, Martha, 188
Scalar, 281, 282n11
Schlesinger, Stephen L., 308
Schmidt, Tyler T., 136
scholarship gaps on Bishop, 2, 266, 303
Schwartz, Lloyd, 34
Schwartz, Pearl, 100–101, 107, 109
science and art, affinities between, 245n7
scrapbooking, 283–284, 287, 293, 300
"Sea and Its Shore, The" (Bishop), 187, 188, 191
"Seascape" (Bishop), 143, 170
Seaver, Robert, 65, 79n5
Secchin, Antonio Carlos, 209, 212, 214
"Secular Masque, The" (Dryden), 260
self-reliance, 163, 166, 168
"Sense of the Sleight-of-Hand-Man, The" (Stevens), 75–76
sentimentality, 46, 47–48, 76–77, 79n11, 97, 135–136
Series II of Elizabeth Bishop Papers, 303–318
  archival mundane, importance of, 316–317
  filing system, 304
Serrano, Jonathas, 224n8
"Sestina" (Bishop), 63n17
sexual abuse, 36, 38–39, 42, 156
sexuality, 40, 41, 66, 115–116
  See also homosexuality; queer poet, Bishop as
Shaw, George Bernard, 30, 61n4

INDEX   353

Shepherdson, George, 38–39, 46, 48, 59–60, 61n1, 156
Shepherdson, Maud (Maude), 38, 48, 59, 61n1, 62n10, 156, 163, 171n2
"Shipwreck and Salvage," *The Body and the Song* (Lombardi), 58–59
shyness, Bishop's, 21, 22, 36, 39, 42
Silent Spring (Carson), 207
sketches, Bishop's, 163, *163, 164,* 165, *253*
Skidmore, Thomas E., 139, 144
Slaughter, Joseph, 142
Slot (Magi), 236
slumming, 132, 150n2, 188
Smith, Barbara Herrnstein, 117
Smith, Martha Nell, 86
Soller, Mallorca, 178, *179*
"Somebody Who's Somebody" (Swenson), 107
"Some Matters of Substance" (Friedel), 93
"Song for the Rainy Season" (Bishop), 229
"Songs for a Colored Singer" (Bishop), 66, 133, 136
"Sonnet" (Bishop), 85, 91, 94
Souza, Decio, 60
Spires, Elizabeth, 47–48
Stanford, Donald, 252, 254–255
Steedman, Carolyn, 2, 79n6, 238
Stein, Gertrude, 254–255, 256–257, 263
St. Elizabeths, 59
Stern, Donnel, 51
Stevens, Marjorie Carr, 47, 49, 54, 169
Stevens, Wallace, 75–76, 143, 185, 187, 188, 190
Stevenson, Anne, 47, 111, 206, 242, 287
"St. John's Day" (Bishop), 282n3
St. John's Day festival, 267, 269, 274, 278
Stone, Julius F, Jr., 187
Sullivan, Harry Stack, 49–50, 62n6–7
Summers, Joseph (Joe), 196, 203, *216,* 221
Summers, U. T., 196, 203, *216,* 221
Summer Seminar for College and University Professors on Elizabeth Bishop and the Literary Archive (Hicok), 3, 6
surprise in Bishop's poetry, 288–289
surrealism, 287
"Survival of the Queerly Fit: Darwin, Marianne Moore, and Elizabeth Bishop" (McCabe), 88
Sweeney Agonistes: Fragments of an Aristophanic Melodrama (Eliot), 251
Swenson, Anna Thilda May
    Bishop, feelings for, 107–108
    Bishop, physical description of, 100–101
    childhood and family, 105–106, 107
    compared/contrasted with Bishop, 100, 105, 108
    critical biography, lack of, 106
    Field on, 114n5
    FSG and, 7
    Grifalconi on, 114n5
    "Her Early Work," 101
    "In the Bodies of Words," 110
    Knudson and, 113
    Lowell-Bishop correspondence on, 100
    Marianne Moore, Elizabeth Bishop & May Swenson: The Feminist Poetics of Self-Restraint, 99
    Mayhall on, 106–107
    To Mix with Time, 102–103
    New and Selected Things Taking Place, 105
    North & South and, 107
    Sarton and, 106
    Schwartz and, 100–101, 107, 109
    "Somebody Who's Somebody," 107
    typing work, 108
Swenson-Bishop correspondence, 100–114, *110*
    Bishop's criticism of Swenson's work, 102–105
    carbon copies, 114n7
    and Guggenheim recommendation, 101
    humor within, 108–109
    last letters, 113–114
    Macedo Soares in, 101
    publication of, 114n1
    "Rapture Letter," 110–112
    Swenson on Bishop's poetry, 100, 110–114
    topics of discussion in, 108–109

Talbot, Kathrine (Ilse Barker), 153, 171n1
Taylor, Jesse Oak, 244
teaching, Bishop on burden of, 313–314

teaching about Bishop, suggested activities for, 300–301
theater. *See* drama, Bishop and
themes in Bishop's work
    children in danger, *292*, 293
    female power, 293
    humble abodes, 164–165
    in-betweens, 151–152
    isolation, 163, 166, 168
    order and chaos, relationship between, 169–170, 273, 278, 288
    outsiderhood, 4, 85
    self-reliance, 163, 166, 168
Theory of the Earth (Hutton), 241–242
Thompson, Clara, 50–51, 62n7
Thompson, Virgil, 254–255
Three Wells, The (Bishop), 250
"Thumb, The" (Bishop), 66, 68, 76
"Time's Andromedas" (Bishop), 19–20, 21, 29, 35
To Mix with Time (Swenson), 102–103
tompung, 294, 301n2
Tortorici, Zeb, 98
tourism, 170, 178–183, *181*, 189–191
Tourist, The (MacCannell), 190, 191
"Tourist Pitch for Recife" (Zenith), 215
Tower of Babel, 218
transcriptions, 94–95, 97, 282n6
    of blues songs, 132–134, *135*, 136, 141
    errors in, 7, 53
translations, Bishop's, 62n11, 194
    Birds, The, 104, 111, 187–192
    Brazilian Bandeirantes (Girl Guides) oath and code of honor, 199
    "Burglar of Babylon, The" and, 195
    of Cabral's poems, 208–210
    "Death and Life of a Severino," 208–210
    "Diary of 'Helena Morley,' The", 144, 149, 199, 200–204, *202*, *204*, 223
    financial concerns and, 203, 205
    Leão and, 200
    Macedo Soares and, 220
    Machova on, 198
    "Magic Barrel, The," 199–200, *201*
    Modern Architecture in Brazil, 203
    in notebook with "The Armadillo" draft, 277, *277*

translating-to-learn, 198
trauma, in childhood, 46, 47, 48, 152
travel, 10–11, 173–192
    ephemera and, 176, 178
    in Europe, 183–186, 190
    Goffman on, 175–176
    Gray on, 175, 191
    Hemingway on, 153
    journals, 54, 153–156, 159, 161–168, *164*, 169
    MacCannell on, 175–176
    picturesque aesthetic and, 175–176, 178, 190–192
    postcards (*See* postcards)
    tourism, 170, 178–179, *181*, 183, 184, 189–191
Travel, 186, *186*
Travisano, Thomas, 68
Treseler, Heather, 52, 316
"Trip to the Mines, A" (Bishop), 143–145, 149
Tropic of Capricorn, 224n11
"Twelfth Morning, Or What You Will" (Bishop), 214

unfinished work, 59, 315–316
    See also individual works
Unraveling Archive: Essays on Sylvia Plath, The (Helle), 8
"Untitled (Elizabeth Bishop's House)" (MacIver), 171n5

"Vague Poem (Vaguely Love Poem)" (Bishop), 243–244
"Valley of Ten Thousand Smokes, The" (Griggs), 24, *25*, *28*, 35
Van Mierlo, Wim, 79n4
Varda, Agnès, 171
Vassar College, 61n1
    drama and, 251
    Elizabeth Bishop and the Literary Archive, graduates as contributors, 13n5
    music and, 266
    Summer Seminar for College and University Professors on Elizabeth Bishop and the Literary Archive, 3, 6
    Vassarion yearbook, *295*, 295–299, *296*, *298*

Vassar College Archives and Special Collections Library, Elizabeth Bishop Papers, 1–13, 2, 13n6, 21, 46
   Foster letters, purchase of, 38, 81, 282n1
   new editions of previously unpublished work, 4, 5
   Patkus and, 13n1
   preservation photocopies, 6, 13n10
   Series II (*See* Series II of Elizabeth Bishop Papers)
Vassarion yearbook, *295*, 295–299, *296*, *298*
Vendler, Helen, 115
Venuti, Lawrence, 194
"Verdigris" (Bishop), 231, 234–236, 237, 238, 245n2
vibrant matter, agency of, 230–231, 235–238
Vider, Stephen, 65–66
"View of the Capitol from The Library of Congress" (Bishop), 35, 234
villanelle form, 235, 327
violence in Bishop's family, 38–39, 42
"Visits to St. Elizabeths" (Bishop), 39
Voyage of the Beagle, The (Darwin), 241

Walnut Hill, 74, 133, 250, 264n4
war
   in Bishop's works, 18–19, 29, 37
   Cold War culture, 18, 218, 222, 234
   World War I, 26, 29
Warren, Eleanor Clark, 254
Washington University, Bishop's archive at, 114n7
"Was It in His Hand?" (Bishop), 66
Watson, Ivory, 54, 63n14

Wehr, Wesley, 227, *228*, 229, 230
"What America Would Be Like without Blacks" (Ellison), 137–138
"What Did I Do To Be So Black and Blue" (Armstrong), 141
Wheatstraw, Peetie, 136
"Where are the dolls who loved me so. . . ." (Bishop), 114n2
White, Gillian, 250, 287, 304
White, Katherine, 153–154, 171n7, 207, 238, 244
White Institute, 50, 51
white paternalism, 136, 139
"Why We Need Things" (Csikszentmihalyi), 93
Wilde, Oscar, 79n11
William Alanson White Institute, 50, 51
Witcher, Heather Bozant, 282n6
women, discrimination against, 317n3
Woolf, Virginia, 86
Worcester, Bishop in, 38, 61n1
Words in Air: The Complete Correspondence between Elizabeth Bishop and Robert Lowell (Logan), 81
Works Progress Administration (WPA), 185
World War I, *26*, 29
WPA (Works Progress Administration), 185
Wright, Hamilton, *186*

Yaddo, 100, 171n1
Yeats, W. B., 127, 159

Zenith, Richard, 215
Zona, Kirstin Hotelling, 32, 33, 99, 101–102, 103–105

CPSIA information can be obtained
at www.ICGtesting.com
Printed in the USA
BVHW010504050220
R10636400002B/R106364PG571274BVX26B/4

9 781643 150116